SOUTHEAST
ASIAN AFFAIRS
2024

SOUTHEAST ASIAN AFFAIRS 2024

EDITED BY

DALJIT SINGH
HOANG THI HA

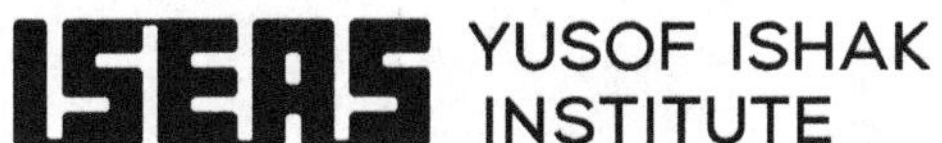

First published in Singapore in 2024 by
ISEAS Publishing
30 Heng Mui Keng Terrace
Singapore 119614

E-mail: publish@iseas.edu.sg
Website: http://bookshop.iseas.edu.sg

The responsibility for facts and opinions in this publication rests exclusively with the authors and their interpretations do not necessarily reflect the views or the policy of the publisher or its supporters.

ISEAS Library Cataloguing-in-Publication Data

Title: Southeast Asian affairs 2024.
Description: Singapore : ISEAS – Yusof Ishak Institute, 2024.
Identifiers: ISSN 0377-5437 | ISBN 9789815203509 (hard cover) | ISBN 9789815203516 (pdf) | ISBN 9789815203516 (epub)
Subjects: LCSH: Southeast Asia—Periodicals.
Classification: LCC DS501 S72A 2020

Typeset by Stephen Logan
Printed in Singapore by Markono Print Media Pte Ltd

Contents

Introduction

Daljit Singh, Hoang Thi Ha and Cha Hae Won

The year 2023 ended with a mixed bag of hopes and frustrations for Southeast Asian countries. The region had left the Covid-19 pandemic behind, but geopolitical tensions such as the ongoing Russia-Ukraine war and the Israel-Hamas war, as well as the subdued performance of the Chinese economy, cast a long shadow over the region's aspirations for a robust post-pandemic recovery. Many countries in the region are currently undergoing leadership transitions, ranging from post-election political consolidation to active campaigning for upcoming elections. Geopolitical tensions between the United States and China, along with the pressure to take sides, are significant sources of concern for many Southeast Asian governments. But foremost among the priorities of Southeast Asian policymakers are efforts to curb inflation, transition towards a more sustainable economic growth model—including by diversifying away from the oil and gas sector and embracing EV industries—and enhance national competitiveness to capitalize on the next wave of FDI diversification from China.

Political Developments

After and Before the Votes: Political Transitions in Malaysia, Thailand, the Philippines, Cambodia, Timor-Leste, Singapore and Indonesia

A number of Southeast Asian states—Malaysia, Thailand, the Philippines, Cambodia and Timor-Leste—were in the process of political consolidation after leadership transitions resulting from elections in 2022 and 2023.

DALJIT SINGH is Visiting Senior Fellow at the ISEAS – Yusof Ishak Institute, Singapore.

HOANG THI HA is Senior Fellow and Co-coordinator of the Regional Strategic and Political Studies Programme at the ISEAS – Yusof Ishak Institute, Singapore.

CHA HAE WON is a Research Officer in the Regional Strategic and Political Studies Programme at the ISEAS – Yusof Ishak Institute, Singapore.

In Malaysia, there was relative political stability after five years of frequent changes of government. National politics was dominated by Prime Minister Anwar Ibrahim and partisan skirmishes over race and religion, as noted by Ariel Tan in her Malaysia overview chapter. The main challenges facing the prime minister were to deliver on his reform agenda, win more Malay support while retaining non-Malay support, and improve the economy. In the six state elections in August, the ruling coalition successfully defended the states under its rule as well as three parliamentary seats but saw an erosion of Malay support. As such, the government enjoyed a strong majority in parliament. However, approval ratings for Anwar and the government declined significantly in 2023 stemming from public concerns about the economy, especially the higher cost of living.

In Thailand, the political divide between the Thaksin-led Pheu Thai Party and the conservative establishment centred on the military and the monarchy, which has been the major source of political instability since 2006, was bridged surprisingly by an alliance between the two. This new alignment, as described by Napon Jatusripitak, reflects a return to old politics driven by the shared interests and common adversaries of the elites, particularly vis-à-vis the Move Forward Party (MFP) and the broader pro-democracy movements. Long-term stability is by no means guaranteed as this delicate balance will face tests. The electoral victory of the MFP—and the denial of its premiership position following Pheu Thai's decision to collaborate with the conservative establishment—underscored the ideological differences in the country over the role of the monarchy and the military. This structural tension in Thai politics will continue to simmer below the surface. These changes have occurred at a time when the economy is vulnerable because of external economic and geopolitical factors, which adds to the uncertainties facing the country going forward.

On the Philippines, Ruth R. Lusterio-Rico highlights the emerging cracks within the political alliance between President Marcos Jr. and Vice-President Sara Duterte, whose "UniTeam" secured a landslide victory in the election of May 2022. These cracks pose uncertainties for the future politics of the country. Issues causing the fissure included the release from jail of former senator and secretary of justice De Lima, and the controversy surrounding Sara's misuse of Confidential Funds. Political manoeuvrings as to who will succeed Marcos Jr. as president in 2027 have already begun. While the country registered impressive economic growth, many Filipinos were unhappy with the increase in prices of basic commodities and utilities, unemployment and underemployment. In the thematic chapter on the country, Yvonne T. Chua analyses the plague of disinformation in which "government, politicians and their allies employ disinformation both online and offline to manipulate public opinion, suppress critics, advance controversial policies and consolidate power".

On Cambodia, David Hutt describes how the country's ruling Cambodian People's Party (CPP) engineered a "once-in-a-lifetime" transfer of power from Hun Sen, who had been the premier since 1992, to his son Hun Manet. It was a meticulously planned and smoothly executed exercise, preceded by the suppression of the political opposition and a landslide win by the CPP in a general election. While no longer the prime minister, Hun Sen still retains significant influence as president of the CPP, president of the Privy Council and possibly the next president of the Senate. The succession exercise embraced a broad spectrum involving the ruling party and the government and state apparatus, including the military. In many instances, the incumbents were succeeded by their children or those trusted by Hun Sen, alongside several non-hereditary cabinet appointments of capable technocrats. Hutt attributes the massive changes to the need to protect the interests of the main political families in the country and to ensure continuity and stability. One of the most difficult challenges facing the new government is to deal with the massive scale of human trafficking, forced labour and international scam syndicates, which have damaged the country's reputation and brought criticism from foreign states whose nationals have been caught up in these nefarious activities.

In Timor Leste, the country's presidential election in 2022 and the parliamentary one in 2023 saw the return of the "old firm" of Jose Ramos-Horta as president and Xanana Gusmao as prime minister. This enhances the prospects for the country's political stability. However, as Michael Leach explains, the team has some daunting challenges to address, especially the solvency of the oil and gas sovereign fund upon which a growing national budget depends—hence the need for diversification of the economy. The issue of youth unemployment is a concern in view of a major demographic "youth bulge". Also, there is a need for a younger generation of leaders to come forward to take the reins of power in the not-too-distant future, which Leach thinks could unfold in the current parliamentary term.

In Indonesia and Singapore, elections and leadership changes will unfold in 2024 and 2025. In Singapore, the succession question had been settled in 2022 with Finance Minister Lawrence Wong being named as successor to Prime Minister Lee Hsien Loong. The handover of the premiership may take place around November or December 2024. Singapore's next general election must be held by 23 November 2025, with the prime minister having the prerogative to call for an earlier election if deemed necessary. Singapore's economy in 2023 was still awaiting a strong post-pandemic recovery. Inflation and the higher cost of living were widespread concerns, especially when the inflation rate exceeded wage growth.

Eugene K.B. Tan, in his Singapore overview chapter, discusses other significant developments in Singapore during the year, including the launch of the Forward SG report outlining government policies to enhance the well-being of the broad middle ground of Singapore society, which largely encompasses the middle class; the presidential election; concerns about the impact of the Israel-Hamas conflict on Singapore society; a corruption scandal and sensational money laundering cases involving foreign nationals; and a financial package to help meet the retirement needs of "young seniors". In the thematic chapter on Singapore, Benjamin Joshua Ong focuses on the 2023 presidential election in which the winner was Tharman Shanmugaratnam. Benjamin also explains the qualifying criteria to participate in the election and the limits of the president's role.

Indonesian politics in 2023 were dominated by contestations, campaigns and horse-trading bargains in the lead-up to the elections scheduled for February 2024. Greg Fealy, in his chapter on Indonesia, provides an analysis of the elections, the presidential candidates and the campaign dynamics. President Joko Widodo continued to enjoy high popularity ratings in the last full year of his presidency, a good deal of it due to public satisfaction with his management of the economy. While acknowledging Jokowi's successes, Fealy also notes dark traits to his presidency, arguing that "[his] gradual but systematic undercutting of democratic principles has made Indonesia less free and less transparent … [leaving] a precedent for succeeding presidents to follow should they wish to grasp greater powers for themselves by eroding institutions created to defend rights and ensure the rule of law".

Challenges Lurking beneath Political Stability in Brunei, Laos and Vietnam

Brunei was politically stable and cautiously optimistic about the near-term future. However, its primary concern lies in the long-term challenge of diversifying its economy away from dependence on oil and gas resources to prepare for the day when these resources are depleted. In 2023, the government and the sultan himself especially emphasized the importance and urgency of realizing Wawasan Brunei 2035 (Brunei Vision 2035), the central agenda of which was economic diversification. So far, the efforts to do so have faced an uphill task. The stakes are significant as the success of these efforts is crucial for maintaining the country's generous welfare benefits and even the survival of the monarchy itself.

Laos saw an unusual change in the leadership in 2023, with Sonexay Siphandone replacing Phankham Viphavanh as prime minister. Sonexay's appointment, which came amid public scrutiny of his predecessor's handling of multiple crises and accusations of extravagance during times of economic downturn, signifies regime continuity given his background from a prominent family with deep political ties. Sonexay inherits significant governance challenges amid the unprecedented dire economic situation in Laos. As outlined by Oliver Tappe, the country has been going through a severe economic and financial crisis, with staggering public debt, currency depreciation and rampant inflation. The younger generation of Laos are losing confidence in the state's promises to deliver a better life. Attempts by the ruling Lao People's Revolutionary Party to mitigate macro-economic problems have not produced any significant improvements.

In neighbouring Vietnam, despite the next party congress being two years away, premature leadership changes have occurred because of the anti-corruption campaign spearheaded by Vietnam Communist Party (VCP) general secretary Nguyen Phu Trong. This so-called "blazing furnace" resulted in the removal of top VCP leaders, including President Nguyen Xuan Phuc and two deputy prime ministers in early 2023. It has led to the consolidation of Trong's power at the expense of the collective leadership structure; the tightening of political control over the press, social media and civil society; and a slowdown in economic decision-making, especially in project and licence approval. Moreover, Nguyen Khac Giang highlights the emerging trend of "securitization of the Vietnamese state"; i.e., the growing dominance of internal affairs institutions such as the ministry of public security and party disciplinary committees. The key question, as articulated by Edward J. Malesky and Thiem Hai Bui in the overview chapter, is "whether the campaign represents a fundamental new beginning or merely opens a window to observe underlying weaknesses in the regime". Inaction—the prevailing response so far of the bureaucracy to the anti-corruption drive—does not amount to fundamental change yet.

Myanmar: Approaching a Failed State

While the rest of Southeast Asia is bouncing back from the Covid-19 pandemic and concentrating on economic revitalization, Myanmar continues its descent into the status of a "failed state". The nation is embroiled in a protracted civil war and teeters on the brink of economic collapse, with no clear resolution on the horizon. Persistent resistance from anti-military forces caused the State Administration Council (SAC), led by coup leader Senior General Min Aung Hlaing, to abandon its election plan in 2023 and extend the state of emergency. The year also witnessed the SAC's most significant military setbacks and territorial losses since the coup, including during the "1027" operation launched by three ethnic armed organizations in October. This has put into question the longstanding belief that "the military was the only national institution that could hold the country together", as Mary Callahan highlights in the overview chapter. The thematic chapter by Sean Turnell and Moe Thuzar sheds light on the country's economic plight and the deteriorating living conditions of Myanmar's people. With a meagre one per cent growth in 2023, the economy remained plagued by foreign investment exits, shrinking manufacturing, high inflation and other financial problems. The SAC's misguided economic policies, which have shifted away from market-oriented ones to more state-centric measures aimed solely at survival, have exacerbated the situation further.

Geopolitical Developments

Southeast Asian countries and ASEAN face the daunting task of navigating the complexities and disruptions brought about by the intensifying Sino-US rivalry. Ian Chong, in his overview of the region, argues that there is just a narrow margin for neutrality and non-alignment, "since even taking a non-position can become siding with the other if major powers increasingly emphasize relative gains". He observes that—apart from the Philippines, which is a US security ally, and Vietnam, which has a hedging strategy—the countries of Southeast Asia have merely been "hiding and freeriding". Most countries in the region have been relatively silent on the contestations in the South China Sea, where maritime communication lines vital to their economies are at risk, hoping that the United States and its allies will deter excessive Chinese claims and action. This passivity discourages the region from taking new initiatives to grapple with the ongoing challenges. In the economic realm, the pursuit of "internal circulation" by China and "on-shoring" and "friend-shoring" by the United States, its allies and close friends means that plugging into key production chains may become more difficult for much of Southeast Asia.

Most states in the region continue to aim for a balance in their relations with China and the United States. Rizal Sukma, in his thematic chapter on Indonesia's foreign policy, points out that a posture of balance is dictated by the two fundamental principles of Indonesia's foreign policy since the country's independence: namely, *bebas-actif* (free and active). This does not mean passively sitting on the fence, but actively seeking creative solutions to address the challenges the country faces in maintaining the balance. In the present context, it requires strengthening Indonesia's national resilience and building up ASEAN's capacity and institutional effectiveness. ASEAN, he says, should go beyond the normative approach in dealing with great powers by developing a strategy "to restrain and deny the legitimacy of any bad actions by great powers towards the region". This can be done through collective action by ASEAN to uphold international law, including the 1982 United Nations Convention on the Law of the Sea. ASEAN needs to speak up and express a collective voice against any acts that violate international law. Indonesia, for its part, while maintaining its *bebas* position, needs to step up its *actif* role in the Indo-Pacific.

In the Philippines, in 2023, there has been a tilt towards its defence treaty ally the United States, especially in terms of closer military cooperation. Ruth R. Lusterio-Rico points out that this tilt has occurred within the broader framework of an "independent foreign policy, with national interest as our primordial guide", as announced by President Marcos. There are strong anti-China sentiments in the country, which intensified further in the wake of ongoing coercive action by China against the Philippines' resupply missions to Sierra Madre, which lies within the country's Exclusive Economic Zone (EEZ).

For Malaysia, Ariel Tan notes that while seeking to balance relations with the United States and China, in 2023 there appeared to be a "slight tilt" towards China. China was the first country Prime Minister Anwar visited after ASEAN countries and Saudi Arabia. It is Malaysia's biggest trade partner and largest foreign investor. The Israel- Gaza conflict was an irritant in relations with the United States. Malaysia also maintained a critical stance on the Australia-UK-US tripartite security partnership (AUKUS), which would enable Australia to acquire nuclear-powered submarines.

According to Eugene K.B. Tan, in 2023 Singapore continued to pursue a self-proclaimed balanced policy between the two great powers. During the year, Prime Minister Lee visited both the United States and China. During his visit to China, the first since 2019, he met top Chinese leaders, including Xi Jinping, and upgraded Singapore-China ties to an "All-Round High-Quality Future-Oriented Partnership". Singapore also deepened cooperation in science and technology with a high-profile visit by Deputy Prime Minister Lawrence Wong to the United States to further collaboration in critical and emerging technologies.

Napon Jatusripitak argues that since the coup of 2014, Thailand has gravitated increasingly towards China, thereby damaging the delicate balancing act that Thailand had traditionally tried to maintain. He is uncertain whether the new civilian-led government will be able to restore the equilibrium because of the importance of China in the prevailing emphasis on economic growth. Nevertheless, Thailand's foreign policy is well diversified beyond the US-China nexus, with strong relations with middle powers, especially Japan, as well ASEAN partners.

In this context, David M. Maliz, in his thematic chapter on Thailand, examines the important Thailand-Japan relationship. While Japan has lost its status as Thailand's paramount foreign partner to China, its ties with Thailand continue to hold significant importance, primarily because of the substantial scale of Japanese investments and the enduring appeal of Japan's soft power.

Cambodia has remained closer to China, its largest trade partner and main provider of foreign investment. Meanwhile, the country's relations with the United States have been adversely affected by the issue of human rights, the suppression of the political opposition, and allegations of possible Chinese military presence at Ream Naval Base. However, Cambodia may seek a more balanced and independent foreign policy, as illustrated by Hun Sen's quick condemnation of Russia's invasion of Ukraine. As David Hutt points out, Hun Manet has also sought to improve relations with Western states, including the United States.

In Laos, China's position is well summed up by Oliver Tappe: "In Laos's foreign relations, China has played and will certainly continue to play a critical yet ambivalent role, eliciting a wide range of perceptions ranging from menace to opportunity.… China definitely wields great influence over Laos, but it falls short of exclusive control. Instead, Laos maintains a diverse network of political, economic and cultural ties with other partners, most notably with its ASEAN neighbours Thailand and Vietnam, as well as with Russia".

Despite conflicting claims in the South China Sea, Brunei's relations with China, its biggest trading partner and investor, have remained smooth and cordial. Jatswan S. Sidhu, in his Brunei chapter, attributes this to Brunei's mild non-confrontational approach to the South China Sea issue, which prompted President Xi Jinping to praise Brunei for prioritizing economic relations rather than the maritime dispute. Brunei's foreign relations are well diversified with ASEAN neighbours and other powers like Japan, the United States and Britain, which prevents any dominant sway of China.

Vietnam meanwhile continued to pursue its omni-directional foreign policy, which cushioned it from excessive dependence on either great power. Diplomatic relations with the United States were upgraded to a "comprehensive strategic partnership", the same status as Russia, China and several other major powers. The upgrade was agreed to during President Biden's historic visit to Vietnam in September 2023. According to Edmund J. Malesky and Thiem Hai Bui, this development was in line with Vietnam's "bamboo diplomacy" of pragmatic flexibility in navigating between the great powers to secure its interests without taking sides. In December, President Xi Jinping paid a state visit to Vietnam and discussed various areas of cooperation. From China's perspective, the most important achievement of the visit was Vietnam's commitment to join China's "community of common destiny". However, Malesky and Bui suggest that it was just another manifestation of Vietnam's "bamboo diplomacy" and policy of assurance to Beijing "without conceding any of its important national interests".

Economic Developments

Post-Covid Resurgence in Tourism

As countries progressively removed Covid-related restrictions, a resurgence in tourism was observed across the region. In 2023, Brunei welcomed its first batch of tourists, the first since the beginning of the pandemic three years ago. Cambodia experienced a surge in tourism, registering a remarkable 179 per cent increase in international visitors during the first ten months of 2023 compared with the same period in 2022. Similarly, Laos saw a notable increase in international tourist arrivals, surpassing three million in 2023. This growth was aided significantly by the return of Chinese travellers and facilitated by the newly opened China–Laos railway. Meanwhile, Singapore's Changi Airport—having endured a decline to the ninety-fifth spot for international passenger traffic in 2021 as the result of pandemic-induced border closures—witnessed a remarkable rebound, receiving 5.12 million passengers by October 2023, the highest since the onset of the Covid-19 pandemic. The Thai government turned to tourism as a major driver for its economic rejuvenation as well, implementing policies aimed at boosting the tourism sector such as exempting visa fees for tourists and extending temporary visa waivers. These measures were designed to attract an estimated 25–30 million visits in 2023. Amidst the resurgence in tourism across the region, Myanmar stood out as an anomaly. Tourist arrivals remained dismally low in 2023, lingering at less than half the levels in 2019, as travellers are deterred by the ongoing armed conflicts and civil unrest stemming from the 2021 coup.

Rampant Inflation across the Region

Inflation, specifically for vital necessities like food, was a serious concern for various Southeast Asian countries in 2023. Ruth R. Lusterio-Rico observes that the Philippines' economic growth rate had only a marginal effect on the average citizen in light of the increasing prices for food and basic commodities. Similarly, Laos encountered food inflation at an average of 45.6 per cent in the first eight months of 2023, with the price of rice increasing from 7,000 kip to 20,000 kip per kilo, and petrol from 8,000 kip to 25,000 kip per litre. Food inflation also lingered in Malaysia, at 3.6 per cent in October 2023. In Singapore, the increase of the Goods and Services Tax (GST) from 7 to 8 per cent in 2023 contributed to inflationary pressures, and real incomes of workers in Singapore declined in 2023 despite a rise in nominal incomes.

In response to the challenges posed by inflation, countries in the region implemented measures aimed at curbing its impact. In Malaysia, the government rolled out the Menu Rahmah initiative—which assists private vendors to provide RM5 budget healthy meals—to address public concerns over the rising cost of living. The Singapore government implemented a range of measures under the SG$8 billion Assurance Package to alleviate the financial burden on its citizens, helping to offset essential expenses such as groceries and utilities. The Bank of Laos tightened monetary conditions and exchange control, increased reserve requirements for foreign exchange, and closed private foreign exchange bureaus to curb the depreciation of the kip, which Oliver Tappe says accounted for two-thirds of the excessive inflation in the country.

Sluggish Export Demand and Fragmentation of Supply Chains

Geopolitical turbulence such as the ongoing Russia-Ukraine war and Israel-Hamas war, coupled with the subdued recovery of the Chinese economy and reduced demand from Western nations, cast a shadow over the region's hopes for a robust post-pandemic rebound. Thailand's manufacturing exports experienced a "softened demand" because of China's "slower-than-anticipated economic rebound", according to Napon. Vietnam also saw a substantial decline of 11.6 per cent in exports, dropping from US$371 billion in 2022 to an expected US$332.82 in 2023. This has led to massive layoffs and unemployment in the country's southern exports hubs. Manu Bhaskaran singled out Singapore and Malaysia as the most affected by China's slump in demand, with double-digit contractions until the end of 2023. Cassey Lee, in the thematic chapter on Malaysia's economy, not only mentions the country's relatively weak export sector in 2023 but also underscores a structural change in the "decline in exports as a driver of Malaysia's growth" going forward.

The region also witnessed growing fragmentation of global supply chains in 2023 because of geopolitical tensions. As highlighted by Manu Bhaskaran in the regional economic overview chapter, "hyper-globalization" during the post–Cold War is transitioning towards industrial policies adopted by both China and Western nations. These policies are driven by the need to reshore manufacturing capacity, particularly in critical sectors such as electrical vehicles (EV) and semiconductors, based on national security concerns rather than comparative advantages. While this accelerating fragmentation causes "efficiency losses", Bhaskaran sees a silver lining in the emergence of new trade and investment patterns that stand to benefit Southeast Asia: global corporations are reconsidering their production locations in favour of places such as Southeast Asia, and a decline in capital flowing into China has corresponded with an increase in investment to other Asian economies. Bhaskaran's views are echoed by Malesky and Bui, who argue that a key factor in Vietnam's surge in FDI was the diversification away from China fuelled by the ongoing US-China trade conflict, as many Trump-era tariffs remain in effect.

While recognizing these potential benefits, Ian Chong highlights long-term challenges stemming from increasingly fragmented global supply chains. At risk, argues Chong, is the old model of Southeast Asia's economic growth, which relies on receiving capital and technologies from the West to manufacture or assemble components, which are then exported around the region and to China, ultimately making end products for the world market. He highlights that both the West's "on-shoring" and "friendshoring" and China's "internal circulation" strategies have the potential to restrict the flow of critical technologies, supply chains, raw materials and market access for Southeast Asian countries. Furthermore, he argues that a waning interest in a globalized approach to the world economy would shift preferences towards more exclusive arrangements at the expense of global institutions such as the WTO.

Riding the EV Wave

In 2023, the region's manufacturing sector was the primary recipient of FDI, driven largely by the burgeoning interest in emerging industries such as EVs. Once a manufacturing hub for internal combustion engine vehicles fuelled by Japanese investments, Thailand is now endeavouring to establish itself as an EV manufacturing hub, focusing on attracting investments from Chinese electric vehicle manufacturers such as BYD Co., Great Wall Motor Co., SAIC Motor Corp, and Chongqing Changan. The industry's momentum was given a boost with a total of US$1.44 billion investment by Chinese EV manufacturers in July 2023 to establish production facilities in Thailand. Focusing on the "Next Generation Automotive" industry as a cornerstone of its economic vision, Thailand ambitiously targets to eliminate internal combustion engines by 2035 and attain a fifty per cent share of EV sales by 2030.

Thailand's "forward-thinking approach towards sustainable transportation solutions", as described by Manu Bhaskaran, is being mirrored elsewhere in the region. Malaysia's 2024 budget charted a new course by adopting environmental, social and governance (ESG) priorities to promote green technology and electric vehicles for sustainable development. The New Industrial Master Plan 2030 (NIMP2030) launched by Anwar Ibrahim with the goal of revitalizing the country's manufacturing sector also featured new growth areas that align with energy transition, particularly the encouragement of EVs.

Indonesia, blessed with abundant reserves of nickel and bauxite, is also keen to expand and upgrade its participation in the EV supply chain. The ambition of the Jokowi administration for the country to become an EV hub, particularly in battery manufacturing, has yielded mixed results. In 2023, Tesla announced its decision not to pursue any significant investment plans in Indonesia, whereas South Korean giant LG was set to build an EV battery cell plant and associated facilities in the country. Vietnam is also gearing up to embrace the EV wave. Biden's visit to Hanoi in September 2023 led to collaboration agreements in EV supply chains, including battery storage and rare earth elements, to foster innovation-driven economic growth.

The Region

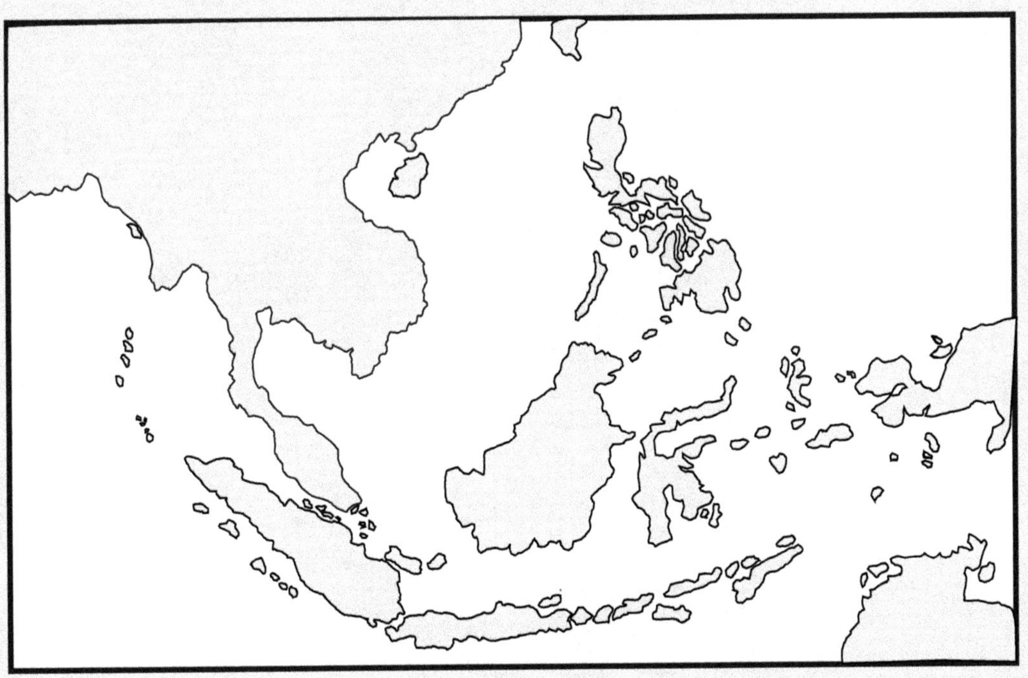

Searching for Direction: Southeast Asia in a Brave New World of Major Power Rivalry

Chong Ja Ian

If 2022 marked the path away from the Covid-19 pandemic, then 2023 provided a glimpse of the contours of a more contentious and uncertain world marked by major power competition. Southeast Asia's integration with the world economy and its location along key access routes between the Indian and Pacific Oceans provided distinct advantages at moments when major power interests converged around a commitment to economic liberalization. Much of the region's economic growth and prosperity over the past three decades lay in accessing capital and technology from North America, Europe and Japan to produce components for export to China or assemble parts from China for the world market. With a focus on economic gains from globalization, territorial disputes could recede into the background while a robust forward US military presence in Asia could coexist with an expanding and modernizing People's Liberation Army (PLA). But given the intensifying friction among major powers and their rethinking of globalization, Southeast Asia's position in the global value chains and the mutual accommodation among major powers in the region are under stress.

Southeast Asia very much felt on edge over the course of 2023. Much of the pressure comes from the fact that the region is a locus of competition between the United States and China, given both geography and its embeddedness in the global supply chains. Persistent pursuit of "internal circulation" by China on the one hand and "on-shoring" and "friend-shoring" among the United States, its allies and close friends on the other meant that plugging into key production chains may become more challenging for much of Southeast Asia. This is despite some Southeast Asian states benefitting somewhat from a general diversification away from China among developed economies. Beijing's

---

CHONG JA IAN is Associate Professor of Political Science at the National University of Singapore and non-resident scholar at Carnegie China.

increasing resolve in establishing a veto over access to maritime East Asia and the desire by the United States, its allies and close friends to prevent such a situation places Southeast Asia in the crosshairs and further complicates the region's fraught politics.

That Southeast Asian states collectively and individually appear generally under-prepared to deal with a more contested and uncertain environment throws a shadow over the region. Claims about "ASEAN centrality" and its supposed importance ring hollow when the grouping and most of its members seem unable to propose a clear plan for navigating the more difficult waters churned up by rising major power competition and global as well as regional instability. The continuing civil war in Myanmar perpetuates a humanitarian crisis and criminality, whereas Russian aggression in Ukraine, conflict in the Middle East and contestation over the maritime space in East Asia potentially place global supply chains at risk. Such conditions exemplify the world to which Southeast Asia must now adapt and where declarations about "not choosing sides" no longer appear to be adequate. Without a clearer sense of direction, Southeast Asia is more dependent on the vagaries of Beijing and Washington's ability and willingness to manage tensions and avoid escalation between them.

The Shadow of Major Power Rivalry

The year 2023 underscored that major power rivalry will be a significant feature of the current international system going forward. On one side is China, which is solidifying relationships with Russia, North Korea, Pakistan and Central Asian members of the Shanghai Cooperation Cooperation—Kazakhstan, Kyrgyzstan, Tajikistan, Turkmenistan and Uzbekistan.[1] Beijing is also actively reaching out to the Middle East, Africa and other states with developing economies.[2] For its part, Washington has made it a point to focus on its allies and closest friends in key economic and security partnerships, which is to say, likeminded states that share its democratic values.[3] When strengthening its most important existing relationships, the United States seeks to consolidate ties with the world's richest and most developed economies and use their varied strengths to appeal to other actors.

Late 2023 witnessed some effort by Washington and Beijing to stabilize relations after a year of mutual testing both diplomatically and militarily. In their first face-to-face meeting after the 2022 G20 summit in Bali, US president Joe Biden and Chinese president Xi Jinping announced a willingness to resume military-to-military contact and continue high-level economic dialogue that had been ongoing throughout the year.[4] As a result, limited senior-level engagement between the defence establishments of both major powers was re-established, and US Defense Department reports indicated a decline in dangerous aerial intercepts of US military aircraft.[5] These developments came after an initial delay triggered by the discovery of a Chinese spy balloon flying over the United States in late 2022 and early 2023, which was later shot down and analysed by the US military over China's objections.[6] Meanwhile, China continued its robust and even threatening actions towards US allies and friends through patrols by its ships and aircraft as well as its non-lethal use of force (or gray zone warfare) in disputed waters.[7]

For Southeast Asia, a world marked by major power competition could well become one of diminishing opportunities. Southeast Asian states approached US-China competition with an idea of not having or wanting to choose sides, based on a premise that there would be a wide berth for non-alignment and neutrality.[8] Even more optimistic views from the region believe that efforts by the United States and its allies as well as China to win over regional states or at least dissuade them from aligning with the opposing side can drive major powers to constantly offer positive inducements.[9] These views may be valid insofar as major power rivals continue to prioritize joint or absolute gains, since even taking a non-position can become siding with the other if major powers increasingly emphasize relative gains. The more major actors see not siding with themselves as deleterious to their interests, whether in terms of economics or security, the less scope for flexibility by third parties in areas under contention they are willing to endure.

The point of "on-shoring" and "friend-shoring" on the one hand and "internal circulation" on the other is to limit the flow of key technologies, supply chains and raw materials as well as market access. Since production in most Southeast Asian states is on contract to commercial entities based in North America, Europe, Japan and China, especially concerning electronics and other technology products, the effects of such limits are twofold. First, limits on production technology, key raw materials and sales dampen the region's own manufacture and sale of advanced products to important markets. Second, restrictions and non-preferential treatment on the transfer of new technology means that the model of absorbing new techniques and skills Southeast Asia has become so accustomed to may have to change. The region may discover opportunities in producing lower-tier technologies for markets other than North America, Europe, Japan and China, but that requires a shift in mindset, commercial networks and supply chains that have yet to visibly occur.

TABLE 1
ASEAN Trade in Goods by Trading Partners, 2013–22

Trading Partner	2013	2014	2015	2016	2017	2018	2019	2020	2021	2022
ASEAN	**617,751.6**	**608,113.8**	**535,380.4**	**517,954.4**	**589,116.7**	**644,654.1**	**632,604.3**	**567,105.8**	**711,839.5**	**856,465.5**
Trading Partner	**1,915,317.6**	**1,927,094.6**	**1,737,481.4**	**1,721,943.0**	**1,982,183.5**	**2,163,451.6**	**2,183,827.8**	**2,102,745.5**	**2,634,971.3**	**2,989,716.9**
Australia	69,053.1	73,395.2	57,492.6	52,878.8	59,108.1	65,633.2	63,090.9	54,876.8	82,162.8	101,098.1
Canada	13,529.3	13,331.2	12,655.2	12,633.6	13,796.7	15,544.7	17,141.9	16,279.5	18,971.1	23,120.3
China	351,583.4	366,711.2	363,496.8	368,567.3	440,973.3	478,535.0	507,963.2	518,617.7	670,255.1	722,103.1
EU-27	214,703.2	218,259.7	201,504.4	205,371.9	230,369.9	252,190.0	245,073.6	226,783.0	269,455.8	295,161.9
India	68,269.4	67,993.1	60,165.7	58,592.2	73,668.7	80,427.7	77,097.8	65,711.1	91,618.2	113,084.2
Japan	240,430.9	229,094.7	202,800.1	202,417.6	218,805.8	230,112.8	226,029.2	204,981.3	241,338.7	268,585.7
South Korea	134,864.2	131,438.3	120,566.7	124,466.9	154,849.5	160,727.7	156,506.5	154,966.7	189,793.5	222,768.1
New Zealand	9,789.0	10,706.0	8,753.0	7,899.6	9,504.6	10,231.8	10,341.3	9,044.7	11,149.5	14,899.4
Russia	19,984.1	22,571.1	13,969.0	11,956.8	16,748.0	19,922.0	18,198.0	14,096.5	18,167.8	15,369.2
United Kingdom	31,831.4	29,919.4	29,150.7	28,207.2	30,389.7	34,678.9	35,744.9	31,805.4	31,660.5	34,321.4
USA	205,313.1	211,507.9	210,582.4	211,810.0	233,833.8	262,126.2	294,793.3	309,088.8	365,599.6	420,444.6
Rest of the world	555,966.6	552,166.6	456,344.9	437,141.2	500,135.5	553,321.8	531,847.1	496,494.0	644,798.5	758,760.9
TOTAL	**2,533,069.2**	**2,535,208.4**	**2,272,861.8**	**2,239,897.4**	**2,571,300.2**	**2,808,105.7**	**2,816,432.0**	**2,669,851.4**	**3,346,810.8**	**3,846,182.4**

Source: *ASEAN Statistical Yearbook 2023.*

TABLE 2
ASEAN Balance of Trade in Goods by Trading Partners, 2013–22

Trading Partner	2013	2014	2015	2016	2017	2018	2019	2020	2021	2022
ASEAN	**59,475.1**	**52,305.1**	**38,832.4**	**37,838.3**	**34,533.8**	**44,359.0**	**32,019.5**	**29,115.9**	**32,120.8**	**43,203.5**
Trading Partner	**−35,711.1**	**461.5**	**31,772.9**	**29,481.7**	**43,756.4**	**19,635.2**	**−791.1**	**94,526.3**	**60,539.9**	**34,886.5**
Australia	21,539.9	17,050.7	14,089.2	13,288.0	10,099.7	12,785.7	7,791.3	7,627.4	3,896.6	2,879.9
Canada	951.0	1,598.2	1,709.7	2,157.3	1,848.3	1,911.6	2,778.9	3,700.8	4,837.6	4,288.4
China	−44,826.4	−58,686.0	−72,914.0	−80,636.6	−66,918.1	−83,176.0	−102,863.3	−80,837.8	−106,628.6	−140,570.0
EU–27	2,170.5	13,432.8	19,440.0	21,592.9	46,601.0	30,190.0	23,950.1	33,813.3	36,325.5	57,593.9
India	16,383.1	19,395.4	20,941.2	16,933.0	17,119.0	20,799.5	19,501.6	13,085.9	16,134.0	28,153.8
Japan	4,676.4	11,222.1	1,082.3	−9,308.0	−6,914.5	−578.3	−6,208.2	499.9	−11,698.9	−1,963.9
South Korea	−29,180.2	−28,187.5	−29,725.0	−32,631.7	−41,385.6	−39,756.3	−37,746.6	−37,807.7	−52,057.8	−61,001.7
New Zealand	1,578.4	2,046.9	1,698.4	1,194.4	1,417.9	1,955.2	1,660.6	1,038.0	2,325.8	3,660.9
Russia	−9,488.6	−11,742.3	−5,431.2	−2,392.5	−5,016.8	−8,003.1	−5,991.9	−2,119.8	−3,472.9	−6,681.1
United Kingdom	385.9	3,400.8	4,678.9	5,694.5	7,972.9	4,498.3	3,447.0	3,613.2	4,682.3	4,522.2
USA	22,258.9	30,918.5	40,303.3	50,342.6	51,128.2	58,396.3	72,795.2	114,089.5	146,999.5	161,484.4
Rest of the world	−22,160.0	11.9	35,900.2	43,247.9	27,804.2	20,612.4	20,094.1	37,823.6	19,196.8	−17,480.2
TOTAL	**23,764.0**	**52,766.6**	**70,605.3**	**67,320.0**	**78,290.2**	**63,994.2**	**31,228.4**	**123,642.2**	**92,660.8**	**78,090.0**

Source: ASEAN Statistical Yearbook 2023.

TABLE 3
Foreign Direct Investment (FDI) Inward Flows to ASEAN by Source Country, 2013–2022

Source Country	2013	2014	2015	2016	2017	2018	2019	2020	2021	2022
ASEAN	**18,464.2**	**22,180.9**	**20,819.3**	**26,358.2**	**26,976.7**	**22,402.8**	**21,348.4**	**22,926.2**	**25,584.8**	**28,081.2**
Rest of the World	**102,501.3**	**107,933.6**	**97,847.9**	**87,113.7**	**129,869.0**	**125,216.6**	**144,708.1**	**96,828.2**	**187,358.7**	**197,712.8**
Australia	2,165.5	4,032.1	1,407.2	960.7	−1,573.2	2,727.1	570.5	396.8	−328.2	2,028.4
Canada	790.0	2,239.7	1,179.7	1,910.3	1,472.1	605.1	5,012.6	3,122.5	3,198.6	3,623.4
China	6,165.2	6,811.7	6,571.8	8,165.8	16,801.7	12,863.6	9,035.7	7,363.3	16,866.2	15,539.0
EU–27	10,715.9	21,877.5	17,011.6	22,751.1	13,156.3	18,884.7	260.7	9,257.2	27,898.6	24,376.3
India	1,731.2	1,163.5	1,473.4	1,470.9	777.9	314.4	1,543.6	2,017.5	1,287.8	677.5
Japan	24,608.6	13,436.1	12,962.3	15,585.2	16,018.3	30,470.9	22,718.3	13,850.3	21,106.0	27,215.0
South Korea	4,302.7	5,257.2	5,608.8	6,990.9	6,289.6	5,737.1	7,653.0	6,035.8	10,127.4	12,546.9
New Zealand	270.0	496.3	−58.3	335.0	155.6	−259.7	185.2	20.7	−275.4	−27.5
Russia	608.0	−113.5	−24.4	63.4	47.8	61.5	88.1	78.0	27.2	166.2
United Kingdom	5,002.5	7,065.8	3,361.5	6,099.9	2,431.0	5,335.9	6,119.5	−1,846.1	−3,005.0	9,800.9
USA	11,457.9	21,141.3	22,912.5	13,415.9	29,134.9	−28,287.0	42,891.8	24,070.2	35,520.7	36,918.1
Others	46,141.7	45,667.3	48,354.3	22,780.5	74,292.0	48,476.1	91,521.0	56,532.2	110,455.4	101,766.6
Total	**120,965.5**	**130,114.5**	**118,667.2**	**113,471.9**	**156,845.7**	**147,619.5**	**166,056.5**	**119,754.3**	**212,943.5**	**225, 794.0**

Vestiges of a Globalized World

Economically, Southeast Asia still displays the globalized ties from which it has benefitted for so long. Overall inbound flows and stocks of direct investment from North America, Europe, Japan and within ASEAN continue to outweigh foreign direct investment from China, Beijing's Belt and Road Initiative (BRI) notwithstanding. ASEAN members export most among themselves and secondarily to China, while importing most from China and then with each other. These patterns suggest the region continues to benefit from capital coming from developed economies that go into the manufacture of components exported around the region and to China or the assembly of parts from the region and China.[10] ASEAN economies as a whole currently run trade deficits with China, South Korea and Russia, but have trade surpluses with other major trading partners. Some of the capital coming to Southeast Asia from Europe, Japan and North America has likely been redirected from China under the diversification and "de-risking" considerations. Southeast Asia's mantra of not wanting to "choose sides" between the United States and China reflects the understandable inertia of not wanting to shift from years of gaining from a growth and employment model based on this ecosystem.

How long Southeast Asia can benefit from existing conditions remains unclear. States like Indonesia, Malaysia, Vietnam and Thailand currently benefit from the redirection of FDI from China, just as Singapore gains from the portfolio

FIGURE 1
ASEAN Top Ten Sources of Foreign Direct Investment by Country, 2022

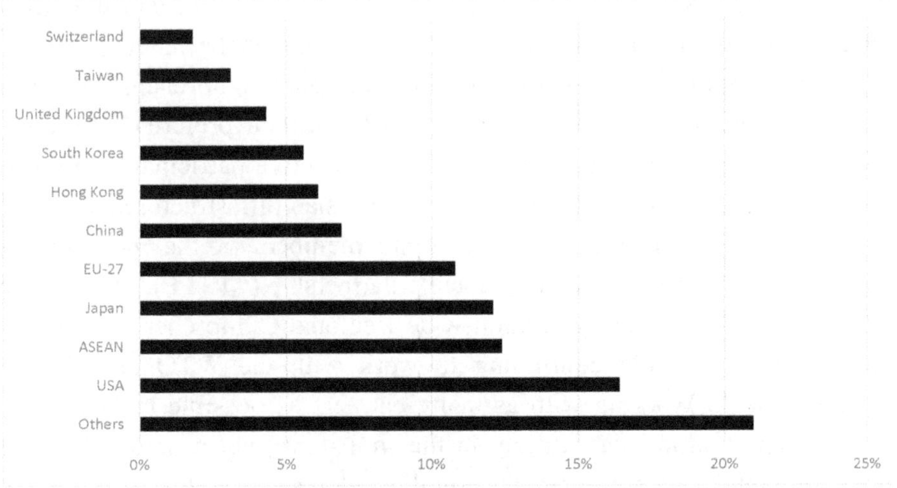

Source: ASEAN Statistical Yearbook 2023.

investment from China and Hong Kong coming to its shores.[11] However, "internal circulation" means that China is seeking to expand domestic production such that it is less reliant on external sources for inputs and components, including from Southeast Asia, leaving the region to export commodities to China.[12] The trends of "on-shoring" and "friend-shoring" by the United States and its closest allies and partners indicate a preference for investing and producing within each other's borders and less so in third areas in Southeast Asia that fall outside these categories.[13] How governments and enterprises in Southeast Asia will adjust to these potentially major economic reorientations remains unclear; if there are indeed plans, they remain unarticulated in public.

Declining interest in a globalized approach to the world economy also spells less interest in governing institutions in favour of more exclusive arrangements. China's use of economic coercion to impose punishment and express displeasure appears to go against most common understandings of trade and commercial activity under a liberal, multilateral regime.[14] Beijing's past targets have so far included Australia, Czechia, France, Japan, Lithuania, Norway, the Philippines, South Korea, Sweden and Taiwan, to name a few. Despite the macro-economic effects of Chinese economic coercion being limited, Southeast Asian states remain nervous about becoming targets of Beijing's ire.[15] Even though the United States reserved its heaviest trade restrictions for China and elicited reciprocation from Beijing, Washington's refusal to allow appointments to the World Trade Organization's appellate body has paralysed the WTO's dispute resolution mechanism.[16] Both the United States and China appear more interested in more restrictive approaches, whether through the Group of Seven (G7) and the Indo-Pacific Economic Framework (IPEF) in the case of the former and the BRI and Shanghai Cooperation Organization (SCO) in the case of the latter.

The participation by Southeast Asian states in both comprehensive and more exclusive economic arrangements is characteristic of their preference to not have to make choices. They have been among the most active participants in the BRI, along with its associated arrangements such as the Asian Infrastructure Development Bank, while several are among the founding members of the more exclusive Comprehensive and Progressive Trans-Pacific Partnership (CPTPP).[17] Concurrently, ASEAN has also led the broad, region-wide Regional Comprehensive Economic Partnership (RCEP) while continuing to work with the WTO and the Asian Development Bank. Working with as many partners as possible makes sense for broadening opportunities, particularly in the short-term, but a gradual fraying of the more comprehensive arrangements could develop as varying sets of competing rules and approaches arise. So far, Southeast Asian states and ASEAN have not given a clear indication of how they intend to use their multiple memberships in economic partnerships to harmonize standards and other rules of the road.

Hiding and Free Riding in Southeast Asia

Within the broader context of intensifying US-China rivalry, noticeable shifts in posture are occurring in the neighbouring regions of Northeast Asia and Oceania. Thanks to a long-term build-up, the PLA Navy now has more vessels than the US Navy, although the United States and its regional allies and partners together still hold a numerical advantage for now.[18] In tandem with a persistent build-up in military and paramilitary capability, China has undertaken increasingly assertive action to press its territorial claims from the East China Sea to Taiwan and the South China Sea. PLA activity includes a greater frequency of aerial and naval military deployments in areas claimed by Beijing and paramilitary action involving coast guard and maritime militia, especially in the South China Sea.[19] They involve risky intercepts of US and allied aircraft, including those on UN sanctioned enforcement operations, as well as the use of lasers, water cannon and ramming against vessels of other Southeast Asian claimant states in the South China Sea.[20] The PLA Air Force has further participated in joint patrols with Russia near Japan and South Korea, causing the latter to scramble fighter aircraft in response.[21]

The United States and its regional allies have taken more action to challenge what they see as aggressive Chinese actions. They involve periodic Freedom of Navigation Operations (FONOPs) to demonstrate that waters and airspace claimed by China are in fact international, and continuing efforts by the Philippines to resupply outposts in contested parts of the South China Sea.[22] Japan, South Korea, Australia, Taiwan and India have been building up their military capabilities through force modernization and expansion. They also regularly share information about Chinese actions, especially those that are exceptionally risky or dangerous.[23] The United States and its allies and friends are supporting capacity building across Southeast Asia through training and the supply of equipment such as radar, drones, aircraft and even missiles.[24] South Korea has become the biggest source of arms supply for Southeast Asia. These developments appear to focus on demonstrating resolve and deterring China from using force to pursue its claims and unilaterally changing the status quo.[25]

The Philippines and Vietnam have borne the brunt of Chinese assertive actions in the South China Sea and have been leading Southeast Asian responses to this challenge. Over the course of 2023, the Philippines has actively shared information, including video, photographic and mapping information relating to Chinese actions to disrupt Manila's attempts to assert its own South China Sea claims.[26] Philippine transparency efforts meant limited diplomatic headway in addressing its maritime disputes with China. These efforts, however, have prompted Beijing to be more restrained in its actions. Chinese paramilitary forces have neither sunk Philippine vessels nor detained civilian fishing vessels and crew, which they did in the past. Manila has further sought to rebuild its air force, enhance its surveillance capability, expand its navy, develop an anti-ship missile capacity, upgrade its coast guard, and bolster defence cooperation with the United States and other US allies such as Japan and Australia, paralleling deterrence efforts in Northeast Asia.[27]

Vietnam's response to the US-China rivalry has been perhaps the closest to hedging as Hanoi announced a comprehensive strategic partnership with the United States and basically accepted China's Global Security Initiative (GSI) within the space of a few months. Over the course of the year, Vietnam hosted a visiting US aircraft carrier and welcomed both US president Joe Biden and Chinese president Xi Jinping for state visits.[28] There were Vietnam-China talks over the management of maritime boundaries in the Gulf of Tonkin, even as the two countries upheld their competing positions over the South China Sea. Chinese vessels continued to harass Vietnamese efforts to survey the South China Sea for hydrocarbons while pressing their own maritime surveys.[29] Hanoi's choices reflect Vietnam's continued and consistent efforts over the years to maintain its interests and claims and maximize autonomy, all while avoiding provocation and escalation of tensions with Beijing to the extent possible.

Other Southeast Asian states have been relatively silent on the above developments, punctuated by claims of progress in negotiations on the South China Sea code of conduct (COC) and the adoption of an ASEAN statement about the South China Sea in December 2023.[30] This quiescence comes despite such contestations occurring in waters and airspace hosting critical channels for Southeast Asia's aerial, maritime and telecommunications traffic upon which the region's economies depend. Rather than some form of hedging, most Southeast Asian states appear to be hiding and hoping to free ride on the efforts by the United States and its friends and allies in Northeast Asia, South Asia and Oceania to deter excessive Chinese claims and action. Such opportunistic behaviour is understandable given the relative lack of capacity across much of Southeast Asia to ensure access, fears of sparking China's backlash and the desire to maintain positive ties with Beijing. Accompanying this passivity is a ceding of initiative on how to shape regional affairs as well as the prevention and management of any crises that may occur.

ASEAN Trudges On

ASEAN entered 2023 with Indonesia as chair. Expectations were high given that Jakarta spent the second half of 2022 planning its leadership role, including ways to address the ongoing civil war in Myanmar triggered by the military coup led by Min Aung Hlaing in 2021. Jakarta had also successfully pulled off a tricky G20 summit in November 2022, which involved Russian participation in the wake of its invasion of Ukraine, and a much-anticipated face-to-face meeting between Joe Biden and Xi Jinping. The year saw ASEAN convene its first Senior Officials' Meeting Working Group on Decision Making Process, which was intended to strengthen the grouping's institutional capacity and effectiveness consistent with the Post-2025 ASEAN Community Vision.[31] On the sidelines of the 78th United Nations General Assembly High Level week in September 2023, Indonesian foreign minister Retno Marsudi called again for the reform of the multilateral system.[32]

Reactions from other ASEAN member states to these calls for institutional change for ASEAN seemed muted. Jakarta's own interest in the agenda seemed to ebb as its presidential and legislative elections began to heat up towards the end of the year. The grouping and its members seemed to go about their normal course of business, including their regular reiterations about the importance of ASEAN centrality. ASEAN did manage to muster the first intra-ASEAN joint military exercise (ASEX-01N), alongside the 2023 ASEAN Multilateral Naval Exercise (AMNEX) hosted by the Philippines, and the first ASEAN-India maritime exercise, co-hosted by Singapore and India. Indonesia also organized several broader multilateral exercises that separately involved the United States, China and other key regional players.[33] Notably, both the 2023 AMNEX and ASEX-01N took place in the territorial seas of the Philippines and Indonesia, respectively, near contested South China Sea waters.[34] While these exercises focused on non-combat operations, they also demonstrated the intent of ASEAN members, albeit subtly, to highlight the lawfulness of military operations in and around the South China Sea despite Beijing's objections.

ASEAN continued to show little movement on ongoing and new global crises over the course of the year. Indonesia assumed its chairmanship with the hope of fostering progress towards peace in the Myanmar civil war, but the fighting and humanitarian crisis persist despite its efforts. The situation has resulted in civilian casualties, displaced persons and a rise in criminality in areas where governance has collapsed, bringing with it an increase in illegal drug production, human trafficking, and scamming being run out of Myanmar.[35] Moreover, the prolonged conflict in Ukraine has drawn international and regional attention and resources away from Myanmar. Adding to the distraction was the attack by Hamas on Israel on 7 October, which elicited a massive and disproportionate armed Israeli response against Palestinians in Gaza, and which has brought official condemnation from several Southeast Asian governments.[36]

Perhaps a bright spark for ASEAN in 2023 came at the end of the year, in the form of a special summit between Japan and the grouping to mark fifty years of the ASEAN-Japan dialogue relations. Japan is consistently popular and trusted in the region despite its invasion and occupation of much of the region during World War II, so the region generally embraced Tokyo's efforts to become more active. Apart from its traditional role of investing in and trading with Southeast Asia, recent changes to legislation meant that Japan can now participate more fully in security, especially capacity building. In this regard, the year witnessed Japan provide maritime surveillance radar and coast guard vessels to the Philippines as well as coast guard vessels and drones to Malaysia. These actions came on top of ongoing training and equipment transfers to Vietnam and Indonesia. The ASEAN foreign ministers' statement at the end of 2023 urged restraint and adherence to prevailing international law as commonly understood in the South China Sea, but a statement remains merely text unless ASEAN and its members are willing to follow through with action.[37]

The receptivity of ASEAN members to Japan's security role may heighten Beijing's suspicion of ASEAN-Japan cooperation, possibly compounding the security dilemma perceived by China in relation to the deepening security ties between the United States and its allies. Leaders in Beijing, including Xi Jinping, on several occasions in the past year described the United States as seeking to contain, encircle and suppress China.[38] The focus of their criticism was on efforts by Washington to deepen the already robust cooperation among US allies and friends around the world, including in Asia. While Beijing could see Japanese outreach to ASEAN as a next step to pushing it into a corner, ASEAN members are unlikely to turn down opportunities to upgrade their defence and law enforcement capabilities at a lower cost. Such a situation contributes to Beijing's views that its major power rivals are seeking to manipulate ASEAN and ASEAN members against China.

Grappling with a Changed World

Most Southeast Asian states and their populations have generally been beneficiaries of globalization and economic liberalization undergirded by the international order after the Cold War. Southeast Asian states that stayed on the non-communist side of the Cold War had benefitted from this US-backed system even earlier, with boosts to their economic growth during the Korean and Vietnam Wars. Of course, these advantages during the Cold War came at the cost of millions of lives in Indochina, repression under the name of anti-communism, and, in the case of Timor Leste, invasion and occupation. As communist parts of Southeast Asia reduced their own authoritarian excesses and moved away from their planned economies, they too began to attain some of the prosperity experienced by their neighbours. That said, even if economic development under the liberal, globalized world order benefitted elites and a growing middle class, it also left many behind and brought about environmental degradation.

Several generations of Southeast Asians and their leaders have grown up accustomed to a globalizing world where major power contestation was contained and there was a pervasive desire for economic integration, for all its strengths and ills. In this respect, they may find it difficult to envision a world that has changed and develop corresponding policies. But if 2023 and the preceding years are any indication, that world is fast becoming a thing of the past. Even if earlier expectations of the terminal decline of the United States and its replacement with China are overly exaggerated, a United States weakened by domestic political distractions and a China facing serious structural economic problems provide little comfort. In such a world, contention between Washington and Beijing will not go away and may even get worse, tugging at the fabric of the integrated world they jointly fostered not so long ago and on which Southeast Asia still depends.

The challenge for Southeast Asian leaders is to formulate an approach that can allow their states and the region to tide over what is likely to be a prolonged difficult period. In an ideal scenario, regional states should be pooling resources and collectively bargaining to increase their leverage and provide themselves with more certainty. But capitals in the region appear unable or unwilling to commit to some sort of joint endeavour, whether this means reforming ASEAN, augmenting it with some other framework, or perhaps even searching for replacements. Part of the issue seems to be that Southeast Asian states seem unsure about whether and how much to put their bets in ASEAN and international institutions undergirding the current, challenged world order, or whether to invest in something new altogether. Even if the answer is some mix of the above, there remains insufficient articulation of what that mix should look like, much less how to pursue it. Addressing such uncertainty with greater direction is perhaps what regional leaders need to be doing, but the window for them to do so with minimal disruption to themselves may be fast closing.

Notes

1. The Shanghai Cooperation Organisation, "Joint Communique Following the 222nd Meeting of the Heads of Government (Prime Ministers) Council of the Shanghai Cooperation Organisation", 26 October 2023, https://eng.sectsco.org/20231026/Joint-communique-following-the-22nd-meeting-of-the-Heads-of-Government-Prime-Ministers-Council-of-963083.html.

2. Dawn C. Murphy, *China's Rise in the Global South: The Middle East, Africa, and Beijing's Alternative World Order* (Stanford: Stanford University Press, 2022).

3. Samantha Power, "How Democracy Can Win: The Right Way to Counter Autocracy", *Foreign Affairs*, 16 February 2023, https://www.foreignaffairs.com/united-states/samantha-power-how-democracy-can-win-counter-autocracy.

4. Emily Feng, John Ruwitch, and Franco Ordnoñez, "Biden and China's Xi Met for Three Hours: Here's What They Talked About", National Public Radio, 14 November 2023, https://www.npr.org/2022/11/14/1136350988/biden-and-xi-are-meeting-in-bali-here-are-the-high-stakes-issues-on-the-agenda; Amy Hawkins, "Planet Earth is Big Enough for Two": Biden and Xi Meet for First Time in a Year", *The Guardian*, 15 November 2023, https://www.theguardian.com/us-news/2023/nov/15/joe-biden-xi-jinping-san-francisco-china-apec.

5. Oren Liebermann, "China's Unsafe Interceptions of U.S. Military Aircraft Have Dropped Off, Defense Officials Say", CNN, 2 January 2024, https://edition.cnn.com/2024/01/02/politics/china-us-unsafe-interactions-fall-off/index.html.

6. Nancy A. Youssef, "Chinese Spy Balloon Used U.S. Tech to Spy on Americans", *Wall Street Journal*, 29 June 2023, https://www.wsj.com/articles/chinese-balloon-used-american-tech-to-spy-on-americans-2e3f5039.

7. Zaheena Rasheed, "In Bid to Counter China, U.S. Ramps Up Efforts to Boost Military Ties in Asia", Al Jazeera, 28 December 2023. https://www.aljazeera.com/news/2023/12/28/in-bid-to-counter-china-us-ramps-up-effort-to-boost-military-ties-in-asia.

8. See Seng Tan, "Consigned to Hedge: Southeast Asia and America's 'Free and Open Indo-Pacific' Strategy", *International Affairs* 96, no. 1 (2020): 131–48.

9. Jonathan Stromseth, "Don't Make Us Choose: Southeast Asia in the Throes of U.S.-China Rivalry", Brookings Institution, October 2019, https://www.brookings.edu/articles/dont-make-us-choose-southeast-asia-in-the-throes-of-us-china-rivalry/.

10. ASEAN Secretariat, *ASEAN Statistical Yearbook 2023*, December 2023, https://www.aseanstats.org/wp-content/uploads/2023/12/ASYB-2023-v1.pdf.

11. Chanyaporn Chanjaroen, Cathy Chan, and David Raml, "Financial Firms are Flocking to Singapore, but Hong Kong Keeps Its Edge", *Time*, 6 October 2023, https://time.com/6321258/singapore-hong-kong-asia-finance-hub/; Huileng Tan, "Supply Chains Moving Out of China Could Create New Winners in the Southeast Asian Middle Class,

Says an Official", *Business Insider*, 15 September 2023, https://www.businessinsider. com/supply-chain-shift-china-create-middle-class-winners-southeast-asia-2023-9.

12. Xianhai Huang, Pan Yu, and Xueyin Song, "Strategic Focus Study on the New Development of 'Dual Circulation' in China under COVID-19", *Transnational Corporations Review* 14, no. 2 (2021): 196–77.

13. Günther Maihol, "A New Geopolitics of Supply Chinas", *SWP Comment* 45 (July 2022), https://www.swp-berlin.org/publications/products/comments/2022C45_Geopolitics_ Supply_Chains.pdf.

14. Vida Macikenaite, "China's Economic Statecraft: The Use of Economic Power in an Interdependent World", *Journal of Contemporary East Asian Studies* 9, no. 2 (2020): 108–26.

15. Jaebeom Kwon, "Taming the Neighbors: Exploring China's Economic Statecraft to Change Neighboring Countries' Policies and Their Effects", *Asian Perspective* 44, no. 1 (2020): 103–38; Audrye Wong, "How Not to Win Allies and Influence Geopolitics", *Foreign Affairs*, 20 April 2021, https://www.foreignaffairs.com/articles/ china/2021-04-20/how-not-win-allies-and-influence-geopolitics.

16. Lorenzo Caliendo and Fernando Parro, "Lessons from the U.S.-China Trade War", *Annual Review of Economics* 15 (2023): 513–47; Lindsay Garner-Knapp, Shaina D. Western, and Henry Lovat, "The US, the WTO, and the Appellate Body: From Great Expectations to Hard Times", in *European Yearbook of International Economic Law*, edited by Jelena Bäumler et al. (2021), pp. 3–32.

17. Angela Tritto and Alvin Camba, "The Belt and Road Initiative in Southeast Asia: A Mixed Methods Examination", *Journal of Contemporary China* 32, no. 141 (2022): 436–54.

18. United States Department of Defense, "Military and Security Developments Involving the People's Republic of China 2023", 2023, https://media.defense.gov/2023/ Oct/19/2003323409/-1/-1/1/2023-MILITARY-AND-SECURITY-DEVELOPMENTS- INVOLVING-THE-PEOPLES-REPUBLIC-OF-CHINA.PDF.

19. Agnes Chang and Hannah Beech, "Fleets of Force", *New York Times*, 23 November 2023, https://www.nytimes.com/interactive/2023/11/16/world/asia/south-china-sea- ships.html; Damien Cave, "China Creates a Coast Guard Like No Other, Seeking Supremacy in Asian Seas", *New York Times*, 12 June 2023, https://www.nytimes. com/2023/06/12/world/asia/china-coast-guard.html; Shuxian Luo and Jonathan G. Panter, "China's Maritime Militia and Fishing Fleets: A Primer for Operational Staffs and Tactical Leaders", *Military Review*, January–February 2021, https://www. armyupress.army.mil/Journals/Military-Review/English-Edition-Archives/January- February-2021/Panter-Maritime-Militia/.

20. Masaaki Yatsuzuka, "China's Advance into the Sea and the Maritime Militia", *NIDS Commentary* 53, 15 July 2023, https://www.nids.mod.go.jp/english/publication/ commentary/pdf/commentary053e.pdf; Sukjoon Yoon and Kim Wonhee, "The Import

of Hybrid Activities in the South China Sea", *Journal of Indo-Pacific-Affairs* (2023): 93–101; "Philippine President Says South China Sea Tension Increasing", NHK, 17 December 2023, https://www3.nhk.or.jp/nhkworld/en/news/20231217_02/.

21. Dzirhan Mahadzir, "Japan Releases Scramble Data against Chinese Aircraft", *USNI News*, 14 July 2023, https://news.usni.org/2023/07/14/japan-releases-fighter-scramble-data-against-chinese-aircraft; "S Korea Scrambles Jets after Chinese, Russian Aircraft Enter Defense Zone", Al Jazeera, 14 December 2023, https://www.aljazeera.com/news/2023/12/14/chinese-russian-warplanes-enter-south-koreas-defence-zone-seoul.

22. Malcolm Cook, "Australia's South China Sea Challenges", Lowy Institute, 26 May 2021, https://www.lowyinstitute.org/publications/australia-s-south-china-sea-challenges; "Philippines, China Trade Accusations over South China Sea Collision", Reuters, 10 December 2023, https://www.reuters.com/world/asia-pacific/philippines-says-china-rammed-water-cannoned-resupply-vessels-2023-12-10/.

23. International Institute for Strategic Studies, *The Military Balance 2023* (London: International Institute for Strategic Studies, 2023).

24. Ministry of Foreign Affairs of Japan, "Tenth Australia-Japan 2+2 Foreign and Defence Ministerial Consultations", 9 December 2023, https://www.mofa.go.jp/press/release/press1e_000352.html; United States Mission in Japan, "Fact Sheet: The Trilateral Leaders' Summit at Camp David. United States Department of State", 18 August 2023, https://jp.usembassy.gov/fact-sheet-trilateral-summit-at-camp-david/.

25. Max Broad and Evan A. Laksmana, "South Korea's Defence Relations in Southeast Asia. International Institute for Strategic Studies", 29 September 2023, https://www.iiss.org/online-analysis/online-analysis/2023/09/south-koreas-defence-relations-in-southeast-asia.

26. Collin Koh, "No China Backlash, So Far: The Philippines New Assertive Transparency Policy in the South China Sea", *Fulcrum*, 6 December 2023, https://fulcrum.sg/no-china-backlash-so-far-the-philippines-new-assertive-transparency-policy-in-the-south-china-sea/.

27. Julio S. Amador III, Deryk Matthew Baladjay, and Sheena Valenzuela, "Modernizing or Equalizing? Defense Budget and Military Modernization in the Philippines, 2010–2020", *Defence Studies* 22, no. 3 (2022): 299–326.

28. Askia Collins, "USS *Ronald Reagan* Carrier Strike Group Visits Vietnam", United States Navy, 25 June 2023, https://www.navy.mil/Press-Office/News-Stories/Article/3438946/uss-ronald-reagan-carrier-strike-group-visits-vietnam/; The White House, "Fact Sheet: President Joseph R. Biden and General-Secretary Nguyen Phu Trong Announce the U.S.-Vietnam Comprehensive Strategic Partnership", 10 September 2023, https://www.whitehouse.gov/briefing-room/statements-releases/2023/09/10/fact-sheet-president-joseph-r-biden-and-general-secretary-nguyen-phu-trong-announce-the-u-s-vietnam-comprehensive-strategic-partnership/; "Vietnam-China Joint Statement", *Vietnam Law*

and Legal Forum, 14 December 2023, https://vietnamlawmagazine.vn/vietnam-china-joint-statement-70965.html.

29. Govi Snell, "Tensions High as Chinese Vessels Shadow Vietnam's Oil, Gas Operations", VOA, 17 June 2023, https://www.voanews.com/a/tensions-high-as-chinese-vessels-shadow-vietnam-s-oil-and-gas-operations-/7141273.html.

30. ASEAN, "ASEAN Foreign Ministers' Statement on Maintaining and Promoting Stability in the Maritime Sphere in Southeast Asia", 30 December 2023, https://asean.org/asean-foreign-ministers-statement-on-maintaining-and-promoting-stability-in-the-maritime-sphere-in-southeast-asia/.

31. Ministry of Foreign Affairs of the Republic of Indonesia, "The First Meeting of ASEAN SOM Working Group on Decision-Making Process", 23 March 2023, https://kemlu.go.id/portal/en/read/4565/berita/the-1st-meeting-of-asean-som-working-group-on-decision-making-process.

32. Ministry of Foreign Affairs of the Republic of Indonesia, "At the United Nations, Foreign Minister Brings the Spirit of Bandung, Raises Global Trust and Solidarity", 24 September 2023, https://kemlu.go.id/portal/en/read/5300/berita/at-the-united-nations-foreign-minister-brings-the-spirit-of-bandung-raises-global-trust-and-solidarity.

33. Maria T. Reyes, "ASEAN Exercise, Naval Chiefs Meeting Demonstrate Unity, 'Voice for Peace'", *Indo-Pacific Defense Forum*, 13 June 2023, https://ipdefenseforum.com/2023/06/asean-exercise-naval-chiefs-meeting-demonstrate-unity-voice-for-peace/.

34. Collin Koh, "ASEX-01N Strengthens the Intra-ASEAN Military Landscape", *East Asia Forum*, 27 October 2023, https://www.eastasiaforum.org/2023/10/27/asex-01n-strengthens-the-intra-asean-military-landscape/.

35. Brookings Institution, "Myanmar's Civil War: Military, Political, and Crime Dynamics", 13 March 2023, https://www.brookings.edu/events/myanmars-civil-war-military-political-crime-dynamics/.

36. Om Prakash Das, "Israel-Hamas Conflict and Southeast Asia Responses", *IDSA Comment*, 8 November 2023, https://www.idsa.in/issuebrief/Israel-Hamas-Conflict-OPDas-081123; Joseph Rachman, "Gaza is a Burning Topic for Southeast Asia's Domestic Politics", *Foreign Policy*, 29 December 2023, https://foreignpolicy.com/2023/12/29/gaza-israel-hamas-war-southeast-asia/.

37. Association of Southeast Asian Nations, "ASEAN Foreign Ministers' Statement on Maintaining and Promoting Stability in the Maritime Sphere in Southeast Asia", 30 December 2023, https://asean.org/asean-foreign-ministers-statement-on-maintaining-and-promoting-stability-in-the-maritime-sphere-in-southeast-asia/.

38. Ministry of Foreign Affairs, People's Republic of China, 习近平同美国总统拜登举行中美元首会晤 [Xi Jinping and US president Biden hold Sino-US leaders' meeting], 16 November 2023, https://www.mfa.gov.cn/zyxw/202311/t20231116_11181125.shtml; Ministry of Foreign Affairs, People's Republic of China, 秦刚：遏制打压不会让美国更伟大，跟阻挡不了中国迈向复兴的步伐 [Qin Gang: Containment

and suppression will not make America great, will definitely not stop China's march toward rejuvenation], 7 March 2023, https://www.mfa.gov.cn/wjbzhd/202303/t20230307_11036890.shtml; 习近平在看望参加政协会议的民建工商联界委员时强调正确引导民营经济健康发展高质量发展 王沪宁蔡奇丁薛祥参加看望和讨论 [Xi Jinping stresses correctly guiding healthy, high quality development when calling on civil and construction industry committee members during Chinese People's Political Consultative Conference Meeting; Wang Huning, Cai Qi, Ding Xuexiang join visit and discussion], 6 March 2023, http://www.news.cn/politics/leaders/2023-03/06/c_1129417096.htm.

Regional Economic Overview for Southeast Asia

Manu Bhaskaran

This chapter provides a review of macroeconomic trends among the member countries of ASEAN in 2023. It first examines how the global environment affected regional economies, assessing the effects of a difficult world economy marked by the adverse effects of monetary tightening, a sluggish Chinese economy, further fragmentations of global supply chains, and the onset of the Israel-Hamas War when the Ukraine War was showing no signs of abating. It then examines why ASEAN economies demonstrated an encouraging degree of resilience in the face of these global headwinds. All the countries studied recorded positive, albeit slowing, growth rates. The reasons for this resilience include sound fiscal and monetary policies from policymakers as well as structural advantages. Finally, the chapter concludes with the cyclical prospects of the region in 2024. The positive outlook is underpinned by a robust trade rebound, supply chain reconfigurations into the region, and increased infrastructure spending.

An Extraordinarily Challenging 2023 for Southeast Asia

A confluence of disturbances hurt the global economy in 2023. Rising inflation that warranted hawkish monetary tightening from central banks, coupled with China's domestic woes, contributed to weak global demand. As a result, global economic growth eased, from 3.5 per cent in 2022 to 3.0 per cent in 2023, according to the International Monetary Fund.[1] In parallel, the world economy saw a pronounced slowing in export demand. Reflecting the difficulties in 2023 to date, the World Trade Organization (WTO) has slashed its forecast for world merchandise trade volume growth to 0.8,[2] less than half of its April forecast of 1.7 per cent. It further concluded that the risks were to the downside given the headwinds created by a sharper-than-expected slowdown in China and the re-

MANU BHASKARAN is CEO of Centennial Asia Advisors and Adjunct Senior Research Fellow at the Institute of Policy Studies, Singapore.

emergence of inflation in advanced economies that would warrant keeping interest rates higher for a longer period.

Lagged Effects of Unprecedented Monetary Tightening

Global monetary tightening has been the key feature of the post-pandemic period, with the world's central banks unleashing a sharp series of interest rate hikes not seen in decades to curb rapidly rising inflationary pressures—since late 2021 to 23 October, policy rates have been raised by an average of 400bps in advanced economies and 650bps in emerging markets, according to the IMF.[3] The hawkish monetary environment brought about several downsides to the global economy. As debts became more expensive to service, this led to a surge in defaults among borrowers who were already in fragile financial positions. Many firms were forced to draw down their cash reserves this year, with many small and mid-sized firms having barely enough to pay interest expenses. Tighter credit conditions also weighed on housing markets, especially in countries with a large share of adjustable-rate mortgages, with several countries witnessing slowing or declining housing prices since the start of the tightening cycle. Higher rates necessitated investment discipline, and together with production overcapacity, hampered capital formation. Coupled with the global demand rotation from goods to services, this meant that export demand, particularly for capital goods, was lacklustre for trade-reliant ASEAN economies, adding to existing difficulties in consumer spending.

The rising rates affected banks too, even though many benefitted from maintaining high rates for borrowers while depressing deposit rates. Financial institutions that had splurged on debt during the heady days of low rates and easy money but had been less than rigorous in their financial discipline suffered stresses as consumers and businesses lost jobs or revenues, with the bank run on tech-focused Silicon Valley Bank (SVB) and its eventual receivership in early 2023 being a notable example. Being a key investor in technology startups, the collapse of SVB dealt another blow to the US technology sector when it was already facing setbacks from rising borrowing costs and difficulties in reversing pandemic-induced over-expansion. Fortunately, the banking scare was limited to regional banks in the United States and Credit Suisse thanks to the swift containment efforts of authorities.

Expected Boost from China's Post-pandemic Reopening Unrealized

China's economic performance was also sub-par as the toxic mix of a deflating property sector, highly leveraged local governments, excessive overall debt, and uncertainty over policy and state ideology hurt the economy and limited the upside from the easing of pandemic controls at the end of December 2022. In June, the country's youth unemployment rate hit an unprecedented 21.3 per cent, prompting authorities to suspend disclosing the depressing statistic. Reflecting the psychosocial malaise affecting the country, movements encouraging disenchanted youths to stop striving for their future gained traction.

Policy response did not help much either. Over fears that stimulating the economy in the old ways could undermine other important objectives such as deleveraging an economy struggling with high debts, policymakers adopted cautious and narrowly focused piecemeal measures that failed to revive confidence. While there has been a ramp-up of stimulus recently, signs of increased party control over the private sector kept investors at bay. Even President Xi Jinping's signature Belt and Road Initiative was not spared from the slowdown, with the Chinese leader pointing to a reduced scale in the second decade of the global infrastructure programme.

As ASEAN economies have capitalized on China's growth over the past few decades by entwining themselves with it, a slumping Chinese economy conversely brought about contagion effects. Coupled with belt-tightening from advanced markets, this led to export contractions across ASEAN markets. Further compounding matters for exporters was the electronics downcycle. In the earlier months of the year, global electronics demand remained subdued because of heightened inventories from depressed sales and prior production ramp-ups. Exporters in Singapore and Malaysia were particularly affected by the slump, with both countries experiencing double-digit contractions that only moderated towards the end of the year. The IMF has since slashed the growth outlook for these export-reliant economies, whereas domestic-oriented economies have seen less-pronounced revisions. Outbound tourism from China also underperformed relative to prior expectations of strong revenge spending, hindering economic recovery in tourism-dependent countries such as Thailand.

Aside from exports, ASEAN currencies were also vulnerable to Chinese economic weakness, reacting to the Chinese yuan depreciating in response to economic travails. For many ASEAN economies, China takes on multiple roles of supplier, buyer and competitor in regional and global trade. Because of their close trade links, when the yuan depreciates, local currencies tend to weaken as well. Widening yield differentials with major economies, particularly the United States, coupled with the departure of equity investors over a lack of substantial stimulus, led to a large depreciation of the yuan this year—more than eight per cent against the greenback since the peak in January 2023. In tandem, Asian currencies fared poorly too, with countries whose exports to China contracted the most, such as Malaysia, leading the pack.

Continuing Adverse Effects of Geopolitical Strains

After a series of high-level exchanges that culminated in a meeting between Xi and his US counterpart Joe Biden at the end of 2022, relations between the two superpowers were off to a rocky start over the appearance of a Chinese spy balloon over America that Biden ordered shot down in February. In the aftermath, secretary of state Anthony Blinken was forced to postpone a planned visit to Beijing to protect the Biden administration from being seen as being too soft on China.

To bolster their position, both superpowers made efforts to strengthen ties with regional partners. Biden helped to broker a series of trilateral defence agreements with the leaders of key treaty allies Japan and South Korea, as Beijing's recent aggressive measures reminded both Tokyo and Seoul of the common threat they face. On China's part, it mobilized countries from the Global South, which have long felt aggrieved by an under-representation of their interests in a Western hegemony, to create groupings that counter the United States. China's successful persuasion of BRICS leaders to invite new members, including US arch-enemy Iran, to expand their fledging organization was a clear attempt at creating a more substantial counterbalance to the US-dominated G7 grouping.

The world breathed a small sigh of relief when Xi and Biden eventually met on the sidelines of the Asia-Pacific Economic Cooperation (APEC) forum in November. Guardrails that prevent unplanned clashes from escalating into more serious confrontations were reinstated as both parties committed to more constructive engagement. Notably, the two presidents agreed to establish direct communication lines between themselves, with commitments to discuss a range of economic and security issues of mutual interest such as the deployment of artificial intelligence in military applications, especially for nuclear weapons. Nevertheless, while the establishment of safeguards was indeed a positive development, the rivalrous nature of US-China relations will remain moving forward.

In 2023, the contest inevitably took on an economic dimension, with the G7 agreeing in May to pursue a strategy of de-risking—reducing a country's reliance on China for the supply of crucial raw materials or as a market for finished products. In the technology arena, this meant restricting the export of "a narrow set of advanced technologies critical for our national security", as President Biden put it. In swift retaliation, Beijing blocked the usage of chips made by US chipmaker Micron Technology across several infrastructure projects, casting a cloud of uncertainty over an industry where it takes at least five years to break even on large amounts of investments. Then, in July, China banned the export of gallium and germanium, two rare metals widely used in semiconductors, a tit-for-tat response to US-led export restrictions on chips and the equipment used to manufacture them. A month later, Biden signed an executive order that restricted outbound investment to China in critical areas, especially concerning "dual-use" technologies that have both commercial and military applications, although US officials took great pains to emphasize that they had no intention of curtailing China's economic growth, using the metaphor "a small yard with a high fence" to describe their strategy of protecting technologies critical to national security.

Accelerated Fragmentation of Globalization with More De-risking Efforts

Worryingly, following Biden's 2022 implementation of the CHIPS Act and Inflation Reduction Act, which provide hefty subsidies to support the country's semiconductor and green energy industries, the rapid adoption of de-risking has further fragmented the post–Cold War era of hyper-globalization. With manufacturing capacity directed along national security concerns rather than comparative advantages, this has resulted in huge efficiency losses. Things took a turn for the worse this year as countries accelerated their efforts to re-shore commodity supply chains. In the critical semiconductors industry, in particular, governments have been proactively offering incentives for domestic chip production.

- The **Chinese** government placed new income tax exemptions for advanced technology process nodes, established import duty exemptions for integrated circuit manufacturers, and resumed operations of the "Big Fund", China's US$50 billion-plus state investment fund for chips.
- In February, the **Japanese** government approved a US$2.8 billion supplement to the annual budget to subsidize private investments in chipmaking equipment, raw materials, power chips and microcontrollers. Then, in April, it allocated an additional US$2.3 billion to Rapidus, a state-organized joint chip venture with eight domestic partners that aims to achieve commercial production of two-nanometre chips by 2027. April's funding came after US$500 million was provided as initial funding for Rapidus last year.
- In March, the **South Korean** government passed the "K-Chips Act", providing 15 per cent tax credits for large corporations and 25 per cent for small and medium enterprises in key national strategic industries, including semiconductors. A month later, the Ministry of Trade, Industry, and Enterprise

announced plans for the Industrial Transformation Super Project, which will allocate 70 per cent of its R&D budget—approximately US$4.7 billion—to core industrial sectors like semiconductors.

- In January, amendments to the Statute for Industrial Innovation, dubbed the "**Taiwan** Chips Act", were passed. The new legislation offered 25 per cent and 5 per cent tax reductions for R&D and new equipment purchases, respectively.

Impact of Wars on the Global Economy

With the Ukraine War showing no signs of ending in 2023, the shocking assault on southern Israel by Palestinian Hamas militants and Israel's bloody retaliation that followed added further chaos to the world. Beyond the near-term risks of rising commodity prices, what was of far more concern for ASEAN nations was the longer-term implications that the Israel-Hamas war would have on the region.

In recent years, the United States has made it clear that its priority is in East Asia as it gears to face a rising and more assertive China. This has had important effects in the region. Smaller nations in this region have gone along with this pivot knowing that it gives them greater leverage to balance between the United States and China. The war in Ukraine has already tested that set of priorities—a broader Middle East conflict involving Israel, with whom the United States has a special relationship, could further test America's resolve to prioritize East Asia. The American political elite is already showing signs of strain over funding Ukraine, with a growing minority within the Republican party reluctant to help fund Ukraine's massive needs. If an Israel in prolonged conflict requires more US funding and supplies of munitions that Ukraine also needs, the United States will be placed in a difficult position. With its fiscal position constrained, the United States might have to make hard decisions that none of its allies will like. In particular, if the United States downgrades assistance to Ukraine in favour of Israel, America's allies in the Indo-Pacific will question how reliable the United States is as a security guarantor against, or counterweight to, China. This could favour China in its contest with the United States.

Reconfigured Supply Chains Because of Geopolitics and Changing Cost Structures

Supply chain reconfiguration picked up steam for several reasons. First, plans for relocation that were interrupted by the pandemic were dusted off and implemented now that the crisis was over. Second, as mentioned, geopolitical risks have worsened, so firms that were hesitating to move are now overcoming that reluctance and have begun moving, and they are willing to restructure their production grids even at some cost to efficiency. Consider the example of India, notorious for a difficult business environment despite some recent progress. Yet, companies, knowing these difficulties of operating in India, are nevertheless still moving there:

- Finland's Salcomp is the world's largest maker of smartphone chargers and is a supplier to Apple. Since 2014, Salcomp's Indian workforce has increased sixfold to 12,000 and it aims to hire 25,000 people in the next two years. Already, the Indian facility produces about 100 million units every year, compared with its China facility that produces about 180 million units.
- In electronics, India has gone from making 9 per cent of the world's smartphone handsets in 2016 to a projected 19 per cent this year, according to Counterpoint Technology Market Research.

Furthermore, with the United States and Europe all adopting industrial policies to encourage domestic production, firms are finding that there are stronger incentives to make the move. Finally, China's continued obsession with national security, which has restricted market opportunities for foreign enterprises, coupled with a shift in consumer sentiment and among corporate buyers, has compelled firms to shift out of the world's second-largest economy. Notably, net FDI inflow into China turned negative in the third quarter of 2023 (3Q23), the first time in data going back to 1998.

A Resilient Southeast Asia in the Face of Global Headwinds

As a sign of resilience, economic growth remained positive despite some signs of slowing across the ASEAN economies. Robust domestic demand and continued recovery in the services sector, particularly the tourism rebound, contributed to keeping employment at healthy levels and staved off a dangerous downward spiral. In fact, except for Singapore and Thailand, ASEAN economies enjoyed remarkably strong economic growth in the face of global headwinds, with Vietnam and the Philippines standing out.

- With a growth of 5.3 per cent in the third quarter of 2023, Vietnam's economy quickly regained its footing after a difficult first half in 2023. While the earlier difficulties had rendered the government's 6.5 per cent growth target for 2023 no longer feasible, there are positive signs that the worst is over and the economy can mount a strong recovery in 2024. Being highly export-dependent, the modest (by Vietnam's pre-pandemic standards) pick-up was driven primarily by manufacturing improvement brought about by the gradual electronics export recovery. Services was another bright spot, performing consistently well in 2023 as it was helped by strong momentum in the commercial and tourism industries. For the latter in particular, visitor arrivals in the year to October already reached 69 per cent of the same period in pre-pandemic 2019 thanks to a combination of easing of visa requirements and the country being a cheaper travel destination.

- The Philippines' robust growth of 5.9 per cent was driven by a strong rebound in government spending, which added 1.0 percentage point to overall growth. In the year to September, state infrastructure expenditure and other capital outlays surged by 19 per cent to PHP857.6 billion. The upswing in government spending can be attributed to the proactive implementation of catch-up expenditure plans by national government agencies and local government units. Foreign investment indicators are on an upward trajectory too, as evinced by a notable increase in investment approvals, which exceeded PHP400 billion in the first nine months of the year.

Even on the currency front, while regional currencies have depreciated, they have done so against a rampant US dollar. Compared with previous economic downturns and rate hike cycles, ASEAN currencies have performed quite well. Notably, real effective exchange rates, which account for price differences across economies, have remained relatively constant throughout the year (Figure 1).

TABLE 1
Real GDP Growth (%)

Economies	2021	2022	1Q23	2Q23	3Q23
Indonesia	3.7	5.3	5	5.2	4.9
Malaysia	3.1	8.7	5.6	2.9	3.3
Philippines	5.7	7.6	6.4	4.3	5.9
Singapore	9.1	3.7	0.4	0.5	0.7
Thailand	1.6	3	2.7	1.8	1.5
Vietnam	2.6	8	3	4.1	5.3

Source: CEIC.

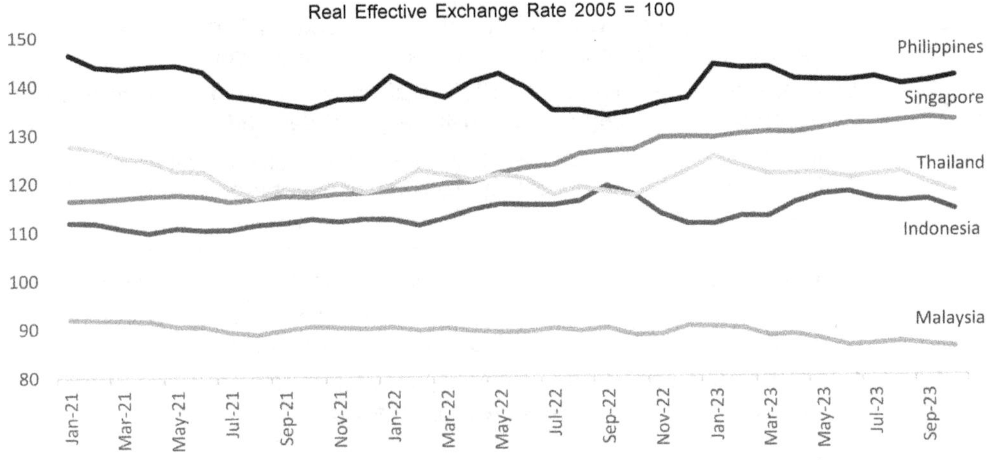

FIGURE 1
Real Effective Exchange Rates

Source: CEIC.

TABLE 2
Current Account Balance, USD millions

Markets	1Q22	2Q22	3Q22	4Q22	1Q23	2Q23	3Q23
Singapore	2,5474	2,4477	2,3413	1,6956	2,3711	2,3547	22,288
Vietnam	−1,677	−4,963	1,661	3,905	4,270	7,860	—
Indonesia	553	3,947	4,629	3,745	2,960	−2,207	−860
Thailand	−2,070	−7,111	−7,305	743	2,028	−2,534	3,299
Philippines	−4,146	−7,974	−6,010	14	−4,619	-3,595	—
Malaysia	1,364	664	4,234	6,018	977	2,015	1,975

Source: CEIC.

Factors behind Southeast Asia's Economic Resilience

Sound Fiscal and Monetary Policies

Sound fiscal and monetary policies had lent credibility, strengthened financial market confidence and given the region more protection against violent financial market moves and disruptive capital outflows. Central banks in the region were forced to raise rates in response to tightening moves by the Fed and other major central banks. With inflation easing and growth headwinds emerging, most of the region's central banks then paused their rate hikes earlier in the year, with Vietnam even slashing rates, understandably so given the growth difficulties in

TABLE 3
Key Economic Trends for Southeast Asia in 2023

GDP	• Most economies saw an improvement in growth in 3Q23, helped by increased private consumption and government spending. • Thailand was a notable exception; GDP growth slowed because of weak government spending and lacklustre external demand. • Indonesia's growth dipped slightly as a result of fiscal contraction. Uncertainty over the upcoming elections clouds the outlook for the final months of the year.
Trade	• Weakening global demand hurt exports across most of the region. • Recent months, however, saw export contractions ease. Imports of inputs grew, signalling a likely pick-up in exports in the coming months. • Through this year, tourism gradually recovered. But the all-important Chinese tourist has not returned in force yet.
Industrial Activity	• Purchasing Manager indices have improved slowly for most Southeast Asian countries since the beginning of the year, but manufacturing activity remains under a cloud. In October, several Southeast Asian countries, such as Vietnam, Myanmar and Thailand, experienced a decline in their PMIs. • Only Indonesia managed to achieve expansion in its PMI, although the rate of growth was notably slower compared with the previous month. • The manufacturing sector was weighed down by weak confidence because of a range of risks, including the conflict in the Middle East, continuing US-China tensions leading to trade and other restrictions, and continued uncertainty in China's economic recovery.
Prices	• Inflation eased across most Southeast Asian countries. In Singapore, inflation rose in October 2023 but is still likely to fall over time.
Currency	• Southeast Asian currencies were pressured by an increase in long-term yields in the United States and weak external demand amidst a tight global monetary policy environment. Risk aversion among investors saw capital flow out of Southeast Asian markets. • The Thai baht was an exceptional underperformer because of poor trade performance, disappointing economic growth and political uncertainty. • The Indonesian rupiah suffered from capital outflows as a result of risk-off sentiment and narrowing interest rate differentials. The export-dependent Malaysian ringgit faced headwinds from the electronic downcycle. • The Singapore dollar continued to strengthen in trade-weighted terms, reflecting the country's strong fundamentals and central bank policy.
Interest Rates	• With inflation easing across all the region's economies, Southeast Asian central banks have kept policy rates unchanged

Source: Centennial Asia Advisors.

its export market. Even with the prior rate hikes, real policy rates continued to be firmly in positive territory for most markets. Another key strength was the region's strong external buffers. The significant accumulation of foreign exchange reserves since the Asian financial crisis proved instrumental in mitigating the effects of potential capital flight.

ASEAN's Long-Term Fundamentals Attracting Global Investors

There was growing confidence in the long-term fundamentals of ASEAN too, given its relative political stability and reforms that could boost the supply-side potential of the economies. Indeed, ASEAN has found itself a main beneficiary of portfolio rebalancing as China's economic woes and geopolitical tensions force investors to divert FDI elsewhere. According to the UNCTAD World Investment Report 2023, ASEAN's share of global FDI exceeded China's by 2.6 percentage points in 2022, a notable development given that the last time the region outperformed China by such a large margin was way back in 1991. Furthermore, the value of announced greenfield projects increased by 35 per cent to US$86.6 billion, with manufacturing receiving the lion's share of investments on the back of emerging industries such as electric vehicles, electronics, biomedical and pharmaceuticals.

Companies are eager to tap into the region's low wages, a result of a burgeoning young population—its median age is thirty, while that of China is thirty-eight. As ASEAN workers are well equipped with specialized skills, after adjusting for productivity, wages in ASEAN economies such as Indonesia, Malaysia and Thailand are some of the most cost-competitive in the world according to the 2019 BCG Global Manufacturing Cost Competitiveness Index. On the demand side, an expanding middle class—ASEAN is forecasted to see 140 million new consumers by 2030—represents immense opportunities for foreign firms. The signing of the Regional Comprehensive Economic Partnership (RCEP) free trade agreement (FTA) in 2020 between ASEAN countries and Australia, China, South Korea, Japan and New Zealand further ensured access to Asia's largest markets. The following are some specific advantages of ASEAN economies.

- In **Vietnam**, beyond the traditional advantages of low operating costs and a growing domestic market, a key advantage is its political stability. The nature of the Hanoi regime gives it significant degrees of freedom in pursuing policies to promote trade and investments through the signing of twenty-seven FTAs, including the RCEP, the Comprehensive and Progressive Agreement for Trans-Pacific Partnership (CPTPP) and the EU-Vietnam FTA. With an average corporate tax rate of only 12.3 per cent, business costs are also one of the lowest in the region. Notably, despite high interest rates curtailing capital expenditure, the country attracted US$18 billion worth of FDI projects in the first eight months of this year, a more than eight per cent year-on-year increase.

- Similarly, **Indonesia**, leveraging its nickel reserves, has positioned itself as a key hub for EVs in Asia. To bolster the EV market, the Indonesian government has implemented a range of robust incentive programmes, like the subsidy for electric motorcycles to stimulate domestic demand and production and to entice foreign investors to set up manufacturing bases. Further underscoring its commitment to this transformative industry, the Indonesian government announced a collaboration with South Korean multinational electronics company LG to fast-track the establishment of a factory for manufacturing EV battery cells and associated facilities.

- In the **Philippines**, the Marcos administration has actively pursued reforms that include the optimization of public-private partnerships (PPPs). On 23 June, the Philippines implemented a new PPP Code, consolidating and streamlining the legal framework governing all PPPs in the country. This aims to create a more conducive and efficient environment for increased private sector participation in crucial infrastructure projects and ease the financial burden on the public sector. Recently, the government also increased foreign ownership limits in telecommunications, enabling significant foreign investment.

- EVs are gaining increased interest in **Thailand**, the largest auto manufacturer in Southeast Asia. Strategically, Thailand has enacted policies to attract FDI into its EV sector, offering tailored corporate tax exemptions for EV types and import tariff waivers for production machinery. These initiatives align with Thailand's broader economic strategy, focusing on the "Next Generation Automotive" industry. Thailand's ambitious plans, aiming to phase out internal combustion engines by 2035 and achieve fifty per cent EV sales by 2030, showcase a forward-thinking approach towards sustainable transportation solutions. Chinese EV manufacturers made a substantial US$1.44 billion investment to establish production facilities in Thailand in July 2023, exemplifying the industry's momentum.

- To set themselves up for the digital revolution, countries are enhancing digital connectivity within industry parks and Special Economic Zones, upgrading factories through digital solutions, robotics and automation, and developing Industry 4.0 clusters linked to technology centres and R&D hubs. **Singapore**'s Jurong Innovation Park and Advanced Remanufacturing and Technology Centre serve as examples.

Crucial Tailwind from Recovery in Tourism

The brisk recovery in tourism activity provided another lift to the region's service exports. According to statistics from the ASEAN+3 Macroeconomic Research Office (AMRO), ASEAN+3 tourist arrivals have, on average, exceeded 70 per cent of pre-pandemic levels as of the second quarter of 2023.[4] The value of service exports also reached 80 per cent of their 2019 levels, with Thailand and Cambodia being the rare exceptions—around 60 per cent—given their large exposure to the slumping Chinese market.

Good Economic Outlook for 2024

Agencies such as AMRO and the Asian Development Bank are projecting economic growth to improve to 4.5–4.8 per cent in the coming year.[5] Several factors contribute to these optimistic expectations, as outlined in the following sub-sections.

A Likely Strong Rebound in ASEAN Trade

The WTO global goods trade barometer, which has a good track record of detecting turning points in world trade, is now indicating that an uptick is nearing. Already, the WTO has reported that the contraction in merchandise trade volume had begun to bottom out in the second quarter of 2023, when it fell by just one per cent, after two quarters of much larger contractions.[6]

Other leading indicators concur. Air and sea cargo volumes, for instance, show early signs of a return to growth after contracting through most of last year (Figure 2). In fact, air cargo volumes expanded in August by 1.5 per cent, its first foray into positive territory since February last year. What was also encouraging for ASEAN was that the trade routes involving Asia, such as Europe–Asia and Middle East–Asia, outperformed global averages. The data also showed that intra-Asian trade flows were making a comeback. Hence, various indicators point to sustained export growth in 2024. Going by WTO estimates, growth in global merchandise trade volumes should rebound to 3.3 per cent in 2024 after a desultory growth of 0.8 per cent in 2023.[7]

Crucially for ASEAN, the critical semiconductors sector is showing signs of approaching a turnaround after a torrid 2022–23. Heightened inventories as a result of depressed sales and earlier production ramp-ups are beginning their slow but steady descent, while sales of semiconductors are also picking up both in the United States and the Asia-Pacific. While it must be emphasized that the recovery process will be a gradual one, the sector can look forward to medium-run sources of healthy demand, including in electric vehicles, but also computing devices with upgraded capabilities, which remain in healthy demand by firms and consumers. That the PMI for Taiwan's new electronics orders returned to growth on 23 September is a key indicator that the worst for the sector is behind it.

Figure 2
Global Air and Sea Cargo Volume

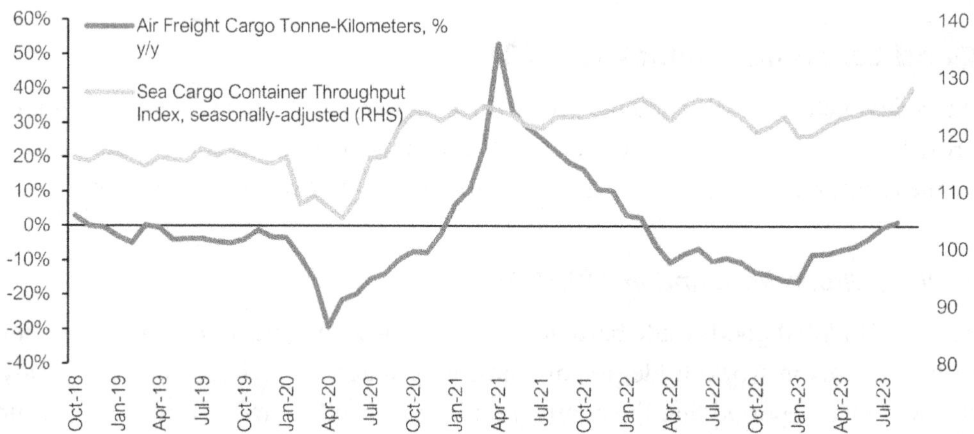

Source: International Air Transport Association, RWI-ISL.

Figure 3
International Arrivals in Asia (thousands)

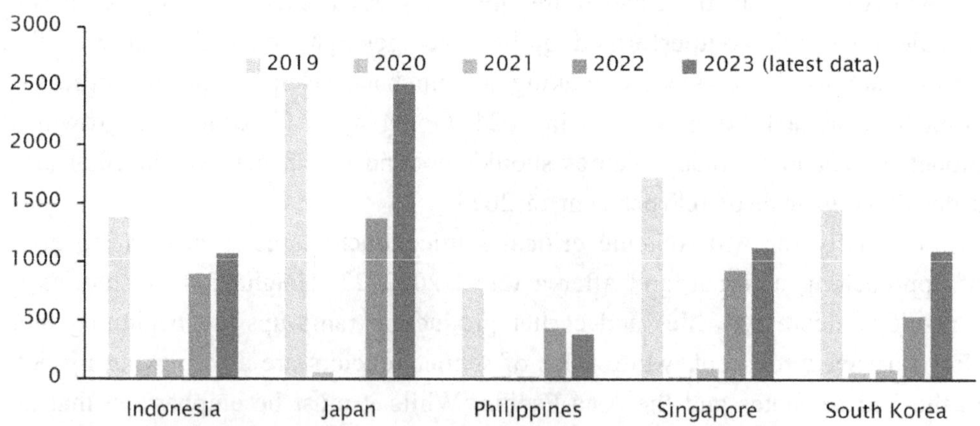

Source: CEIC.

Further Room for Tourism to Pick Up

As international borders continue to open and travel restrictions ease, the tourism sector is poised to further regain its vitality, contributing significantly to economic growth (Figure 3). A return to pre-Covid levels in 2024 is now likely.

Even though China's outbound travel has not yet rebounded to pre-pandemic levels, a strong recovery in domestic travel is under way (Figure 4). Domestic travel volume has reached ninety per cent of 2019 levels, with spending bouncing back to around seventy per cent of pre-pandemic figures. As Chinese consumers regain confidence and travel restrictions continue to ease, the return of Chinese tourists to Southeast Asia will provide a boost to the region. Thailand and Cambodia, with their heavy reliance on Chinese tourists, will particularly benefit from the rebound.

Figure 4
China's Domestic Visitor Arrivals (mn)

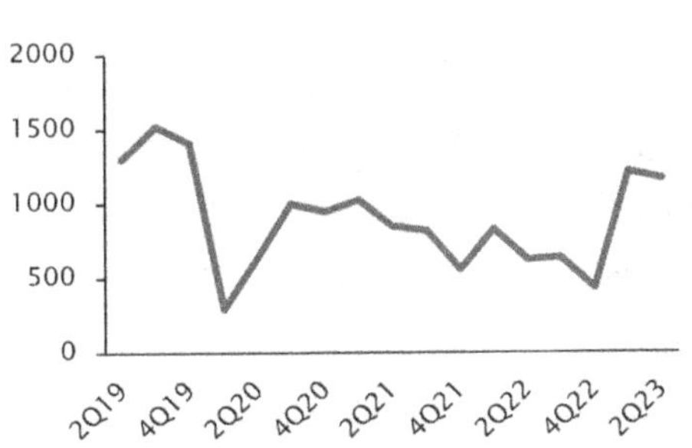

Figure 5
China's International Flights

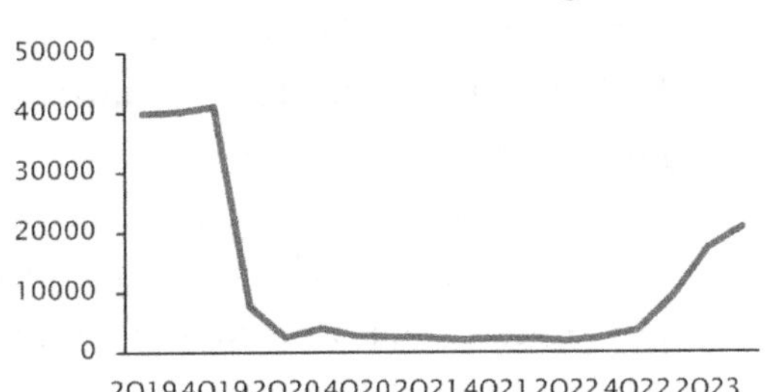

Source: Ministry of Culture and Tourism, OAG.

Benefits for Southeast Asia from Supply Chain Reconfigurations amid Tense US-China Relations

New trade and investment patterns are emerging, indicating trade diversion away from China. Between 2018 and 2022, China's share of US imports declined by over 4 percentage points, while Vietnam, Thailand and Indonesia experienced an increase. Similarly, the United States' share of Chinese imports decreased by approximately 2 percentage points, benefiting Taiwan and Vietnam. Corporate announcements regarding capital allocation and business operations restructuring suggest a shifting landscape of foreign investment, with less flowing into China and more into other Asian and emerging economies.

Bilateral electronics trade between the United States and China decreased by 5.6 per cent from 2017 to 2021. This shift is notable as there was a steady increase of 2.7 per cent in the years preceding the trade war, from 2012 to 2016.

During this period, the United States reduced its electronics imports from China and turned primarily towards ASEAN for final electronics goods, along with NEA-2 (South Korea and Taiwan) for intermediate products, particularly semiconductors.

As such, we anticipate the following future trends:

- **Reallocation of capital and restructuring of business operations**: Global corporations are reconsidering their production locations and are likely to reduce their allocation to China in favour of places such as Southeast Asia. Western firms are separating their Chinese businesses, while Chinese firms may establish entities in friendly locations like Singapore to mitigate potential American restrictions.
- **Increased governmental initiatives**: Governments are likely to enhance their attractiveness to firms undergoing this transition. For instance, the Philippines is considering a constitutional amendment to introduce new laws aimed at attracting foreign investment.
- **Robust infrastructure spending** across ASEAN will boost economic growth and investments in ASEAN by enhancing the region's connectivity, efficiency and competitiveness. This strategic investment not only creates a more conducive environment for businesses but also positions ASEAN as a prime destination for global investors seeking robust returns.

What Can Go Wrong in 2024?

The immediate concern is the impact of the Middle East crisis. The greatest risk is that the war in Gaza broadens in such a way as to disrupt the production or transportation of oil, causing energy prices to soar. In practical terms, this could happen if Iran were to be sucked into the conflict. So far, however, this seems unlikely. Iran and its allies such as Hezbollah have been relatively restrained in their reactions, and the statements from both parties suggest a strong desire to avoid a direct clash with Israel or the United States. So long as that remains the case, the risk of serious damage to an Asian recovery from events in the Middle East will be low.

Another source of concern is that if the US-China power struggle worsens it could produce more restrictions on trade and investment as the two big powers engage in a long period of contestation. But the evidence also shows that both powers are keen to contain the risks of escalation and are making progress in building the guardrails necessary to ensure this. That Xi agreed to meet with Biden in November—essentially shifting away from the previous strategy, which was to withhold cooperation with the United States—also suggests that Xi has calculated that China's current predicament requires him to focus on its domestic challenges and not be distracted by escalating tensions with the United States.

While the above concerns are manageable in our view, China's shaky economic recovery warrants a pause. As mentioned, there is a toxic mix of a deflating property bubble, worsening financial stresses in over-leveraged firms, and declining confidence among households and private businesses. The key to containing these risks is the policy response, which has been growing in intensity. The authorities seem to have a plan to contain financial risks, basically by getting financial institutions to bail out the large property developers whose collapse could cause widespread damage. In addition, local governments—the other major area of concern—are also being given greater financial support by the central government, which is also deploying more of its fiscal resources to boost the economy. All things considered, it looks like policy support will be further expanded. If this is executed efficiently—and the track record of the Chinese authorities is good in this regard—then the downside risks to Chinese growth can be contained and ASEAN can look forward to a much better 2024.

Notes

1. International Monetary Fund, "World Economic Outlook, October 2023", 2023, https://www.imf.org/en/Publications/WEO/Issues/2023/10/10/world-economic-outlook-october-2023.
2. World Trade Organisation, "Global Trade Outlook and Statistics, October 2023", 2023, https://www.wto.org/english/res_e/booksp_e/gtos_updt_oct23_e.pdf.
3. IMF, "Global Financial Stability Report, October 2023", 2023, https://www.imf.org/en/Publications/GFSR/Issues/2023/10/10/global-financial-stability-report-october-2023.
4. ASEAN+3 Macroeconomic Research Office, "Quarterly Update of the ASEAN+3 Regional Economic Outlook (AREO)", 2023, https://amro-asia.org/wp-content/uploads/2023/10/REG_AREO-2023-October-Update-Report_Oct-4.pdf.
5. Ibid.; Asian Development Bank, "Asian Development Outlook, September 2023", 2023, https://www.adb.org/outlook/editions/september-2023#:~:text=Asian%20Development%20Outlook%20(ADO)%20September,South%20Asia%20and%20Southeast%20Asia.
6. World Trade Organisation, "Global Trade Outlook and Statistics, October 2023", 2023, https://www.wto.org/english/res_e/booksp_e/gtos_updt_oct23_e.pdf.
7. Ibid.

Decoding China's Global Governance Initiatives: Insights from Southeast Asia

Bowen Yao and Mingjiang Li

In recent years, China has embarked on an ambitious path to not only consolidate its own development model but also to project its norms and values across the global stage. This projection is embedded in a series of initiatives that collectively aim to reorient the axes of global governance, potentially forging an alternative architecture replete with "Chinese characteristics". Central to this architecture are the Global Development Initiative (GDI), Global Security Initiative (GSI) and Global Civilization Initiative (GCI), which are complemented by the expansive Belt and Road Initiative (BRI) and China's growing economic clout.

These initiatives do not operate in isolation but interlock to promote a comprehensive suite of norms and values that China deems conducive to its vision of a harmonious global order. While the BRI lays the physical groundwork for connectivity, the GDI, launched by Chinese president Xi Jinping in September 2021, seeks to catalyse a more equitable, balanced and inclusive development paradigm. Meanwhile, the GSI, introduced in 2022, offers a Chinese formula to counter what it perceives as a security dilemma exacerbated by zero-sum alliances. The GCI, though less concrete in its early form, proposes a dialogue-of-civilizations approach that appears to challenge the Western-centric narrative of global governance.

Southeast Asia, with its dynamic economies[1] and complex security landscape,[2] serves as an influential testing ground for the reception and integration of these initiatives. The diverse responses from the region, ranging from receptive collaboration to cautious hedging,[3] provides a nuanced canvas to evaluate the traction these initiatives might gain and the potential reshaping of Southeast Asia's

BOWEN YAO is a PhD student at the S. Rajaratnam School of International Studies (RSIS), Nanyang Technological University, Singapore.

MINGJIANG LI is Associate Professor at RSIS, Nanyang Technological University, Singapore.

political, economic and strategic domains. As China continues to promote its narratives and approaches with vigour and an assertive diplomatic posture, the fabric of Southeast Asian governance structures, development models and geopolitical alignments could be subject to significant influence, if not transformation.

This chapter will dissect the layers of this influence, contemplating the extent to which Southeast Asian states might align with, adapt or counterbalance the outreach of Chinese initiatives. It aims to unravel these norms and values and critically examine their implications for Southeast Asia, a region that is both geographically proximate and strategically pivotal to China's global aspirations. The interplay of these developments is not merely regional but bears the weight of global significance, posing fundamental questions about the future trajectory of international order. This analysis will, therefore, not only spotlight the Southeast Asian perspective but also reflect on the broader implications of a global governance structure that continues to evolve and to be contested under the shadow of a rising China.

China's Norms and Values in Global Governance

China's ascent to global prominence has been accompanied by the articulation and promotion of distinctive norms and values that aim to recalibrate international relations and global governance. Central to this reorientation are the GDI, GSI and GCI, which collectively seek to offer an alternative paradigm to the prevailing liberal international order.

The GDI underscores a vision for equitable and sustainable development. It emphasizes a multipolar world where development is not a zero-sum game but a collaborative pursuit for mutual benefits. The GDI's core principles include promoting a people-centred approach, fostering green and low-carbon development, and advancing a global partnership for development. By advocating for the reduction of the North-South development gap and calling for the implementation of the 2030 Agenda for Sustainable Development, China positions itself as a leader in addressing global development challenges.[4]

Complementing the GDI is the GSI, which promises to foster a new security architecture by challenging the traditional security paradigms characterized by military alliances and power politics. Instead, it proposes the concept of common, comprehensive, cooperative and sustainable security. The initiative underscores non-interference in the internal affairs of states, peaceful resolution of disputes, and upholding of equity and justice in the international arena. This initiative represents a strategic narrative from China that seeks to reshape global security policies in line with its worldview.[5]

The GCI, though less defined than its counterparts, is a cultural and ideological proposition that invites a "dialogue among civilizations". It responds to the perceived dominance of Western cultural narratives and promotes the idea of cultural diversity and civilizational exchange on equal terms. Through this initiative, China promotes the notion of building "a community with a shared future for mankind", one that China claims to be harmonious and inclusive.[6]

In concert with these initiatives, the BRI serves as the economic arm of China's global strategy. As the most visible of China's international projects, the BRI seeks to enhance global economic development through infrastructure investment and connectivity on a transcontinental scale.[7] While the BRI is framed as an economic project, its geopolitical implications are profound, fostering deep-seated linkages that could potentially translate into political influence.

In Southeast Asia, these initiatives find a receptive yet cautious audience. The region's developing economies see the potential for accelerated development through Chinese investments and partnerships. The GDI's emphasis on sustainable development and poverty reduction finds resonance in many Southeast Asian countries, which are still grappling with development challenges such as infrastructure deficits, poverty, economic disparities and the need for sustainable growth.[8] The GDI's offerings of development cooperation, green transformation and technological advancement are appealing and align with the region's economic goals.

The GSI's non-confrontational approach to security resonates with Southeast Asia's preference for consensus-based diplomacy. The initiative's emphasis on the principle of non-interference also echoes the region's long-standing norm, as articulated in the Treaty of Amity and Cooperation in Southeast Asia.[9] However, the region's embrace of the GSI has not been without reservations. Southeast Asian states are acutely aware of their strategic position between the competing interests of major powers. Thus, while they may align with China's development narrative, they also seek to maintain autonomy and balance in their foreign policies. The ASEAN Outlook on the Indo-Pacific, which emphasizes inclusivity, sovereignty and the centrality of ASEAN, is indicative of this balancing act.[10] The traction that China's initiatives gain in Southeast Asia will be contingent upon how they intersect with the region's own aspirations and challenges.

The broader geopolitical currents also affect the traction of these Chinese initiatives in Southeast Asia. The United States' pivot to Asia, coupled with the increasing engagement of other powers like the European Union and Japan, provides Southeast Asian states with an array of options. The United States' Indo-Pacific strategy, which emphasizes freedom of navigation, democratic values and the rule of law, presents a counter-narrative to the GSI. The Quad—an informal strategic forum comprising the United States, Japan, India and Australia—further underscores the competing visions for regional security architecture. These powers' narrative of a rules-based international order is deeply entrenched in the strategic thinking of regional states, such as Singapore and Vietnam.[11] The contestation between these divergent narratives is playing out across diplomatic forums, development projects and security dialogues. It is a contestation that goes beyond mere power politics; it encompasses a battle of ideas and principles for the future of global governance. Southeast Asia, with its historic interplay of external influences and its own rich tapestry of norms, sits at the forefront of this unfolding dynamic.

China's initiatives, backed by its economic heft and strategic patience, have the potential to create enduring shifts in the region's landscape. Whether these shifts will lead to a reconfiguration of Southeast Asia's governance structures and regional order is a question that only time will answer. But it is clear that the region is engaging with China's narratives on development, security and cultural exchange with a mix of opportunism and strategic caution. As these initiatives unfold, they will continue to test the resilience of the existing liberal international order and the adaptability of Southeast Asian states. The outcome of this test will have profound implications not only for the region but also for the architecture of global governance as a whole.

Security and Strategic Implications

The geopolitical landscape of Southeast Asia is marked by a delicate equilibrium, where nations tread a fine line between asserting strategic autonomy, balancing relations with major powers, managing historical disputes, and engaging in cooperative security arrangements as well as a patchwork of alliances.

China's GSI proposes a recalibration of traditional security concepts that have long underpinned the region's strategic landscape. At its core, the GSI advocates for the principles of common, comprehensive, cooperative and sustainable security. It challenges the dynamics of military alliances, power politics and the perceived unilateral security measures often associated with Western influence. China's narrative positions the GSI as a more inclusive and equitable approach, eschewing the zero-sum game mentality in favour of collective action and mutual respect for sovereignty and territorial integrity.[12] This recalibration is not merely a shift in security paradigms but an endeavour to align regional security perspectives with a set of principles that resonate with China's worldview and security interests.

For Southeast Asia, a region historically fraught with territorial disputes, varying degrees of political stability and diverse economic landscapes, the GSI offers an intriguing and complex proposition. The GSI's principles of common and cooperative security resonate with the ASEAN-centric security architecture and the ASEAN Way, which emphasizes non-intervention, consensus-building and respect for national sovereignty. Reception of the GSI is complicated, however, by the region's own security alliances and partnerships; notably, those with the United States, which has been a longstanding security guarantor through its network of bilateral alliances and defence agreements.

China's increasing assertiveness in the South China Sea, which includes territorial and maritime claims overlapping with those of several Southeast Asian states, tests the GSI's principle of respect for sovereignty and peaceful resolution of disputes. While China promotes dialogue and negotiation through forums like the ASEAN-China talks on a Code of Conduct in the South China Sea, the ongoing militarization and island-building efforts present a stark contrast to the cooperative security narrative espoused by the GSI. Vietnam, for example, is wary of giving full support to the proposal in light of its territorial and maritime disputes with China in the South China Sea.[13] Such concerns are also shared by Indonesia out of its interests in the North Natuna Sea.[14]

Furthermore, the GSI's implications for Southeast Asia extend into the domain of cybersecurity, space, and the digital economy—areas of growing importance to regional security. China's prowess in technology and its initiatives in cyber governance present both opportunities for cooperation and challenges in ensuring a free, open and secure digital domain in the region.[15]

The region's response to the GSI is nuanced, reflecting a diverse set of national interests and strategic priorities. Countries like the Philippines and Singapore, which maintain a security alliance or strong defence ties with the United States, approach the GSI with a degree of caution, seeking to maintain a balance between their traditional security partnerships and the potential benefits of engagement with China. Conversely, nations like Cambodia and Laos, with closer economic ties to China, might view the GSI more favourably, seeing it as an opportunity to enhance their security infrastructure and capabilities through Chinese investment and support.

As Southeast Asian states continue to hedge between different security paradigms, the GSI's prospects hinge on China's capacity to deliver tangible security benefits while mitigating regional concerns over its strategic intentions. China needs to demonstrate that its approach to security complements existing security mechanisms and effectively addresses the region's security challenges such as maritime disputes and transnational crime without undermining the autonomy and interests of regional nations. It will also depend on how China's actions, particularly in contested spaces like the South China Sea, correspond with the cooperative ethos of the GSI.

The long-term traction of the GSI in Southeast Asia will be determined by the unfolding geopolitical contest between the major powers, the evolving nature of security threats, and the region's collective response to the complex interplay of power, principles and partnership. As China presses on with the GSI, this would be a litmus test for the adaptability of regional security structures, the resilience of ASEAN unity and Southeast Asian states' balancing act in leveraging the GSI for regional security while maintaining strategic relationships with other major powers. Whether the GSI will redefine Southeast Asia's security landscape or simply add another layer to the intricate tapestry of regional security remains an open question, one whose answer will shape the contours of regional and global governance for decades to come.

China's Economic Influence and Southeast Asia

In the contemporary geopolitical theatre, the economic dimension of statecraft has become a predominant force in shaping international alliances and regional dynamics. The effects of China's ascendance as a global economic powerhouse have been particularly significant in Southeast Asia, a region that has become a focal point for Beijing's economic outreach and strategic interests. The intersection of the BRI and the GDI has the potential to not only bolster economic development within the region but also to recalibrate existing power structures and influence the geopolitical landscape.

The BRI has been instrumental since its inception in establishing a network of infrastructure projects, including railways, highways, ports and energy projects across Asia, Africa and beyond. In Southeast Asia, the BRI has been received with a mix of enthusiasm and apprehension. On one hand, it offers access to substantial Chinese investments, which promise to accelerate industrialization, improve connectivity and promote economic growth.[16] On the other hand, there is wariness about the potential for debt-induced dependency and the strategic implications of China's increasing footprint in the region.[17]

China's economic influence in Southeast Asia is not merely transactional; it also has a transformative effect on the developmental trajectories of countries in the region. To complement the BRI, which places emphasis on hard infrastructure, the GDI seeks to position China as a champion of sustainable and equitable development and advocates for a more balanced and inclusive global development architecture.[18] The synergy between the BRI and GDI in Southeast Asia is evident in the way China leverages its economic might to foster a development-oriented partnership with the region. Projects under the BRI—such as the China–Laos railway, the Jakarta–Bandung high-speed rail in Indonesia and the New Yangon City in Myanmar—are emblematic of the development-centric approach that the GDI aims to promote. These projects are poised to reshape the economic landscape of the region, enhancing intra-regional trade and fostering closer economic ties between Southeast Asia and China. As Lee Hsien Loong, prime minister of Singapore, put it, Asian states "reciprocate China's desire to deepen economic integration" and "look forward to participating in new growth opportunities in China's dynamic economy".[19]

The GDI also functions as a diplomatic and narrative instrument for challenging the security-focused strategy of the United States in the Indo-Pacific. It aims to resonate with developing countries that perceive the United States and Europe as overly focused on the conflict in Ukraine, allocating disproportionate attention and resources there, while neglecting the development requirements of the Global South.[20]

However, the economic engagement championed by China through these initiatives also intersects with the strategic concerns and national interests of Southeast Asian states, which are mindful of maintaining their sovereignty and economic independence. The principle of "high-quality development" promoted by the GDI must be reconciled with the on-the-ground realities of these states, where the capacity to absorb investment, manage debt and maintain control over strategic assets varies.

The implications of China's economic influence in Southeast Asia are multifaceted. Economically, the infusion of Chinese capital and technology has the potential to catalyse development and integration within the region. At the same time, it raises questions about the long-term sustainability of such investments and the ability of recipient countries to negotiate terms that protect their national interests. There is also the concern of "debt-trap diplomacy", a term used by critics to describe a situation where countries become overly indebted to China and potentially susceptible to Beijing's influence.[21]

The strategic implications are equally significant. As Southeast Asia's infrastructure and economies become more intertwined with China, the region's strategic autonomy could be affected. The dual-use potential of many infrastructure projects, such as ports and communication networks, has not gone unnoticed by regional states and external powers. The possibility of such projects facilitating greater Chinese military or strategic presence in the region adds another layer of complexity to Southeast Asia's engagement with the BRI and GDI.[22]

The effect of China's economic initiatives on the regional order is also a subject of considerable debate. While the economic benefits of projects under the BRI and GDI can contribute to regional stability and prosperity, they also have the potential to shift the balance of influence in favour of China. This shift could see Southeast Asian states recalibrating their foreign policies, potentially at the expense of traditional alliances and partnerships.

The reception of China's economic initiatives in Southeast Asia has not been uniform across the region. Cambodia and Laos have embraced the BRI and GDI with little reservation, attracted by the promise of development and the prospect of closer ties with China. Others, like Vietnam and Indonesia, have approached it with more caution, balancing the economic benefits with a desire to maintain their strategic autonomy and diversify their partnerships.

In conclusion, China's economic influence in Southeast Asia, channelled through the BRI and GDI, is a powerful force with the capacity to alter developmental paths and influence regional geopolitics. The success of these initiatives will depend largely on China's ability to provide tangible benefits without imposing onerous debt obligations or compromising the autonomy of recipient nations. China's developmental partnerships must be perceived as equitable and mutually beneficial to gain lasting traction. The outcomes of these initiatives will shape not only the economic futures of individual Southeast Asian states but also the strategic orientation of the region as a whole. The challenge for Southeast Asian countries lies in harnessing this influence for their own economic growth and development while safeguarding their strategic autonomy and navigating the complex waters of great power rivalry.

Cultural and Ideological Engagement

Southeast Asia, with its rich tapestry of cultures and histories, has always been a vibrant confluence of civilizational currents. China's introduction of the GCI represents a strategic foray into this cultural milieu, with implications far beyond the realm of traditional statecraft. The GCI, while less clearly defined than its economic and security counterparts, is predicated on the promotion of cultural exchange, mutual learning, and the coexistence of diverse civilizations. It targets the soft power dimension of China's engagement with Southeast Asia, seeking to foster a deeper cultural understanding and affinity between China and regional states. It also marks an attempt by China to reshape the global narrative and present an alternative to the Western-centric discourse on culture and ideology.

The GCI's cultural overtures towards Southeast Asia manifest in various forms, including Confucius Institutes, cultural exchanges, media partnerships and educational collaborations. These initiatives are designed to build soft power and foster a positive image of China, presenting it as a benign and culturally rich neighbour. By promoting the learning of the Chinese language and facilitating cultural programmes, China aims to create cultural affinity and a deeper understanding of its traditions, modernization narrative and governance model.

In Southeast Asia, the response to China's cultural initiatives has been mixed. The region's own cultural confidence and diversity mean that while there is openness to engagement with Chinese culture, there is also a desire to preserve local identities and traditions. Southeast Asian states are aware of the soft power dimensions of cultural engagement and are cautious about the potential for cultural influence to translate into political or ideological sway.

The GCI's emphasis on a "community with a shared future for mankind" reflects China's aspiration for a form of global governance that acknowledges the legitimacy of different governance models. This narrative, which subtly challenges the universality of Western democratic values, has resonated with some governments in the region, particularly those that favour a more state-centric model of development and governance. For these nations, the Chinese model offers an example of how to pursue modernization without wholesale adoption of Western political systems.[23] However, for Southeast Asia, the GCI's promotion of cultural exchange must be balanced against the safeguarding of democratic principles and institutions.[24] The success of China's cultural and ideological engagement in these countries depends on its ability to present its initiatives as complementary to local values rather than as replacements.

China's cultural diplomacy also extends to regional media landscapes. Through partnerships and content-sharing arrangements with local media outlets, China disseminates its development narrative and perspective on global affairs. The penetration of Chinese media content into Southeast Asian information spaces is part of a broader strategy to influence public opinions and shape perceptions of China's role in the world.[25] The proliferation of digital media and the internet has amplified the potential for cultural exchange, but it has also raised concerns about information sovereignty and the protection of national cyber spaces.[26] The digital aspect of the GCI, through the promotion of Chinese technology and digital platforms, presents both opportunities for connectivity and challenges in terms of data security and the preservation of information ecosystems free from external influence.

The GCI's approach to promoting dialogue among civilizations is particularly salient in the context of Southeast Asia's multicultural societies. China's narrative of respecting cultural diversity and promoting harmonious coexistence aligns with the region's ethos of cultural pluralism. Yet, there is an underlying wariness about the GCI's potential to foster dependencies or erode local cultures.[27] As Southeast Asia grapples with the cultural dimensions of China's initiatives, it must navigate a complex landscape where cultural engagement intersects with geopolitics. Countries in the region are tasked with maximizing the benefits of cultural exchange while maintaining the integrity of their cultural and ideological spheres.

In the long term, the success of the GCI in the region will require a nuanced approach from China that respects the cultural sovereignty of Southeast Asian states and promotes genuine bilateral and multilateral cultural exchanges. The GCI should support the region's cultural agency and not merely serve as a vehicle for spreading Chinese culture and ideology. On their part, Southeast Asian countries need to strengthen their ability to engage critically with the Chinese cultural and civilizational narratives, foster their own cultural diplomacy and promote intra-regional exchanges so as to contribute to a genuine dialogue among civilizations.

The vibrancy and resilience of Southeast Asian cultures, along with the region's commitment to maintaining a diverse and open cultural space, will ultimately shape the trajectory and impact of China's cultural and ideological engagement. As China continues to present its civilization narrative, it is the response of Southeast Asian states—rooted in their own rich cultural heritages and values—that will determine the region's cultural future in the face of global shifts.

Conclusion and Outlook

The GDI, GSI and GCI are China's strategic policy frameworks that aim to redefine global cooperation and governance in line with Chinese perspectives. The integrated nature of the GDI, GSI and GCI paints a holistic picture of China's efforts to promote and project its interwoven economic, security, cultural and ideological influence onto the global stage.

The engagement of Southeast Asia with China's GDI, GSI and GCI thus far signifies a region at a crossroads, navigating the complexities of a shifting global order. The GDI offers economic prospects that are cautiously welcomed, given the region's development needs and China's ability to fulfil them. The GSI, with its alternative security paradigm, presents a vision that aligns with ASEAN's cooperative security and ethos of non-interference. Yet, it is weighed against traditional security alliances and the hedging strategies of Southeast Asian nations. Meanwhile, the GCI extends China's cultural and ideological engagement, and its success will be measured by China's ability to resonate with and respect the rich cultural mosaic of the region.

Going forward, engagement by Southeast Asian countries with these initiatives will likely continue to be selective, aligned with their national interests and regional priorities, and based on a combination of economic pragmatism, strategic caution and cultural assertiveness. The degree to which these initiatives are adopted will depend on the perceived value addition to the region's pursuit of autonomous, sustainable and inclusive growth and development. The GDI's infrastructure and development projects must demonstrate a commitment to sustainable practices and respect for local conditions. The GSI's security propositions need to show that they can contribute to regional stability without undermining existing security frameworks and alliances. The GCI's cultural engagements must enrich the region's cultural fabric without eroding its diversity.

As these initiatives unfold, the prospect of Southeast Asia adopting or adapting to these narratives will depend on a nuanced interplay of regional autonomy, economic pragmatism, and the strategic balance of power. The initiatives are not just about the expansion of China's influence; they are also a test of the region's ability to assert its own agency and shape the contours of its engagement with major powers. In other words, the trajectory of China's GDI, GSI and GCI in Southeast Asia will be a critical indicator of the region's openness to alternative governance models and its willingness to embrace a multipolar global order.

Given its strategic and economic significance, Southeast Asia is emerging as a key arena for the contestation and collaboration of twenty-first-century powers and as a pivotal player in the international community's pursuit of a more balanced and multipolar world. The evolving relationship between Southeast Asia and China's suite of initiatives will, therefore, be a bellwether for China's broader global influence, which, in turn, will be telling of the future trajectory of global governance. The region's response will not only reflect its own developmental, security and cultural priorities but also set precedents and references for other regions of the world. Whether Southeast Asia's engagement with China leads to a recalibration of the international order or reinforces the existing global governance structures, the implications will reverberate far beyond Southeast Asia's immediate geopolitical theatre.

Notes

1. Denis Bugrov, Debadrita Dhara, and Kamaruzaman Kamarudin, "Southeast Asia's Economies: Softening but Still Strong", October 2023, https://www.mckinsey.com/featured-insights/future-of-asia/southeast-asias-economies-softening-but-still-strong#/; Amanda Murphy, "Southeast Asia's Economic Outlook is Only Brightening", *Nikkei Asia*, 25 July 2023, https://asia.nikkei.com/Opinion/Southeast-Asia-s-economic-outlook-is-only-brightening.

2. Rahman Yaacob, "Not Only the Dragon: Understanding Southeast Asia's Complex Security Landscape", *The Interpreter*, 26 October 2023, https://www.lowyinstitute.org/the-interpreter/not-only-dragon-understanding-southeast-asia-s-complex-security-landscape; ASEAN Secretariat, "ASEAN Security Outlook", 2021, https://asean.org/book/asean-security-outlook/.

3. In the field of international relations, the term "hedging" refers to a strategy that combines balancing and bandwagoning to minimize risks imposed by great power competition. For more details on the concept, see David Martin Jones and Nicole Jenne, "Hedging and Grand Strategy in Southeast Asian Foreign Policy", *International Relations of the Asia-Pacific 22*, no. 2 (2022): 205–35; and John D. Ciorciari and Jürgen Haacke, "Hedging in International Relations: An Introduction", *International Relations of the Asia-Pacific 19*, no. 3 (2019): 367–74.

4. Ministry of Foreign Affairs of China, "习近平出席第七十六届联合国大会一般性辩论并发表重要讲话" [Xi Jinping attended the general debate of the 76th United Nations General Assembly and delivered an important speech], 22 September 2021, https://www.fmprc.gov.cn/zyxw/202109/t20210922_9584018.shtml.

5. Ministry of Foreign Affairs of China, "The Global Security Initiative Concept Paper", 21 February 2023, https://www.fmprc.gov.cn/mfa_eng/wjbxw/202302/t20230221_11028348.html.

6. Cai Aimin, "Remarks by Chinese Ambassador to Sweden Cui Aimin at the Webinar 'A Call for a Global Civilization Initiative'", 28 June 2023, https://www.mfa.gov.cn/mfa_eng/wjb_663304/zwjg_665342/zwbd_665378/202306/t20230630_11106077.html; Han Zheng, "Build a Community with a Shared Future for Mankind and Jointly Deliver a Brighter Future for the World", 22 September 2023, https://www.fmprc.gov.cn/eng/wjdt_665385/zyjh_665391/202309/t20230922_11148422.html.

7. Ministry of Foreign Affairs of China, "Chair's Statement of the Third Belt and Road Forum for International Cooperation", 18 October 2023, https://www.fmprc.gov.cn/mfa_eng/zxxx_662805/202310/t20231020_11164505.html.

8. Hoang Thi Ha, "Why Is China's Global Security Initiative Cautiously Perceived in Southeast Asia?", *ISEAS Perspective*, no. 2023/11, 22 February 2023, https://www.iseas.edu.sg/articles-commentaries/iseas-perspective/2023-11-why-is-chinas-global-security-initiative-cautiously-perceived-in-southeast-asia-by-hoang-thi-ha/.

9.   Treaty of Amity and Cooperation in Southeast Asia, 24 February 1976, https://asean-aipr.org/wp-content/uploads/2018/07/Treaty-of-Amity-and-Cooperation-in-Southeast-Asia-1976-TAC.pdf.

10. ASEAN Secretariat, "ASEAN Outlook on the Indo-Pacific", 23 June 2019, https://asean.org/asean2020/wp-content/uploads/2021/01/ASEAN-Outlook-on-the-Indo-Pacific_FINAL_22062019.pdf.

11. Dylan M.H. Loh, "Singapore's Conception of the Liberal International Order as a Small State", *International Affairs* 99, no. 4 (2023): 1499–1518; Thuy T. Do, "Vietnam's Prudent Pivot to the Rules-Based International Order", *International Affairs* 99, no. 4 (2023): 1557–73.

12. Ministry of Foreign Affairs of China, "The Global Security Initiative Concept Paper", 21 February 2023, https://www.fmprc.gov.cn/mfa_eng/wjbxw/202302/t20230221_11028348.html; Ian Seow Cheng Wei, "The Global Security Initiative of China", 4 August 2023, https://www.rsis.edu.sg/rsis-publication/rsis/the-global-security-initiative-of-china/.

13. Paul Haenle and Huong Le Thu, "Vietnam's Response to China's Global Security Initiative", Carnegie Endowment for International Peace, 18 October 2023, https://carnegieendowment.org/2023/10/18/vietnam-s-response-to-china-s-global-security-initiative-pub-90793.

14. Aristo Darmawan and Jefferson Ng Jin Chuan, "China's Global Security Initiative: A View from Indonesia", *RSIS Commentary*, 8 November 2022, https://www.rsis.edu.sg/rsis-publication/idss/ip22064-chinas-global-security-initiative-a-view-from-indonesia/.

15. Liaw Siau Chi, "A Shared Vision for Security: Asean and China's Global Security Initiatives", *The Star*, 14 August 2023, https://www.thestar.com.my/opinion/columnists/search-scholar-series/2023/08/14/a-shared-vision-for-security-asean-and-china039s-global-security-initiatives.

16. Wang Zheng, "Assessing the Belt and Road Initiative in Southeast Asia amid the COVID-19 Pandemic (2021–2022)", *Fulcrum*, 10 June 2022, https://fulcrum.sg/assessing-the-belt-and-road-initiative-in-southeast-asia-amid-the-covid-19-pandemic-2021-2022/.

17. CIMB ASEAN Research Institute, "China's Belt and Road Initiative (BRI) and Southeast Asia", October 2018, https://www.lse.ac.uk/ideas/Assets/Documents/reports/LSE-IDEAS-China-SEA-BRI.pdf.

18. Ministry of Foreign Affairs of China, "习近平出席第七十六届联合国大会一般性辩论并发表重要讲话" [Xi Jinping attended the general debate of the 76th United Nations General Assembly and delivered an important speech], 22 September 2021, https://www.fmprc.gov.cn/zyxw/202109/t20210922_9584018.shtml; Wang Yi, "Jointly Advancing the Global Development Initiative and Writing a New Chapter for Common Development", 21 September 2022, https://www.fmprc.gov.cn/eng./wjdt_665385/zyjh_665391/202209/t20220922_10769721.html.

19. Lee Hsien Loong, "PM Lee Hsien Loong at the Boao Forum for Asia Annual Conference 2023", 30 March 2023, https://www.pmo.gov.sg/Newsroom/PM-Lee-Hsien-Loong-at-the-Boao-Forum-for-Asia-Annual-Conference-2023.

20. Hoang Thi Ha, "Why Is China's Global Development Initiative Well Received in Southeast Asia?", *ISEAS Perspective* no. 2023/9, 21 February 2023, https://www.iseas.edu.sg/articles-commentaries/iseas-perspective/2023-9-why-is-chinas-global-development-initiative-well-received-in-southeast-asia-by-hoang-thi-ha/.

21. Toshiro Nishizawa, "China's Double-Edged Debt Trap", *East Asia Forum*, 19 September 2023, https://www.eastasiaforum.org/2023/09/19/chinas-double-edged-debt-trap/.

22. Daniel R. Russel and Blake H. Berger, "Weaponizing the Belt and Road Initiative", Asia Society Policy Institute, September 2020, https://asiasociety.org/sites/default/files/2020-09/Weaponizing%20the%20Belt%20and%20Road%20Initiative_0.pdf.

23. Hoang Thi Ha, "The Global Civilisation Initiative: Are 'Asian Values' Back with a Chinese Vengeance?", *Fulcrum*, 28 April 2023, https://fulcrum.sg/the-global-civilisation-initiative-are-asian-values-back-with-a-chinese-vengeance/.

24. Ibid.

25. Prashanth Parameswaran, "Could China's Southeast Asia Media Offensive Get Even Better?", *ASEAN Wonk*, 22 September 2023, https://www.aseanwonk.com/p/china-southeast-asia-media-asean-influence.

26. Amir Yusof, "Despite China's Media Influence in Southeast Asia, Public Remains Sceptical: US-Based Think-Tank", CNA, 15 September 2022, https://www.channelnewsasia.com/asia/china-media-influence-malaysia-indonesia-philippines-2939906.

27. Chang-Yau Hoon and Ying-Kit Chan, "Reflections on China's Latest Global Civilisation Agenda", *Fulcrum*, 4 September 2023, https://fulcrum.sg/reflections-on-chinas-latest-global-civilization-agenda/.

Brunei Darussalam

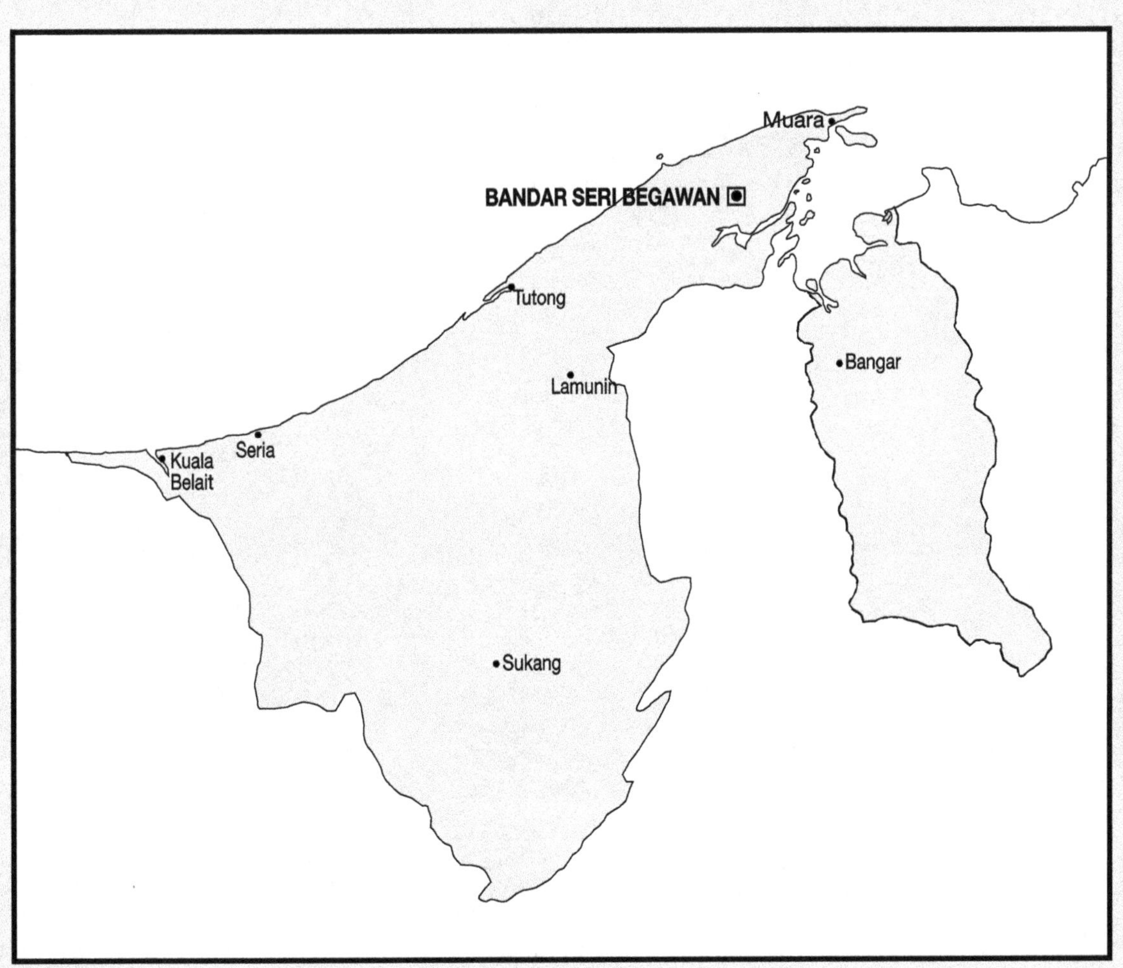

BRUNEI DARUSSALAM IN 2023:
A Year of Cautious Optimism and Hope

Jatswan S. Sidhu

As the year 2023 arrived, the mood in Brunei, as around the world, turned from one of doom and gloom to cautious optimism and hope. The reason for this was the steady downward trend in the number of Covid-19 cases and the eventual return to normalcy in February 2023. This air of cautious optimism and hope was reflected in Sultan Hassanal Bolkiah's New Year speech to the nation on 1 January, in which he called on all Bruneians to express their utmost gratitude to Allah for being able to successfully weather the storm of the Covid-19 pandemic. He also highlighted the silver lining behind the pandemic, which provided the country with the opportunity to build its resilience in sectors such as food security, education, finance and health. He expressed hope that this would in turn encourage Bruneians to work harder towards achieving the national agenda of economic diversification, especially in realizing Wawasan Brunei 2035 (Brunei Vision 2035).[1]

Two major events in early 2023 that perhaps signalled the return to normalcy in Brunei were a royal wedding in January and the country's national day celebrations in February. It is often said that whatever happens in Brunei centres mainly on the royal family. As such, the year started with a gala royal wedding when Sultan Hassanal's fifth daughter from his second wife, Princess Azemah Ni'matul Bolkiah, married her first cousin, Prince Bahar, a son of the sultan's brother, Prince Jefri Bolkiah, on 25 January. The opulent and grand ceremony, held at the sultan's official residence, the Istana Darul Iman, was marked by much pomp and pageantry. Lasting a week, it was attended by foreign dignitaries, including members of Brunei's foreign diplomatic community.[2]

The other event was Brunei's 39th National Day celebrations on 23 February. The theme for the event was "Menjayakan Wawasan Negara" (Achieving the National Vision), which emphasized that every Bruneian had a role in realizing

JATSWAN S. SIDHU is Professor of International Relations with the School of Liberal Arts and Sciences (SLAS), Taylor's University in Subang Jaya, Malaysia.

the country's national vision. The theme for 2023 was the same as in 2022, which underscored the importance of Wawasan Brunei 2035. The event was marked by a massive parade and performances by seven thousand participants.

The Covid-19 Pandemic and the Return to Normalcy

After battling the Covid-19 pandemic since 2020 with the whole-of-nation and whole-of-government approach, in 2023 the situation improved dramatically when the number of Covid-19 cases declined further. As a result, on 6 February, Brunei's Ministry of Health revealed its latest amendments to Covid-19 control measures, including removing mandatory isolation for positive Covid-19 cases, replacing the Quarantine Order with the Self Isolation Advice, and reducing the period of mandatory isolation of five to ten days to self-isolation of between three and five days. On 15 February, the Ministry of Health announced that its weekly media briefing on the Covid-19 pandemic situation would cease and would only be reinstated if necessary.[3] It was because of these relaxations that, in July 2023, Brunei welcomed its first batch of 110 Chinese tourists, the first in three years since the beginning of the pandemic. In 2019, tourists from China accounted for 22 per cent of total tourist arrivals in Brunei.

As of 30 April 2023, the national vaccination rate was 79.2 per cent for persons with three doses and 12.1 per cent for those with four doses. It was also reported that there was no Covid-19 case in Category 4 (those in need of respiratory assistance and under close monitoring) or Category 5 (those receiving treatment in an intensive care unit).[4] It is noteworthy that Brunei is the only Southeast Asian country to have recorded a hundred per cent Covid-19 vaccination rate (not inclusive of the booster doses).

The Economy – Moving Ahead amidst Global Uncertainties

As was the case with countries around the world, Brunei too had to confront the economic headwinds from the outbreak of the pandemic. But as the number of Covid-19 cases decreased both globally and domestically, Brunei opened its international borders on 1 August 2022. With the further removal of restrictions in February 2023, Brunei's economy was expected to surge ahead faster towards post-pandemic recovery after seven consecutive quarters of contraction. This was not the case, however, as it still faced slow economic growth and persistent inflation. Although the inflation rate in 2023 had declined to 1.7 per cent compared to 3.7 per cent in 2022, it remained a concern for the government. The unemployment rate was also a cause of concern. It showed only a slight decrease from 5.2 per cent in 2022 to 4.9 per cent in 2023. Mohd Amin Liew, the second minister of finance and economy, emphasized, therefore, "the urgency for Brunei's economy not only to be diverse and sustainable but also fundamentally resilient".[5]

On the same note, the International Monetary Fund (IMF) cautioned that while the post-pandemic economic recovery in Brunei had begun, it was "expected to be uneven and uncertainty surrounding the outlook remains high".[6] The IMF also highlighted several key challenges for Brunei, which include public spending constraints, the need to ensure intergenerational equity, volatility of the oil and gas sector, and global decarbonization pressures. It called on Brunei to implement prudent policies, sustain microeconomic stability, undertake structural reforms in support of recovery, boost economic diversification and ensure climate resilience.

To cushion the impact of Covid-19 on the economy, the government undertook several proactive relief measures, which included tax relief, deferment of loan payments, and wage subsidies. Nevertheless, perhaps the most important lesson learnt was the urgency to diversify Brunei's economy. More importantly, as the country is still overly reliant on the oil and gas sector, there is the dire need to create a buoyant and diversified energy sector. To this end, the government has begun to undertake steps for digitalization of the sector and to explore renewable energy sources; namely, solar energy.[7] That said, on 17 October, Brunei was hit by a major power outage as a result of a power grid failure, which was only restored the next day. Most parts of the country, including the national capital, were affected.

Brunei maintains a procyclical fiscal policy where spending is increased when energy prices are high and reduced accordingly when prices decline. On 7 March 2023, the government tabled a supply bill of BND$5.96 billion (US$4.47 billion) for the 2023/24 financial year (FY). This marked a slight increase over the FY2022/23 figure of BND$5.7 billion (US$4.27 billion). While tabling the bill to the Legislative Council, Brunei's second finance and economy minister, Mohd Amin Liew, stated that national revenues grew at 25 per cent in 2022/23 amounting to BND$6 billion (US$4.49 billion). He also noted that, while oil prices remained high, the government decided to provide a conservative projection of state revenues for 2023/24 at just BND$2.99 billion (US$2.24 billion), primarily because of the weak global outlook. In addition, he revealed that for FY2023/24, the country was expected to register a BND$2.97 billion (US$2.22 billion) deficit.[8]

Since the beginning of 2023, Brunei's economy had begun to show signs of improvement. For the first quarter, it posted a 0.8 per cent year-on-year growth rate, mainly attributed to a significant expansion of the non-oil and gas sector, which recorded a 6.2 per cent growth. For the second quarter of 2023, however, the GDP regressed to −3.1 per cent. The main reason for the backslide was the 10.7 per cent decline in the oil and gas sector, which was largely the result of a decrease in oil and gas production on account of delays in exploration, development, production and rejuvenation works. Nonetheless, the non-oil and gas sector recorded a 4.3 per cent growth. In the lead was the air transport services sub-sector, with a 131.9 per cent growth, followed by the finance sub-sector (79.9 per cent) and the manufacturing sub-sector (34.2 per cent).[9] Despite the economy showing a growth rate of 0.7 in the third quarter, the oil and gas sector still recorded a decline of 3.7 per cent because of the reasons mentioned above.[10]

In October 2023, the ASEAN+3 Macroeconomic Research Office (AMRO) released a report projecting an annual growth rate of 1.1 per cent for Brunei for 2023 and an expected growth rate of 2.0 per cent for 2024. The inflation forecast for 2023 was raised to 1.0 per cent (from the earlier 0.9 per cent), and the projected inflation in 2024 was 1.1 per cent.[11] The AMRO forecast was far more conservative than that of Brunei's Centre for Strategic and Policy Studies (CSPS), which gave a projected growth rate of 2.6 per cent for 2023.

Brunei's total trade volume as of October 2023 stood at BND$3 billion (US$2.3 billion), with exports at BND$1.6 billion (US$1.2 billion) and imports at BND$1.4 billion (US$1.1 billion), and a trade balance of BND$162.2 million (US$122.07 million). Brunei's three main export destinations were Australia (27.9 per cent), Singapore (26 per cent) and China (18.4 per cent). Its main export items were mineral fuels, amounting to BND$1.3 billion (US$948.53) and accounting for 79.5 per cent of exports. Its main import sources were Malaysia (32.6 per cent), Russia (16.4 per cent) and China (11.2 per cent). Intermediate goods topped the imports at BND$866.8 million (US$652.37 million), or 60.9 per cent.[12]

China remains Brunei's top foreign investor and amongst its largest trading partners. Brunei is often regarded as the most enthusiastic partner in the Belt and Road Initiative (BRI) in Southeast Asia. While some BRI projects in the region "have been criticised, renegotiated or even cancelled due to concerns over high costs and debt liability, BRI-related projects in Brunei have not, at least thus far, sparked similar controversy".[13]

China's multi-billion-dollar investments in Brunei are concentrated mainly in a refinery and petrochemical complex located at Pulau Muara Besar, near Bandar Seri Begawan. The project is a joint venture between China's Zhejiang Hengyi Group and Brunei's Damai Holdings (a fully government-owned subsidiary company), with ownership shares of 70 per cent and 30 per cent, respectively. The first phase of the project, costing US$3.45 billion, started operations in November 2019 with a crude oil refining capacity of 175,000 barrels a day (8 million tonnes a year). On 8 November 2023, both parties entered into the Implementation Agreement for the Pulau Muara Besar Phase 2. Upon completion, this project will enhance crude oil refining capacity by an additional two million tonnes a year. In fact, it was also noted that in 2022, 55 per cent of Brunei's total exports were contributed by this industry alone.[14]

To further stimulate the growth of trade between the two countries, in July 2023, Brunei launched a container shipping route between its sole deep-water port in Muara and China's Beibu Gulf Port in the Guangxhi Zhuang Autonomous Region. This was the result of a joint venture initiated in February 2017 between Darussalam Assets, a state-owned company in Brunei, and the Guangxhi Beibu Gulf International Port Group Company Ltd. This was a significant event as the venture not only provides Brunei the opportunity to enhance its trade with China, but it is also, according to Xinhua, the first such route between China and a Southeast Asian country.[15]

To further enhance internet services in the country, on 22 June 2023, the 5G service was launched in Brunei to provide ultra-high-speed internet of up to 300BM per second. The journey towards this began in 2020 when a 5G Taskforce was created under the country's Authority for Info-communications Technology Industry. Following this, in April 2021, a 5G pilot project was launched to gauge the needs of consumers and the viability of launching 5G services in the country.[16] There was no mention of the 5G service provider at the launch, though Huawei had been involved with the construction of the telecommunication infrastructure. While the internet penetration rate in Brunei was at 36.8 per cent in 2010, by 2019 it had increased more than threefold to 95.3 per cent and is currently at 98.1 per cent—the highest in Southeast Asia.

Another notable economic initiative was the minimum wage policy in the private sector for both residents and non-residents. This came into effect on 12 July 2023 through the enactment of the Employment (Minimum Wage) Order 2023 as an addendum to the Employment Order 2009. The new law covers both part-time and full-time workers, with the full-time minimum wage benchmarked at BND$500 (US$370) per month, while part-time wages were set at BND$2.62 (US$1.94) per hour. The policy was introduced in two major phases, with the first phase covering the information and communication technology, banking and financial sectors. Employers have been given a six-month transitional period to comply with the new law, and those who fail to do so can be jailed for up to one year and fined BND$3,000 (US$2,224). In a speech on 15 July in conjunction with his seventy-seventh birthday, the sultan urged employers to support the policy as it was "a step towards strengthening the lives and well-being of the people".[17]

Brunei's performance in its efforts to combat human trafficking showed improvements. Between 2019 and 2021, Brunei had been on the Tier 2 Watchlist but was downgraded to Tier 3 in 2022. In 2023 it was reinstated to the Tier 2 Watchlist thanks mainly to several significant initiatives by the government to combat this menace. Despite the impact of Covid-19, some key achievements of the government included the referral of two alleged traffickers for prosecution, the identification of fourteen labour trafficking victims and the provision of special passes for alternative employment in the country for these victims, the establishment of two shelters for trafficking victims, the passage of a regulation that limited worker-paid recruitment fees for domestic labour, and the inking of a bilateral Memorandum of Understanding (MoU) with Bangladesh for the purpose of recruitment of Bangladeshi migrant workers.[18] Brunei is a destination for human trafficking rather than a source or transit country. The problem of human trafficking in Brunei centres primarily on forced prostitution and forced labour, and even includes minors. The victims are mainly from Bangladesh, China, India, Indonesia, Malaysia, Pakistan, the Philippines and Thailand.

Wawasan Brunei 2035: Taking Stock and Intensifying Efforts

The agenda of economic diversification to steer Brunei away from over-reliance on the oil and gas sector has been a top priority for the sultanate for at least three decades now. Various efforts have been in place since the 1990s through the country's five-year national development plans and other long-term plans. One such long-term plan is the Wawasan Brunei 2035, which was initiated in 2007. It aims to create a dynamic and sustainable economy and in turn reduce the country's dependency on the oil and gas sector through a whole-of-nation approach. The three major thrusts of Wawasan Brunei 2035 are creating a highly educated and competent population, achieving a standard of living amongst the top ten globally, and having a dynamic and sustainable economy with a high income per capita. All these are aimed at facilitating the progression of Brunei into a progressive Islamic state within the framework of the state philosophy of Melayu, Islam, Beraja (Malay, Islamic, Monarchy) and Maqasid Sya'riah (an Islamic legal doctrine).[19]

To expedite the realization of this vision, the Majlis Tertinggi Wawasan Brunei 2035 (Brunei Vision 2035 Supreme Council), or MTWB 2035, was created in 2014, chaired by the sultan himself. In March 2023, the government released a periodic review of Wawasan Brunei 2035. According to the review, for the first goal of creating a holistic first-class education system, the country was ranked 53rd out of 77 in the Programme for International Student Assessment 2018 by the Organisation for Economic Co-operation and Development. For the second goal of creating a high quality of life, Brunei achieved a high human development index as it was ranked 51 out of 191 countries in 2021. For the third goal, the *World Economic Outlook October 2022* report by the IMF disclosed that in 2021 Brunei was ranked 10th out of 195 countries in GDP per capita in PPP terms.[20]

On 22 February 2023, while chairing the first MTWB 2035 for 2023, the sultan reminded Bruneians that Wawasan Brunei 2035 was the core national development agenda and not mere rhetoric or an empty dream. While acknowledging that much had been achieved thus far, the sultan called on all parties concerned to intensify efforts at attaining Wawasan Brunei 2035 and reminded them that the country was a mere twelve years away from the dateline.[21] One day later, on the occasion of Brunei's 39th national day, the sultan once again reminded Bruneians of the urgency to expedite efforts at achieving Wawasan Brunei 2035. He also announced that the Ministry of Finance and Economy had already formulated the roadmaps for the food, downstream oil and gas and maritime services industries and was currently in the process of designing the roadmaps for the information technology and info-communications sector. This was in line with the Brunei Economic Blueprint, launched by the said ministry in January 2021, which was a part of Wawasan Brunei 2035. In addition, the sultan revealed that the government was in the process of formulating a policy on micro, small and medium enterprises aimed at increasing productivity in these sectors. To further enhance the quality of its education and create a world-class education system, the sultan reiterated that skills in science, technology, engineering, arts and mathematics would be expanded.[22]

Foreign Relations—Business as Usual

As a small state, Brunei maintains friendly and cordial relations with all countries and is also a member of various international organizations. Nevertheless, it places special emphasis on the Southeast Asian region as well as the Association of Southeast Asian Nations (ASEAN). Brunei's membership in ASEAN and its friendly relations with other Southeast Asian neighbours are considered of paramount importance to the sultanate. This is especially so given that its past relations with some countries in the region, such as Malaysia, have not always been smooth sailing. Additionally, as a small state surrounded by larger neighbours like Indonesia, Malaysia and the Philippines, Brunei views ASEAN as providing an additional layer of security guarantee to the country.

Brunei shares a 266-kilometre land border as well as maritime borders with Malaysia, which is also amongst its largest trading partners. As such, bilateral ties with Malaysia often take centre stage in Brunei's external relations. The first major foreign dignitary to visit Brunei in 2023 was Malaysian prime minister Anwar Ibrahim, who made a two-day official trip on 24 and 25 January. This was Anwar's second official visit after taking office as prime minister, the first being to Singapore. During the visit, Anwar expressed hope that the two countries would enhance cooperation in areas such as *syariah* judiciary, education as well as youth and sports and he promised to strive to identify new areas of strategic cooperation. He also called on the Brunei Investment Agency—the investment arm of the sultanate—to increase its investments in Malaysia.[23]

In return, on 2 August 2023, Sultan Hassanal Bolkiah arrived in Kuala Lumpur on a three-day state visit that also coincided with the 24th Malaysia-Brunei Darussalam Annual Leaders' Conference (ALC). The ALC is an annual meeting between the leaders of both countries to discuss matters of bilateral interest. A highlight of the visit was the discussion on the demarcation of the Malaysia-Brunei land boundary, with significant progress made by the Joint Technical Committee on the Demarcation and Survey of the Land Boundary between Malaysia and Brunei in surveying and demarcating a total distance of 132.25 kilometres, or 25 per cent, of their boundary. The committee was expected to complete the task by 2034. In addition, the Terms of Reference for the Working Committee on Security Related Matters to the Brunei Darussalam-Malaysia Land Boundary were finalized. The ALC also acknowledged the progress made towards fostering greater economic cooperation between Brunei and the Malaysian states of Sabah and Sarawak as well as the need to enhance connectivity between Brunei and Sarawak.[24]

On 8 and 9 October 2023, Japanese foreign minister Yoko Kamikawa made a working visit to Brunei and had an audience with Sultan Hassanal Bolkiah. The trip was aimed at deepening bilateral relations. Kamikawa also held discussions with Brunei's foreign affairs minister II, Awang Erywan Mohd Yusof. Among the issues discussed were cooperation in a number of areas and Japan's offer to assist Brunei in coming up with a roadmap for decarbonization. In addition, Japan pledged its support and commitment to work with the ASEAN Centre for Climate Change. The centre, initiated by ASEAN in 2021 and based in Bandar Seri Begawan, was scheduled to begin operations in September 2023.[25] Japan's relations with Brunei go back to 2 April 1984 when both countries established official diplomatic relations. Japan is also Brunei's largest importer of liquified natural gas (LNG), while Brunei is Japan's sixth-largest supplier of LNG. The LNG plant in Lumut, Brunei, is owned on a 50-50 per cent basis by Brunei LNG and Japan's Mitsubishi Corporation.

Another prominent visitor to Brunei in late 2023 was the president of Timor-Leste, Dr Jose Ramos-Horta, who arrived in Bandar Seri Begawan on 5 November for a four-day state visit. Among the highlights of the visit were discussions on initiatives to expand bilateral trade relations and cooperation in forest conversation and the oil and gas sector. The trip also saw the signing of an MoU on labour mobility from Timor-Leste to Brunei. The visit was obviously related to shoring up support for Timor-Leste's pending membership of ASEAN. On this, Ramos-Horta was quoted as saying that "we are looking forward to joining ASEAN" and, "for Timor-Leste to develop further, we have to integrate into regional and international economies".[26] Official diplomatic relations between the two countries were established in 2002, two years after Timor-Leste gained its independence from Indonesia.

On 13 May 2023, Brunei became the eleventh nation (and the fourth ASEAN country) to ratify the Comprehensive and Progressive Agreement for Trans-Pacific Partnership (CPTPP). One of the world's largest free trade pacts, the CPTPP membership currently includes eleven countries; namely, Australia, Brunei, Canada, Chile, Japan, Malaysia, Mexico, New Zealand, Peru, Singapore and Vietnam. Signatories to the treaty benefit from market access to a region encompassing 600 million people and a combined GDP of US$13.5 trillion, or 13.4 per cent of the global economy. In its press release on Brunei's ratification of the agreement, the Ministry of Finance and Economy noted that the deal provides Brunei with "new market access to Canada and Latin American countries such as Chile, Peru and Mexico" and "will also enhance Brunei Darussalam's attractiveness as a destination for foreign direct investment".[27]

Notwithstanding its close economic relations with China, Brunei is also a claimant state in the Spratly Islands dispute and asserts its maritime jurisdiction over the Lousia Reef (Terumbu Semarang Barat Kecil), which is located within its exclusive economic zone. Brunei is often categorized as a silent claimant and at times even makes conflicting claims. One such example was in 1992 when the country's foreign minister, Prince Mohamed Bolkiah, asserted that the country was only claiming the waters around the Lousia Reef and not the feature itself.[28] When China unveiled its 2023 China Standard Map in late August 2023 reasserting its claim over the entire area, Brunei's Ministry of Foreign Affairs and Trade issued a mildly worded statement on 2 September 2023, which merely reiterated its two-step approach to the dispute that should be addressed through peaceful dialogue and consultations on a bilateral basis and in accordance with international law; namely, the United Nations Convention on the Law of the Sea. In addition, Brunei reaffirmed its "commitment to the full and effective implementation of the 2002 Declaration on the Conduct of Parties in the South China Sea" and called on all parties concerned to work for the conclusion of "an effective and substantive Code of Conduct in the South China Sea".[29] Some may argue that this low-key and non-confrontational position can be attributed to the fact that China is currently Brunei's largest foreign investor and trading partner and that Brunei does not want to derail its cordial relations with Beijing by raising the issue. But this is probably not the main reason because Brunei's position on the issue has been quite consistent even prior to the arrival of large Chinese investments in the country. Chinese President Xi Jinping praised Brunei for prioritizing economic relations rather than the South China Sea dispute when he met Sultan Hassanal on the sidelines of the Asia-Pacific Cooperation Meeting (APEC) Economic Leaders' Meeting in San Francisco on 17 November 2023. Xi also promised to increase imports from Brunei, increase investments and encourage more Chinese enterprises to establish business in the country.[30]

Brunei has always been an ardent supporter of a peaceful resolution to the Israel-Palestine conflict on the basis of a two-state solution; namely, the creation of a State of Palestine with its capital in East Jerusalem. On the recent outbreak of violence in the region, Brunei supported the adoption of the Resolution on Protection of Civilians and Upholding Legal and Humanitarian Obligations during the Tenth Emergency Special Session of the United Nations General Assembly on the Illegal Israeli Actions in Occupied East Jerusalem and the Rest of the Occupied Palestinian Territory on 12 December 2023.[31] On 3 November, Brunei issued a strong condemnation of the violence in Gaza, especially the attack on the Jabalia refugee camp, which resulted in many civilian casualties. On 6 November, Brunei issued another strong statement condemning the violence in Gaza and called for an immediate cessation of hostilities. Further, on the sidelines of the APEC summit in San Francisco in November 2023, Brunei, together with Indonesia and Malaysia, issued a joint statement calling for an "immediate, durable and sustained humanitarian truce leading to a cessation of hostilities in the Gaza Strip".[32]

As Sultan Hassanal Bolkiah is also Brunei's foreign minister, he takes it upon himself to attend major meetings around the world and often makes state visits aimed at strengthening bilateral relations. One such trip in early 2023 was his official visit to Türkiye, between 6 and 9 March. During the visit, Sultan Hassanal held talks with Recep Tayyip Erdogan, Türkiye's President. Five agreements were signed in areas such as research, education, defence, culture and bilateral consultations. The two leaders also held discussions on a wide array of issues, which included the Rohingya, Palestine, efforts to mediate in the Russian-Ukraine war, Türkiye's role in the Organisation of Islamic Cooperation, and developments in ASEAN. Two key outcomes from the visit were the signing of a declaration of intent aimed at enhancing military cooperation and an MoU on cooperation in higher education and scientific research.[33] Brunei and Türkiye established official diplomatic relations on 1 January 1984.

The sultan also made a three-day state visit to Australia in June 2023, where he held talks with Australian prime minister Anthony Albanese. The aim of the trip was to create a comprehensive partnership between the two countries, and the key takeaway was the initiative to enhance cooperation in defence and the climate. Other issues discussed related to food security, maritime security, trade and investment, and the transition to net-zero carbon emissions.[34] Relations between Brunei and Australia were established in 1984, and in 2023 Australia was Brunei's second-largest export and import partner.

Conclusion

While oil prices are high and the danger from the Covid-19 pandemic has receded, Brunei remained cautiously optimistic through 2023. Its post-pandemic economic recovery was on track, but the global economic outlook remains rather bleak. As its oil and gas resources continue to deplete, creating a sustainable diversified economy remains an uphill battle. In a state where citizens have continuously enjoyed generous welfare benefits that are sustained with oil and gas revenues, the depletion of these resources may eventually see the cessation of such benefits. More importantly, the very survival of the regime hinges on how successfully it can steer the country away from overdependence on the hydrocarbon industry. That said, and amidst all these uncertainties, Bruneians are probably eagerly anticipating yet another gala royal wedding—this time of Prince Abdul Mateen, the sultan's son from his second wife, which is scheduled for January 2024.

Notes

1. Information Department, Prime Minister's Office, "Titah KDYMM Sempena Menyambut Tahun Baru Masihi 2023" [His Majesty's royal proclamation in conjunction with the 2023 New Year celebration], 1 January 2023, https://www.information.gov.bn/Lists/TITAH/ ItemDisplay.aspx?ID=917&Source=https%3A%2F%2Fwww%2Einformation%2 Egov%2Ebn%2FPages%2FTitah%2DView%2Easpx& ContentTypeId=0x0100422E821 587FC974C9DFFAF38C117CE34.

2. Lyana Mohamad, "New Envoys Wowed by Royal Wedding", *Borneo Bulletin*, 17 January 2023, https://borneobulletin.com.bn/new-envoys-wowed-by-royal-wedding-2/.

3. "Brunei Govt Announces that Mandatory Self-Isolation due to Covid-19 to be Scrapped", *The Star*, 6 February 2023, https://www.thestar.com.my/aseanplus/aseanplus-news/2023/02/06/brunei-govt-announces-that-mandatory-self-isolation-due-to-covid-19-to-be-scrapped.

4. Brunei Darussalam Ministry of Health, "Media Statement – COVID-19 in Brunei", 1 May 2023, https://www.moh.gov.bn/Lists/Latest%20news/NewDispForm.aspx?ID=1379#:~:text=ii)%20As%20of%20yesterday,having%20received%20the%20fourth%20dose.

5. "Brunei's Economy Needs to Be Resilient to Face Global Challenges, Says Economic Minister", *The Star*, 1 September 2023, https://www.thestar.com.my/aseanplus/aseanplus-news/2023/09/01/brunei039s-economy-needs-to-be-resilient-to-face-global-challenges-says-economic-minister.

6. International Monetary Fund, "IMF Executive Board Concludes 2023 Article IV Consultation with Brunei Darussalam, Press Release No. 23/336", 6 October 2023, https://www.imf.org/en/News/Articles/2023/10/04/pr23336-brunei-imf-executive-board-concludes-2023-article-iv-consultation-with-brunei-darussalam.

7. Lawrence Webb, "The Impact of COVID-19 on Brunei's Energy Sector", EnergyPortal.eu, 19 June 2023, https://www.energyportal.eu/news/the-impact-of-covid-19-on-bruneis-energy-market/38396/#gsc.tab=0.

8. Ain Bandial, "Gov't Tables $5.96 Billion Budget, Remains Cautious on Economic Outlook", *The Scoop*, 7 March 2023, https://thescoop.co/2023/03/07/govt-tables-5-96-billion-budget-remains-cautious-on-economic-outlook/.

9. Department of Economic Planning and Statistics and Ministry of Finance and Economy, *Brunei Darussalam Key Economic Developments, Second Quarter, Q2 2023*, 2023, p. 1.

10. Department of Economic Planning and Statistics, Ministry of Finance and Economy, *Gross Domestic Product Third Quarter 2023*, pp. 1–3.

11. "Brunei Poised for 1.1 Percent Economic Growth in 2023, Says AMRO", *The Star*, 7 October 2023, https://www.thestar.com.my/aseanplus/aseanplus-news/2023/10/07/brunei-poised-for-11-per-cent-economic-growth-in-2023-says-amro#:~:text=BANDAR%20SERI%20BEGAWAN%20(Borneo%20Bulletin,per%20cent%20growth%20in%202024.

12. Department of Economic Planning and Statistics, Ministry of Finance and Economy, *International Merchandise Trade Statistics October 2023*, October 2023, pp. 2–7.

13. Sufrizul Husseini, "Why is Brunei Hedging between the U.S. and China", United States Institute of Peace, 26 October 2023, https://www.usip.org/publications/2023/10/why-brunei-hedging-between-us-and-china.

14. Xue Fei, "China-Brunei Joint Venture Sign Phase 2 Petrochemical Project Deal", *The Star*, 9 November 2023, https://www.thestar.com.my/news/world/2023/11/09/china-brunei-joint-venture-signs-phase-2-petrochemical-project-deal#:~:text=BANDAR%20SERI%20BEGAWAN%2C%20Nov.,for%20the%20flagship%20petrochemical%20project.

15. "Brunei Launches 1st Direct Container Shipping Company to China", Xinhua, 9 July 2023, https://english.news.cn/asiapacific/20230709/4beed985ecb6492290169f317536d7e1/c.html

16. Rasidah Hj Abu Bakar, "Brunei Launches 5G Network, Hope to Spur Digital Transformation", *The Scoop*, 23 June 2023, https://thescoop.co/2023/06/23/brunei-launches-5g-network-hopes-to-spur-digital-transformation/.

17. Ain Bandial and Hazirah Zainuddin, "Brunei Introduces Phased Introduction of Minimum Wage", *The Scoop*, 15 July 2023, https://thescoop.co/2023/07/15/brunei-announces-phased-introduction-of-minimum-wage/.

18. US Department of State, "2023 Trafficking in Persons Report: Brunei", https://www.state.gov/reports/2023-trafficking-in-persons-report/brunei.

19. Brunei Vision 2035 Supreme Council, Prime Minister's Office, *Laporan Wawasan Brunei 2035, 2015–2022* [Brunei Vision 2023 report, 2015–2022], p. 18.

20. James Kon, "Towards National Goals", *Borneo Bulletin*, 14 April 2023, https://borneobulletin.com.bn/towards-national-goals/.

21. "Don't Treat Vision 2035 as an Empty Dream: Sultan", *The Star*, 22 February 2023, https://www.thestar.com.my/aseanplus/aseanplus-news/2023/02/22/dont-treat-brunei-vision-2035-as-an-empty-dream-sultan.

22. Prime Minister's Office Brunei Darussalam, "Titah Perutusan KDYMM Sempena Hari Kebangsaan Negara Brunei Darussalam Kali Ke-39 Bagi Tahun 1444H/2023M" [His Majesty's royal proclamation in conjunction with Negara Brunei Darussalam's 39th National Day], 23 February 2023, https://www.pmo.gov.bn/Lists/TITAH/NewDispform.aspx?ID=423&Source=https%3A%2F%2Fwww%2Epmo%2Egov%2Ebn%2FPMO%2520 Pages%2FTitah%2DView%2Easpx& ContentTypeId=0 x0100422E821587FC 974C9DFFAF38C117CE34.

23. "Anwar Hopes 24th Malaysia-Brunei ALC Will Finalise Several Matters of Mutual Interests", *The Star*, 25 January 2023, https://www.thestar.com.my/news/nation/2023/01/25/anwar-hopes-24th-malaysia-brunei-alc-will-finalise-several-matters-of-mutual-interest.

24. Ministry of Foreign Affairs Malaysia, "Joint Statement on the 24th Annual Leaders' Consultation between the Honourable Dato' Seri Anwar Ibrahim, Prime Minister of Malaysia and His Majesty Sultan Hassanal Bolkiah Mu'izzaddin Waddaulah, Sultan and Yang Di-Pertuan of Brunei Darussalam", 3 August 2023, https://www.kln.gov.my/web/guest/-/joint-statement-on-the-24th-annual-leaders-consultation-between-the-honourable-dato-seri-anwar-ibrahim-prime-minister-of-malaysia-and-his-

majesty-sult#:~:text=Both%20Leaders%20reaffirmed%20their%20commitment,the%20 Field%20of%20Digital%20Cooperation.

25. "Brunei, Japan Ministers Highlight Importance of Cooperation", *The Star*, 10 October 2023, https://www.thestar.com.my/aseanplus/aseanplus-news/2023/10/10/brunei-japan-ministers-highlight-importance-of-cooperation.

26. "Timor-Leste Seeks Closer Ties with Brunei", *Borneo Bulletin*, 7 November 2023, https://borneobulletin.com.bn/timor-leste-seeks-closer-ties-with-brunei/.

27. "After 5 Years, Brunei Ratifies CPTPP Trade Deal", *The Scoop*, 15 May 2023, https://thescoop.co/2023/05/15/brunei-ratifies-cptpp/.

28. The National Bureau of Asian Research, "Country Profile from the Maritime Awareness Project", https://www.nbr.org/publication/brunei/.

29. Ministry of Foreign Affairs Brunei Darussalam, "Statement on the Latest Development in the South China Sea", 2 September 2023, https://www.mfa.gov.bn/Lists/Press%20 Room/news.aspx?id=1067&source=https://www.mfa.gov.bn/site/home.aspx.

30. "China's XI Offers More Investments in South China Sea Claimant Brunei", Reuters, 17 November 2023, https://www.reuters.com/world/asia-pacific/chinas-xi-offers-more-investment-south-china-sea-claimant-brunei-2023-11-17/.

31. United Nations General Assembly, "Protection of Civilians and Upholding Legal and Humanitarian Obligations – GA 10th Emergency Special Session Draft Resolution (Adopted)", 10 December 2023 (adopted on 12 December 2023), https://https://www. un.org/unispal/document/protection-of-civilians-and-upholding-legal-and-humanitarian-obligations-ga-10th-emergency-special-session-draft-resolution/.

32. Ministry of Foreign Affairs of the Republic of Indonesia, "Joint Statement of Brunei Darussalam, Indonesia and Malaysia on the Occasion of the 30th APEC Economic Leaders' Meeting (AELM), San Franciso, United States of America, 16–17 November 2023", 18 November 2023, https://kemlu.go.id/portal/en/read/5513/siaran_pers/joint-statement-of-brunei-darussalam-indonesia-and-malaysia-on-the-occasion-of-30th-apec-economic-leaders-meeting-aelm-san-francisco-united-states-of-america-16-17-november-2023.

33. "Brunei, Turkiye Strengthen Ties through MoU Signing", *The Scoop*, 9 March 2023, https://thescoop.co/2023/03/09/brunei-turkiye-strengthen-ties-through-mou-signings/.

34. "The Leaders of Australia and Brunei Meet in Canberra to Discuss Their Cooperation on Maritime Security and Other Issues", ABC News, 20 June 2023, https://www.abc.net. au/news/2023-06-20/albanese-sultan-of-brunei-renew-strategic-partnership/102498446.

Cambodia

Stueng Treng
Siem Reap
Battambang
Tonle
Sap
Kompong
Cham
Koh Kong
PHNOM PENH
Takeo
Kampot

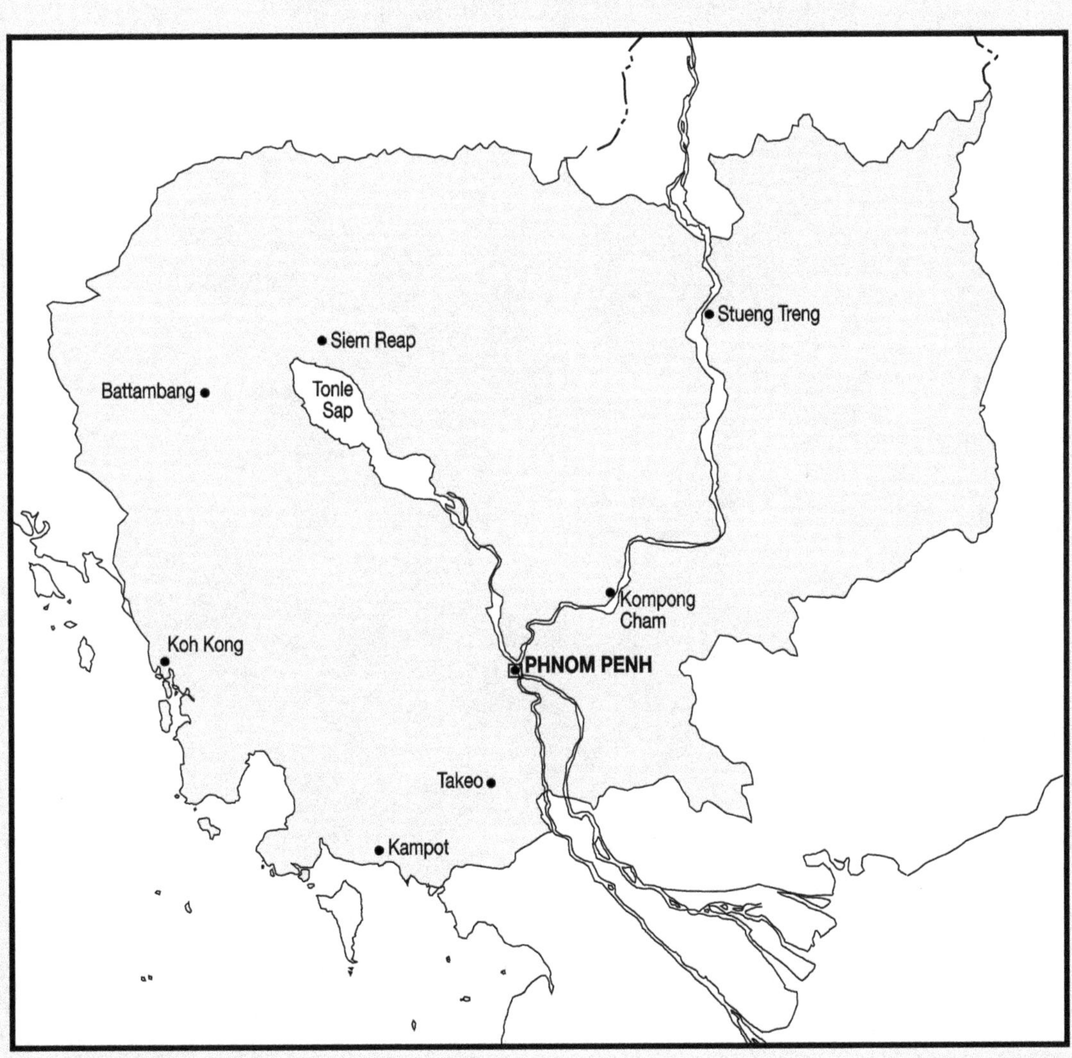

CAMBODIA IN 2023:
A Once-in-a-Lifetime Transfer of Power

David Hutt

In 2023, Cambodia's ruling party managed to hand over political power without sparking an intra-regime conflict, something many other authoritarian governments have failed to achieve. It did so via a vast and meticulously planned "generational succession" that saw the ageing grandees of the Cambodian People's Party (CPP) and of state institutions transfer power to their children or younger political elites. Hun Sen, 71, Cambodia's prime minister since 1985, resigned on 26 July, three days after the CPP won by a landslide in general elections. Hun Manet, 45, his eldest son, was officially anointed prime minister on 22 August. Meanwhile, the Council of Ministers, which is the Cambodian cabinet, underwent a significant reshuffling to make way for a hereditary succession of younger leaders—the so-called "second generation" of the CPP, most of whom are in their forties. For instance, Tea Banh, 78, the defence minister since 1987, resigned and gave power to his son Tea Seiha, 43. Sar Kheng, 72, the interior minister since 1992, handed his son Sar Sokha, 42, the ministerial reins.[1] The same process was replicated throughout the bureaucratic apparatus, as a younger generation progressed through the ranks of secretaries and under-secretaries of state.

For more than a decade, Hun Sen has been non-committal over when he would step down. In 2013, he said he would be in power until at least 2025; in 2020, he said for another decade. But the die was cast in December 2021 when the ruling CPP unanimously voted Hun Manet, then the army chief, as its future prime ministerial candidate. Still, analysts were not sure whether Hun Sen would step down immediately after the July 2023 general elections or sometime closer to the subsequent national ballots in 2028. Events in early 2023, however, indicated the process would be fast-tracked. The groundwork was laid via three elements: (1) crushing dissent within society, (2) uniting the CPP behind a vast

Dᴀᴠɪᴅ Hᴜᴛᴛ is Research Fellow at the Central European Institute of Asian Studies, Czech Republic.

generational succession, and (3) forcing its opponents to defect. According to Mun Vong, "Regime stability, achieved through the ruthless repression and co-optation of political opposition, gave Hun Sen and the CPP the confidence that a transfer of power could finally occur."[2]

Crushing Dissent within Society

After narrowly winning the 2013 general elections, the CPP underwent a reformation. It adopted many populist and welfarist policies advocated by its political rivals and promoted a new cadre of competent and technocratic officials through the bureaucracy. It also launched a brutal crackdown on all political alternatives. At the 2018 general elections, the CPP won all 125 seats in the National Assembly, cementing a de facto one-party state after having forcibly dissolved the Cambodia National Rescue Party (CNRP), its only viable opponent, the previous year on spurious charges of plotting a US-backed "colour revolution". Like all authoritarian governments, the CPP must only get one thing right to stay in power: deny any space to political opponents.

On 13 February 2023, the Ministry of Information revoked the media operating licence of *Voice of Democracy*, one of the last remaining independent outlets, after it published an article alleging that Hun Manet, as army chief, had interfered in government policy surrounding aid relief given to Türkiye after a deadly earthquake. The following month, the information ministry revoked the licences of three Khmer-language media outlets for allegedly violating journalistic ethics. It then threatened legal action against *CamboJA News*, another independent outlet. In July, a week before the general elections, the government ordered internet service providers (ISPs) to block the news outlets Radio Free Asia and *Cambodia Daily* as well as the new site Kamnotra.

The authorities also continued to harass civil society organizations (CSOs). In January 2023, for instance, they threatened legal action against the Cambodian League for the Promotion and Defence of Human Rights and several other CSOs for sharing a politically charged music video. Chhim Sithar, the leader of the Labour Rights Supported Union of Khmer Employees of NagaWorld, was arrested in early 2022 for alleged incitement to commit a felony. On 25 May 2023, a court found her and eight other trade unionists guilty; she received a two-year prison sentence. The same month, a Cambodian court brought charges against three land rights activists from the Coalition of Cambodian Farmer Community, a community organization, which was threatened with an outright ban until Hun Sen intervened and elicited a promise from the organization that it would no longer hold protests. Also, in May, the authorities banned a planned conference of the Centre for Peace and Conflict Studies.

The authorities ramped up their repression of the political opposition. On 3 March, Kem Sokha, the former CNRP president who had been detained on treason charges since 2017, was convicted and sentenced to twenty-seven years in prison (commuted to house arrest) by the Phnom Penh Municipal Court for "conspiring with [a] foreign power". He was also banned from politics. Exiled CNRP leaders, including Sam Rainsy, were hit by several more criminal convictions *in absentia*. In July, Sam Rainsy, who has lived in France since 2015, was banned from running for office for twenty-five years after he urged people to spoil their ballots at that month's election. Some sixteen other exiled senior opposition members were also banned from running for office for twenty years.

The Candlelight Party (CP), which emerged as the largest opposition party at the 2022 local elections, in which it won 22 per cent of the vote, faced several lawsuits against its top brass that year. It went into 2023, however, thinking it could pick up a similar tally at the national elections. But the death knell came on 15 May when the National Election Committee (NEC) disqualified the main opposition party from the ballot over claims that it had not filed the correct paperwork. The CP, which was first registered as the Sam Rainsy Party in the late 1990s, asserted that it could not locate its original registration documents, which it said were confiscated by the authorities during a 2017 raid on its headquarters.

Certain events, however, also demonstrated the CPP's frailties. From 5 to 17 May, Cambodia hosted the 32nd Southeast Asia Games and the 12th ASEAN Para Games. The run-up to the event provided another opportunity for Phnom Penh to elicit investment from China, including funding for the US$150 million, sixty-thousand-seat Morodok Techo National Sports Complex in the north of the capital. In early April, Hun Sen said that all events would be free for attendees. The Games were generally popular and well-attended, and they provided the CPP with an occasion to boast about how much Cambodia had progressed and developed under its watch. But there were also negative reports of spectators being unable to access tickets and poor conditions for workers who built the athletes' village.[3] Hun Sen asserted that the Games "are not a matter for the government or the Cambodian People's Party, but for our people". Yet eyebrows were raised when Hun Sen, not King Norodom Sihamoni, opened the Games, and the narration during the opening ceremony extolled the "win-win policy of the extraordinary founder", referring to Hun Sen.[4] Moreover, the government irked the public when the Ministry of Education instructed all public and private educational institutions to close from 20 April until 18 May so that children could attend the sporting events. Private schools complained that they had been forced to close for much of 2020 and 2021 because of the Covid-19 pandemic and were still suffering financially. Parents complained that they would have to take time off work to care for their children and still had to pay tuition fees for private schools. Within hours of the announcement, the Ministry of Education said that schools could host exams and then slowly walked back the forced holiday for students, an indication that the CPP government is vulnerable to public pressure, especially when it comes from the middle classes.

Hun Sen also waded into a personal controversy in June when Facebook's independent Oversight Board recommended that his account be suspended for six months because of a public speech he gave in January in which he had warned political opponents that he could "rally CPP people for a demonstration and beat you guys up".[5] At first, Hun Sen banned Facebook representatives from the country and threatened to block the social media platform in Cambodia, but he walked back on this threat after a public outcry; Facebook is by far the most popular platform in the country. He then said he would close his account (but didn't) and recommended that all Cambodians start using alternative social media platforms such as Twitter/X and Telegram, where he likes to post long, rambling monologues to more than 800,000 followers. In September, he returned to using Facebook after Meta, Facebook's parent company, rejected the Oversight Board's recommendation to ban him.

Uniting the CPP

Hun Manet's rise through the CPP was gradual. After years in the military, in 2018, the graduate of America's elite West Point academy was appointed the deputy commander-in-chief of the Royal Cambodian Armed Forces and the commander of the Royal Cambodian Army. The following year, he became head of the CPP's youth wing, allowing him to build his own personal power base within the party. During the Covid-19 pandemic, he gained more control of parts of the ruling party's charity wing. He and his wife, Pich Chanmony, run the Samdech Techo Voluntary Youth Doctor Association, a supposedly independent organization that played a leading role in Cambodia's vaccination scheme during the Covid-19 pandemic and brought a good deal of publicity for the future first couple. In March 2023, Hun Manet announced that he would run as the CPP's top candidate in Phnom Penh in the July elections. On 20 April, he was made a four-star general. He then stepped down from his military positions to run for office.

Some within the CPP, however, were thought to be sceptical about the succession, given that Hun Manet had never held a governmental or elected office before being designated as the party's future prime ministerial candidate. Sar Kheng, arguably the most powerful figure within the party other than Hun Sen, was the last to sign up to Hun Manet's nomination as the party's future candidate when it was put to a vote in late 2021.[6] Tea Banh was also thought to have reservations. But these intra-party tensions appeared to have faded by 2022. For the most part, the "first generation" CPP grandees were placated by Hun Sen's promise of an institution-wide succession process, which guaranteed that all political families would keep the spoils of power.

According to Neil Loughlin, a hereditary succession process "allows the ruler to protect himself against other elites who may seek to seize power as his authority wanes with age. It also dispels other elites' fears of a power vacuum upon his death and mitigates the risk of a subsequent power struggle, in which coalition members' own powers may be curtailed in an alternative future arrangement".[7] With Tea Banh and Sar Kheng passing down their positions directly to their children in August, for instance, "the Hun family has maintained stability by dividing the country's spoils among the next generation of CPP elites", stated Will Brehm.[8]

Nonetheless, Hun Sen moved to secure his own power base ahead of the transfer of power. In May, for instance, he announced that Mao Sophan, the leader of Brigade 70, his de facto private bodyguard unit, would succeed Hun Manet as the next army chief. Another of Hun Sen's sons, the military intelligence chief Hun Manith, was made deputy army chief at the same time.

In June, a number of *oknha*—an honorific title that translates as "tycoon" or "lord" and is given to people who donate at least US\$500,000 to the state or ruling party—established the Cambodian Oknha Association. Ly Yong Phat, a senator, was named president of the group, and Hun Sen became the honorary president. While ostensibly a vehicle for the ruling party to extract even more donations from the tycoons, it is also a way for Hun Sen to maintain his power over the influential private sector bosses and for the *oknha* to self-manage their own ranks. As of June 2023, there were 1,299 people with the honorific title, although the number grew after the July general elections.[9]

Defections to the CPP

According to one estimate, some 6,473 members of opposition parties defected to the CPP between January and June 2023.[10] That included CNRP youth leader

Yim Sinorn and opposition activist Hun Kosal, both of whom joined the CPP days after being released from detention on bail, as well as most of the leadership of the Grassroots Democratic Party—Yang Saing Koma, Sam Inn, Leok Sothea and Sem Hak. Defections also extended to civil society. Preap Kol, a former head of Transparency International's Cambodia office, joined the CPP and was awarded the position of government advisor in May. When Voice of Democracy was forcibly closed by the authorities in February, Hun Sen publicly offered government posts to the outlet's laid-off staff members. Within a matter of weeks, at least twenty-five had accepted government positions, with Hun Sen waiving the normal government entrance examination for them.

An Election and a Succession

Against this backdrop, the CPP went into the 23 July general elections without any real challenger. A lingering concern, however, was whether there would be a repeat of the 2018 general elections, when 8.5 per cent of voters spoiled their ballots (a higher percentage than the votes secured by the second-place FUNCINPEC party), or whether there would be a sizeable boycott of the elections, which would have discredited the party's succession plans, not least because the CPP framed the elections as a de facto "plebiscite" on the succession process. To ward off a boycott, on 23 June, the National Assembly passed an amendment to the Law on Elections. It ruled that anyone who did not vote in the July elections could be barred from running as a candidate in future ballots, while anyone charged with encouraging others to boycott the election could be fined between US$1,200 and US$4,800.

Without its main challenger, the CP, on the ballot, the ruling CPP won 82.3 per cent of the vote, which translated into all but 5 of the 125 seats in the National Assembly. The royalist FUNCINPEC party, which had not controlled a seat in parliament for a decade, won 9.2 per cent of the vote and the remaining 5 seats. Of the sixteen other competing parties, only three gained more than 1 per cent of the total vote. According to the NEC, the voter turnout was 84 per cent, up 1.5 percentage points from the 2018 general elections.

While Western governments and international organizations refused to send election monitors in protest of the pre-election repression, most offered relatively mild criticism after the election. The United States, an exception, dubbed the elections "neither free nor fair" and complained about "a pattern of threats and harassment against the political opposition, media, and civil society".[11] Three days after the ballots, Hun Sen announced his resignation as prime minister. The new administration was formally ushered in on 22 August after a unanimous vote from the rubber-stamp National Assembly.

Most of the cabinet was reshuffled, with many of the children or relatives of the "first generation" CPP leaders taking up ministerial roles. Some were direct successions from fathers to sons, such as Hun Manet and the new interior minister Sar Sokha and defence minister Tea Seiha. Others were diagonal moves, with the children of party grandees like Say Chhum, Heng Samrin and the late Sok An becoming ministers or secretaries of state of departments not controlled by their fathers. There were also dynastic successions elsewhere in society. Chea Chantho, the governor of the National Bank of Cambodia, the central bank, was replaced by his daughter, Chea Serey. Lower down the rankings, family members of party elites also became secretaries or under-secretaries of state, with the number of such positions growing from 641 to 1,422 during this succession process in July and August.[12]

There were, however, several non-hereditary cabinet appointments. Keo Rottanak, the new minister of mines and energy, is not from a political family and had been managing director of the state-owned electricity provider Electricite du Cambodge since 2008. Chheang Ra, the new health minister, was formerly the director of the state-run Calmette Hospital. Moreover, while many "princelings" rose through the ranks, much of the power of the government remains in the hands of their predecessors or elder, technocratic politicians. Aun Pornmoniroth, 58, the minister of economy and finance since 2013, was one of almost a dozen cabinet ministers to keep his post. He is widely regarded as a competent technocrat who will keep the new government on a tight ship, financially speaking. He also heads many of the CPP's internal committees. Vongsey Vissoth, 58, a close partner of Aun Pornmoniroth in his former post as a secretary of state at the Ministry of Economy and Finance, was promoted to minister for the Council of Ministers in August, so essentially in charge of the agenda and activities of the cabinet. Both have an ally in the new foreign minister, Sok Chenda Sophea, 67, formerly president of the Council for the Development of Cambodia, the government body tasked with attracting and managing foreign investment. These three experienced and non-dynastic ministers, who are focused on economic development, form a "trifecta" tasked with guiding their younger and less-experienced cabinet colleagues, including Hun Manet.[13] There was also a reshuffle of deputy prime ministers in August, with Neth Savoeun, the former National Police chief and a Hun Sen loyalist, and Sun Chanthol, a trusted former commerce minister who has close connections with China, moving up to this rank.

Although many of the children of party grandees inherited their father's positions, the fathers are expected to retain control of their families' patronage and influence networks. As for Hun Sen, he no longer reigns, but he still rules. He remains the CPP president, a position afforded even more power over party and government personnel after constitutional changes made in 2022 limited the National Assembly's ability to censure or dismiss ministers. He also took up the position of president of the Privy Council, a rank equal to prime minister. Hun Sen also said that he intends to become the next president of the Senate, the upper chamber of parliament, a position that would make him acting head of state when King Norodom Sihamoni is out of the country. Senate elections were scheduled to take place in February 2024.

A Reformist Administration?

After the parliament voted unanimously to make him the new prime minister on 22 August, Hun Manet stated that his administration would continue to guarantee "peace, stability, security and safety" to the Cambodian people and he pledged more investment to improve healthcare, social welfare and job security for low-skilled workers.[14] After the first hundred days of his tenure, there were debates about whether anything had really changed.

Many commentators saw continuity in how his administration dealt with dissent and potential political rivals. Phil Robertson of Human Rights Watch called Hun Manet's administration "the dictatorial version of 'old wine in a new bottle'".[15] In September, for instance, the prominent activist Ny Nak was beaten severely in the streets of Phnom Penh, while the agriculture ministry threatened to close *CamboJA News*. The following month, the Phnom Penh Municipal Court barred three members of Mother Nature Cambodia, an environmental activist group, from travelling to Sweden to collect the Right Livelihood award, which is often termed the "Alternative Nobel". At the time of writing, it remains unclear whether the authorities will also try to stymie the CP's efforts to run in the Senate elections in February 2024. The CPP and opposition parties formed new coalitions late in the year.

The Hun Manet administration also made progress, however, on judiciary and administrative reforms. Keut Rith, the well-regarded minister of justice and a deputy prime minister since August, announced a ten-year plan for judicial reform. Amongst the biggest problems for the judiciary is a considerable backlog of cases. In October, the cabinet approved a draft law on the Establishment of the National Authority for Out-of-Court Dispute Resolution to encourage local officials, such as commune chiefs or district governors, to solve petty disputes so that they do not end up in the courts.

On 10 November, Vongsey Vissoth announced a package of administrative reforms following a meeting of the National Committee for Promoting the Implementation of Key Measures for Public Administration Reform. Ministries and state institutions will have until the third quarter of 2024 to prepare their structural reviews, which will be evaluated over the following four years. This chiefly will streamline the number of civil servants and fold different ministerial departments into larger units, potentially dissolving some ministries in the process, to limit bureaucratic overlap. Hun Many, Hun Manet's younger brother, was made minister of civil service in August and will spearhead these reforms.

One of the most difficult challenges the Cambodian governments faced in 2023, however, was responding to eye-wateringly horrific revelations about the scale of human trafficking, forced labour and international scam syndicates, which greatly damaged the reputation of several Southeast Asian states in 2022 and 2023. According to a report released in August 2023 by the UN High Commissioner for Human Rights, "credible estimates" indicate at least a hundred thousand people are being kept in slave-like conditions in compounds in Cambodia.[16] Estimates vary, but the online scam industry in Cambodia could be worth between US$12.5 billion and US$20 billion annually.[17] To put that into perspective, Cambodia's GDP was US$28.5 billion in 2022.

Cambodia had become a hub for online gambling in the late 2010s, although Phnom Penh made it illegal in 2019, leading to a mass exodus of Chinese nationals from the country. But from 2022 onwards, journalists began reporting on a vast array of online scam compounds within Cambodia that were leading to a spike in human trafficking and reports of workers being forcibly detained in conditions described as modern-day slavery. In August 2022, after months of international scrutiny, the then interior minister, Sar Kheng, finally admitted that a more aggressive approach was needed to tackle the problem. Over the following twelve months, the authorities reportedly rescued more than two thousand foreign nationals, shut down five scam companies and detained ninety-five people. Nonetheless, in June, the US State Department's annual report on global human trafficking placed Cambodia in Tier 3, meaning it had made insufficient efforts to address human trafficking and did not meet the minimum standards. Investigations by journalists in 2023 linked these scam compounds to senior Cambodian officials and tycoons. In August, for instance, *The New York Times* insinuated a link with Senator Ly Yong Phat, one of Cambodia's wealthiest tycoons and a personal adviser to Hun Manet.[18]

Some progress on this front was made in 2023. Phnom Penh engaged with foreign governments and police in joint operations, including foiling an Indonesian "organ harvesting" syndicate operating out of a state-run hospital in Phnom Penh. In September, Hun Manet instructed all twenty-five provincial governors to do more to tackle drugs and human trafficking. The National Committee for Counter Trafficking prepared a 2024–28 initiative to tackle the problem. Some corrupt officials were jailed, including the former deputy chief of the Anti-Drug Police Department in November. A new centre for victims of trafficking was set up by Hun Manet and his Thai counterpart, Srettha Thavisin, in September. Phnom Penh also stepped-up cooperation with Vietnam and Laos on this matter. According to one news report, "The diplomatic circuit is now saying that 'the tone' of the government has changed since Hun Manet took power in August and a slew of arrests, a bureaucratic shake-up, and a five-year counter-trafficking strategy seem to support arguments that a sterner effort is being made."[19] It is possible that Phnom Penh took a tougher line in 2023 because international news headlines about slave-like conditions in the country as well as movies like *No More Bets*, a Chinese blockbuster in 2023 that warned of the dangers of human trafficking in Southeast Asia (which was banned in Cambodia), severely hampered the recovery of Cambodia's vital tourism sector and investor confidence. But Cambodian officials also continued to downplay reports about the scale and size of the alleged scam industry in the country. This will be an ongoing problem for the Hun Manet administration in the years to come.

A More Balanced Foreign Policy?

Cambodia's relations with Western governments deteriorated significantly over the CNRP's forced dissolution in 2017 and Phnom Penh's more overtly pro-China stance. Relations with the United States were particularly tense because of Washington's accusations since 2018 that Cambodia may allow China to station its troops at the Ream Naval Base in Preah Sihanouk Province, something Phnom Penh and Beijing deny. However, Cambodia's chairmanship of ASEAN in 2022 allowed Hun Sen to partially renew engagement with the United States and, particularly, with France. Western states were also appreciative of Hun Sen's quick condemnation of Russia's invasion of Ukraine in early 2022, which made Cambodia an outlier in Southeast Asia.

As already noted, many Western governments issued relatively weak condemnations of the conduct of the July general elections. For the most part, this was because they took a wait-and-see approach to the new Hun Manet administration, which some in the West thought would be more amicable and far less instinctively anti-Western than the Hun Sen government. Some pointed to the fact that Hun Manet and several other incoming ministers were educated in American, British or German universities. According to some commentators, the Hun Manet administration wants to prioritize "economic diplomacy" as the defining feature of foreign policy, thus shifting the foreign ministry's attention away from its alleged fixation with geopolitics. This was likely why Sok Chenda Sophea was appointed foreign minister in August.[20]

In late September, Hun Manet visited New York for a UN General Assembly session and met Victoria Nuland, the acting US deputy secretary of state, on the sidelines. There, Hun Manet appears to have extracted some concessions from Washington. Hours after the July election results were announced, the US Department of State said that US$18 million in aid earmarked for the Cambodian government would be withheld and visa restrictions would be imposed on Cambodian individuals.[21] But hours after Hun Manet's meeting with Nuland in September, Cambodia's foreign ministry briefed that Washington had agreed to resume the aid programmes.

In 2023, Washington was also quieter than in previous years regarding allegations that Cambodia will allow access by Chinese troops to the Ream Naval Base. For instance, the Pentagon's 2022 Report on Military and Security Developments Involving the People's Republic of China described the Ream Naval Base as the "first PRC overseas base in the Indo-Pacific".[22] But the 2023 iteration of the same report dropped this categorization and stated, more prosaically, "In June 2022, a PRC official confirmed that the PLA would have access to parts of Cambodia's Ream Naval Base."[23]

Although the Hun Manet administration sought to improve relations with Western governments in 2023, Cambodia remained committed to its partnership with China, its largest trading partner and the main provider of foreign investment, throughout 2023. Before becoming prime minister, Hun Manet twice visited Beijing as part of his father's entourage—in February 2020 and February 2023. On 14 September, he arrived in Beijing on his first official trip abroad since taking office and met with President Xi Jinping and other senior Chinese officials. He then headed to Nanning for the 20th ASEAN-China Expo. He returned to China in mid-October for the 3rd Belt and Road Forum, where numerous memoranda of understanding were signed with Chinese companies. Cambodia's government also continued to improve relations with Vietnam in 2023. In part, this is because Cambodia now sees a future for its manufacturing sector to become a key node of Vietnam's supply chains, especially as Vietnam has become oversaturated with investment in low-end manufacturing, which is now cheaper to perform in Cambodia. The Cambodian government laid out plans in 2023 for a new expressway to connect Phnom Penh and Bavet, which is situated on the border with Vietnam, and a new railway that will run between Cambodia's border with Thailand and Vietnam. The latter project is currently awaiting formal investment offers.

A Recovering Economy

The World Bank's "East Asia and Pacific Economic Update", published on 2 October 2023, forecasts Cambodia's GDP growth at 5.5 per cent in 2023 and 6.1 per cent in 2024.[24] The country's inflation is expected to average 2.3 per cent for the whole of 2023 and its fiscal deficit to widen to 3.6 per cent.[25] Paramount to the government's economic plans was the finalization in early 2023 of the "Pentagonal Strategy – Phase 1", an economic masterplan that succeeds the Triangular Strategy (1998–2003) and Rectangular Strategy (2004–23).[26] It aims to make Cambodia an upper-middle-income country by 2030 and a high-income country by 2050, as well as setting out a series of administrative reforms that are expected to be carried out across government. The masterplan was officially launched in late August, just days after Hun Manet took office.

The economy continued to suffer from similar economic problems in 2023 as in previous years. Cambodia welcomed 4.4 million international visitors in the first ten months of the year, a 179 per cent increase from the same period in 2022.[27] The majority of them, however, were Southeast Asian visitors, who typically spend less than Chinese tourists, who constituted the bulk of foreign visitors before the pandemic. In mid-October, the Siem Reap–Angkor International Airport was opened, which has a capacity to handle seven million travellers annually. It was built over three years at a cost of nearly US$1 billion, paid for by a consortium of Chinese state-owned companies from China's Yunnan province, which will operate the airport under a fifty-five-year build-operate-transfer deal.

Exports from the vital garment, footwear and travel sector fell by 18.6 per cent year-on-year in the first half of 2023 because of continuing weak demand from Western purchasers. But exports of non-garment products, especially automotive parts and solar panels, increased by 22.9 per cent year-on-year over the same period.[28]

Perhaps more consequentially, private debt and a stalling property sector remained considerable problems throughout 2023. Cambodia has one of the highest rates of private debt to GDP in Asia, estimated to be near 182 per cent in 2022. For comparison, in China, private debt is about 220 per cent of GDP.[29] Cambodia's property sector was severely damaged by the Covid-19 pandemic as pre-pandemic speculation by Chinese investors and then local Cambodians—as property prices soared in the 2010s—came to a shuddering stop. Property prices have fallen considerably since 2020, leaving many investors, including middle-class Cambodians, with sizeable mortgages or loans but depreciating assets. Many real estate developers have gone bankrupt. Others are badly in debt yet continue to owe money to investors. Several prominent tycoons—including Hy Kimhong, director of Piphup Deimeas Investment and director of microfinance institution AMZ—were arrested in 2023 because of alleged fraud related to non-payment of money owed to local investors.

On a positive note, Cambodia secured important foreign investment, principally from China, for several infrastructure schemes in 2023. In November 2022, China's then premier, Li Keqiang, gave assurances that Beijing would fund the planned US$1.6 billion expressway from Phnom Penh to Bavet. Ground was broken on this expressway project in June 2023, with construction being carried out by the state-run China Road and Bridge Corporation (CRBC). In January, the CRBC also presented its feasibility study to upgrade the Phnom Penh–Poipet railway into Cambodia's first express railway, which is estimated to cost US$4 billion.

The government continued to implement new economic reforms. In May, a new Law on Taxation came into effect, which consolidated fifteen types of existing taxes under one regulation and created new mechanisms to improve revenue collection. In July, a new Law on Rules of Origin was promulgated. In late September, the government agreed to raise the monthly minimum wage for garment workers to US$204.

Cambodia also continued to make progress on its green transition. In March, Hun Sen stated that renewable energy makes up over sixty-two per cent of the country's installed electricity capacity. Several new solar power projects and Chinese-funded hydropower schemes were announced in 2023. In November, energy minister Keo Rottanak announced a decision to abandon plans to build a US$1.5 billion 700-megawatt coal-fired power project in a protected reserve and said Cambodia would instead build an 800-megawatt plant fired by natural gas. The same month, the government launched its new circular strategy on the environment for 2023–28, which is in line with the Pentagonal Strategy's aim of making Cambodia a carbon-neutral country with sixty per cent forest cover by 2050.

Conclusion

The year 2023 saw the consolidation of the Hun family's march through Cambodia's institutions, a process that had begun in the 1990s. Hun Manet has become the head of government, while Hun Sen—although not serving in frontline positions—continues to maintain his dominance over all areas of political life. He remains the CPP president, a post that allows him to dictate government policy. In his resignation speech, he indicated that he would become the next Senate president, a post that would make him acting head of state. He is expected to take up this position in April 2024. At the same time, Hun Sen's other sons, Hun Many and Hun Manith, also moved up the political ladder. The ruling party has become ever more dominant over all areas of political and social life, while the opposition parties continue to suffer constant setbacks, raising questions about the future of opposition politics in Cambodia. Economically and socially, in 2023 Cambodia was well on track towards post-pandemic recovery, and conditions are expected to remain stable over the coming years. But questions remain about the impact of vast public debt and how the government can re-normalize relations with the West, which saw some improvements in 2023.

Notes

1. For more information on the new cabinet, see "An Overview of New Ministry Leaders and Their Family and Business Ties", *CamboJA News*, 22 August 2023, https://cambojanews.com/an-overview-of-new-ministry-leaders-and-their-family-and-business-ties/; "Ministers '23", Kamnotra, 2023, https://kamnotra.io/en/succession/succession-2023/.

2. Mun (Mark) Vong, "Can Competitive Elections Come Back to Cambodia?", *East Asia Forum*, 5 September 2023, https://www.eastasiaforum.org/2023/09/05/can-competitive-elections-come-back-to-cambodia/.

3. Fiona Kelliher and Mech Dara, "SEA Games in Cambodia: Workers and Athletes Call Buildup 'a Mess'", *Nikkei Asia*, 4 May 2023, https://asia.nikkei.com/Spotlight/Sports/SEA-Games-in-Cambodia-Workers-and-athletes-call-buildup-a-mess.

4. "Hun Sen Feted at Cambodia's SEA Games Opening Ceremony", Radio Free Asia, 5 May 2023, https://www.rfa.org/english/news/cambodia/cambodia-sea-games-05052023163507.html.

5. Sebastian Strangio, "Meta Rejects Recommendation to Suspend Former Cambodian PM from Facebook", *The Diplomat*, 30 August 2023, https://thediplomat.com/2023/08/meta-rejects-recommendation-to-suspend-former-cambodian-pm-from-facebook/.

6. Andrew Nachemson, "Hun Sen Stands in the Way of His Own Succession Plan", *Foreign Policy*, 15 June 2022, https://foreignpolicy.com/2022/06/15/cambodia-hun-sen-succession-hun-manet/.

7. Neil Loughlin, "Beyond Personalism", *Contemporary Southeast Asia* 43, no. 2 (August 2021): 246.

8. Will Brehm, "How Did Hun Sen Engineer a Seamless Succession in Cambodia?", *East Asia Forum*, 9 September 2023, https://www.eastasiaforum.org/2023/09/09/how-did-hun-sen-engineer-a-seamless-succession-in-cambodia/.

9. The figure was stated by the Cambodia Oknha Association, cited in "16 More Oknha Titles Granted in Year's First Dozen Royal Gazettes", Kamnotra, 9 August 2023, https://kamnotra.io/en/2023/08/16-more-oknha-titles-granted-in-years-first-dozen-royal-gazettes/.

10. "Pro-government Media Claims Thousands of Defections to CPP", Kamnotra, 6 July 2023, https://kamnotra.io/en/2023/07/pro-government-media-claims-thousands-of-defections-to-cpp/.

11. US Embassy in Cambodia, "Press Statement by Department Spokesperson Matthew Miller on National Elections in Cambodia", 24 July 2023, https://kh.usembassy.gov/press-statement-by-department-spokesperson-matthew-miller-on-national-elections-in-cambodia/.

12. "Only 15% of Top Ministry Officials Are Women", Kamnotra, 23 August 2023, https://kamnotra.io/en/2023/08/only-15-of-top-ministry-officials-are-women/.

13. David Hutt, "Policy Veterans in Charge behind Succession of Cambodia's Princelings", Radio Free Asia, 27 July 2023, https://www.rfa.org/english/commentaries/cambodia-succession-07272023135143.html.

14. Shaun Turton, "Hun Manet Pledges 'Peace, Stability' as New Cambodian PM", *Nikkei Asia*, 22 August 2023, https://asia.nikkei.com/Politics/Cambodia-s-new-leadership/Hun-Manet-pledges-peace-stability-as-new-Cambodian-PM.

15. Quoted in Sebastian Strangio, "Cambodian Court Sentences Opposition Figure to 3 Years Prison", *The Diplomat*, 19 October 2023, https://thediplomat.com/2023/10/cambodian-court-sentences-opposition-figure-to-3-years-prison/.

16. Office of the United Nations High Commissioner for Human Rights, "Online Scam Operations and Trafficking into Forced Criminality in Southeast Asia: Recommendations for a Human Rights Response", August 2023, https://bangkok.ohchr.org/wp-content/uploads/2023/08/ONLINE-SCAM-OPERATIONS-2582023.pdf.

17. "Is Cambodia Finally Moving on Human Traffickers?", *UCANews*, 16 November 2023, https://www.ucanews.com/news/is-cambodia-finally-moving-on-human-traffickers/103278.

18. Sui-Lee Wee, "They're Forced to Run Online Scams. Their Captors Are Untouchable", *New York Times*, 28 August 2023, https://www.nytimes.com/2023/08/28/world/asia/cambodia-cyber-scam.html.

19. "Is Cambodia Finally Moving on Human Traffickers?", *UCANews*, 16 November 2023, https://www.ucanews.com/news/is-cambodia-finally-moving-on-human-traffickers/103278.

20. Sokvy Rim, "The West's Impact on the Future of Cambodia's Democracy", *East Asia Forum*, 7 September 2023, https://www.eastasiaforum.org/2023/09/07/the-wests-impact-on-the-future-of-cambodias-democracy/.

21. This was made in a press statement by Matthew Miller, a US State Department spokesperson, 23 July 2023, https://www.state.gov/national-elections-in-cambodia/.

22. US Department of Defence, "Military and Security Developments Involving the People's Republic of China 2022", 29 November 2022, https://www.defense.gov/News/Releases/Release/Article/3230516/2022-report-on-military-and-security-developments-involving-the-peoples-republi/.

23. US Department of Defence, "Military and Security Developments Involving the People's Republic of China 2023", 19 October 2023, https://media.defense.gov/2023/Oct/19/2003323409/-1/-1/1/2023-MILITARY-AND-SECURITY-DEVELOPMENTS-INVOLVING-THE-PEOPLES-REPUBLIC-OF-CHINA.PDF.

24. World Bank, "Services for Development: East Asia and Pacific Economic Update, October 2023", 17 October 2023, https://openknowledge.worldbank.org/server/api/core/bitstreams/e9a7d669-f854-4de6-8afb-a0a01ae85e21/content.

25. International Monetary Fund, "IMF Staff Completes 2023 Article IV Mission to Cambodia", 31 October 2023, https://www.imf.org/en/News/Articles/2023/10/30/pr23365-cambodia-imf-staff-completes-2023-article-iv-mission.

26. For an English language copy of the document, see https://mfaic.gov.kh/files/uploads/1XK1LW4MCTK9/EN%20PENTAGONAL%20STRATEGY%20-%20PHASE%20I.pdf.

27. Hin Pisei, "Foreign Tourist Numbers Skyrocket", *Phnom Penh Post*, 30 November 2023, https://www.phnompenhpost.com/business/foreign-tourist-numbers-skyrocket.

28. Asian Development Bank, "ADB Adjusts 2023 Growth Forecast for Cambodia, Maintains 2024 Outlook", 20 September 2023, https://www.adb.org/news/adb-adjusts-2023-growth-forecast-cambodia-maintains-2024-outlook.

29. World Bank, "East Asia and Pacific Economic Update, October 2023", 17 October 2023, https://openknowledge.worldbank.org/server/api/core/bitstreams/e9a7d669-f854-4de6-8afb-a0a01ae85e21/content.

Indonesia

Banda
Aceh
Medan
Batam
Palembang
JAKARTA
Yogyakarta
Surabaya
Bali
Banjarmasin
Balikpapan
Makassar
Manado
Ambon
Biak
Jayapura

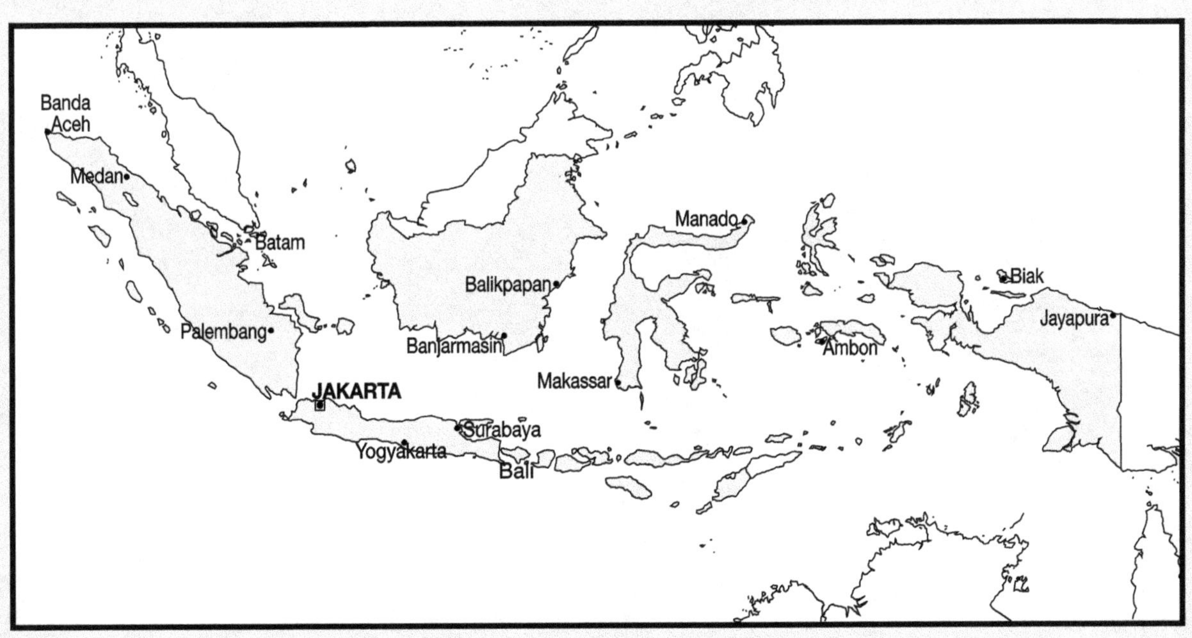

INDONESIA IN 2023:
Jokowi's Dominance – Power without Principle

Greg Fealy

Upon winning re-election in 2019, Indonesian president Joko Widodo (Jokowi) was preoccupied with one pressing question: how to avoid becoming a lame-duck president in his second term, as his predecessor, Susilo Bambang Yudhoyono, had been. Jokowi is an ambitious, impatient politician fired with a determination to transform Indonesia into an advanced and economically powerful nation. In his first term, he had committed himself to a significant programme of infrastructure, welfare, health and educational reforms, achieving success in many of these or making considerable progress. But he has far bigger plans for his second term, including a proposed new capital city, high-technology industrialization, and raising the quality of Indonesia's workforce and innovation capacity. As Eve Warburton has observed, Jokowi sees himself as a latter-day Soeharto, the authoritarian president who ruled Indonesia from 1966 till 1998.[1] Just as Soeharto had a profound impact on the nation through his developmental policies and restoration of its international reputation, so too does Jokowi wish to be remembered as bringing a dramatic improvement to the lives of Indonesians and presiding over Indonesia's ascent to becoming a major global power.

With four years of his second five-year term now elapsed, Jokowi has banished any threat of political diminution. Indeed, as he prepares for his final year in office, he has become the commanding figure within the nation's politics, enjoying greater power and public approbation than any president of the post-1998 Reformasi period. He is widely regarded as having managed the Covid-19 pandemic capably, the economy is healthy, Indonesia's international profile has never been higher, and the country has been largely peaceful and stable. A measure of how

---

GREG FEALY is Emeritus Professor of Indonesian Politics at the Australian National University, Canberra.

highly he is regarded can be found in public opinion surveys, which for most of 2023 have shown his approval ratings in the seventy to eighty per cent range—an unprecedented level for the past twenty-five years. He has a firm grip on political processes and an ability to bend parliament and political parties to his will. His governing coalition contains seven of the nine parliamentary parties, or eighty-three per cent of seats, providing the president with a compliant legislature. His authority is such that his coalition and parliament readily endorse his legislative agenda and his appointment of loyalists to a wide range of key positions within the cabinet, the bureaucracy and the military, thereby ensuring that his wishes and interests are safeguarded by trusted figures. Most media magnates are also close to coalition parties or Jokowi, resulting in largely positive reporting of his and his government's actions.

Despite his soaring popularity and tight grip on power, there is a dark side to Jokowi's political dominance. His concentration of political influence and determination to assert himself has come at a high cost: in effect, he has sacrificed many of the principles of Reformasi that once defined his presidency, including a commitment to democratization, human rights, freedom of expression and probity in government. Increasingly, Jokowi has used his position, or allowed those around him, to intimidate opponents and critics, to manipulate and coerce parties within his coalition and to undermine the independence and effectiveness of key institutions within the political system, most notably the Anti-Corruption Commission (KPK) and the Constitutional Court, two of the central institutions of Reformasi.[2] In some cases, he has undertaken these actions in concert with the support of broad sections of the political elite; in other cases, he has acted primarily out of his own or family interests but drawn the support of others keen to win his favour and advance their own prospects. Political opponents and civil society groups who criticize the president routinely suffer retribution, often in the form of cyber-harassment or intimidation, but sometimes also entailing threats to their careers or businesses.[3] Most seriously of all, prominent figures who cross the president can find themselves subject to police or KPK investigation and perhaps prosecution.[4] These reversals in democratic rights have been recorded by major democracy research institutes such as Freedom House and the Economist Intelligence Unit and are reflected in Indonesia's declining ranking across the nine years of Jokowi's presidency.

Jokowi appears to regard this overturning of Reformasi principles as necessary to ensure rapid economic development. Moreover, he has come to associate his own continuing influence as critical to Indonesia's advancement, providing justification for his manoeuvres to establish a political dynasty that will entrench him and his family within the nation's leadership for many years to come. Much as Jokowi has sought to transform his country, he has also, in effect, transformed himself into a far different politician from the one who won office in 2014. The Jokowi of a decade ago captured the imagination of voters by embodying a new type of Reformasi leadership. He was of humble background, had painstakingly built a successful business before entering politics as mayor of Solo in Central Java, and then became governor of Jakarta and finally president. He was a non-elite politician who had risen rapidly based primarily on merit and astuteness rather than wealth or powerful connections. Indeed, his rhetoric was of a champion of ordinary people and an opponent of oligarchic status quo interests. But the Jokowi of 2023 is nepotistic, self-interestedly manipulative and increasingly autocratic. He has brought a whatever-it-takes ruthlessness to advancing his own family as a force in elite politics and has bent or broken rules that have limited his exercise of power. He has gone from an icon of Reformasi to a Machiavellian architect of democratic regression.

Economic and Diplomatic Ascendancy

In August 2022, Jokowi proudly announced at his annual state of the nation address that Indonesia had reached the "pinnacle of global leadership", because "we hold the presidency of the G20, an international forum made up of the world's largest economies", and "next year we will assume the chairmanship of ASEAN".[5] Thus, a combination of economic and diplomatic achievements had taken his country to unprecedented international standing and influence. In 2023, Indonesia applied for membership in the OECD, which, if granted, as appears likely, will further enhance the nation's status within prestigious global institutions.[6] When Jokowi speaks of his legacy, it will be attainments such as these that he cites as tangible evidence of success.

The economy has always been central to Jokowi's political legitimacy, and it is the high public satisfaction with how he has managed economic and development issues that underlies his extraordinary end-of-term approval ratings. The economic news in 2023 was reasonably positive, though growth is slower than in the past two years. The economy grew at 4.94 per cent year-on-year in the third quarter, slightly below the predicted 5.1 per cent, with inflation lower than expected at 3.6 per cent because of easing fuel prices and good harvests in much of the agricultural sector. The main economic change was the fall of resource exports and the rise in domestic demand. The high global prices that prevailed during 2021–22 for Indonesian commodity exports—such as coal, iron, nickel and palm oil—have now moderated, leading to a contraction in exports from 4.2 per cent to 2.9 per cent, accompanied by a reduction in revenue. In its place, Indonesia's rapidly growing middle class is driving a boom in consumption, which now makes up over half of GDP.[7] The unemployment rate fell from 5.86 per cent in 2022 to 5.32 per cent this year, and overall employment grew by 3.77 per cent, with the workforce now numbering 139.8 million. Labour participation was also up modestly from 68.6 per cent in 2022 to 69.8 per cent in 2023. Poverty levels continued to fall slowly, registering 9.5 per cent in 2022, down by 0.6 per cent in 2021. But it was also notable that Indonesia's Gini Index has declined since 2013, from 40.8 to 37.9. Overall, Indonesia's post-Covid performance is better than most countries in the region and it achieved upper middle income status in mid-2023.

Some aspects of Jokowi's economic policies have attracted closer international scrutiny over the past two years. Despite the president's strong pro-market comments to foreign audiences, his government's policies have tended towards greater protectionism that inhibits participation in global supply chains. Indonesia's ban on the export of raw resources, such as nickel and bauxite, and its insistence that value-added processing occur in-country, commonly referred to as "downstreaming", has been popular domestically but it has drawn an adverse ruling from the World Trade Organization on grounds of restriction of trade.[8] Similarly, the government's plans to establish an electric vehicle battery manufacturing capacity have met with little success. Attempts to lure major battery producers, such as Tesla, have failed, and Indonesia appears to be losing out to other nations that have more highly skilled workforces and stronger records within global value chains.

Diplomatically, the past two years have been the high point of Jokowi's presidency. Following his presidency of the G20 in 2022, he took over the chairmanship of ASEAN in late 2022. Jokowi came to office knowing little about international affairs, and his primary foreign policy focus was on generating greater economic opportunities for Indonesia. For much of his presidency, he had shown only tepid interest in major regional and international issues. Thus, expectations were low when he assumed the G20 leadership. Jokowi faced two challenges in his G20 role: to manage the fallout from the Ukraine War, particularly to prevent open divisions or a partial boycott of the November 2022 summit; and to seek tangible outcomes in the fields of global health, sustainable energy transition and digital transformation. He showed some deftness in his management of the Ukraine issue, pursuing a neutral position that involved him visiting both Moscow and Kyiv and inviting Ukrainian president Volodymyr Zelenskyy to the summit at which Russian president Vladimir Putin had declared he would also be present. In the end, neither president attended: Zelenskyy gave an online address and Putin was represented by the Russian foreign minister. While many Western states had wished Jokowi had taken a more critical stance towards Russia, his approach nonetheless won approval for assuring a smooth summit. He was also successful in winning a commitment of US$20 billion from various Western countries to decarbonize Indonesia's economy.

Jokowi's 2023 chairing of ASEAN has gone less smoothly. The two most important concerns over the past year have been the continuing escalation of China-US tensions, particularly in the South China Sea, and the status of Myanmar following the 2021 military coup. Many major powers have, over the past decade, increasingly questioned the effectiveness of ASEAN in dealing coherently with both of these issues. The bloc has been openly divided between member nations that are close to China, such as Cambodia and Laos, and those in ASEAN who have tense relations with it, such as the Philippines and Vietnam. The lack of progress on initiatives such as a code of conduct in the South China Sea has frustrated those countries that face significant intervention and harassment by Chinese vessels. Doubts about ASEAN's importance were reflected in, among others, US president Biden's decision not to attend the 2023 ASEAN-US summit. Meanwhile, Jokowi, having hosted the ASEAN-China summit in Jakarta in September, travelled to Beijing for the Third Belt and Road Forum in October, drawing private disapproval from some ASEAN members that he was more interested in economic opportunities than attending to regional strategic issues.[9]

If little progress was made on China-related strategic issues, Myanmar proved an even greater frustration. Despite intensive diplomatic efforts by Indonesia over the past year, the Min Aung Hlaing regime refused to halt its violent repression of dissent or enter into dialogue with civilian groups seeking a return to democracy. Jokowi conceded at the ASEAN meeting that no progress had been made in negotiations with the regime, and for the second year running the Myanmar leadership was excluded from the summit. The Myanmar issue is becoming more pressing for various ASEAN members, as growing numbers of refugees, particularly displaced Rohingya, come to their shores. Malaysia says it is hosting more than 200,000 Rohingya, and Indonesia has also experienced an upsurge in refugee arrivals, leading some local communities to protest and push boats back to sea.[10]

2024 Election Overview

The 2024 elections have dominated Indonesian politics over the past year and a half. To be held on 14 February, the event will feature five simultaneous elections for the presidency, the national, provincial and district legislatures and the Regional Representative Council (DPD). More than 204 million people are registered to vote, making this the world's largest single-day election. For the presidential election, pairs of presidential and vice-presidential candidates can be nominated if they secure support from 20 per cent of parliamentarians or have the backing of parties that won 25 per cent of the national vote at the 2019 general election. To win the election, a pair of candidates must gain a majority of the national vote as well as 20 per cent of the vote in half of Indonesia's thirty-eight provinces. If no ticket wins a majority on 14 February, a second run-off round will be held on 26 June, with the new president to be installed on 20 October. Seventeen parties will contest the elections for the 580-seat parliament, and they need to clear a threshold of 4 per cent of the national vote in order to win representation.

Most public and media attention has been focused on the presidential election, with three candidates in particular, according to opinion polls, standing out as frontrunners: Prabowo Subianto, who was Jokowi's rival in 2014 and 2019 but is now his defence minister; Ganjar Pranowo, the two-term governor of Central Java; and Anies Baswedan, the former governor of Jakarta. Only one party, the Indonesian Democratic Party of Struggle (PDIP), had sufficient parliamentary numbers to nominate candidates by itself; all other parties would have to form coalitions to do so. The path to nomination seemed straightforward for Prabowo, who led his own party, the Greater Indonesia Party (Gerindra), which had 13 per cent of parliamentary seats and needed only one or two other parties to reach 20 per cent. Ganjar was the expected nominee for PDIP, in which he had been a career politician, but the party chair, former president Megawati Sukarnoputri, delayed anointing him until she was certain of his deference to her. Anies faced the greatest difficulty as he had no party of his own and thus had no automatic basis of support.

This situation set up a battle of wills between the parties and the three candidates, especially Prabowo and Anies, who needed coalitions behind them. The parties were determined to put the highest possible price on their support, with the aim of raising their vote in the general election and trying to maximize their stake in a new government. For a number of parties, their primary concern was to have their leader secure a vice-presidential nomination, thereby giving rise to a supposed "coat-tail effect" in which the party's vote would be bolstered by virtue of having its chair in a high-profile position. Examples of parties nominating their general chairmen included Golkar, which championed Airlangga Hartarto, the coordinating minister for the economy; the National Awakening Party (PKB), which touted Muhaimin Iskandar; and the Democrat Party, which advocated for Agus Harimurti Yudhoyono. Other parties had patrons for whom they campaigned, such as the National Mandate Party (PAN), which promoted the state-owned enterprises minister, Erick Thohir, a generous benefactor of the party. More generally, all parties sought to lock in deals over future ministerial portfolios or other spoils of office should they be part of a winning coalition.

For the presidential candidates, there were good reasons to hold off in deciding their running mates. If the election is tight, a strong vice-presidential candidate could mean the difference between victory and defeat. But it was difficult to know many months in advance of the October 2023 registration deadline what type of vice-presidential nominee might best complement their own campaigns; for example, by drawing support from constituencies where the presidential candidate was weak. Thus, candidates had to balance between enticing parties to coalesce behind them while keeping their vice-presidential options open.

From mid-2022, there was a flurry of coalitions forming and dissolving as parties jostled to best position themselves in a rapidly changing political environment. Space does not permit a detailed account of the many alignments and re-alignments, but describing several of the moves may allow some insight into the fluidity of the process. Perhaps the most striking set of manoeuvres were those surrounding Anies Baswedan, who, in October 2022, was the first candidate to be nominated. His coalition was led by the National Democrats party (NasDem) and its media-magnate founder Surya Paloh, but it also included the mildly Islamist Prosperous Justice Party (PKS), which had no competitive candidate of its own, and the Democrat Party, which was confident that Agus Harimurti would be Anies's running mate. Meanwhile, PKB had entered into a coalition with Gerindra in August 2022 and persistently pressed for Muhaimin to be Prabowo's running mate. Prabowo dutifully talked up the possibility of running with Muhaimin without ever committing to it, much to PKB's chagrin. When Golkar and PAN suddenly joined Prabowo's coalition in August 2023, Muhaimin realized his prospects were dimming so he entered into quiet negotiations with Paloh about becoming Anies's vice-presidential candidate.[11] On 1 September 2022, Paloh shocked unsuspecting political observers when he announced an Anies-Muhaimin ticket. Anies, himself, was cool on the idea and preferred Agus as his partner, but without a party of his own, he had little leverage against Paloh. The Democrats, infuriated by what they saw as Paloh's betrayal, withdrew from the NasDem coalition and threw their support behind Prabowo. PKS was also initially nonplussed by the prospect of having to back Muhaimin as his constituency was the Nahdlatul Ulama (NU) community, which had often pilloried PKS as radical and intolerant.

Other coalition manoeuvres were less dramatic but nonetheless pointed to the pragmatism of Indonesia's party system. Prabowo ended up assembling an alliance of nine parties by the time of his formal nomination in October 2023. In addition to his own Gerindra and the late-joining Golkar and PAN, his coalition included a string of smaller parties, most of which were unlikely to win parliamentary seats. As will be recounted in greater detail below, Prabowo's preferred vice-presidential candidate was Jokowi's eldest son, Gibran Rakabuming Raka, who was also the mayor of the Central Java city of Solo. But Golkar and PAN nonetheless continued to advocate for their respective candidates—Airlangga Hartarto and Erick Thohir—in the hope that Gibran was ineligible or overlooked. Eventually, on 22 October, Prabowo and his coalition announced Gibran as their vice-presidential candidate.

PDIP was much less interested in coalition deals, partly because its 128 parliamentary seats already met the nomination threshold, and partly because Megawati remained aloof in her dealings with other potential allies. The only significant party to join PDIP was the Islamic United Development Party (PPP), which was hoping that its recent star recruit, the tourism and creative economy minister, Sandiago Uno, might become PDIP's vice-presidential candidate. Megawati declared Ganjar to be her party's presidential candidate on 21 April 2023, and in October the coordinating minister of politics, law and security, Mahfud MD, was announced as his running mate. The following section will discuss in greater detail the three presidential candidates, their strategies and prospects.

Prabowo's Reset

Prabowo has been a high-profile figure in Indonesia's public life for almost half a century, whether as a controversial senior military officer and son-in-law to former president Soeharto, or as a civilian politician during the Reformasi era. Throughout most of this time, his reputation has been that of a highly intelligent, ambitious, forceful and at times volatile person. Although regarded by some observers as a brave and brilliant army commander, his military career ended ignominiously with his dishonourable discharge on grounds of human rights abuses. It was in the 2014 and 2019 presidential elections, where he was Jokowi's sole rival, that he carved out a distinctive political identity. In contrast to the quietly spoken and reserved Jokowi, Prabowo projected an image of emphatic resoluteness and self-confidence. His speeches were rousing, often angry, and filled with hortatory nationalist—even xenophobic—language. He and his campaign team assailed Jokowi, accusing him of being a lackey to foreign economic interests and questioning his Islamic credentials and willingness to defend Indonesia's majority Muslim community. And he appeared bent on reversing many of the democratic reforms of the post-1998 period by, among other things, seeking a return to the original 1945 constitution, which gave extensive powers to the executive branch and offered minimal protection of citizens' rights.

All this changed in July 2019 when Prabowo surprised the nation by reconciling with Jokowi and agreeing to become defence minister in the new government. His about-face was borne of an awareness that time was running out on his political career and that a new strategy was needed if he was to finally secure the presidency, something that he had long believed was his destiny. Jokowi's presidential term would end in 2024, by which time Prabowo would be seventy-two years old, and facing possibly his last chance to win a presidential election. Thus, he set about transforming himself from a fiery oppositional figure railing against the status quo to a senior, responsible cabinet minister who was willing to work constructively within the existing system and collaborate with many whom he had previously regarded as foes.

Prabowo has largely succeeded in his makeover, to judge by his electability figures in opinion surveys. For the past two years he has been among the top three prospective presidential candidates, and since mid-2023 he has been the leading candidate. As defence minister, he has performed ably and avoided major controversies. Most importantly, he has avoided the kind of intemperate displays that previously had raised questions in the minds of the public about his suitability for high office. His only blunder occurred at the IISS Shangri-la Dialogue in Singapore in June 2023, where, contrary to government policy, he proposed to end the war between Russia and Ukraine via a negotiated peace process. Both Jokowi and Retno Masudi, the foreign minister, admitted to being blindsided by the off-the-cuff remarks, and Prabowo was summoned to the palace to explain his statement.[12]

The single most important element of Prabowo's 2024 election strategy is Jokowi. The incumbent president has gone from being the primary obstacle to Prabowo's political ambitions to now being their guarantor. Prabowo has systematically cultivated Jokowi over the past year using various means, including effusive praise of the president's achievements and showing submissiveness to Jokowi at every turn. He has promised to continue "Jokowi-nomics", maintaining the president's policy settings on such things as infrastructure development, down-streaming of resource production and construction of the new capital, Nusantara, in Kalimantan. He admits to "learning much" from Jokowi because the president "was a winner". Prabowo called his campaign committee "Team Jokowi" and renamed his coalition the Advance Indonesia Coalition (Koalisi Indonesia Maju), mimicking the Advance Indonesia title that Jokowi gave to his current cabinet.[13]

Perhaps Prabowo's most astute initiative was to propose choosing Gibran as his running mate. No doubt mindful of Jokowi's dynasty-building ambitions as well as his determination to maintain influence with government after his term ends, Prabowo likely calculated that having Gibran as his running mate would ensure the president's support. There was, however, one major hurdle. The 2017 Election Law, which governed the conduct of the presidential election, specified that presidential and vice-presidential candidates must be at least forty years old; Gibran was thirty-six. The only means by which he could stand would be if the Constitutional Court changed the election law. The court considered several petitions seeking amendments to the law, dismissing all but one: a proposal from a professed "admirer" of Gibran that an exemption to the age limit be granted to any directly elected regional head, such as a governor, regent or mayor. The court approved this exemption petition with a 5-4 majority, thereby opening the way for Gibran, who had been elected mayor in 2021, to run as vice-president. The court decision drew widespread criticism, but it did not assure Gibran's nomination. Both Prabowo and Jokowi were wary that there might be a backlash and closely monitored survey results and social media discourses for signs of voter disapproval. On the eve of the deadline for nominations, having received reassurance from pollsters that there was no significant adverse reaction, Jokowi gave his blessing to Gibran and Prabowo duly announced the president's son would be his running mate.

Prabowo's actions tell of a striking change of behaviour and a willingness to suppress traits that had been apparent throughout his career. He has deep pride in his attainments, both as a military officer and a politician. In all likelihood, he sees himself as better equipped to be president than any of his rivals, including Jokowi. He probably harbours considerable resentment towards Jokowi, the man who has twice defeated him and consigned his chance of becoming president to the twilight of his career. Moreover, taking on Gibran, a political neophyte who was the least qualified vice-presidential candidate available to him, must also irk Prabowo. But he has nonetheless put aside any such sentiments and shown enormous self-discipline in his pursuit of Jokowi's favour and endorsement. For a man who has kowtowed to few others in his life, his fawning cultivation of the president is evidence of how badly he wants victory in 2024.

Anies and Ganjar

From mid-2022, Ganjar Pranowo led most surveys on the electability of presidential candidates but suffered a sharp fall in popularity in February and March 2023. The immediate cause was a public backlash against his role and that of other leading PDIP politicians in the loss of the FIFA Under-20 World Cup, which Indonesia was awarded to host in late 2023. Ganjar, under pressure from the PDIP leadership, spoke out against the involvement in the tournament of the Israeli team, claiming that this ran counter to Indonesia's long-standing objection to relations with the Jewish state. Eventually, FIFA withdrew the event from Indonesia, causing widespread anger among Indonesia's many soccer fans.[14]

Other problems also eroded his public standing. Megawati was reluctant to approve Ganjar's nomination until he had proven his fealty to her by reportedly agreeing in advance to allocate particular portfolios to PDIP and comply with party policy positions. She regularly lectured him at length in public and made him go through displays of obeisance to her. By the time she formally endorsed his nomination, he seemed a somewhat diminished figure, with serious questions asked about his independence and character. Finally, Ganjar's popularity suffered as Jokowi showed increasing favour to Prabowo. Initially, Jokowi had appeared equally supportive of Ganjar and Prabowo, but as Megawati sought to exclude the president from PDIP's deliberations on Ganjar's nomination, he drew nearer to the ever-receptive Prabowo. The party's nomination of Mahfud as vice-presidential candidate was due primarily to its belief that he would bolster Ganjar's vote among Muslim voters in Java. Mahfud was from Madura in East Java and he had links to NU, the largest Islamic organization in East and Central Java. He also brought immense executive and legal experience, being not only a senior minister in the Jokowi government but also a former law professor and ex-chief justice of the Constitutional Court.

Anies Baswedan's nomination as president in late 2022 was a bold stroke by Surya Paloh aimed at stealing a march on other candidates and also avoiding the possibility of Jokowi dictating to NasDem whom to support. Paloh had once been a staunch ally of Jokowi's, but their relations have cooled in recent years. In backing Anies, whom Jokowi dislikes intensely, Paloh risked incurring the president's wrath. Paloh foisted Muhaimin on Anies, with the rationale that the PKB leader could lift Anies's low poll numbers in the NU-dominated areas of East and Central Java.

Campaign Dynamics

A major point of discussion among observers has been whether the 2024 election campaign would be marred by acrimony and polarization, as had been the case in the two previous presidential elections. The 2014 and 2019 elections had strong sectarian and sometimes racist overtones, with especially vituperative social media discourses. Leading politicians and their campaign teams played up identity differences, particularly on religion, in order to mobilize voter sentiment in their favour. Prabowo's camp did this with powerful effect against Jokowi in 2014 and somewhat less potently in 2019; Jokowi's campaign resorted to similar, though less virulent, measures against Prabowo in 2019.

All indications to date are that the 2024 election will be conducted in a more civil manner than the two before it. Survey data shows that many of the cleavages created during those preceding elections have given way to a renewed desire to bridge divisions and emphasize common national purpose. Candidates and parties that had previously used polarizing tactics are now speaking the language of unity and accommodation of difference. Prabowo's 2019 rapprochement with Jokowi helped this process, but there has also been a wider sentiment in political circles and society that the weaponizing of religion risks unleashing destructive forces. Jokowi and the other candidates have also backed this 'counter-polarization' trend.[15] To date, none of the presidential candidates has used sectarian messaging.

At the time of writing, all credible polls show Prabowo and Gibran with a healthy and growing lead over the other two pairs of candidates. Indeed, Prabowo has been well ahead of the field since April, when the U20 Cup fiasco cut away at Ganjar's popularity. Most surveys give Prabowo between a 6 per cent and 12 per cent advantage. These figures reflect the success of Prabowo's efforts to remake his image. He has spoken well at public events, has been good-humoured on the hustings, and has even produced short dance videos for TikTok that have gone viral. The partnership with Gibran, far from being a burden, has bolstered Prabowo's support among younger voters, a crucial constituency given that people under forty make up over half the electorate. Polling from *Kompas* and LSI shows that much of Prabowo's rising support comes from former Jokowi voters who are abandoning Ganjar and PDIP, thus confirming that the Jokowi factor is a powerful element in the election.[16] Given that some polls published in late December have Prabowo with roughly 45 per cent of the vote and extending his lead over his rivals, it is possible that he and Gibran may win in a single round if the current trend continues.

Ganjar's candidacy appears to be flagging. Although most polls have him placing second, many suggest the gap between Ganjar and Anies is narrowing, and some have Anies slightly ahead. Ganjar has been unable to halt the drift of loyal Jokowi voters to Prabowo. While smooth and affable on the campaign trail, he had made little impact on undecided or swing voters, a group that some pollsters suggest could be as great as 28 per cent of the electorate.[17] He has made few memorable statements during the campaign and has been mediocre when discussing policy details. Mahfud, while estimable, is not a skilled retail politician and often seems bemused at the endless demands and rituals of campaigning. Meanwhile, Anies and Muhaimin have proven effective campaigners, though they have the least funds of the three teams. They have campaigned with vigour, especially in the populous Javanese electorates where Anies was previously weak. Anies is an articulate campaigner who has a good grasp of policy issues but is regarded with suspicion by minority religious communities after his perceived courting of conservative Islamist groups during his Jakarta gubernatorial campaign in 2017. He has sharpened his criticisms of Jokowi's policies and style of leadership, questioning the wisdom and scale of the Nusantara project and accusing the government of growing repression. If Ganjar fails to re-energize his campaign, Anies could overtake him in the new year.

Jokowi's Machinations

By far the most important person in shaping the dynamics of the presidential election has been Jokowi himself. He has done this through a growing range of interventions in the political process, particularly using state institutions or supporter groups to manipulate, intimidate and sometimes coerce his coalition partners or political enemies to do what he wants. Jokowi does not do this directly as he strives to maintain a buffer of deniability and appear above the fray of practical politics. Instead, he uses different figures within his trusted inner circle, such as his coordinating minister of maritime affairs and investment, Luhut Panjaitan, and state secretary, Pratikno, to convey his wishes.[18] Politicians and businesspeople have learned that resisting or ignoring the president's wishes can be hazardous, and anecdotes of the palace's punishments for non-compliance circulate freely in elite circles. The pattern of Jokowi's interventions has become increasingly clear in recent years as his intrusions have become bolder and more details emerge in the media and academic publications about the president's exercise of power.

Early instances of Jokowi's manipulative style came with his strategy to prolong his presidency, either by extending his second term to seven or eight years rather than the constitutionally specified five years, or amending the constitution to allow a third five-year term. Initially, several coalition parties—including Golkar, PKB and PAN—publicly floated the idea of an extension; some of their leaders later made it known to journalists that they had been threatened with either corruption investigations or possible court challenges to the legality of their party boards if they failed to endorse a longer term. Luhut also backed the proposal, claiming to have "meta data" that showed strong public support for the idea. He was ridiculed by the media when he subsequently refused to provide details. In the end, adverse public opinion, as well as Megawati's own emphatic rejection of a term extension, forced its abandonment. All the parties involved, as well as Luhut, suffered reputational damage.[19] Throughout the entire controversy, Jokowi gave the impression of being a disinterested observer, claiming the extension idea had come from those around him and that he was leaving it to the public to decide.

Such manipulation of politicians and party leadership became more intense in mid-2022. In July, a number of parties came under pressure from "the palace" to support Prabowo rather than Anies or Ganjar. A salient example of this was Golkar, which endured orchestrated destabilization. Airlangga found himself under investigation by the Anti-Corruption Commission over his alleged role in a scheme to manipulate palm oil prices in order to defraud the state of some Rp6 trillion, details of which appeared in various media. Though no charges have been laid, Airlangga's image has been badly tarnished. At the same time, Golkar politicians who were close to Jokowi, including Luhut and Bahlil Lahadalia, the investment minister, informed journalists that they were prepared to challenge Airlangga's position as chair, and pressure grew for an extraordinary party conference to decide the matter.[20] In the face of such pressure, the Golkar board broke off negotiations with NasDem and PDIP and instead swung their backing behind Prabowo.[21] PAN similarly followed Golkar in backing Prabowo, reportedly after pressure from Jokowi's lieutenants. Golkar was also the first party in Prabowo's coalition to formally nominate Gibran as Prabowo's running mate.

NasDem's actions in supporting Anies also made it a target. Two of its cabinet members—Johny Plate, information and communication minister, and Syahrul Yasin Limpo, agriculture minister—came under investigation; they were both charged with corruption and forced to stand down. Plate has since been jailed for fifteen years and Limpo is awaiting trial.[22] Suryo Paloh's extensive business interests also came under pressure, with the loss of government contracts, difficulty in gaining credit and seeming advertiser boycotts of his media outlets. Paloh was so worried by the retaliation that he made repeated efforts to assuage Jokowi, but without success.[23]

Anies, himself, was subject to a KPK investigation into his management of the Formula E electric car race in Jakarta in 2022. Many observers and ex-KPK investigators believe there was little substance to the allegations, and no charges have been laid.[24] Muhaimin also found that long-dormant investigations into allegations of corrupt behaviour in 2011 when he was employment and transmigration minister were quickly revived by the KPK following his joining of Anies's ticket.[25]

Numerous other cases could be cited, but the central point is that the Jokowi government has established a pattern of retributive action against politicians and parties that defy it. The KPK, in particular, features prominently in these campaigns. This is not to say that the KPK cases are without legal merit. Elite political corruption is commonplace and a great many senior officials may be guilty of malfeasance. Rather, it is the timing and the selective targeting of politicians who have fallen foul of the president or act contrary to his urgings that has drawn criticism of KPK's apparent politicization. The charging of the KPK chair, Firli Bahuri, in November 2023 with corruption linked to the Limpo case has further underscored the serious integrity problems of the commission.[26]

Jokowi's behaviour runs counter to the precedents set by his two predecessors, Susilo Bambang Yudhoyono and Megawati, both of whom avoided meddling in the 2004 and 2014 elections while being incumbent presidents. Indeed, Jokowi's behaviour bears some similarities to Soeharto's approach. While Jokowi operates within a broadly democratic system, unlike the authoritarian New Order regime, he has increasingly adopted Soeharto's patrimonial style of appointing loyalists to key positions and regarding security agencies and institutions of state as instruments of his personal authority rather than autonomous, professional agencies governed by statutes and regulations.

Two recent cases highlight the problematic nature of Jokowi's approach of the end justifying the means. The first concerns the independence of the Constitutional Court. In mid-2022, the chief justice of the court, Anwar Usman, married Jokowi's sister in a lavish wedding in the president's home city of Solo. At the time, many commentators bemoaned the most senior judge of the paramount court marrying into the president's family, but most expected that Anwar would recuse himself from any cases in which there were apparent conflicts of interest. But when the court considered petitions relating to Gibran's eligibility to run in the presidential election, Anwar only excluded himself from some deliberations and decided to sit in judgement of the sole petition seeking an exemption for mayors, such as Gibran. When the court's verdict was handed down and it emerged that Anwar's vote had helped to deliver the 5-4 granting of the petition, the outcry was immediate. Media outlets were soon reporting that Anwar had lobbied fellow judges in favour of the exemption and that various procedural irregularities accompanied the filing of the petition.[27] Eventually, an Honour Council of the Constitutional Court was formed to rule on the appropriateness of Anwar's actions. It found him guilty of serious ethical breaches and removed him as chief justice. Nonetheless, the ruling on the exemption stands. Investigative reporting by the well-regarded *Tempo* magazine claimed that Jokowi had spoken to Anwar about the case and seemingly did not object to his brother-in-law's involvement—something Jokowi strenuously denies.[28] Many Reformasi activists regard this court ruling as Jokowi's most blatant abuse of authority and that he should have insisted on Anwar's recusal.

The second case relates to cutting corners to elevate a loyalist to high office, a practice Soeharto commonly adopted later in his rule. General Agus Subiyanto, whom Jokowi had known when mayor of Solo, has enjoyed a meteoric rise, becoming head of the presidential guard, then army chief of staff in October 2023 for just one month, before being appointed armed forces commander in November. He has jumped from being a two-star to a four-star general in a matter of months, a process usually taking years, having leap-frogged many other well-regarded senior officers.[29]

Whatever the ethical issues surrounding Jokowi's behaviour in the past year, current polling suggests he is likely to succeed in his dynastic ambitions. While most opinion surveys show voter disapproval of dynastic politics, they also show concomitant acceptance of Gibran's nomination. For example, a Charta Politika poll in November 2023 showed that 59 per cent of respondents disagreed with dynastic politics and 49 per cent regarded Gibran's nomination as constituting dynastic politics. But two other polls probably better captured the mood of voters. Populi found 46 per cent of respondents regarded dynastic politics as "normal" (*biasa saja*), with only 18 per cent finding it unacceptable. Indikator revealed that 53 per cent regarded it as unproblematic provided candidates submitted themselves to direct election.[30] At least two conclusions are possible from these results. The first is that, while many voters view Gibran's rise as constituting dynastic politics, they do not have strong objections, quite possibly because they are uncertain as to how directly involved the president has been. His repeated denials of intervention may incline many voters to give him the benefit of the doubt. Second, even if Jokowi were directly involved, voters who admire his leadership may welcome Gibran's prospective vice-presidency as ensuring the perpetuation of existing policies and a style of governance that they see as successful. Though they may not like the way Gibran's elevation was secured, their objections are insufficient for them to vote against him.

Closing Reflections

Jokowi has attained much during his nine years as president and looks set to leave office in late 2024 with a higher public approval than any of his predecessors. He has indeed delivered on many of his promises of economic growth and development, and most Indonesians are better off currently than when he became president in 2014. Indonesia is now poised to become a far more significant player in regional and global economic and diplomatic affairs than at any time in its past. However, Jokowi's gradual but systematic undercutting of democratic principles has made Indonesia less free and less transparent. His country is now a semi-democracy rather than a full democracy, and Jokowi has left a precedent for succeeding presidents to follow should they wish to grasp greater power for themselves by eroding institutions created to defend rights and ensure the rule of law.

Notes

1. Eve Warburton, "Jokowi and the New Developmentalism", *Bulletin of Indonesian Economic Studies* 52, no. 3 (2016): 297–320.

2. Liam Gammon, "Flying Too Close to the Son?", *Inside Story*, 27 October 2023, https://insidestory.org.au/flying-too-close-to-the-son/; and "Sebut Mahkamah Konstitusi Kebobolan, Ujang Singgung Nama Gibran" [The Constitutional Court burgled, Ujang mentions Gibran's name], *Jawa Pos (JPNN)*, 27 October 2023, https://www.jpnn.com/news/sebut-mahkamah-konstitusi-kebobolan-ujang-singgung-nama-gibran-jleb.

3. Robertus Robet, Ihsan Ali-Fauzi, and Raditya Darningtyas, "NGO's Say Civic Space Shrinking Fast in Indonesia", *Indonesia at Melbourne*, 26 September 2023, https://indonesiaatmelbourne.unimelb.edu.au/ngos-say-civic-space-shrinking-fast-in-indonesia/.

4. Ruth Meliana Dwi Indriani and Fita Nofiana, "'Jokowi Punya Cara Balas Dendam Tak Terduga', Gatot dan Prabowo Pernah Jadi Korban, Selanjutnya Surya Paloh?" ["Jokowi has unexpected ways of retribution", Gatot and Prabowo have been victims, Surya Paloh also?], *Suara.com*, 17 November 2022, https://www.suara.com/news/2022/11/17/140713/jokowi-punya-cara-balas-dendam-tak-terduga-gatot-dan-prabowo-pernah-jadi-korban-selanjutnya-surya-paloh.

5. "'Indonesia at the Pinnacle of Global Leadership', President Says", Reuters, 16 August 2022, https://www.reuters.com/world/asia-pacific/indonesia-pinnacle-global-leadership-president-says-2022-08-16/.

6. "OECD Response to Indonesia's Membership Request Positive: Minister", Antara, 2 August 2023, https://en.antaranews.com/news/290082/oecd-response-to-indonesias-membership-request-positive-minister.

7. World Bank, "Indonesia Economic Prospects: The Invisible Toll of Covid-19 on Learning", June 2023, https://openknowledge.worldbank.org/server/api/core/bitstreams/

e276a12e-4a4c-4429-812f-fd14f77337c5/content; and Cameron Cooper, "What's Driving Indonesia's Economic Boom?", *Intheblack*, 1 October 2023, https://intheblack. cpaaustralia.com.au/economy/whats-driving-indonesias-economic-boom.

8. Arianto Patunru, "Trade Policy in Indonesia: Between Ambivalence, Pragmatism and Nationalism", *Bulletin of Indonesian Economic Studies* 59, no. 3 (2023): 311–40.

9. M. Habib Abiyan Dzakwan, "President Jokowi's October 2023 Visit to China: Interpreting Mixed Signals", *CSIS Commentaries*, 25 October 2023, https://www. csis.or.id/publication/president-widodos-october-2023-visit-to-china-interpreting-the-mixed-signals/.

10. Edna Tarigan and Jim Gomez, "Indonesia's President Admits ASEAN Has Made No Progress on Myanmar Crisis", *The Diplomat*, 11 May 2023, https://thediplomat. com/2023/05/indonesias-president-admits-asean-has-made-no-progress-on-myanmar-crisis/.

11. "Golkar, PAN Resmi Bergabung Dukung Prabowo Capres 2024" [Golkar, PAN officially join to support Prabowo], *Detik.com*, 13 August 2024, https://www.detik. com/sumbagsel/berita/d-6873834/golkar-dan-pan-resmi-bergabung-dukung-prabowo-capres-2024.

12. "Prabowo Melangkahi Jokowi?" [Prabowo Goes Past Jokowi?], *Republika*, 7 June 2023, https://news.republika.co.id/berita/rvv2ik377/prabowo-melangkahi-jokowi.

13. "Mengapa Mesin Kampanye Ganjar Pranowo Macet" [Why is Ganjar Pranowo's campaign machine stalled?], *Majalah Tempo*, 4 July 2023, https://majalah.tempo.co/ read/laporan-utama/168993/kampanye-ganjar-pranowo.

14. John Duerden, "How Bali Governor's Israel Protest Ended Indonesia's U20 World Cup Dream", *The Guardian*, 30 March 2023, https://www.theguardian.com/football/2023/ mar/30/indonesia-mens-u20-world-cup-bali-israel-fifa.

15. Greg Fealy, Sally White, and Burhanuddin Muhtadi, "Counter-Polarisation and Political Expediency", *New Mandala*, 1 July 2022, https://www.newmandala.org/ counter-polarisation-and-political-expediency/.

16. Bambang Setiawan, "Prabowo-Gibran Unggul; Pemilih Bimbang Meningkat" [Prabowo-Gibran ascendant; undecided voters increase], *Kompas,* 11 December 2023, https://www.kompas.id/baca/riset/2023/12/10/prabowo-gibran-unggul-pemilih-bimbang-meningkat?open_from=Section_Terpopuler.

17. Ibid.

18. "Siapa Calon Wakil Presiden Prabowo Subianto?" [Who is Prabowo Subianto's vice-presidential candidate?], *Koran Tempo*, 22 October 2023, https://majalah.tempo.co/ read/laporan-utama/169980/cawapres-gibran-rakabuming-raka.

19. "Mengenal Big Data yang Disinggung Luhut di Isu penundaan Pemilu" [About big data mentioned by Luhut regarding the issue of delaying the election], CNN Indonesia, 13 April 2023, https://www.cnnindonesia.com/nasional/20220413144935-617-784334/ mengenal-big-data-yang-disinggung-luhut-di-isu-penundaan-pemilu-2024.

20. "Apa Peran Airlangga Hartarto dalam Kasus Korupsi Minyak Goreng" [What was Airlangga Hartarto's role in the palm oil corruption case?], *Majalah Tempo*, 30 July 2023, https://majalah.tempo.co/read/laporan-utama/169369/dana-sawit-airlangga-hartarto; "Mengapa Airlangga Hartarto Hendak Dilengserkan dari Kursi Ketua Golkar?" [Why the desire to remove Airlangga Hartarto as Golkar chair?], *Majalah Tempo*, 30 July 2023, https://majalah.tempo.co/read/laporan-utama/169362/airlangga-hartarto-golkar.

21. "Mengapa Jokowi Makin Condong Mendukung Prabowo?" [Why Jokowi is increasingly inclined to support Prabowo?], *Majalah Tempo*, 16 July 2023, https://majalah.tempo.co/read/laporan-utama/169266/jokowi-untuk-prabowo-subianto.

22. "Johny G Plate Divonis 15 Tahun Penjara dalam Kasus Korupsi Menara BTS 4G Kemeninfo" [Johny G Plate jailed for 15 years in the BTS 4G tower corruption case], BBC News Indonesia, 8 November 2023, https://www.bbc.com/indonesia/articles/cxr17w4yrdvo.

23. "Dibongkar Habis-Habisan! Anies Baswedan Beber Situasi Bisnis Surya Paloh Pasca Dukung Dirinya" [Completely dismantled! Anies Baswedan opens up about Surya Paloh's business situation after supporting Anies], *Warta Ekonomi*, 19 June 2023, https://wartaekonomi.co.id/read504484/dibongkar-habis-habisan-anies-baswedan-beber-situasi-bisnis-surya-paloh-pasca-dukung-dirinya-iklan-dari-bumn-drop.

24. Nina A. Loasana, "Anies Answers Call for Summons over Formula E Irregularities", *Jakarta Post*, 7 September 2022, https://www.thejakartapost.com/indonesia/2022/09/07/anies-answers-call-for-summons-over-formula-e-irregularities.html.

25. Rosseno Aji Nugroho, "Cak Imin Blak-Blakan Usai 5 Jam Diperiksa KPK, Bilang ini" [Imin bluntly has this to say after 5 hours' KPK interrogation], CNBC Indonesia, 7 September 2023, https://www.cnbcindonesia.com/news/20230907153215-4-470427/cak-imin-blak-blakan-usai-5-jam-diperiksa-kpk-bilang-ini.

26. "Polisi Beber 4 Alat Bukti Jerat Firli Bahuri Jadi Tersangka" [Police set out 4 pieces of evidence to charge Firli Bahuri], CNN Indonesia, 15 December 2023, https://www.cnnindonesia.com/nasional/20231215111916-12-1037629/polisi-beber-4-alat-bukti-jerat-firli-bahuri-jadi-tersangka.

27. "Bagaimana Anwar Usman Mengatur Putusan Mahkamah Konstituti" [How Anwar Usman arranged the Constitutional Court decision], *Majalah Tempo*, 22 October 2023, https://majalah.tempo.co/read/laporan-utama/169981/anwar-usman-mahkamah-konstitusi.

28. "Bentuk Cawe-Cawe Jokowi dalam Pemilihan Presiden 2024" [Jokowi's interventions in the 2024 presidential election], *Majalah Tempo*, 29 October 2023, https://majalah.tempo.co/read/laporan-utama/170030/jokowi-pemilihan-presiden.

29. Rizky Adha Mahendra, "KSAD Agus Subiyanto Cerita Kedekatan dengan Jokowi Saat Masih Jabat Dandim" [Army commander Agus Subiyanto speaks of closeness to Jokowi since serving as district commander], *Detik.com*, 8 November 2023, https://

news.detik.com/berita/d-7024994/ksad-agus-subiyanto-cerita-kedekatan-dengan-jokowi-saat-masih-jabat-dandim.

30. "Ragam Hasil Survei Sikap Publik atas Isu Politik Dinasti" [Diverse public survey results on the dynastic politics issue], CCN Indonesia, 23 November 2023, https://www.cnnindonesia.com/nasional/20231128182348-617-1030207/ragam-hasil-survei-sikap-publik-atas-isu-politik-dinasti.

Poverty Trends during the Jokowi Era: Achievements, Challenges and Prospects

Latif Adam and Siwage Dharma Negara

Indonesia has made considerable progress in reducing poverty over the past decade. In 2006 the poverty rate was still 17.8 per cent of the total population, meaning around 40 million people were classified as poor. Gradually the poverty rate was reduced to 9.4 per cent, or around 25 million people, by 2019, before the Covid-19 pandemic (Figure 1).

There are many factors contributing to Indonesia's success in reducing its poverty. Its stable political situation is arguably the most critical factor. With political stability, Indonesia has sustained its robust economic growth above five per cent annually since 2005, until the Covid-19 pandemic hit. The pandemic has reversed some of the progress made in poverty reduction. The poverty rate increased to 9.8 per cent and 10.1 per cent in 2020 and 2021, respectively. The pandemic has led to widespread unemployment and rising poverty levels, especially among women and young workers. Nonetheless, thanks to various policy mitigation measures and economic stimulus, Indonesia managed to lower its poverty rate again after the pandemic (Figure 1).

During the era of President Joko "Jokowi" Widodo, there has been a strong political commitment to address poverty. The administration has implemented social assistance programmes and safety nets to support the poor and vulnerable groups, including cash transfer programmes, health insurance schemes, and subsidies for basic needs. Nonetheless, poverty remains one of Indonesia's main development challenges, and better policies are required to address this social problem fully. According to the latest survey by the Central Statistics Agency (BPS) in March

Latif Adam is Senior Researcher at the Economic Research Centre for Macroeconomic and Finance, Indonesia's National Research and Innovation Agency (BRIN).

Siwage Dharma Negara is Senior Fellow at the ISEAS – Yusof Ishak Institute, Singapore.

FIGURE 1
Poverty Rate, 2005–23 (% of population)

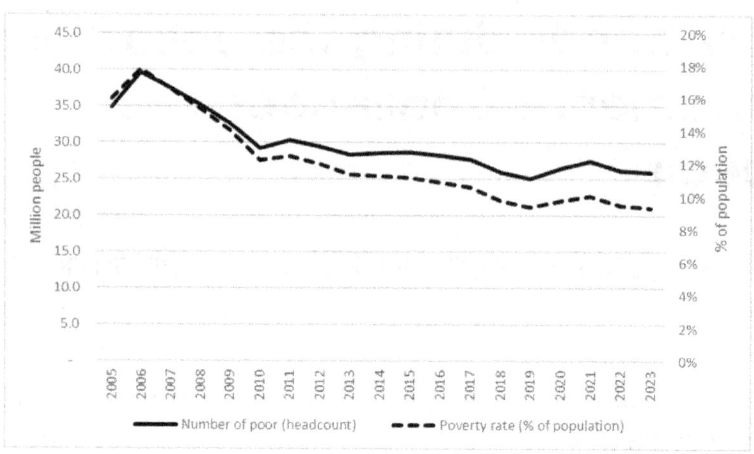

Source: BPS via CEIC.

2023, the poverty rate in Indonesia was 9.36 per cent, which means around 26 million people were still classified as poor.[1]

In the 2020–2024 National Medium-Term Development Plan (RPJMN), the government has targeted bringing down the poverty rate to below 7 per cent and achieving zero extreme poverty by 2024.[2] Perhaps what is more important than setting such an ambitious target is to ensure sustained poverty reduction continues from Jokowi to the new government.

This essay examines key programmes related to Indonesia's poverty reduction strategy during the Jokowi era. It also discusses the challenges of implementing the programmes effectively and in achieving poverty eradication targets. Finally, it examines the prospects of Indonesia's goal to eradicate extreme poverty.

Key Strategies for Poverty Eradication

To address poverty, the Indonesian government implemented three strategies. First, it provides social assistance programmes through direct assistance to the poor to meet their basic necessities. Second, it offers empowerment programmes for the poor to improve their income and economic capacity. Third, it creates development in the disadvantaged regions by providing basic services like education, healthcare, clean water and sanitation.

These three main strategies comprise various programmes. Each programme has its own specific goals, coverage and disbursement mechanism. Unfortunately,

TABLE 1
Indonesia's Anti-poverty Programmes

Programme	Start Year	Description	Benefits
Social Assistance Programmes			
PIP (Program Indonesia Pintar, or Smart Indonesia Programme)	2015	School assistance for 21.7 million poor students (bottom 25% of pop.); formerly BSM (Bantuan Siswa Miskin, or Poor Student Assistance, 2008)	Elementary: IDR 0.45 million/year Junior high: IDR 0.75 million/year Senior high: IDR 1 million/year
BIDIKMISI/KIP (Kartu Indonesia Pintar, or Smart Indonesia Card) Kuliah	2010	Scholarship programme for 0.82 million financially disadvantaged and academically talented tertiary students	Education fee: IDR 2.4 million/semester Living costs: IDR 4.2 million/semester
PKH (Program Keluarga Harapan, or Family Hope Programme)	2007	Conditional cash transfer for 10 million poor families (bottom 20% of pop.)	IDR 1.9 million/year (regular household) IDR 2.0 million per year (households with elderly or disabled members)
BPNT (Bantuan Pangan Non-Tunai, or Non-cash Food Assistance)	2018	Food assistance programme for 16 million households (bottom 25% of pop.); formerly Rastra (Rice for the Prosperous Population, 2015), Raskin (Rice for poor households, 2002), OPM (Cheap Market Operation, 1998)	10 kg rice (Rastra) or IDR 110,000 per month (non-cash food assistance)
PBI-JKN (Jaminan Kesehatan Nasional, or National Health Insurance)	2014	Health insurance assistance for 96.8 million people (bottom 40% of pop.); formerly Jamkesmas (Public Health Insurance, 2007), Askeskin (Health Insurance for the Poor, 2005)	IDR 23,000/month
Electricity Subsidy	2000	Electricity subsidies for 23.43 million households (450 VA) and 6.54 million households (900 VA)	IDR 90,000/month average
LPG Subsidy	2007	LPG Subsidy for 54.9 million people and 2.29 million SMEs	IDR 60,000/month average
Diesel Fuel Subsidy	1967	Diesel fuel subsidy	IDR 1,000 subsidy per litre
Empowerment Programmes			
Kartu Prakerja (Pre-employment Card)	2020	Skill development programme targeting 5.6 million jobseekers aged 18 or above not in formal education and not receiving PKH, BPNT or BST (Cash social assistance),	Training with a value of IDR1 million (one time) Post-training benefit of IDR 600,000 per month (4 months) Post-programme survey incentives of IDR50,000 per survey (3 surveys)
Interest Subsidy	2015	Interest subsidies to support MSMEs in accessing financial services, previously using guarantee scheme (2007–15)	15% for KUR Super Mikro 13.5% for KUR Migrant Worker Placement 10% for KUR Mikro 5.5% for KUR Kecil

Note: Average exchange rate in 2023: US$1 = IDR 15,255.
Source: Authors' compilation

except for social assistance programmes, there are limited reports or detailed information about the programmes under these strategies.

Table 1 briefly describes each programme, specifically those included as social assistance initiatives. It shows that the oldest anti-poverty programme is Beras Sejahtera (Rastra), formerly known as Operasi Pasar Khusus (OPK), which was launched in 1997/98 when the country was hit by the Asian financial crisis. Since then, various other anti-poverty programmes have been introduced. The programme that offers the most generous financial assistance for each participant is Kartu Indonesia Pintar Kuliah, or Smart Indonesia Card for Tertiary Education Students (BIDIKMISI/KIP Kuliah). Meanwhile, Penerima Bantuan Iuran–Jaminan Kesehatan Nasional (PBI-JKN) is the most extensive programme in terms of participants, with around forty per cent of the total population enrolled. This programme contributes significantly to Indonesia's health insurance programme (JKN, or Jaminan Kesehatan Nasional; also known as BPJS Kesehatan).

By the mid-2000s, some programmes—like food assistance programmes and subsidy-based programmes—were adjusted to support the purchasing power of people experiencing poverty. More recently, the government designed and implemented more sophisticated anti-poverty initiatives, such as PKH (a conditional cash transfer programme), school assistance and assistance for health insurance contributions. These programmes aim to address the human capital dimension of

FIGURE 2
State Spending for Anti-poverty Programmes, 2013–23 (IDR trillion)

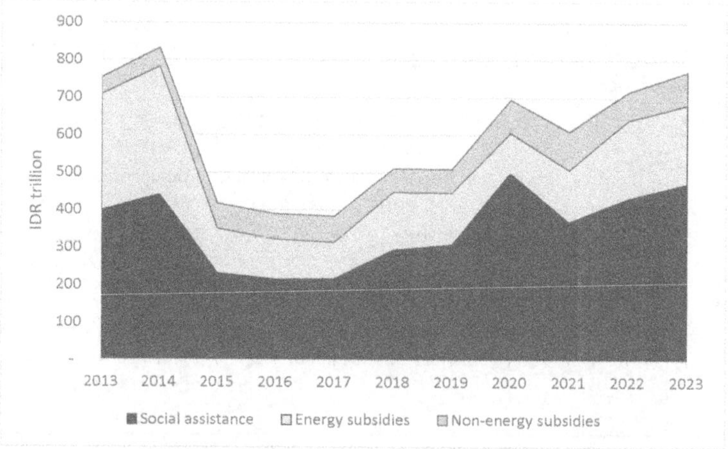

Source: Ministry of Finance.

poverty. The idea being that building healthy and intelligent human capital will eventually address the long-term poverty challenge.

The government has gradually increased state spending for anti-poverty programmes to achieve its poverty reduction target. Figure 2 shows that between 2013 and 2023, government anti-poverty spending grew from IDR 398 trillion in 2013 to IDR 470 trillion by 2023. Part of the funding comes from reallocating energy subsidies to social assistance programmes.

Figure 2 also indicates that—although gradually decreasing—energy subsidies (for electricity, LPG and diesel fuel) persist and still account for a significant proportion of Indonesian anti-poverty programmes. Several studies argue, however, that the subsidies have been ineffective in addressing poverty and that they lead to inefficient resource allocations.[3] This is because—unlike social assistance programmes, which are designed to provide direct financial and non-financial assistance for targeted poor households—the subsidies, which are broad-based, benefit primarily the middle-class. This suggests that subsidy-based programmes are not well targeted to the poor, as every household can purchase subsidized commodities regardless of income level.[4]

Some studies found that the number of poor people who benefit from subsidies was much lower than that of the non-poor.[5] Therefore, shifting the government budget from subsidies to more targeted programmes for people experiencing poverty will be more effective for poverty reduction goals.[6] Below, we explain some of the targeted programmes implemented in Indonesia, their achievements and challenges.

PKH (Program Keluarga Harapan)

PKH (Program Keluarga Harapan, or Family Hope Programme) is the first conditional cash transfer initiative in Indonesia. It gives income support to poor households through cash handouts. To be eligible, a household must fulfil at least one of the following conditions: (1) a mother who is pregnant or nursing; (2) children under the age of six; (3) elementary school children; or (4) junior high school children.[7]

Studies on the PKH programme produced mixed findings. Nazara and Rahayu highlighted some issues with the programme, which appear to persist today, including (1) unequal programme extension and inadequate institutional setup, (2) inadequate complementarity with other programmes aimed at eradicating poverty, and (3) unclear programme exit strategy.[8] Lee and Hwang found that PKH had no discernible impact on child labour or the enrolment rate of youngsters.[9] Because of the inadequate and temporary nature of the stipend, children continued to work instead of attending school. A more recent study by Cahyadi et al., however, showed that PKH produced a favourable result by significantly decreasing the risk of physical stunting and increasing the probability rates of high school graduation.[10]

PIP (Program Indonesia Pintar)

PIP (Program Indonesia Pintar, or Indonesia Smart Programme) targets human development by encouraging poor children to continue their education. PIP replaced BSM (Bantuan Siswa Miskin, or Poor Students Assistance), which aimed to narrow the educational gap between students from poor families and those from non-poor families. PIP and BSM are not quite identical, however; PIP is dedicated to all low-income school-age children regardless of their enrolment status (i.e., school-age children who do not continue their studies, those who have dropped out of school and children with social welfare problems). In contrast, BSM targeted low-income pupils still attend schooling. Children between the ages of six and twenty-one are eligible for PIP, which helps them complete their mandatory twelve years of education.[11]

A World Bank study shows that in 2018 this programme did not correctly target people with low incomes, since thirty-six per cent of PIP beneficiaries were not poor or not even near poor.[12] In high school, the mistargeting was more severe. Another issue was from the supply side, as educational services were insufficient to meet the increasing demand generated by PIP. This was especially true in rural regions, where there are only a few schools and teachers.[13] A study by Wicaksono, however, reveals that poor students who enjoyed PIP assistance completed more years of study than those who did not receive PIP benefits.[14]

PBI-JKN (Penerima Bantuan Iuran–Jaminan Kesehatan Nasional

PBI-JKN (Penerima Bantuan Iuran–Jaminan Kesehatan Nasional, or Recipients of National Health Insurance Contribution Assistance) is a national health insurance system that integrates various disparate insurance schemes (health insurance for poor people—Jamkesmas; health insurance for civil servants—Askes; health insurance for military personnel—Asabri; and health insurance for private employees—Jamsostek). Enrolment in the programme is mandatory for all Indonesians. PBI-JKN or insurance contribution support is given to households in the bottom four deciles considered poor or near poor. The aim is to increase the access of poor households to healthcare by reducing out-of-pocket medical expenses.[15]

PBI-JKN is arguably the most extensive single-payer system in the world owing to a significant and continuous increase in its beneficiaries and expenses.[16] But whilst PBI-JKN is supposed to focus on poor and vulnerable households, only thirty-two per cent of programme recipients in 2018 came from the poorest twenty per cent of households.[17]

BPNT (Bantuan Pangan Non-Tunai)

BPNT (Bantuan Pangan Non-Tunai, or Non-cash Food Assistance) is a food-based assistance programme introduced in response to the 1997/98 Asian financial crisis. At that time, because of the subsequent seventy per cent loss in the value of the Indonesian currency, many poor households faced significant food price inflation. In response, the government implemented Operasi Pasar Khusus (OPK, or Special Market Operation) by providing subsidized rice to poor households. After the financial crisis, the programme was continued, rebranded as Beras Miskin (Raskin, or Rice for the Poor) in 2002 and later as Beras Sejahtera (Rastra) in 2015.[18] Rastra's goals expanded to include (1) stabilizing rice prices, especially in urban markets, and (2) providing direct food subsidies to poor households.[19] Rastra beneficiaries receive ten kilogrammes of rice monthly. Both Hastuti et al. and Timmer et al. found some inefficiencies in the supply chain and distribution of the Rastra programme.[20] Moreover, despite over twenty years of existence and multiple rebranding exercises, the policy adjustments did not significantly enhance the quality of the programme. Mistargeting of recipients and inaccurate quantity and quality of rice disbursed were persistent problems that hampered the effectiveness of the programme.[21]

In 2018, the government replaced Rastra with BPNT, shifting to non-cash food assistance, although Rastra distribution continued alongside BPNT that year. Under BPNT, beneficiaries receive IDR 110,000 monthly deposited directly into their bank accounts, designated for rice and egg purchases.[22] BPNT and Rastra, like other cash transfer programmes, suffer from mistargeting, which extends beyond the intended bottom twenty-five per cent income group.[23]

Challenges in Eradicating Extreme Poverty

In March 2023, Statistics Indonesia reported that poverty and extreme poverty rates were 9.36 per cent and 1.12 per cent, respectively. The government is optimistic that further reduction in these rates can be achieved by continuing the anti-poverty programmes. Nevertheless, if we look at the government's targets stated in the

FIGURE 3
BPS's Social Assistance Program Effectiveness Survey (SEPBS), December 2021

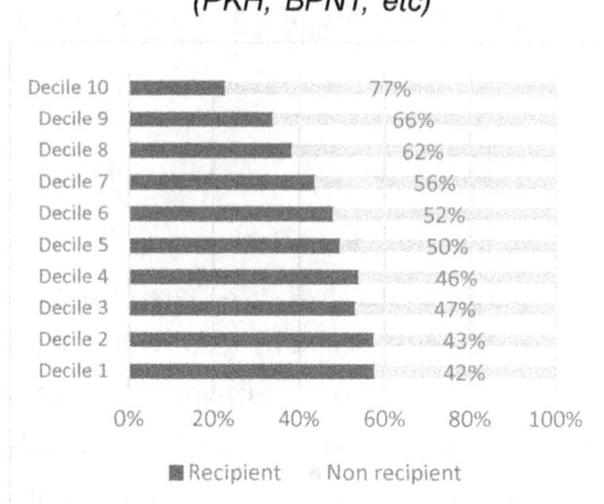

*a. Routine Social Assistance
(PKH, BPNT, etc)*

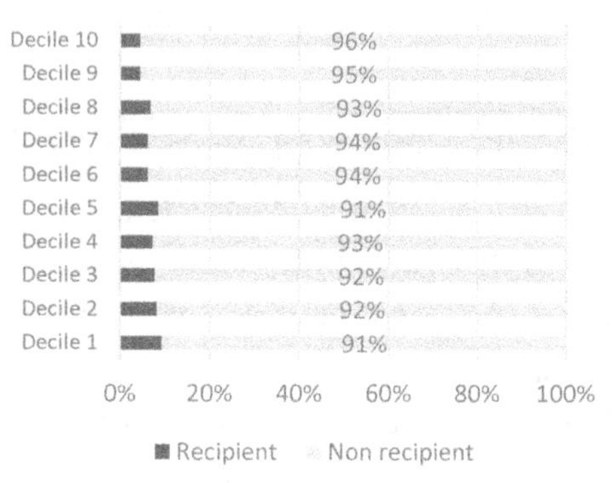

*b. Additional Social Assistance
(BLT-DD, Basic staple food)*

Note: Decile 1 is the poorest expenditure group. The higher the decile, the less poor the group is.
Source: BPS, Social Assistance Program Effectiveness Survey (SEPBS) 2022.

2020–2024 National Medium-Term Development Plan (RPJMN)—that the poverty rate will be around 6–7 per cent by 2024 and the extreme poverty rate approaching zero—those targets will be difficult to achieve with the current strategies. Without significant improvement in the targeting mechanism and improved coordination and programme convergence, we will not see the target being achieved very soon. These steps are particularly crucial in a country like Indonesia, characterized as it is by vast territories, challenging geographical topography and a predominant informal sector.

In fact, poverty eradication has been growing more slowly recently. The rate of reduction had declined from 0.8 per cent (2008–15) to 0.37 per cent (2015–22). This means much more effort is required to accelerate poverty reduction progress. Below, we explain some of the critical challenges in anti-poverty programmes.

Targeting Mechanism

The targeting mechanism is a critical aspect of anti-poverty programmes. The programmes will not be effective if they fail to reach the intended targets. Conceptually, two types of mechanism errors result in anti-poverty programmes failing to reach their intended targets. First, *inclusion error* refers to targeting errors that could result in non-poor households receiving the benefits of the

FIGURE 4
Exclusion and Inclusion Errors in PKH and Food Programmes

	Recipient	Non recipient
Decile 10		97%
Decile 9		93%
Decile 8		88%
Decile 7		84%
Decile 6		80%
Decile 5		76%
Decile 4		72%
Decile 3		68%
Decile 2		63%
Decile 1		57%
Poor		58%
Extreme poverty		52%

Source: TNP2K 2023.

programmes. Second, *exclusion error* refers to a targeting error that could lead to poor households not receiving the programmes.

Several studies emphasized that the targeting mechanisms of Indonesia's anti-poverty programmes need to be improved so as to minimize the two types of mechanism errors.[24] BPS, through its Social Assistance Program Effectiveness Survey (SEPBS), reported that a high percentage of families in decile 1 (poor) did not receive social assistance (exclusion error). Conversely, many families from deciles above 4 (non-poor) enjoyed the programme's benefits (inclusion error) (Figure 3).[25]

The targeting accuracy of the programmes is questionable, as regular and additional programmes were accessible to all expenditure decile groups (deciles 1–10). Figure 3a highlights a notably high exclusion error in the anti-poverty programme, in which 42 per cent of families in the poorest category (decile 1) did not receive any routine social assistance programme benefits (such as PKH or BPNT). Figure 3b depicts a bigger problem, indicating that 91 per cent of the poorest families (decile 1) did not receive additional social assistance (BLT-DD and/or basic food).

Using data from the National Economic Survey (SUSENAS) 2021, TNP2K identified elevated exclusion errors in the PKH and Sembako (Basic staple food) programmes.[26] The findings revealed that 52.4 per cent of households in the extremely poor category did not receive the benefits of either the PKH or

Sembako programmes. Interestingly, 2.5 per cent of households in the wealthiest group received the benefits of one of these programmes (Figure 4).

Given the omission of a substantial proportion of poor people in the bottom decile, it is crucial to update the national social registry system. The existing database—Data Terpadu Kesejahteran Sosial, or DTKS (Integrated Social Welfare Data)—which is used to implement social assistance programmes, was last updated in 2015. While efforts were made to update the system in 2021, the focus was solely on updating data related to the Population Identification Number (NIK), not changes in social and economic status. Because of this narrow focus, socio-economic variables crucial to developing the ranking system (to determine the poor groups) have not undergone improvements or updates in the DTKS. It is critical, therefore, to update the DTKS to enhance data quality and adapt to evolving demographic, social and economic changes, particularly those affecting the conditions of poor households.

Delivery Mechanism

Another issue concerning the implementation of anti-poverty programmes is the delivery mechanism. Cash transfers to programme beneficiaries should be made through the banking system for a more effective and efficient delivery mechanism.[27] Beneficiaries would then be able to receive the correct government social assistance benefits on time.

The problem is, cash transfer delivery in Indonesia faces challenges on account of the limited financial infrastructure, especially in rural and remote areas. Many beneficiaries have no bank account and only limited financial literacy.[28] According to the Kemenko PMK monitoring report, around 28.6 per cent of respondents had to withdraw their PKH benefits in villages other than their own since there was no bank branch in their area.[29] The report also revealed that nearly half of the respondents shared their card identification numbers with merchants. This suggests the government must consider a more effective delivery mechanism.

Programme Convergence

Most anti-poverty programmes are scattered and spread across government agencies without proper interconnection. There is a lack of complementarity among different anti-poverty initiatives. This absence of complementarity makes it challenging for the anti-poverty programmes to be effective.

Nugroho et al. argued that, while the bottom income households in Indonesia are entitled to all social assistance programmes, many did not receive them.[30] For instance, 4 per cent of the bottom decile households receive no social assistance, and 36.4 per cent receive the benefits of only one programme. Expanding the analysis to the bottom four deciles, 5.5 per cent received no anti-poverty programme assistance, and 44 per cent received assistance from only one programme. This highlights the lack of complementarity in programme distribution. Despite PKH targeting the poorest households in the community, most PKH beneficiaries do not receive other programme assistance, such as BPNT/Sembako, PBI-JKN or PIP.

According to a TNP2K simulation, to achieve near zero extreme poverty by 2024, Indonesia needs to improve the convergence and targeting mechanisms of its anti-poverty programmes.[31] Programme convergence refers to various social assistance programmes to ease the expenditure burdens of the poor as well as the notion that various economic empowerment programmes must complement each other.

Rural vs Urban Poverty: Challenge of Low Productivity

Indonesia has diverse geographical conditions. This results in significant regional disparities in living conditions, income levels and access to services. A World Bank study demonstrated that poverty levels in rural and urban areas had converged from 46 per cent in urban regions and 73 per cent in rural regions in 2002 to 16 per cent in both urban and rural areas by 2022.[32] It is important to note that the World Bank used $3.20 expenditure per day as the poverty line for both rural and urban areas. Meanwhile, Statistics Indonesia (BPS) used a different methodology to measure the poverty line, and it uses different poverty lines for rural and urban areas. In 2022, BPS used poverty rates of IDR 521,494 (US$ 34.8) per capita per month and IDR 484,209 (US$32.3) per capita per month for urban and rural areas, respectively.[33]

If we use the poverty measures from BPS, presently, more than half of the impoverished population (54 per cent) resides in rural areas. Between 2011 and 2023, rural areas continued to have a higher poverty rate than urban areas, even after the government introduced the village fund in 2015 (Figure 5).

The village fund provides village governments with additional financial resources to support their development, including eradicating poverty and empowering their communities. Annual adjustments have been made in the village fund allocation scheme to encourage village governments to utilize the funds for poverty alleviation and community empowerment. The issue is, village governments could not fully utilize the village fund to assist and empower the poor, meaning the programme had an insignificant impact on rural poverty reduction. Furthermore, most poor people in rural areas were employed in agriculture, low-skilled services and informal sectors, indicating lower productivity. This suggests that village funds should also be allocated to encourage more productive and sustainable economic activities in rural areas.

FIGURE 5
Number of Poor People, Rural vs Urban (million people)

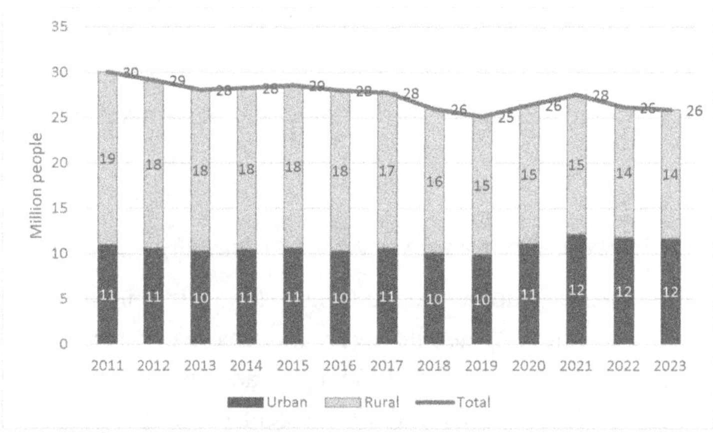

Source: BPS.

FIGURE 6
Number of Poor People, by Select Regions (million people)

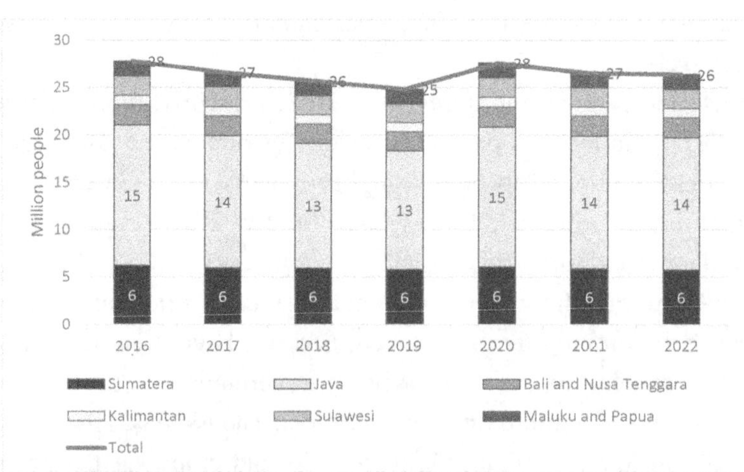

Source: BPS.

Similar, albeit slower, convergence has been observed among regions. The primary lagging regions, Nusa Tenggara and Maluku-Papua, experienced a reduction in poverty rates of 50 percentage points, decreasing from around 80 per cent in 2002 to below 30 per cent in 2022.[34] This compares with a drop of approximately 40 percentage points in the remaining regions.[35] But rural areas in Nusa Tenggara and Maluku continue to lag in poverty reduction despite government initiatives to build infrastructure and invite investment into these regions. This suggests that simply building infrastructure is insufficient to uplift those regions from poverty.

Figure 6 shows that more than half of people experiencing poverty in Indonesia live on Java Island. Sumatra is the island that accounts for the second-largest incidence of poverty. This pattern aligns with population distribution in the country, in which Java and Sumatra are the two most populated islands. This means addressing poverty in Java and Sumatra will have a significant effect on the national poverty reduction goals.

It is worth noting that in 2019, forty per cent of the population in both rural and urban areas experienced economic insecurity. Over a third of the population experienced a low level of economic stability, which means they could easily slip into poverty when confronted with economic or health-related shocks. The majority of people in this category, while not currently in poverty, are vulnerable to falling into it should they be exposed to unexpected challenges.[36] Economic insecurity forces them to resort to unfavourable coping methods such as taking loans from illegal moneylenders. Often they will exhaust their physical and human capital assets to address day-to-day financial needs.

Furthermore, these vulnerable groups often adopt conservative or risk-averse production (agricultural and low-skilled services sectors) and investment strategies. These adverse coping strategies contribute to a sustained decrease in long-term productivity, lowering their likelihood of escaping poverty.[37]

Despite being crucial for short-term poverty reduction, agriculture and low-value-added services often provide insufficiently productive jobs and sustainable income. Agricultural incomes primarily drive the decline of rural poverty. But many farmers remain impoverished because of subsistence farming and limitations in rice cultivation. Some regions face obstacles transitioning to more profitable cash crops because of poor incentives and various restrictions in the sector. In urban areas, the increasing proportion of workers in low-value-added services contributes to poverty reduction in the short term. But the informal and low-productivity nature of this employment leaves many workers in vulnerable positions when there are economic crises.[38]

To improve economic security for the vulnerable group, Indonesia needs to create more high-skilled jobs, which are currently very limited. Despite more productive opportunities in manufacturing and high-value-added services, the shortage of skilled workers hinders their exploitation. The number of high-value-added jobs in manufacturing needs to be increased. The problem, however, is that Indonesia is facing premature deindustrialization, in which the share of its manufacturing sector to GDP has decreased from 27.9 per cent in 2002 to 16.3 per cent in 2022. Meanwhile, the service sector expanded from 36 per cent in 2002 to 58 per cent in 2022. This rapid increase has been driven primarily by growth in two sectors: wholesale and retail trade, and information and communication.[39]

Because of its inward-looking industrial policy, Indonesia has missed out on productivity gains from global value chain integration and export competition. This resulted in a drop in service productivity from 4.0 per cent (2000–2013) to 1.7 per cent (2014–19).[40] The lack of a productivity-increasing structural transformation may undermine Indonesia's potential for sustainable poverty reduction and economic security.

Moreover, rapid urban migration without sufficient high-quality job opportunities hampers productivity gains as limited workers benefit from positive agglomeration forces. Currently, urban areas in Indonesia have experienced greater productivity driven by agglomeration forces rather than an influx of more productive workers. The official urbanization trend primarily resulted from the reclassification of sub-urban areas to urban areas rather than rural households actually moving. Despite being a vital force, urbanization faces challenges such as insufficient opportunities for higher productivity work, high living costs (especially housing), traffic congestion, and air pollution. These factors may discourage more productive workers from moving to urban areas, thus limiting agglomeration gains.[41]

Cultural norms and home care responsibilities put many women in disadvantaged positions in the labour market. This in turn limits household livelihood opportunities. Currently, around fifty per cent of the labour force participation is by men, vastly outnumbering women. Only around fifty per cent of women workers are employed or seeking employment. Gender-based discrimination, reflected in lower earnings for women, further contributes to the gender disparity. Women's care responsibilities for household members, especially around child-bearing age, persistently result in a small gender poverty gap. Encouraging more women to participate in the labour market will have a positive effect on household livelihoods and increase economic security for the family.

Concluding Thoughts

Despite the current global turmoil, Indonesia's economy is expected to grow by around five per cent for the next few years. If Indonesia can sustain its stable growth and continue creating higher-quality jobs for the population, it will support further poverty eradication.

Indonesia must watch out, however, for the future risk of higher inflation as a result of the global economic situation. Escalating global tensions because of the war in Ukraine and the Israel-Hamas war may affect worldwide energy and food prices. The impact of El Niño will also affect domestic food production. All these factors can put pressure on domestic inflation. Certainly, the poor will be the ones who suffer most from the sudden rise in food and energy prices.

Going into an election year in 2024, Indonesia must maintain its political stability. This is critical for sustained economic development. A stable political environment can foster economic growth and create an atmosphere conducive to poverty reduction initiatives. Also, government policies and social assistance programmes to reduce poverty should be sustained and improved. If Indonesia manages to develop effective social safety nets, education and healthcare programmes, it may contribute to a faster reduction in poverty. Finally, further improvements in education and healthcare services are important for long-term poverty reduction. The two sectors are vital elements for enhancing human capital and productivity growth. Therefore, improving access to quality education and healthcare services is crucial.

Learning from Jokowi's administration, the upcoming government must enhance the effectiveness of anti-poverty programmes by undertaking several crucial steps. First, *prioritizing targeted social protection programmes*. Indonesia needs to shift its strategies away from broad and regressive subsidies, such as those for fuel, and move towards social programmes with a more targeted approach. This shift is critical to increasing the efficiency of targeted programmes, ensuring that assistance reaches only those genuinely in need. Furthermore, transitioning to targeted programmes would allow the government to allocate additional fiscal resources for building a sustainable and equitable social protection system.

Second, *adopting programme integration*. To effectively address poverty, the social protection system must engage multiple government sectors. Collaborative efforts across ministries and government agencies and between central and regional authorities are vital for integrating the various programmes, thereby enhancing their efficiency and effectiveness in addressing poverty and welfare issues. Integration also entails combining those programmes with similar goals and target groups.

Finally, *developing a social registry*. The current social registries (DTKS) is outdated, affecting the accuracy of the targeting mechanism. Thus, Indonesia needs a social registry with a dynamic approach to updating data. Developing a social registry requires a clear division between those government agencies responsible for data collection, hosting and maintenance. Moreover, the DTKS was developed top-down, missing poverty dynamics. To address this issue and exclusion errors, a bottom-up self-registration system using an on-demand application (ODA) is essential. ODA should be integrated into a social registry for data collection, regular updating, and a reporting mechanism.

Notes

1. BPS, "Profil Kemiskinan di Indonesia Maret 2023" [Poverty profile in Indonesia, March 2023], https://www.bps.go.id/id/pressrelease/2023/07/17/2016/profil-kemiskinan-di-indonesia-maret-2023.html.

2. Peraturan Presiden Republik Indonesia Nomor 18 Tahun 2020 [Regulation of the president of the Republic of Indonesia number 18 of 2020], "Rencana Pembangunan Jangka Menengah Nasional 2020–2024" [The medium-term national development plan, 2020–24], https://bappeda.bondowosokab.go.id/uploads/image/Lampiran_1__Narasi_RPJMN_2020-2024.pdf. In March 2023, the national poverty rate was about US$36.7 per capita per month, whilst the extreme poverty rate was at about US$21.5 per capita per month (less than a dollar per day).

3. O.D. Lasserve, L. Campagnolo, J. Chateau, and R. Dellink, "Modelling Distributional Impacts of Energy Subsidy Reforms: An Illustration with Indonesia", OECD Environment Working Paper no. 86 (Paris: OECD, 2015); P.J. Burke and S. Kurniawati, "Electricity Subsidy Reform in Indonesia: Demand-Side Effects on Electricity", *Energy Policy* 116 (2018): 410–21.

4. A. Nugroho, H. Amir, I. Maududy, and I. Marlina, "Poverty Eradication Programs in Indonesia: Progress, Challenges and Reforms", *Journal of Policy Modeling* 43 (2021): 1204–24.

5. Lasserve et. al., "Modelling Distributional Impacts".

6. Ibid.; Nugroho et al., "Poverty Eradication".

7. SMERU, *Review of Government's Poverty Reduction Strategies, Policies, and Programs in Indonesia* (Jakarta: SMERU, 2010); W. Utomo, S.K. Rahayu, I. Marlina, and S. Sumarto, "Protecting the People", in *Keeping Indonesia Safe from the COVID-19 Pandemic: Lesson Learnt from the National Economic Recovery Programme*, edited by S.M Indrawati, S. Nazara, T. Anas, C.F. Ananda, and K. Verico (Singapore: ISEAS – Yusof Ishak Institute, 2022), pp. 257–90.

8. S. Nazara and S.K. Rahayu, "Program Keluarga Harapan (PKH): Indonesian Conditional Cash Transfer Program", *Policy Research Brief* 42 (October 2013): 5.

9. K.W. Lee and M. Hwang, "Conditional Cash Transfer against Child Labor: Indonesia Program Keluarga Harapan", *Asia Pacific Education Review* 17, no. 3 (2016): 391–401.

10. N. Cahyadi, R. Hanna, B.A. Olken, R.A. Prima, E. Satriawan, and Ekki Syamsulhakim, "Cumulative Impacts of Conditional Cash Transfer Programs: Experimental Evidence from Indonesia", NBER working paper series (2018).

11. Nugroho et al., "Poverty Eradication".

12. World Bank, *Indonesia Public Expenditure Review Spending for Better Results* (Jakarta: World Bank, 2020), https://www.worldbank.org/en/country/indonesia/publication/indonesia-public-expenditure-review.

13. Ibid.

14. E. Wicaksono, *The Impact of School Assistance for the Poor on School Enrolment in Indonesia* (Venice: ECOMOD, 2018).

15. Utomo et al., "Protecting the People".

16. R. Agustina, T. Dartanto, S. Sitompul, K.A. Susiloretni, M.K.M. Suparmi, and E.L. Achadi, "Universal Health Coverage in Indonesia: Concept, Progress, and Challenges", *The Lancet* 393, no. 10166 (2019): 75–102.

17. World Bank, *Indonesia Public Expenditure*.

18. Nugroho et al., "Poverty Eradication".

19. P.C. Timmer, H. Hastuti, and S. Sumarto, "Evolution and Implementation of the Rastra Program in Indonesia", InMPRA paper no. 81018 (2016).

20. H. Hastuti, S. Sumarto, A. Madi, and R. Prama, "The Effectiveness of the Raskin Program" (2008), http://www.smeru.or.id/en/content/effectiveness-raskin-programHorridge; Timmer et al., "Evolution and Implementation".

21. Timmer et al., "Evolution and Implementation".

22. Nugroho et al., "Poverty Eradication".

23. Badan Kebijakan Fiskal, "Melaju Di Tengah Gejolak Global. Tinjauan Ekonomi, Keuangan dan Fiskal" [Advancing amidst global turmoil. Economic, financial and fiscal review] (2019), https://fiskal.kemenkeu.go.id/publikasi/tekf/2019/tekf1/edisi1 2019.pdf.

24. Utomo et al., "Protecting the People"; TNP2K, "Upaya Percepatan Penghapusan Kemiskinan Ekstrem" [Efforts to accelerate the elimination of extreme poverty] in *Kesiapan Daerah dan Perbaikan Sasaran Program Studi Kasus di 8 Kabupaten/Kota Prioritas* [Regional readiness and improvement of case study programme targets in 8 priority districts/cities] (Jakarta: TNP2K, 2024).

25. BPS, "Kemiskinan Ekstrem: Hasil Survei Efektivitas Program Bantuan Sosial" [Extreme poverty: Results of a survey on the effectiveness of social assistance programmes] (December 2021); Presentation material at the coordination meeting with the Coordinating Minister for Economic Affairs, 26 January 2022.

26. TNP2K, "Upaya Percepatan Penghapusan".

27. E. Kim and J. Yoo, "Conditional Cash Transfer in the Philippines: How to Overcome Institutional Constraints for Implementing Social Protection", *Asia and the Pacific Policy Studies* 2, no. 1 (2015): 75–89. TNP2K, "The Future of the Social Protection System in Indonesia: Social Protection for All" (Jakarta: TNP2K, 2018).

28. Utomo et al., "Protecting the People".

29. Kemenko PMK, "Hasil Pemantauan Program Sembako dan PKH", presentation, Jakarta, 2021.

30. Nugroho et al., "Poverty Eradication".

31. TNP2K, "Strategi Percepatan Pengurangan Kemiskinan Ekstrem" [Strategy for accelerating extreme poverty reduction] (Jakarta: TNP2K, 2022).

32. World Bank, *Indonesia Poverty Assessment* (Jakarta: World Bank, 2023), https://documents.worldbank.org/en/publication/documents-reports/documentdetail/099041923101015385.

33. BPS, "Profil Kemiskinan di Indonesia September 2022" [Poverty profile in Indonesia, September 2022] (2023); *Berita Resmi Statistik*, no. 07/01/Th. 26, 16 January 2023.

34. World Bank, *Indonesia Poverty Assessment*.

35. Ibid.

36. Utomo et al., "Protecting the People".

37. World Bank, *Indonesia Poverty Assessment*.

38. Ibid.

39. BPS, *PDB Seri 2010, 2010–2023* (Jakarta: Badan Pusat Statistik, 2023), https://www.bps.go.id/indicator/11/65/1/-seri-2010-pdb-seri-2010.html

40. World Bank, *Indonesia Poverty Assessment*.

41. Ibid.

"Do Not Be a Proxy": Indonesia, ASEAN and the Sino-US Rivalry

Rizal Sukma

Like many other Southeast Asian countries, Indonesia has been increasingly worried about the state of great power relations and the direction it may take in the region. The country's leaders have raised the issue more frequently in recent years. They are concerned that the intensification of great power rivalry would inevitably threaten the stability and prosperity of Southeast Asia. For example, in his speech at the opening of the 43rd ASEAN Summit in September 2023 in Jakarta, President Joko Widodo (Jokowi) warned great powers "not to turn our ASEAN ship into an arena for rivalry that is destructive".[1] A year earlier, as Indonesia started its presidency of the G-20, President Jokowi also warned that "it is not the time for rivalry, it is not the time to create a new tension".[2] Foreign Minister Retno Marsudi often expresses similar messages of concern about the intensification of US-China rivalry and warns the two great powers that "we don't want to get trapped by this rivalry".[3]

The focus of concern is clearly on the state of the relationship between the United States and China. For Indonesia, the preferred default position has always been described as *tidak memihak* (not taking sides). That position is seen as the natural manifestation of the principle of *bebas* (free/independent) in the twin principles of *bebas-aktif* (free and active) of Indonesia's foreign policy. Indonesia is still committed to the vision of a Southeast Asia that is free from great power rivalry. But as the rivalry has intensified over the last few years, Indonesia finds itself in a more challenging strategic environment. Indeed, navigating the US-China rivalry whilst maintaining a close and equidistant relationship with each of them has now become a difficult task for Indonesia's foreign policy. As Southeast Asia becomes the arena for the competition for influence between the two great

Rizal Sukma is Senior Fellow at the Centre for Strategic and International Studies (CSIS), Jakarta.

powers, Jakarta sees it as crucial to ensure that Indonesia and the region remain *bebas*. President Jokowi, on more than one occasion, warned ASEAN "not to be a proxy for any great power".

In order to stay *bebas*, Indonesia must be *aktif*. In order to pursue the twin imperatives of *bebas* and *aktif*, Indonesia cannot just sit on the fence and hope the challenge will simply go away. It must formulate an active and creative response to that challenge. This essay examines Indonesia's strategic concerns and predicaments emanating from the great power rivalry, explains Indonesia's response to the challenge and discusses some changes that Indonesia needs to consider if it wants to cope with the intensification of great power rivalry in Southeast Asia in an active way. It is imperative, however, to also understand that the expression of Indonesia's foreign policy towards great powers will continue to be affected and tempered by its domestic politics and national economic interests.

Indonesia's Strategic Concerns

Indonesia's concerns about great power rivalry are no longer confined to just Southeast Asia. For Indonesia, its core strategic interests should now be located and pursued within the emerging geopolitical space of the Indo-Pacific. This strategic framework makes sense not only because the majority of great and major world powers are located in the region, but also because of the reality of interconnectedness between the Pacific and Indian oceans. As states begin to formulate, articulate and execute their strategic policies within the Indo-Pacific framework, it is hard not to see Southeast Asia as both the fulcrum of the Indo-Pacific and the locus of great power rivalries in the region. Indonesia believes, therefore, that any understanding of the impacts of great power rivalry on Southeast Asia cannot be separated from the wider geopolitical developments in the Indo-Pacific.

In this regard, there are four key elements of Indonesia's concerns about the intensification of great power rivalry in the region. First, Indonesia is particularly concerned about the state of US-China relations and its effects on regional stability in general. While most Indonesian foreign policy elites believe the possibility of a fully fledged war between the two great powers seems remote, a limited military confrontation and conflict cannot be ruled out. President Jokowi was worried that "if not managed, [the rivalry] could lead to open conflict or even war".[4] Of course, while rarely stated in public, cross-strait relations over Taiwan have always been an issue that raises grave concerns in the region.[5] The risk of incidents leading to a limited military confrontation between the United States and China over Taiwan cannot be underestimated. Similarly, incidents in the South China Sea, such as the ongoing tussles between China and the Philippines, are clearly escalating the tensions. Recent developments could spark armed clashes between China and the Philippines and, in turn, would become more complicated if Manila, in the face of growing pressure from China, invoked its defence treaty with the United States. Indeed, the Taiwan issue and the South China Sea disputes cannot be separated from the Sino-US rivalry.

Second, as the rivalry intensifies, the strategic challenges and risks that ASEAN faces are becoming more overwhelming. For one, the possibility for the marginalization of ASEAN—often praised as the most successful regional organization after the European Union—from geopolitical and geo-economic dynamics in the Indo-Pacific is becoming real. ASEAN also finds it more difficult to maintain unity among its member states, and intra-ASEAN polarizations on strategic preferences vis-à-vis the Sino-US rivalry are becoming increasingly likely. The need to choose might become more difficult to resist. Attempts by the two great powers to woo ASEAN countries have become more frequent. Indonesia's President Jokowi had to warn his fellow ASEAN leaders not to become a proxy of the rivalry of big powers.[6] For Indonesia, preventing Southeast Asia from becoming an arena for great power rivalry is still a key strategic interest. In other words, Indonesia is worried that Sino-US rivalry would compromise ASEAN unity and therefore undermine its strategic autonomy.

The third strategic concern, related to the second one, is about the usefulness, effectiveness and utility of ASEAN-centred institutions. For decades, especially more so since the end of the Cold War, Indonesia has been a strong proponent of ASEAN-centred processes as the platform to attain regional peace and security, which involves both ASEAN member states and extra-regional powers. The ASEAN Regional Forum, ASEAN Plus Three (APT), ASEAN Post-Ministerial Conferences with its individual Dialogue Partners, ASEAN Defence Ministers Meeting Plus, and East Asia Summit (EAS) were expected to serve continuously as ASEAN's main instruments to manage regional order in the era of great power rivalry. But this expectation seemingly needs a serious reassessment. Indonesia believes a stronger ASEAN is now needed. This awareness was the reason behind Indonesia's support and proposals on how ASEAN can strengthen its capacity and institutional effectiveness.[7]

The fourth concern is the impact of the Sino-US rivalry on Indonesia's position between the two great powers. Indonesia, as a matter of principle, would try to sustain its ability to stay "neutral". In reality, however, Jakarta faces the growing difficulty of avoiding the impression of "leaning to one side" in its relations with the two. For some critics, close and growing economic relations with China, for example, have been cited as evidence Indonesia is now leaning towards China. On the other hand, the decision to purchase US military weapons is cited as evidence Indonesia is still closer to the United States. For this reason, Indonesia is seen simplistically as a country that depends on China for its economic needs and on the United States for its security interests. Finding a balance in positioning itself between the two great powers—the essence of a *bebas-aktif* principle in the context of Sino-US rivalry—constitutes a strategic challenge for Indonesia.

Characteristics of Indonesia's Response

How then has Indonesia responded to the challenges brought about by the intensification of the Sino-US rivalry? What are the main characteristics of that response? The most important characteristic of Indonesia's response towards the Sino-US rivalry, in practice, is to maintain the appearance of *bebas* (independent). Indonesia's policy towards great powers will always be dictated by the normative principle of *bebas-aktif,* which requires Indonesia to not take sides in any rivalry between great powers. Indeed, this response towards great power rivalry has been shaped by "a familiar sense of distrust towards extra-regional powers, driven by historical experience that breeds a strong sense of nationalism, competitive domestic politics and a sense of regional entitlement".[8] In the context of domestic politics, the appearance of not bowing to any great power becomes an important element of foreign policy.

The appearance of not kowtowing to any great power can be observed in many statements and policy pronouncements of Indonesia's officials. In an attempt to dismiss suggestions that Indonesia has bowed to China, for example, Luhut B. Panjaitan, coordinating minister for investment and maritime affairs, stated that "no way I would allow myself to be dictated by China.... No country can dictate Indonesia."[9] In responding to a report by the US Department of Defense that China might consider Indonesia for locating a People's Liberation Army military logistics base, Foreign Minister Retno Marsudi quickly asserted that "Indonesia territory cannot and will not be used as a military facility base for any country."[10]

One manifestation of *bebas* has been expressed in terms of the need and the ability to strike a *keseimbangan* (balance) in Indonesia's relations with both great powers. But it is not always easy to demonstrate how a "balanced" relationship might look in practice. Indonesia has been seen, for example, as tilting closer to China since President Jokowi came to power. This closeness to China is measured by economic indicators such as trade, investment and other aspects of economic cooperation, especially in infrastructure development. This, of course, is natural as

Indonesia has been working to strengthen its economic ties with China since the early 2000s. But even though growing economic cooperation with China reflects Indonesia's economic needs and agenda, Indonesia felt obliged to "balance" that trend with a series of decisions. While these could also be based on Indonesia's own interests, policies such as joining the negotiation on the US-initiated Indo-Pacific Economic Framework, postponing the decision to join BRICS, and applying to join the OECD can be seen as creating the impression of "balance" in dealing with China and the United States.

A "balanced" approach is also visible on the political-security front. Even though Indonesia's relationship with China is deepening and expanding fast, the relationship with the United States remains important for Indonesia. Indonesia's defence and security ties with the United States are still strong and in fact have been improving over the last few years. The United States is still the main source of defence equipment for Indonesia. It is also a close security partner and its participation in military exercises such as Garuda Shield has been warmly welcomed. But close cooperation with the United States does not deter Indonesia from expressing its concerns against some aspects of US policy in the region. For Indonesia, the US Indo-Pacific strategy, which priorities the military component of its engagement in the region, is not very assuring. Indonesia has also been critical of the tripartite Australia-UK-US security partnership (AUKUS) and is worried that mini-lateral arrangements such as the Quad would undermine ASEAN centrality. This, again, displays a sense of balance and the appearance of *bebas*.

Another characteristic of Indonesia's response is displayed in its preference to work with and through the regional vehicle ASEAN. The key aspect of this response is the conviction that normative order and institution building in the region provide the best hope for peace and stability to prevail in Southeast Asia and beyond. In this regard, Indonesia believes that regional relations must take place in a web of regional institutions with ASEAN at the centre. Consequently, Indonesia's approach to great power politics has been characterized by a strong desire and suggestion that the ASEAN-centred processes of regional dialogue and cooperation must be strengthened. This explains why norm setting, norm sharing, rule making and rule socialization, and institutional building are of paramount importance for ASEAN.

Indonesia also expects ASEAN to try to mitigate and moderate great power rivalry. Here, Indonesia believes ASEAN can be a great bridge-builder that recognizes geopolitical and geo-economic complexity and which accommodates regional diversity. It wants to emphasize the importance of the principle of inclusivity in regional order, where all powers—both intra- and extra-regional—are accommodated. Jakarta's proposal for the ASEAN Outlook on the Indo-Pacific (AOIP) was driven by this preference. Through the AOIP, Indonesia expects to provide an alternative vision of regional order that is unique to ASEAN, is more inclusive, and hence will be more acceptable to all players in the region. When China extended its support to the AOIP, following other Dialogue Partners that had expressed their support earlier, ASEAN felt its sense of centrality had to a certain degree been vindicated.

Such characteristics in Indonesia's responses to great power rivalry—the appearance of *bebas*, maintaining *keseimbangan*, its normative and institutional-building approach with and through ASEAN, and the inclusive accommodation of all powers—might not be adequate as the rivalry intensifies and the challenges discussed earlier demand more strategic responses. The situation has exposed two problems of inadequacy. First, internally, Indonesia's domestic politics would always ensure that any government would be expected to uphold the position of "not taking sides" in great power rivalry. Operationalizing that expectation into practical policy, however, is not an easy task. Second, ASEAN is excessively reliant on normative and institutional approaches in managing regional relations. The dynamics of strategic rivalry have created regional uncertainty, affected regional stability, and shaped a strategic environment less favourable to middle and smaller powers in the region. In such circumstances, ASEAN centrality is under pressure, and neither ASEAN unity nor ASEAN's strategic autonomy can be guaranteed.

On the domestic front, Indonesia's relations with China and the United States have always been dictated by domestic politics. Domestic public concerns over the growing economic relationship with China serve as an impediment to close bilateral ties between the two countries. Coupled with rising nationalism at home, these sentiments could fuel strong nationalist responses to China's incursions into Indonesia's exclusive economic zones in the North Natuna Sea and deepen Indonesia's suspicion of Beijing's intentions. The 2023 State of Southeast Asia survey by the ISEAS – Yusof Ishak Institute found that 50 per cent of Indonesian elites were worried about China's growing regional economic influence and 61.1 per cent were worried about China's political and strategic influence. Anti-American sentiments are also strong, with 67.4 per cent of Indonesian elites worried about US political and strategic influence in the region.[11] Indonesian politicians and officials would work hard to avoid being perceived as an *antek Amerika* (American stooge) serving American interests in Indonesia. At the centre of this rather permanent suspicion against great powers stands a strong sense of non-aligned and free Indonesia.[12] As Indonesia enters the election year in 2024, when Indonesians will choose a new president and a new parliament, no one wants to be portrayed as either a pro-China or pro-America candidate.

At the regional level, while Indonesia seeks to manage great power rivalry with and through ASEAN, it must also recognize that ASEAN's approach is problematic and under pressure. In managing regional relations, ASEAN often invokes, and overestimates, the importance of ASEAN centrality; namely, an idea that places ASEAN at the centre of regional architecture and regional diplomatic processes. ASEAN centrality is a useful concept to describe where ASEAN wants to be in managing great power rivalry, but it says little about how to turn that aspiration into reality. Simply chanting the mantra of ASEAN centrality does not guarantee that ASEAN can be in that position, and addressing great power politics requires more than hope and expectations. The preservation of ASEAN centrality requires collective strategic autonomy. Achieving strategic autonomy demands a clear policy, strategy and plan of action. Unfortunately, ASEAN is still struggling on this front.

Next Directions: Can Indonesia Navigate Better?

How then can Indonesia cope with and better navigate the intensification of Sino-US rivalry? We know the greatest challenge facing Indonesia is to resist both the temptation and pressure to choose a side. The application of such resistance needs to place strategic autonomy—namely, the freedom and capacity to act independently without depending heavily on others—at the centre of Indonesia's strategy. This strategic autonomy needs to be built, nurtured, accumulated and enhanced continuously. Indonesia will need to craft a new strategy for coping with great power rivalry, one that would (1) enhance its own strategic autonomy and (2) encourage its fellow ASEAN members to also enhance ASEAN's collective strategic autonomy.

To enhance its own strategic autonomy, Indonesia needs to consider the following steps. First, it should strengthen national resilience. Indonesia needs to focus on building economic resilience at home, especially in the energy and food sectors. This condition is important if Indonesia wants to avoid heavy reliance on one great power, be it in the economic sector or the political and security domain.[13] It should also diversify economic cooperation and ties with key major powers inside and outside the region. It must expand market access to international markets and strengthen its role in regional economic integration through multilateral economic cooperation frameworks such as ASEAN, the APT, Asia-Pacific Economic Cooperation (APEC), and the Regional Comprehensive

Economic Partnership (RCEP). Indonesia will not be able to sustain its strategic autonomy without active participation in regional economic integration. On the political-security front, Indonesia should continue its undeclared hedging strategy by building strategic partnerships and cooperation with all great and major powers, bilaterally or multilaterally through the existing ASEAN-centred institutions. Indeed, strategic autonomy is easier to sustain in an interdependent world and through multilateral engagements.

Second, Indonesia cannot work alone in addressing the strategic challenges emanating from great power rivalry. It needs to work with and through ASEAN, especially in building ASEAN's strategic autonomy. To develop the collective strategic autonomy of ASEAN, Indonesia needs to convince fellow ASEAN members to consider three issues. First, ASEAN needs to deepen intra-ASEAN economic integration through various ASEAN economic cooperation frameworks so that its members can reduce heavy reliance on extra-regional powers. Second, ASEAN needs to change, transforming itself to become a resilient ASEAN. This should start by revising the ASEAN Charter, addressing its flaws, and strengthening ASEAN's capacity and institutional effectiveness. It should address the absence of a crisis management mechanism, the cumbersome and outdated decision-making process, the role of ASEAN's organs such as the secretary-general and the ASEAN Secretariat, among others. Third, ASEAN needs to institutionalize the EAS and turn it into a premier multilateral platform where ASEAN's preference for dialogue and norms/values on the one hand, and the reality of power politics among the major powers on the other, can be reconciled.

Fourth, Indonesia should encourage ASEAN to go beyond the normative approach in dealing with great powers. ASEAN needs to develop a strategy to restrain and deny the legitimacy of any bad actions by great powers towards the region. This can be done through a collective action by ASEAN to uphold rules. The rules of the sea—i.e., the United Nations Convention on the Law of the Sea (UNCLOS)—is a case in point. To ensure that the South China Sea does not become a stage of US-China rivalry and conflict, ASEAN should find creative ways to bypass the protracted talk on a Code of Conduct in the South China Sea. ASEAN can also take the initiative to form a coalition of UNCLOS defenders at both regional and global levels to deny the possibility of any great power dominating the area. More importantly, ASEAN needs to speak up and express a collective voice against any acts deemed to violate international law. ASEAN's silence on the tension over the Second Thomas Shoal in the South China Sea between China and the Philippines does not augur well for ASEAN centrality.

Fifth, while encouraging ASEAN to reform, Indonesia should also reset its relationships with great powers and regional major powers. It is important for Indonesia to sustain its *bebas* position, but that needs to be accompanied by being *aktif* as well. If Indonesia really sees its strategic interests to have expanded into the Indo-Pacific, then its *mandala keterlibatan* (space of engagement) must also expand. Here, relations with the United States, China, Japan and India should be brought to the centre of Indonesia's engagement in the Indo-Pacific. Indonesia should also work closely with fellow middle powers in the Indo-Pacific, especially Malaysia, South Korea and Australia, and find initiatives that could facilitate dialogues and cooperation between the United States and China. In other words, as the Indo-Pacific has now become a single strategic space, it is time for Indonesia to formulate its policy and strategy in line with that reality.

Concluding Remarks

Indonesia has been concerned about the delicate problem of responding to and positioning itself within the Sino-US rivalry. As this rivalry intensifies, it is no longer adequate to continue engaging in the habit of declaring that Indonesia would not take sides and would always maintain its non-aligned position. There have been those who expressed concerns that Indonesia, in the event of war between China and the United States, would get dragged into great power military conflict.[14] This clearly points to the importance of maintaining strategic autonomy for Indonesia. It also strongly suggests that Indonesia should seek ways to strengthen its national resilience as the foundation of that strategic autonomy, and extend it into Southeast Asia and ASEAN.

ASEAN has been beset by differences among its member states in their strategic orientations when it comes to the roles and engagement of great powers. Some members are treaty allies of the United States, some are non-aligned, and some are close partners of it. Some are close to China politically, and all ASEAN members have developed close economic ties with China. Some have even become too reliant on China's economy for their economic growth and development. These differences make it hard for ASEAN to have a unified position in responding to US-China competition beyond the mantra of "hoping not to choose sides" and "hoping to maintain strategic autonomy". ASEAN needs to turn those mantras into reality by considering the steps and issues discussed in the previous section. ASEAN urgently needs to build its strategic autonomy so that the region would not become a proxy to any great power. ASEAN member states should keep in mind that the notion of "centrality" was included in ASEAN's strategic lexicon in order for the grouping to stay in the driver's seat and play the role of a manager of regional order. ASEAN, as President Jokowi keeps reminding us, should never allow itself to be a proxy of a great power.

Notes

1. Stanley Widianto and Kate Lamb, "Indonesia Warns ASEAN on 'Destructive' Rivalry", *Jakarta Post*, 5 September 2023, https://www.thejakartapost.com/world/2023/09/05/indonesia-warns-asean-on-destructive-rivalry.html.

2. Dezy Rosalla Piri, "Jokowi to G20 Nations: 'It Is Not the Time for Rivalry", *Kompas*, 17 February 2022, https://go.kompas.com/read/2022/02/17/215425774/jokowi-to-g20-nations-it-is-not-the-time-for-rivalry.

3. Tom Allard and Stanley Widianto, "Indonesia to U.S., China: Don't Trap Us in Your Rivalry", Reuters, 8 September 2020, https://www.reuters.com/article/us-indonesia-politics-foreign-minister-idUSKBN25Z1ZD/.

4. Sui-Lee Wee, "Once Inward-Looking, Joko Widodo Casts Himself as a Global Statesman", *New York Times*, 13 November 2022, https://www.nytimes.com/2022/11/13/world/asia/indonesia-joko-widodo-g20.html.

5. In an interview with the *Economist* in November 2022, President Jokowi admitted that he was very worried about Taiwan. See "The Economist Interviews Joko Widodo", *The Economist*, 11 November 22, https://www.economist.com/jokowi-interview.

6. Haeril Halim, "Don't Let ASEAN Become 'Proxy' of Rivalry between Big Powers: Jokowi", *Jakarta Post*, 11 November 2022, https://www.thejakartapost.com/seasia/2017/04/30/dont-let-asean-become-proxy-of-rivalry-between-big-powers-jokowi.html.

7. ASEAN had set up a High-Level Task Force to look at how ASEAN can strengthen its capacity and institutional effectiveness. The task force submitted its recommendations to ASEAN leaders at the 41st summit in Cambodia in November 2022. But the extent to which ASEAN can undertake necessary changes in order to strengthen its capacity and institutional effectiveness remains to be seen.

8. Rizal Sukma, "Indonesia and the Emerging Sino-US Rivalry in Southeast Asia", in *The New Geopolitics of Southeast Asia*, LSE Ideas Special Report, SR015, November 2012, p. 45.

9. Ade Miranti Karunia and Yoga Sukmana, "Dituding Kerap Diatur oleh China, Luhut: Anggak Ada Sama Sekali Saya Mau Diatur" [Often accused of bowing to China, Luhut: No way I would allow myself to be dictated], *Kompas*, 3 December 2022, https://money.kompas.com/read/2022/12/03/165000426/dituding-kerap-diatur-oleh-china-luhut--enggak-ada-sama-sekali-saya-mau-diatur.

10. Budi Sutrisno, "'Indonesia Won't Be Military Base for Any Country', Retno Says, Dismissing Pentagon Report", *Jakarta Post*, 4 September 2020, https://www.

thejakartapost.com/news/2020/09/04/indonesia-wont-be-military-base-for-any-country-retno-says-dismissing-pentagon-report.html.

11. Sharon Seah, Joanne Lin, Melinda Martinus, Sithanonxay Suvannaphakdy, and Pham Thi Phuong Thao, *The State of Southeast Asia: 2023 Survey Report* (Singapore: ISEAS – Yusof Ishak Institute, 2023), p. 27.

12. For a brief discussion on this point, see Johannes Nugroho, "Indonesia Standing between Great Powers", *The Intepreter*, 26 January 2022, https://www.lowyinstitute.org/the-interpreter/indonesia-standing-between-great-powers.

13. Concerns about heavy reliance on great powers, especially China, have of late been voiced by segments of the public in Indonesia. See, for example, Jaayanti Nada Shofa, "Indonesia's Growing Reliance on Chinese Investments Could Backfire", *Jakarta Globe*, 15 June 2023, https://jakartaglobe.id/business/indonesias-growing-reliance-on-chinese-investments-could-backfire#:~:text=Indonesia%27s%20Growing%20 Reliance%20on%20Chinese%20Investments%20Could%20Backfire,-Jayanty%20 Nada%20Shofa&text=Jakarta.,and%20Road%20Initiative%20(BRI).

14. See Abdul Rahman Yaacob, "Even a Neutral Indonesia Could Get Dragged into a China-US War", *The Diplomat*, 5 August 2023, https://thediplomat.com/2023/08/even-a-neutral-indonesia-could-get-dragged-into-a-china-us-war/.

Laos

Phongsali
Louang Namtha
Muang Xai
Ban Houayxay
Louangphrabang
Muang Pakxan
VIENTIANE
Savannakhet
Pakxe
Champasak

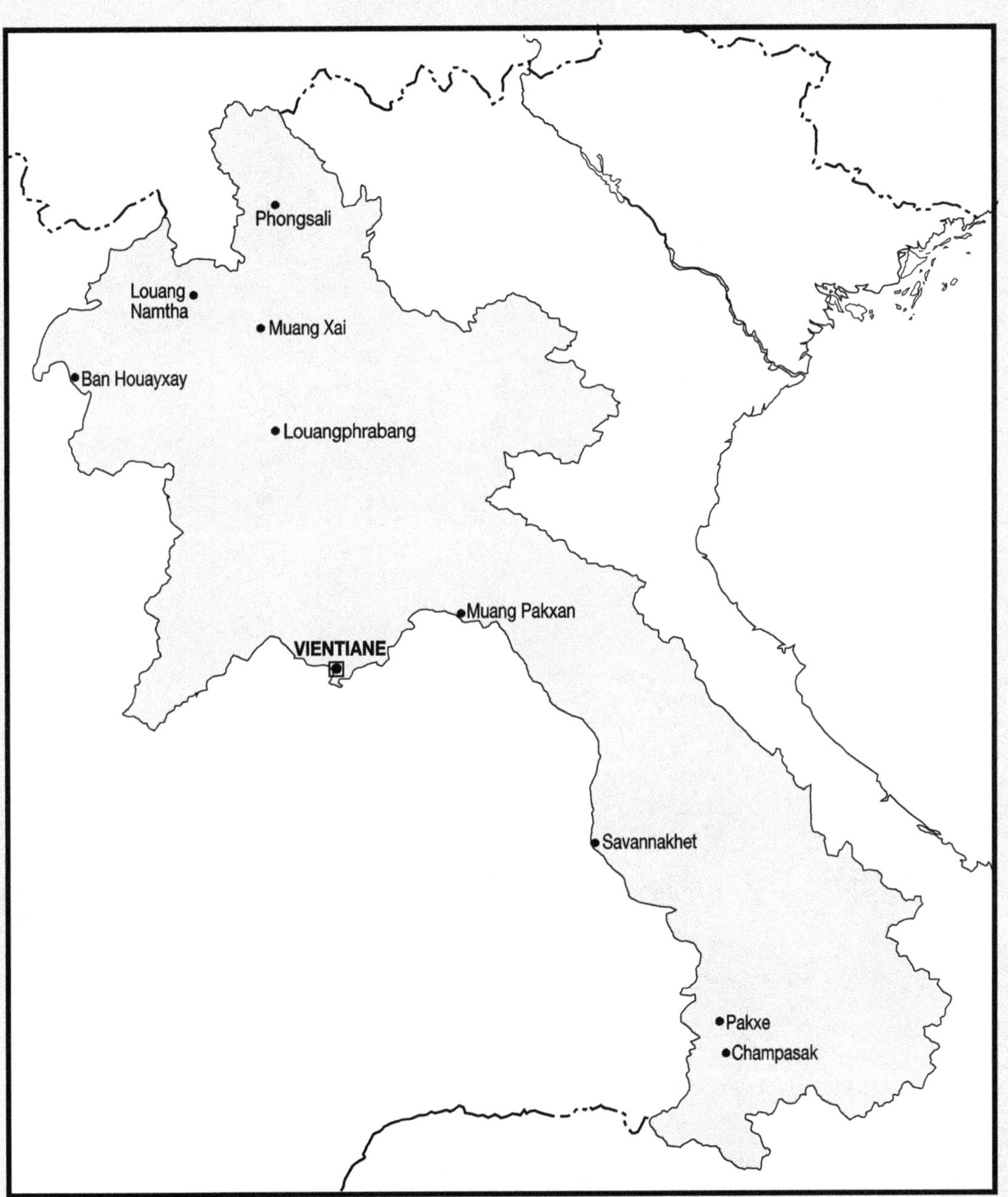

LAOS IN 2023:
Debts and Doubts

Oliver Tappe

The year 2023 saw Laos drifting through its most severe economic and fiscal crisis since the late 1970s. According to recent estimates, public debt has reached a staggering 123 per cent of GDP. Ongoing currency depreciation and rampant inflation plagued the population. This crisis laid bare the country's macroeconomic vulnerabilities and had negative impacts on already pressing problems such as environmental degradation, economic and legal inequalities, and precarious labour migration. To mitigate the economic woes, the ruling Lao People's Revolutionary Party (LPRP) has initiated a number of fiscal measures, the effectiveness of which remains to be seen.

On the surface, everyday life in the cities appears like business as usual. Construction projects fuelled by Chinese or Vietnamese investment keep operating. But in conversations with local people, the foreign observer can sense disillusionment and uncertainty. In the capital city Vientiane, civil servants and skilled workers look for second jobs to cope with the price hikes of key commodities such as food and petrol. Petty corruption is on the rise again despite attempts by state authorities to enforce anti-corruption laws. Luang Prabang is experiencing a fresh tourism boom, which indeed nurtures hopes for new economic opportunities. The rural population, meanwhile, faces precariousness and insecurity because of inflation, land acquisition and environmental risks.

On the positive side, the Laos–China Railway (LCR) performed well and raised hope for new commercial dynamics (while the social and environmental costs of large-scale infrastructure construction also became evident). With the Covid-19 crisis having petered out, the tourism sector has gained momentum this year, seeing an estimated three million visitors. Chinese tourists and businesspeople were crossing the border again, embodying the ambiguous nature

---

OLIVER TAPPE is Senior Researcher at the Institute of Social Anthropology, University of Heidelberg, Germany.

of Chinese influence in Laos, which is perceived both as a catalyst of economic development and as a domineering force. At the same time, the spectre of the Chinese "debt trap" was looming large, dominating international media coverage. As in the previous year, Laos in 2023 was still far removed from any "post-pandemic bounce".[1]

The Lao Party-State: Leadership Change and Continuity

The year began with a premature change in the political leadership, unprecedented in Lao PDR history: on 3 January 2023, Sonexay Siphandone, Politburo member (since 2016) and seen by many observers as the next man on the Lao political stage, replaced Phankham Viphavanh as prime minister. Phankham had officially resigned a few weeks before for health reasons, but it seemed that he had also fallen from grace within the inner circles of the party-state. Blamed for being incapable of handling the country's multiple crises and subjected to public scrutiny, it did not help that he built a pompous residence amidst an economic crisis that forced many Lao citizens to tighten their belts.[2]

A scion from one of the most influential families in Laos—his father, Khamtay Siphandone, was a prominent leader of the Lao revolution—Sonexay (born in 1966) received education in China and the Soviet Union before starting an impressive career in the party-state. He served as governor of Champasak Province, minister of planning and investment, and deputy prime minister.[3] He inherits his father's excellent connections with key partners such as China, Vietnam, Russia and Thailand, and it will be interesting to see how he is going to leverage them. The immense economic influence of the extended Siphandone family is an open secret in Laos.[4]

Sonexay embodies regime continuity. An occasion in 2024 to celebrate the LPRP's revolutionary legacy will be certainly the centennial of his father, Khamtay—who has not been seen in public for some time and apparently is very frail. Forming part of the regime's commemorative activities, Khamtay's former housing in Champasak Province will be developed into an educational and touristic site.[5] It is to be expected that the new prime minister will take advantage of this opportunity to showcase the power of his family.

Regime continuity is also represented by the president of the Lao National Assembly, Xaisomphone Phomvihane (son of the LPRP's first leader, Kaysone Phomvihane), other party-state veterans such as longstanding Politburo members Pani Yathotou and Bounthong Chitmany, and, not least, state president Thongloun Sisoulith. Like Sonexay, Thongloun studied in the Soviet Union and has good relations with Russian president Vladimir Putin, Chinese leader Xi Jinping and the leadership of Vietnam. Those connections are certainly vital for Laos to deal with the current economic crisis.

Economic and Fiscal Troubles

Stable political continuity notwithstanding, the regime is increasingly concerned about the impact of the precarious economic and financial situation, and about public perceptions of its inadequate crisis management. Most observers agree that the Lao government had blatantly mishandled the crisis in 2022–23. Perhaps even worse, the crisis brought macroeconomic structural deficiencies to the fore, which cannot be mitigated in the short run. Instead of building profitable and sustainable agricultural and manufacturing sectors, the Lao political elite concentrated, rather, on developmental megaprojects and generous Chinese loans—an irresistible source of convenient wealth creation "too alluring" for the political elite and their patronage networks, as journalist David Hutt points out.[6]

In September 2023, the ADB's "Asian Development Outlook" presented a devastating picture of the Lao economy. The estimated GDP growth of 3.7 per cent (down from a previous 4 per cent forecast) was overshadowed by dramatic numbers such as the average annual inflation at 28 per cent, by far the highest in the region (peaking at 41.3 per cent year-on-year in February). Public debt accounted for approximately 100 per cent of GDP (US$15.47 billion) by end-2022. The ongoing depreciation of the kip has further aggravated this situation. Recent reports indicated that the public and publicly guaranteed debt stood at 123 per cent of GDP, with state default remaining a realistic scenario.[7]

Meanwhile, the depreciation of the kip continued at an alarming rate. In 2022, the Lao currency fell by half against the US dollar and by 44 per cent against the Thai baht. This decline went on from January to August 2023 by a further 13.6 per cent against the US dollar (14.8 against the Thai baht). Currency depreciation accounted for two-thirds of the staggering inflation. This development is dramatic given the dependence by Laos on imports (mainly from Thailand and China) that include essential commodities such as food, petroleum, fertilizers and various consumer goods. In August 2023, the trade deficit stood at US$88 million.

The stable economic growth that Laos sustained throughout the 2000s and 2010s did not translate into sustainable macroeconomic structures. The regime's constant invocation of "development" (*kanphatthana*) has degenerated into an empty phrase. The Lao government now faces the dire consequences of its failures to build efficient and sustainable political-economic mechanisms that might have cushioned the current crisis. Did the Lao political and economic elite focus too much on skimming off the profits instead of investing in sustainable economic policies? Recent tendencies towards oligarchic structures, nepotism and growing social inequalities are becoming increasingly conspicuous and hard to overlook.

The Lao government remains confident about the country's capacity to generate renewable energy and it still cultivates the image of the "Battery of Southeast Asia". Exports from the growing hydro-energy sector indeed constitute the most important state revenue (about one fifth of total export value, generated by more than eighty operational dams). But concerns exist about the country's reliance on hydropower because of its seasonal fluctuations (for instance, at the peak of domestic energy demand in the dry season, hydropower production is low), the impact of hydropower dams on the local environment and livelihoods, and public discontent over the controversial dam project near Luang Prabang. Solar and wind energy are promoted as alternatives, as in the case of the ambitious Monsoon Wind Farm project (run by Japanese and Thai companies) in southeast Laos, with a generation capacity of 600 megawatts.[8]

Among the few bright spots is the recovery of the tourism sector. In anticipation of the Visit Laos Year 2024 campaign, international tourism arrivals are projected to exceed three million in 2023, almost doubling the numbers from the previous year. The UNESCO World Heritage Luang Prabang hosted the large part of international visitors, not least as the Lao-Chinese border opened again in April 2023—just in time for the Lao New Year festival—after years of pandemic-induced closure. Tourism authorities are optimistic that the flow of tourists will increase significantly in 2024. The Visit Laos Year 2024 campaign seeks to draw in 4.6 million visitors, thus boosting the service sector and generating much needed revenue for the country.[9]

Against this backdrop, the LCR constituted another success story, with impressive numbers both for passenger and freight transport. In the first eighteen months of operation since December 2021, the cross-border railway handled an impressive twenty-one million tons of cargo. In the same period, the high-speed trains transported 16.4 million passengers. Tourism authorities in Luang Prabang expect a further hike of arrivals from China. Not surprisingly, the LCR fuels hopes for more aggregate income and GDP growth in Laos. However, this massive infrastructure project is also widely regarded as a primary factor behind the current Lao debt crisis.[10]

In the "Debt Trap"?

The 422-kilometre section of the LCR within Laos has cost US$5.9 billion, of which Laos took a US$3.54 billion loan through a credit arrangement with the Export-Import Bank of China. More generally, an estimated half of Laos's external debt is owed to China. Laos is confronted with annual external debt service payments totalling US$1.3 billion until 2027. Given insufficient foreign exchange reserves and general macroeconomic vulnerabilities, this burden would push Laos perilously close to a state of default. The country could find itself in a veritable debt crisis, even in the absence of a fully fledged "debt trap", which some analysts consider a "myth" and not in China's interest at all.[11]

At the same time, Chinese media described the LCR as a pure success story that brings development and prosperity to Laos. In an interview with the Chinese online paper *Global Times*, Sonexay used positive phrases that resonated with the Chinese narrative, such as "mutual trust", "mutual benefit" and "brotherly cooperation", and vehemently resisted the "debt trap" narrative. Instead, he said that the BRI "has promoted the economic and social development of participating countries". Another *Global Times* article highlighted that the railway project helped clear 459 pieces of unexploded ordnances (UXO) along the track, and criticized US warnings about debt traps as hypocritical.[12]

In any case, it is unlikely that China will jeopardize its relationship with Laos by resorting to measures like asset seizure. Instead, Chinese business interests will exploit the leverage that this relationship of dependency brings about. The Lao government offers new development zones and concessions, such as those for mining, plantations or hydropower projects, to Chinese investors, with insufficient monitoring—or no monitoring at all in the case of the Golden Triangle Special Economic Zone (SEZ).[13] As revenues from these investments will flow mainly into Chinese coffers, this approach does little to alleviate the public debt problem. Meanwhile, local Lao communities bear the social and environmental costs of these investments, which usually do not translate into job opportunities for the Lao population.[14]

What are the Lao government's practical measures to address the precarious debt situation besides insisting that a debt trap does not exist? Its responses included tightening borrowing and fiscal policies, actively seeking debt deferrals, and introducing bonds to enhance liquidity and alleviate debt service pressures. However, baht-denominated bonds issued in August received only a lukewarm reception. The Lao government had to rely on short-term loans from domestic banks to cover maturities. To reduce dependence of fuel imports, a shift to e-vehicles was proposed, but the specific steps to realize this transition remain unclear. Meanwhile, boosting local industrial production remains an ambitious goal, and expectations of reaping easy revenues for the state through crypto-mining have not been fulfilled so far.[15]

The Lao government also aims to buy time with debt deferrals, especially through agreements with Chinese banks. Next to China, key creditors for concessional loans include the ADB and IDA (World Bank Group), which have committed to help Laos restructure its debt. China and several commercial banks hold accounts for non-concessional loans. A large portion of these loans is held by the struggling SOE Electricité du Laos, raising particular concern among analysts evaluating current debt risks. While hoping for economic recovery, the government is busy negotiating with creditors to further defer and restructure its debt, including opaque "behind-the-scenes debt relief deals" with China.[16]

The Lao News Agency (KPL) announced 4.5 per cent GDP growth in 2023 without providing compelling evidence to support this claim (the ADB's projection of only 3.7 per cent is less optimistic, as is the modest 4 per cent forecast for 2024). In November 2023, Sonexay at least acknowledged that the current challenges were caused by "both internal and external factors", and he characterized the government's goals as "very ambitious".[17] Debt repayment obligations definitely remain a huge challenge as they constrain the already limited public investments in health, education and road maintenance, as evident in the poor state of key routes such as the north–south Route 13.

The regime relies on a small group of well-trained economists to grapple with the accumulated macroeconomic deficiencies that are hampering any attempts of recovery. In an almost prophetic paper published in 2019 shortly before the Covid-19 pandemic kicked in, Lao economist Buavanh Vilavong warned that the country's low score on the economic vulnerability index would prevent its elevation from Least Developed Country (LDC) status. He wrote that "macroeconomic instability remains a worry due to growing public debt, revenue shortfalls, financial sector risks and limited buffers to shocks".[18]

Four years later, Buavanh and his co-author Chanhsy Samavong highlighted the need for mid- and long-term reforms to address underlying structural problems. Their recommendations include broadening the tax base, stabilizing exchange rates, promoting domestic production (not least to tackle import dependency) and reducing demand for foreign exchange reserves, given that the ongoing flight into dollar and baht is dramatic. Like many observers, they agree that fighting inflation must be a priority—a goal that was sorely missed in 2023.[19]

The Kip Crisis

On 31 October, the sixth ordinary session of the National Assembly's 9th legislature started with a serious debate on how to mitigate the current economic and fiscal crisis. Prime Minister Sonexay Siphandone highlighted currency depreciation and inflation as key challenges. He reassured the National Assembly that Laos would not slide into default despite the high debt level. He indicated that maximizing revenue collection will be key to keep state-funded development projects, and thus local contractors, alive. But given the poor state of revenue collection and the loopholes, especially for well-connected elites, it remains to be seen if these words are more than mere lip service.[20]

Experts doubt that inflation will recover, while national debt will remain a burden for years. The currency decline causes a loss of purchasing power for the Lao population. Perhaps even more critical for the regime is the loss of public trust, as many people began to question the *kanphatthana* narrative. Cost hikes for petrol and food aggravated the precarious income situation for many Lao households, some of which have had to cut back on spending on health and education.[21]

Food inflation, averaging 45.6 per cent in the first eight months of 2023, weighed heavily on Lao households as many food items and agricultural inputs are imported from Thailand. In urban areas, the proportion of food-insecure households increased from 58 per cent to 66 per cent, with detrimental effects to people's diet and health.[22] One measure to address this issue involved minimizing the importation of certain vegetables and other agricultural produce to help boost the cultivation of these crops in Laos. But the results of these policies remain uncertain.

To provide context on the inflation data, in October 2023 the author communicated with an old friend working for a monthly salary of 2 million kip (US$96) in the provincial administration of Houaphan. He highlighted the increase in consumer prices, noting that rice had climbed from 7,000 kip up to 20,000 kip per kilo, petrol from 8,000 kip to 25,000 kip per litre, and cement from 600,000 kip to 1.8 million kip per ton. Some of his colleagues with very low salaries got a modest increase to reach the new minimum wage of 1.6 million kip (US$77) established earlier this year. But for his salary tier, he has not received any salary increase so far to cope with inflation, which weighs heavy on his household income.

The governor of the Bank of Laos (BoL), Bounleua Sinxayvoravong, announced that the bank will try to push inflation down to a single-digit level by the end of 2024.[23] To achieve this, the BoL has started to tighten monetary conditions; for example, by increasing the policy rate from 3.0 to 7.5 per cent by February 2023, increasing reserve requirements for foreign exchange from 5.0 to 8.0 per cent in 2023, tightening exchange control, and closing private foreign exchange bureaus.[24] But even if fiscal consolidation will slow the accumulation of public debt, it is unclear whether this will be sufficient to reverse the rising debt-to-GDP ratio.

Social Problems and Precariousness

The Lao labour market remains weak despite a gradual recovery of the tourism sector following the end of the pandemic. The ongoing construction boom, while providing some job opportunities for Lao workers, offers very low wages. Furthermore, local workers face competition from Vietnamese and Chinese migrant workers, who are often given preference by their respective contractors. The younger Lao generations are left with very limited options, which include self-employment, agricultural business—possibly returning to subsistence farming—or seeking employment abroad, primarily in Thailand.

After a reduction of border fees that made Thailand even more attractive for migrant workers from ASEAN countries, the number of Lao migrants to Thailand in 2023 is projected at 100,000. In Thailand, Lao workers can earn three to four times the Lao minimum wage of 1,600,000 kip (US$77). Some argue that this outflow of human resources might be beneficial for regime stability because this would constitute an economic valve for the disaffected youth.[25] According to ADB estimations, 39 per cent of youth aged 15–24 years are neither employed nor in school or training, while an estimated half of households in Laos depend on remittances (1.3 per cent of GDP in 2022).[26]

The government's land-into-capital policies have yielded satisfying results for the regime, especially in terms of infrastructure development. While it is true that land privatization and commodification resulted in increased land values over the past several decades, the downside of this process has been dispossession and social inequalities. These processes include land acquisition for economic development zones in urban areas (sometimes at least reasonably compensated), or for mining and plantation concessions in rural areas—where incomplete land titling programmes have encouraged land expropriation without proper compensation. Another tendency is accumulation of land by wealthier people, in particular the urban political and business elites. In contrast, land loss as a result of indebtedness or the need to sell land just to get by is the fate of many impoverished people in Laos.[27]

Public protests remain an exception. As a rare example, recent protests in Xieng Khouang province were directed against a Chinese company that attempted to register village land as its own after the end of the concession period. The campaign was deliberately formulated more as a request to the government than as criticism.[28] In contrast, open dissatisfaction among the younger generation is increasingly manifest through critical social media posts. In response, the party-state has strengthened social media surveillance and is dealing harshly with opponents. Its arrests of dissidents in recent years and an as yet unexplained shooting of the operator of a critical Facebook page in April 2023 have attracted international media attention.[29]

Amidst an atmosphere of precariousness and disillusionment, drug abuse has resurfaced as a major social problem. The notorious *ya ba* (Lao term for a variety of chemical drugs including methamphetamines) has been spreading across the country at an alarming rate. Largely produced in conflict-ridden Myanmar—where local warlords finance themselves with drug production—the pills make their way to even the most remote upland villages. The Lao government is severely concerned about the social effects of drug abuse and seeks to strengthen counter-trafficking efforts through border patrols.[30] Conversely, the popularity of Beerlao and the influence of the Lao Brewery Company, a joint venture company of the Carlsberg Group and the Lao government, have hindered any effective anti-alcohol policies despite the increasing number of accidents caused by drunk driving.[31]

Droughts and floods have plagued many provinces in Laos this year, heightening concerns about food security. Meanwhile, in rural Laos, cassava has become the dominant cash crop, accounting for US$408 million out of the US$901 million total export value of agricultural produce in the first months of 2023. Many farmers have shifted from rice and rubber to cassava to take advantage of the strong demand from China and Vietnam. This has exposed them to the risks of price crashes, which will seriously jeopardize their household subsistence. Cassava is notorious for depleting soil fertility, and the burning of its dry remnants in the fields contributes to the immense haze problem in Laos at the end of the dry season, negatively affecting public health and tourism.[32]

Infrastructure development projects have involved large-scale land acquisitions, accompanied by inadequate compensation programmes, which have contributed to a worrying rate of deforestation. The issue is further compounded by the problem of "conversion timber", which is caused by illegal logging along road construction and at mining concessions. Corrupt relations between contractors and authorities are commonplace. Documents by Vietnamese customs reveal that the volume of exported timber from Laos by far exceeded the harvest quotas. As new rail connections and roads cross the mountainous habitats of bats, environmental experts are concerned about the spillover of infections similar to the Covid-19 virus.[33]

Laos is also grappling with a looming education crisis as poor households must cut spending by not sending children to school. Less than 10,000 students enrolled at Lao universities in 2023, the lowest number in years, even though more than 49,000 students graduated from high school during the same period. At the same time, the number of applications to online courses of overseas institutions has risen, and the Confucius Institute announced the tripling of applications, indicating increasing interest in Chinese language classes.[34] Together with scholarship programmes for Lao students, this forms part of China's soft power strategy in Laos.

Foreign Relations

In a recent insightful paper, Simon Rowedder quotes a sentence that he often heard from Lao interlocutors in the province of Luang Namtha, bordering China: "Soon, northern Laos will be part of Southern China!" While this remark could be linked to the simplistic discourse of Chinese expansion, Rowedder also highlights its complex and ambiguous nature, which "might refer to a simple joke, anger, uncertainty, fear, worry, fatalism, resilience, pragmatism and aspiration all at the same time".[35] In Laos's foreign relations, China has played and will certainly continue to play a critical yet ambivalent role, eliciting a wide range of perceptions ranging from menace to opportunity.

China definitely wields great influence over Laos, but it falls short of exclusive control. Instead, Laos maintains a diverse network of political, economic and cultural ties with other partners, most notably with its ASEAN neighbours Thailand and Vietnam, as well as with Russia, which offers a certain counterweight to Chinese influence.[36] The relationship with Russia is particularly delicate these days as Laos (alongside Vietnam) has abstained from UN resolutions condemning the Russian invasion of Ukraine. For the majority of the Lao population, however, this conflict does not seem relevant to their everyday lives.

Russia is the main provider of military aid to Laos. In addition, Russia plays a significant role as a destination for Laotians' education abroad and as a promising source of foreign tourists. New direct airline connections between Laos and Russia have been established, and Russian travellers are allowed to stay in Laos for thirty days without a visa following the example of Thailand to attract wealthy Russian tourists. Notably, the Lao government protested against the US delivery of cluster bombs to Ukraine, a stance that is grounded in the tragic legacy of these weapons in Laos, but which also demonstrates Laos's allegiance to Russia.[37]

China and Russia play important roles in sustaining the Lao regime. Chinese investments in mining and plantation concessions have contributed to the country's GDP growth, with a value of Chinese investments in concessions and special economic zones amounting to US$13.67 billion.[38] Ten years into the BRI, the close cooperation between the two countries was celebrated on the occasion of the 3rd BRI Forum for International Cooperation in Beijing, which was held under the theme "High-Quality Belt and Road Cooperation: Together for Common Development and Prosperity". Lao president Thongloune Sisoulith attended the forum, where he also held meetings with Chinese president Xi and with Russian president Putin.

Beyond China and Russia, Vietnam and Thailand remain important political and economic partners for Laos. Laos is dependent on many imports from Thailand, which accounted for more than half of total imports (valued at US$7.67 billion, with refined petroleum the top import) in 2021.[39] Meanwhile, Vietnam continues to invest in various development projects, including a new railway connection between Tan Ap in central Vietnam with Thakhaek in south-central Laos, aligning with historical colonial plans. Looking forward, the 2024 ASEAN chairmanship will provide an opportunity for Laos to act as a reliable partner, but it also constitutes a diplomatic challenge given the diverging interests across ASEAN member states and among its dialogue partners, particularly in relation to the Myanmar conflict.[40]

Conclusion

In 2023, the Lao government grappled with severe economic and fiscal problems, including a rampant debt crisis. Debt restructuring agreements may offer some short-term remedy. The public debt is poised to become a heavy burden for future Laotian generations, particularly as state expenditures in education and health are at risk of being further reduced. Younger generations are increasingly losing confidence in the promises of the Lao party-state to deliver prosperity, as demonstrated in their critical comments on social media. Meanwhile, both its ASEAN partners and China have no interest in an unstable and bankrupt Laos.

Apart from the debt problem, Laos must also cope with currency depreciation and widespread inflation. To this end, the government needs to address the macroeconomic vulnerabilities of the country, which will otherwise continue to hamper economic recovery in the long run. Efforts towards tax reforms and expenditure efficiency are among the key goals recommended by analysts. Meanwhile, the smoothly operating LCR and a renewed tourism boom raise hopes for future revenue generation (which, though, will still lag debt repayments).

Social and environmental problems add to the bleak outlook for 2024. The effects of climate change continue to afflict the Lao population, especially in the countryside, who are already grappling with escalating costs of petrol, fertilizers and other imported goods. Laos is stagnating in its implementation of the Sustainable Development Goals (currently ranked 115 of 166 countries) and will certainly miss the goal of shedding its LDC status by 2026. While celebrating the "Visit Laos 2024" campaign, the regime needs to come up with effective solutions to address the mounting discontent among the population.

Notes

1. Nick Freeman, "Laos in 2022: No Post-pandemic Bounce Just Yet", in *Southeast Asian Affairs 2023*, edited by Hoang Thi Ha and Daljit Singh (Singapore: ISEAS – Yusof Ishak Institute, 2023).

2. David Hutt, "New Lao PM Inherits Multiple Poison Chalices", *Asia Times*, 2 January 2023, https://asiatimes.com/2023/01/new-lao-pm-inherits-multiple-poison-chalices/.

3. Martin Stuart-Fox, Simon Creak, and Martin Rathie, *Historical Dictionary of Laos*, 4th ed. (Lanham: Rowman & Littlefield, 2023), pp. 458–59.

4. Family members hold key positions in many commercial enterprises, including the well-known Lao Brewery Company. For a fascinating study on the history of this powerful company, see Martin Rathie, "'Love Me, Love My Beer: National Heritage in a Bottle': The Social and Economic Engineering of the Lao Beer Industry", in *Beer in East Asia – A Political Economy*, edited by Paul Chambers and Nithi Nuangjamnong (London: Routledge, 2023), pp. 186–211. Present-day elite family networks in the Lao PDR bear a striking resemblance to pre-revolutionary sociopolitical configurations, albeit with different families; see Joel Halpern, *The Lao Elite: A Study of Tradition and Innovation* (RAND Corporation, 1960), https://www.rand.org/pubs/research_memoranda/RM2636.html.

5. Chono Lapuekou, "Former President's Centenary Spurs Transformation of Historic Residence", *Laotian Times*, 20 November 2023, https://laotiantimes.com/2023/11/20/former-presidents-centenary-spurs-transformation-of-historic-residence/. For a biography of Khamtai Siphandone, see Martin Stuart-Fox, Simon Creak, and Martin Rathie, *Historical Dictionary of Laos*, 4th ed. (Lanham: Rowman & Littlefield, 2023), pp. 245–46.

6.   David Hutt, "Can Laos' Communist Party Recover from the Current Economic Crisis?", *The Diplomat*, 31 October 2023, https://thediplomat.com/2023/10/can-laos-communist-party-recover-from-the-current-economic-crisis/.

7.   ADB, "Asian Development Outlook September 2023 – Southeast Asia", September 2023, https://www.adb.org/sites/default/files/publication/908126/southeast-asia-ado-september-2023.pdf; Alastair McCready, "Laos Debt at 'Critical Level' with China Payments Still Opaque", *Nikkei Asia*, 22 September 2023, https://asia.nikkei.com/Economy/Laos-debt-at-critical-level-with-China-payments-still-opaque.

8.   Ekaphone Phouthonesy, "Laos Looks to Renewables as Inflation Hits Energy Prices", *Mekong Eye*, 23 October 2023, https://www.mekongeye.com/2023/10/23/laos-renewables-inflation/; Kosuke Inoue and Tomoya Onishi, "Southeast Asia's 'Battery' Laos Embraces Wind Power to Sustain Energy Exports", *Nikkei Asia*, 15 April 2023, https://asia.nikkei.com/Business/Energy/Southeast-Asia-s-battery-Laos-embraces-wind-power-to-sustain-energy-exports; Tom Fawthrop, "Laos' Luang Prabang May Lose Unesco Status amid Fears Dam Will Cause 'Irreversible Damage'", *South China Morning Post*, 5 March 2023, https://www.scmp.com/week-asia/health-environment/article/3212250/laos-luang-prabang-may-lose-unesco-status-amid-fears-dam-will-cause-irreversible-damage.

9.   "Luang Prabang Eyes 1.7 Million Tourist Arrivals during Visit Laos Year 2024", *Vientiane Times*, 16 January 2024, https://www.vientianetimes.org.la/freefreenews/freecontent_11_Luang_y24.php; Phontham Visapra, "Lao Tourism 2023 Highlights: A Year of Recovery, Growth", *Laotian Times*, 25 December 2023, https://laotiantimes.com/2023/12/25/lao-tourism-2023-highlights-a-year-of-recovery-growth/.

10. Tan Hui Yee and Lim Min Zhang, "'We Have Clients All Year Round': New Railway Line Brings Chinese Travelers to Ancient Laos Town", *Straits Times*, 2 September 2023, https://www.straitstimes.com/multimedia/graphics/2023/09/belt-and-road-initiative-laos-china-railway/index.html?shell; Geoff de Freitas, "BRI Success Stories: The Laos–China Railway Remains Clearly Well on Track", *HKTDC Research*, 22 December 2023, https://research.hktdc.com/en/article/MTU1NTUzNTAwOQ.

11. Toshiro Nishizawa, "China's Double-Edged Belt and Road Debt Trap", *Asia Times*, 25 September 2023, https://asiatimes.com/2023/09/chinas-double-edged-belt-and-road-debt-trap/; Nyshka Chandran, "Laos Is Spiraling toward a Debt Crisis as China Looms Large", CNBC, 8 November 2023, https://www.cnbc.com/2023/11/09/laos-is-spiraling-toward-a-debt-crisis-as-china-looms-large.html.

12. "China-Laos BRI Cooperation a Successful Model for Participating Countries", *Global Times*, 15 October 2023, https://www.globaltimes.cn/page/202310/1299858.shtml; Ding Gang, "US Dropped Bombs in Laos, China Builds Railways", *Global Times*, 12 July 2023, https://www.globaltimes.cn/page/202307/1294231.shtml?id=11. The number of cleared UXO is not that impressive if we consider the size of the

railway project. The target sites of the US bombing raids in the Second Indochina War were located elsewhere, anyway.

13. Only recently, the notorious casino town of Boten (Luang Namtha Province) has been revealed as a hotspot of cybercrime schemes: Chono Lapuekou, "Joint Police Operation Takes Down 462 Online Fraud Suspects in Golden Triangle SEZ", *Laotian Times*, 6 December 2023, https://laotiantimes.com/2023/12/06/joint-police-operation-takes-down-462-online-fraud-suspects-in-golden-triangle-sez/.

14. In addition, the operation of Chinese security agents on Lao territory, and Chinese control of the electrical grid in Laos, is seen as "a trade-off in lieu of debt repayments": Shibani Mahtani and Ore Huiying, "China's Promise of Prosperity Brought Laos Debt — And Distress", *Washington Post*, 12 October 2023, https://www.washingtonpost.com/world/interactive/2023/laos-debt-china-belt-road/.

15. ADB, "Asian Development Outlook September 2023 Economic Forecasts", September 2023, https://www.adb.org/outlook/editions/september-2023; Kit Yin Boey, "Laos Turns Home as Thai Route Shuts", *IFR Asia*, 7–13 October 2023, https://www.ifre.com/story/4159285/laos-turns-home-as-thai-route-shuts-cnn5fcv0fb; Manyphone Vongphachanh, "Laos Suspends Power Supply to Cryptocurrency Mining Businesses", *Laotian Times*, 25 August 2023, https://laotiantimes.com/2023/08/25/laos-suspends-power-supply-to-cryptocurrency-mining-businesses/.

16. Marwaan Macan-Markar, "Laos' ASEAN Chairmanship Faces Chinese Reality Check", *Nikkei Asia*, 16 January 2024, https://asia.nikkei.com/Politics/International-relations/Laos-ASEAN-chairmanship-faces-Chinese-reality-check; Keith Barney, "Laos' Economic Reckoning", *East Asia Forum*, 24 January 2024, https://eastasiaforum.org/2024/01/24/laos-economic-reckoning/.

17. "Lao Government Targets Economic Growth of 4.5 pct in 2024", KPL online, 23 November 2023, https://kpl.gov.la/EN/detail.aspx?id=78429; David Hutt, "Laos' Economic Woes Will Continue in 2024", *The Diplomat*, 18 December 2023, https://thediplomat.com/2023/12/laos-economic-woes-will-continue-in-2024/.

18. Buavanh Vilavong, "Laos' Rapid Economic Growth Path Has So Far Avoided Macroeconomic Cliffs", *East Asia Forum*, 9 February 2019, https://www.eastasiaforum.org/2019/02/09/laos-rapid-economic-growth-path-has-so-far-avoided-macroeconomic-cliffs/.

19. Chanhsy Samavong and Buavanh Vilavong, "Laos Must Address Rising Inflation in 2023", *East Asia Forum*, 1 February 2023, https://www.eastasiaforum.org/2023/02/01/laos-must-address-rising-inflation-in-2023/.

20. Souksakhone Vaenkeo, "National Assembly Opens, Govt Vows to Stabilise Economy, No Debt Default", *Vientiane Times*, 1 November 2023, https://www.vientianetimes.org.la/freefreenews/freecontent_213National_23.php.

21. World Bank, "Lao Economic Monitor, May 2023: Addressing Economic Uncertainty – Key Findings", May 2023, https://www.worldbank.org/en/country/lao/publication/lao-economic-monitor-may-2023-addressing-economic-uncertainty-key-findings.

22. ADB, "Asian Development Outlook September 2023 Economic Forecasts", September 2023, https://www.adb.org/outlook/editions/september-2023; World Bank, "Household Welfare Monitoring in the Lao PDR", 12 September 2023, https://www.worldbank.org/en/country/lao/brief/monitoring-the-impact-of-covid-19-in-lao-pdr.

23. "The Bank of Laos Will Attempt to Lower the Rate of Inflation in 2024", KPL online, 2 November 2023, https://kpl.gov.la/EN/detail.aspx?id=77853.

24. IMF, "Lao People's Democratic Republic: 2023 Article IV Consultation-Press Release; Staff Report; and Statement by the Executive Director for Lao PDR", https://www.elibrary.imf.org/view/journals/002/2023/171/article-A001-en.xml.

25. David Hutt, "Migration Throws Laos' Communist Government a Lifeline", Radio Free Asia, 28 October 2023, https://www.rfa.org/english/commentaries/laos-migration-10282023095444.html; Jonathan Meadley, "Thailand's Aging Population Drives Lao Labor Market across the Border", *Laotian Times*, 4 January 2024, https://laotiantimes.com/2024/01/04/thailands-aging-population-drives-lao-labor-market-across-the-border/.

26. ADB, "Asian Development Outlook", September 2023, https://www.adb.org/outlook/editions/september-2023. See also, World Bank, *Lao PDR Economic Monitor*, May 2023, https://www.worldbank.org/en/country/lao/publication/lao-economic-monitor-may-2023-addressing-economic-uncertainty-key-findings. It is clearly the need to acquire cash that keeps large parts of the Lao population moving, leaving schools and fields behind, seeking new income opportunities that the labour market in Laos cannot provide.

27. Miles Kenney-Lazar, "Turning Land into Capital? The Expansion and Extraction of Value in Laos", *Environment and Planning A: Economy and Space* 55, no. 6 (2023): 1565–80, https://doi.org/10.1177/0308518X211063493; Philip Hirsch, Kevin Woods, Natalia Scurrah, and Michael B. Dwyer, eds., *Turning Land into Capital: Development and Dispossession in the Mekong Region* (Seattle: University of Washington Press, 2022).

28. Namfon Chanthavong, "Villagers Protest in Xieng Khouang over Alleged Land Grab", *Laotian Times*, 24 January 2024, https://laotiantimes.com/2024/01/24/villagers-protest-in-xieng-khouang-over-alleged-land-grab/.

29. In a controversial article, Kearrin Sims linked such incidents to a general decline of public safety and security in Laos: Kearrin Sims, "Is Laos a Criminal State?", *The Diplomat*, 5 May 2023, https://thediplomat.com/2023/05/is-laos-a-criminal-state/.

30. "PM Calls for Joint Efforts to Combat Drugs", *Vientiane Times*, 26 June 2023, https://www.vientianetimes.org.la/freeContent/FreeConten121_PM_y23.php; Alastair McCready, "'Cheaper than Beer': Laos Meth Prices Plummet as Myanmar Chaos Fuels Trade", Aljazeera online, 7 November 2023, https://www.aljazeera.com/news/2023/11/7/cheaper-than-beer-laos-meth-prices-plummet-as-myanmar-chaos-fuels-trade.

31. Martin Rathie argues that Beerlao "helps to sedate the populace on a broad scale. When underpaid civil servants are able to clock off work early and enjoy a group

drinking session with either colleagues, family or friends it helps distract their attention from chronic problems such as delayed salaries, deteriorating workplaces, virtually non-existent welfare and a casual regard for law." Rathie, "'Love Me, Love My Beer", p. 202.

32. Latsamy Phonevilay, "Cassava Profits Conceal Alarming Environmental Threat in Laos", *Laotian Times*, 17 July 2023, https://laotiantimes.com/2023/07/17/cassava-profits-conceal-alarming-environmental-threat-in-laos/.

33. Ryan McNeill, Deborah J. Nelson, Allison Martell, and Michael Ovaska, "China, Birthplace of the COVID Pandemic, Is Laying Tracks for Another Global Health Crisis", Reuters, 16 May 2023, https://www.reuters.com/investigates/special-report/global-pandemic-bats-deforestation/.

34. Chono Lapuekou, "Chinese Institute in Laos Sees Increase in Applications Despite Overall Low University Enrollment", *Laotian Times*, 15 August 2023, https://laotiantimes.com/2023/08/15/chinese-institute-in-laos-sees-increase-in-applications-despite-overall-low-university-enrollment/.

35. Simon Rowedder, "Dreaming the 'Chinese Dream': Local Productions of and Engagements with Chinese Infrastructures in Northern Laos", *Journal of Southeast Asian Studies*, forthcoming.

36. Joanne Lin, "Changing Perceptions in Laos Toward China", *ISEAS Perspective* no. 2023/55, 17 July 2023.

37. Jonathan Meadley, "Laos Issues Statement on Delivery of Cluster Munitions to Ukraine", *Laotian Times*, 11 July 2023, https://laotiantimes.com/2023/07/11/lao-foreign-ministry-gives-statement-amid-us-decision-to-send-ukraine-cluster-bombs/.

38. "PM Seeks More Investment from China", *Vientiane Times*, 31 March 2023, https://www.vientianetimes.org.la/freeContent/FreeConten64_PM_y23.php.

39. OEC, Laos Country Profile, https://oec.world/en/profile/country/lao.

40. David Hutt, "ASEAN Gives Laos a Reprieve over Myanmar Crisis", *The Diplomat*, 15 September 2023, https://thediplomat.com/2023/09/asean-gives-laos-a-reprieve-over-myanmar-crisis/; Joanne Lin, "Is Laos Able to Make a Difference in the Myanmar Crisis?", *Fulcrum*, 13 October 2023, https://fulcrum.sg/aseanfocus/is-laos-able-to-make-a-difference-in-the-myanmar-crisis/.

Malaysia

Kudat
Kota Kinabalu
Sandakan
Kota Bahru
Kuala Terengganu
Penang
Miri
Ipoh
Kuantan
Bintulu
KUALA LUMPUR
Sibu
Mersing
Melaka
Kuching
Johor Bahru

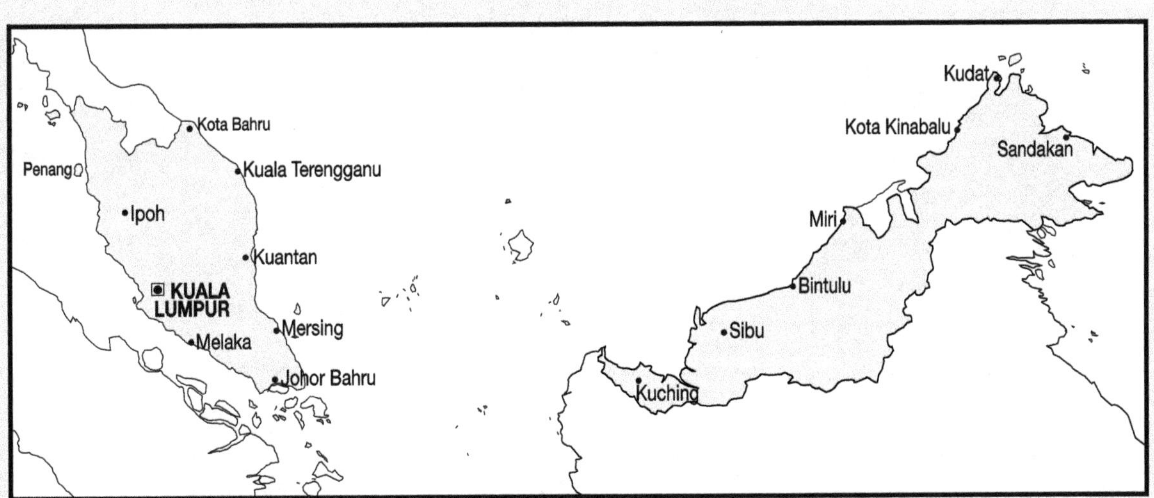

MALAYSIA IN 2023:
Full Throttle on Politics,
Reforms in Back Seat

Ariel Tan

The year 2023 saw Malaysia return to political stability after five years of dramatic changes of government and a general election in 2022 that produced a hung parliament and the Pakatan Harapan–led Unity Government. National politics was dominated by new prime minister Anwar Ibrahim and partisan skirmishes over race and religion. On its one-year anniversary in November, the government faced criticism for having made little progress to reform Malaysia's governance and socio-economic system, and for failing to deliver a strong economy.

Pakatan Harapan is a multiracial coalition comprising Anwar's Parti Keadilan Rakyat (PKR), the Democratic Action Party (DAP), Amanah and Pertubuhan Kinabalu Progresif Bersatu (UPKO). It was joined by three main coalitions—Barisan Nasional led by the United Malays National Organisation (UMNO), Gabungan Parti Sarawak (GPS) and Gabungan Rakyat Sabah (GRS)—and smaller parties to form the governing coalition after the 15th general election (GE15) in 2022. The opposition, Perikatan Nasional, is a Malay-centric coalition formed by Parti Islam Se-Malaysia (PAS) and Parti Pribumi Bersatu Malaysia (Bersatu), with token representation by the multiracial Parti Gerakan Rakyat Malaysia (Gerakan).

Anwar spent much of his first year in office campaigning for the six-state elections in August. The ruling coalition gained breathing space as it successfully defended the states under its rule and the three parliamentary and state seats it had controlled in by-elections this year, but it lost ground with Malay voters. With five Bersatu parliamentarians expressing support for Anwar as prime minister in November, the government enjoyed the support of 152 parliamentarians out of 222 seats.

ARIEL TAN is Senior Fellow at the Institute of Defence and Strategic Studies, S. Rajaratnam School of International Studies, at the Nanyang Technological University, Singapore.

After the state elections, the government stepped up with a series of medium-term plans on the economy and tabled the 2024 Budget in October, but Anwar then turned to the Israel-Palestine conflict and vigorously pressed the issue both domestically and internationally in October and November. The issue resonated with the Muslim-Malay population but overshadowed the government's messaging on the economy. Its approaches to money politics, religion and human rights, reminiscent of previous Barisan administrations that Harapan had criticized when in the opposition, also disappointed its base.

Internationally, Malaysia was well represented by Anwar. He sought to engage key partners in Asia, the Middle East and the West to promote investments and bolster his political legitimacy domestically.

Politics

The stumbles of the Harapan government 1.0 (2018–20) loomed over this second administration in 2023. Harapan 1.0 had been painted as dominated by the Chinese-majority DAP and hostile to Malay-Muslim interests. It collapsed when its Malay-centric partner Bersatu and the anti-Anwar faction from PKR abandoned the government. Harapan's weak support among Malay voters continued in GE15 and the 2023 state elections. Mollifying Malay distrust was critical for the ruling coalition in 2023. While Harapan's multiracial base was disappointed with this approach, the spectre of a repeat of government collapse encouraged discipline in the leadership and patience among their supporters.

State Elections and By-elections

State elections were held on 12 August 2023 in Selangor, Penang, Negri Sembilan, Kelantan, Terengganu and Kedah. The former three were retained by Harapan, the latter by PAS. The other states had earlier called snap elections (Sabah, Melaka, Sarawak and Johor) or held theirs in conjunction with GE15 (Pahang, Perak and Perlis).

In Selangor, a Harapan stronghold led by PKR since 2008, there had been concerns that the state could fall as a result of the support of more Malays for PAS and Bersatu, particularly in the more rural areas. Harapan-Barisan dropped 11 seats (from 45 at the point of dissolution), settling with 34 seats out of 56. Four seats—Sungai Kandis, Gombak Setia, Taman Medan and Dengkil—were lost by PKR to Perikatan by fewer than 500 votes. There were discussions that PKR might file a petition to challenge the results.

Perikatan had drummed up expectations that it could beat Harapan-Barisan, with former Selangor *mentri besar* ("state chief minister") Azmin Ali running as Bersatu's candidate for Hulu Kelang and, potentially, *mentri besar* if Perikatan clinched the state. Azmin won and became the opposition leader in the state assembly.

In Penang, a Harapan stronghold led by the DAP, Harapan-Barisan lost 6 seats, largely in Malay-majority areas, falling to 29 out of a total of 40 seats. Chow Kon Yeow was reappointed chief minister despite his clashes with former chief minister and DAP chairman Lim Guan Eng. Their public backbiting and controversies such as a questionable land deal involving the Penang government undermined Chow and the DAP's vaunted discipline and incorruptibility.

In Negri Sembilan, Harapan-Barisan dropped from a total of 36 to 31 seats—losing the total control of the state assembly they previously had. It was a laudable result, however, given the national trend. The election was contested by senior leaders of the coalition; namely, Anthony Loke, secretary-general of the DAP and transport minister, and Mohamad Hasan, deputy president of UMNO and then defence minister.

Terengganu saw a total wipe-out of UMNO and Harapan, with the popular incumbent *mentri besar* Dr Samsuri Mokhtar leading PAS to victory. Perikatan swept all 32 seats. In Kedah, the high-profile incumbent *mentri besar* Muhammad Sanusi Md Nor from PAS grabbed 33 out of 36 seats, gaining 13 more seats than their previous 20, leaving 3 for Amanah/Harapan. Both Kedah and Terengganu had been ruled by UMNO before it lost these states to PAS; UMNO still had significant presence there, but it lost all the seats it contested in the two Malay-majority states.

Kelantan, as expected, was won by PAS, and the party saw a significant jump from 37 to 43 seats out of 45 despite pockets of unhappiness among residents with PAS over the state's underdeveloped infrastructure and economy. Voters who lived outside the state but returned to vote reportedly tended to support PAS.

Overall, Harapan and Barisan saw their seat holdings drop from 145 to 99. Perikatan gained ground from 85 to 146. Harapan and Barisan won the popular vote against Perikatan (49.5 per cent vs. 49.3 per cent) by a small margin.[1]

In the three parliamentary by-elections held in 2023, all seats were successfully defended by the incumbent parties. Kuala Terengganu (Terengganu) returned to PAS/Perikatan, Pulai (Johor) to Amanah/Harapan, and Kemaman (Terengganu) to PAS. The decision by PAS to field Dr Samsuri Mokhtar in Kemaman signalled its grooming of him for national politics. Formerly the political secretary to PAS president Hadi Awang, Dr Samsuri is seen to be close to Hadi. He is well respected and has a doctorate in aero-engine ignition and combustion from Leeds University. While he is touted as a potential candidate for prime minister, he would have to overcome potential concerns in the party that the highest political position would be held by a PAS leader who is not from their powerful *Ulamak* (clerics) wing.

In the state by-elections, Simpang Jeram (Johor) was retained by Amanah/Harapan, Pelangai (Penang) by UMNO/Barisan, and Jepak (Sarawak) by Parti Pesaka Bumiputera Bersatu/GPS.

Analysts found that Malay voters continued to abandon UMNO. While Harapan supporters were prepared to vote for UMNO and against PAS and Bersatu, there was less transfer of votes from UMNO supporters to Harapan candidates. Nevertheless, this was the first major campaign where UMNO, PKR, Amanah and the DAP worked together on the ground. The question remained as to whether this socialization would foster cooperation in the next general election due in 2027.

The campaign by Harapan-Barisan was dominated by Anwar, who campaigned across the states. The opposition had painted these elections as a referendum on the new unity government. Anwar went along with the narrative that the unity government was at stake and essentially put his personal brand on the ballot. This reinforced perceptions that the government was precarious and distracted. The popular Harapan-led state governments had a longer record and closer connections with their electorates than the federal government, but they were overshadowed by Anwar and national partisan skirmishes over race and religion.

Pakatan Harapan

The coalition was more cohesive than Harapan 1.0. First, the DAP, knowing that it was a useful bogeyman for PAS and Bersatu, kept a low profile. DAP secretary-general Anthony Loke, who was proficient in Malay, was more accepted by Malays than his predecessor, Lim Guan Eng. DAP supporters were less vocal against the government's moves to placate Muslim sensitivities. The "green wave", denoting the growing electoral success of PAS in GE15 and the 2023 state elections, continued to play on their mind.

Second, PKR was a more cohesive party, with the excision of the Azmin faction and the party election in 2022 reinforcing Anwar's control. Anwar fielded primarily his allies in GE15. While PKR deputy president and economy minister Rafizi Ramli was a potential challenger to Anwar, he was constrained by the limited remit of his portfolio and beholden to Anwar for his government appointment. In November, Rafizi defended Anwar passionately at their party congress.

Third, Amanah maintained its cohesion despite murmurings of dissatisfaction with its president, agriculture and food security minister Mohamad (Mat) Sabu. A progressive Islamist party, Amanah had failed to gain ground among PAS supporters, but its leaders did succeed in forming the federal government through their steadfast support for Anwar and Harapan. Following their party election in late December, Mat Sabu was returned as president for his last term. His close rival, former vice president Mujahid Yusof Rawa, who was previously minister in the prime minister's department overseeing religious affairs, was elected deputy president. Mujahid had called for party renewal, and his elevation reflected an acknowledgement that the party needed to do more to cultivate Malay support.

The most serious hit taken by Harapan was the dropping by the government in September of forty-seven graft charges against UMNO president and deputy prime minister Ahmad Zahid Hamidi involving Yayasan Akalbudi funds. It was left to the High Court to grant Zahid a discharge not amounting to acquittal. Amidst a public outcry, new attorney general Ahmad Terrirudin clarified that the Attorney General's Chambers had not withdrawn the case but that it required time to scrutinize new documents and representation before making any new decision.

It was believed that Anwar only trusted Zahid to keep UMNO in line and within the unity government. Should UMNO abandon the government, it could collapse as it could not count on GPS or GRS staying on. Other UMNO leaders like deputy president Mohamad Hasan and vice-president Johari Abdul Ghani might be amenable to keeping UMNO in the unity government, but neither man had full control of the party.

UMNO

Zahid continued to consolidate his position in the party since forcing the GE15 and sidelining internal detractors in the election. UMNO delivered its worst results, winning 26 seats, down from the previous low of 54. Party leaders like Khairy Jamaluddin and Noh Omar then called for Zahid's resignation. Instead, he delivered UMNO to Anwar in forming the unity government and won positions for himself and his colleagues in the federal and state governments led by Harapan. There remained the belief among UMNO grassroots that it would continue to lose Malay support as a result of Zahid's leadership and the decision to join the DAP in government.

In January, the UMNO general assembly consented to a no-contest for the posts of president and deputy president, keeping Zahid and Mohamad Hasan in position until at least 2026. The UMNO supreme council then sacked Khairy and Noh Omar from the party, and suspended others, including former defence minister Hishammuddin Hussein and deputy youth chief Shahril Hamdan for six years. While a number of UMNO parliamentarians were reportedly aligned with Hishammuddin, the anti-hopping law, the benefits of being part of the ruling coalition, and uncertainty that Perikatan could unseat the unity government discouraged members from hopping to Perikatan.

In November, Zahid hinted that he might stop running for public office but did not say when.[2] Following subsequent rumours of a cancer diagnosis, Zahid stated that he had had prostate surgery but continued with his official duties and gave no indications that he planned to step down. UMNO's inability to attract Malay voters was a drag on the government. Anwar's reference in October to his early open invitation for PAS to join the unity government could be seen in this context. PAS president Hadi Awang, however, had ruled out cooperating with Anwar and the DAP.

Bersatu

Bersatu was led by its experienced president and former prime minister Muhyiddin Yassin, and secretary-general and former home minister Hamzah Zainuddin. It ran a very well-resourced campaign in GE15. But Muhyiddin's rejection of the king's invitation for him to form a unity government with Harapan left Perikatan out in the cold. He was slapped with multiple graft charges in March. He was acquitted of four charges of abuse of power (involving US$50 million) by the High Court in August, but still faced three charges of money laundering (involving US$43 million). Other Bersatu politicians, including parliamentarian and former party information chief Wan Saiful Wan Jan, also had pending court cases.

While their supporters believed the leaders' claim that the charges stemmed from the government's selective political prosecution, these incidents took some shine off Bersatu. PAS appeared to be distancing itself from Bersatu. Its appointment of Mahathir Mohamad—a recent virulent critic of Muhyiddin—as unofficial advisor to the four states under PAS's control was seen as a slight at Muhyiddin.

Indeed, the state elections were far more critical for Muhyiddin and Perikatan than the unity government. Perikatan needed to win big to attract more allies to take over the government. Bersatu had not developed a strong grassroots and relied on PAS for ground mobilization. Questions remained over Bersatu's viability as a party.

In November, five members of parliament from Bersatu declared their support for Anwar while remaining in Bersatu, thereby avoiding losing their seats under the anti-hopping law. At Bersatu's general assembly in November, Muhyiddin declared his intention to run for president (after saying he would step down the day before) at party elections postponed to 2024, perhaps to warn off challengers. Further disarray in the party could trigger realignments in national politics.

PAS

Being the largest party in parliament, with 43 seats, and receiving greater support from Malay voters than UMNO, PAS could claim to be the true representative of Malays. While UMNO had painted it as a provincial and extremist party confined to the north, PAS was gaining ground southwards. Meanwhile, UMNO appeared to be on the retreat, secure only in Melaka, Negri Sembilan and Johor, with help from Harapan. A PAS-led federal government was no longer beyond the realm of possibility.

PAS held its party election in October. Incumbent president Hadi Awang, deputy president Tuan Ibrahim Tuan Man, and vice presidents Idris Ahmad, Mohd Amar Abdullah and Dr Samsuri Mokhtar all retained their positions unopposed. This reinforced PAS's image as a unified and disciplined party. At their annual congress, Hadi noted that Perikatan had failed to form the government after GE15 because of the shortfall in non-Malay support; PAS needed to win over non-Malays and non-Muslims in the next general election.

Rulers

A significant player on any party's path to power would be the king. PAS has had a complex relationship with the rulers, partly given its ambiguous position on the role of royalty in Islam and government. In July, Kedah *mentri besar* Sanusi criticized the Selangor sultan's appointment of Amirudin Shari as *mentri besar*, adding that the Kedah sultan would not have done so. He was charged with sedition.

The king had promoted the idea of a unity government to resolve the hung parliament after GE15, thereby facilitating the deal between Harapan and Barisan to join forces. The incoming king, slated to be enthroned in January 2024, the sultan of Johor, had signalled his approval of Anwar as prime minister since March. Anwar's solicitous posture towards the rulers contrasted him well against his rivals. But the rulers would also be careful in safeguarding their own position by paying heed to the democratic will of the people.

Governance

General Assessment

In January, Anwar unveiled "Malaysia Madani" (or Malaysia Modern and Civilized, inspired by Islamic civilizational ideals) as his government's policy framework for good governance and racial harmony. It denoted six core values: sustainable development, prosperity, innovation, respect, trust and compassion.

From the start, Anwar was perceived to prioritize proving his Malay-Muslim credentials for political legitimacy. More than his predecessors, he often donned traditional Malay garb both in Malaysia and abroad, made publicized visits to mosques, and highlighted his personal links with foreign Muslim leaders such as Türkiye's president Recep Erdogan. In addition, he assiduously cultivated the Malay establishment: the Malay rulers and civil service, including the Islamic bureaucracy. This surprised some supporters of Harapan, which had for years campaigned against Barisan's alleged Malay-centric authoritarianism.

Reforming the government would be a massive undertaking. The auditor general's 2022 report released in November showed the enormity of the challenge of simply curbing waste and the leakage of public funds. It reported more than RM600 million (US$64 million) in losses of public funds from audits of fourteen ministries, spanning programmes from rice planting to the management of foreign workers.

The administration's need to contend with legacy issues was exemplified by 1MDB debts paid thus far (US$9.4 billion) and the littoral combat ship project. In May, it announced it would pay an additional US$430 million for five rather than the originally contracted six ships for the Malaysian navy, on a delayed schedule. The original contract awarded in 2011 was for US$1.96 billion, with reports that US$300 million had been misappropriated and with no ship delivered thus far.[3] In October, the parliamentary public accounts committee revealed that the government planned to take over the troubled shipbuilders Boustead Naval Shipyard as part of efforts to salvage the project.

Positive Developments

In 2023, trust in the judiciary remained high. There were no serious allegations of political interference. Sensitive cases with racial or religious dynamics were processed straightforwardly. They included the granting of citizenship to the stateless Wong Kueng Hui, Loh Siew Hong's fight against her children's unilateral conversion, and Sam Ke Ting's exoneration.[4] Parliament continued to develop its separate personality and agency from the executive, with the public accounts committee and other select committees increasingly fulfilling their mandated roles.

Notable government achievements included the passing of the Abolition of Mandatory Death Penalty Bill 2023 in April; a new provision in March, Section 507A of the Penal Code, to criminalize stalking; and the Control of Smoking Products for Public Health Bill 2023 in November for more updated and comprehensive regulations of all tobacco products, including electronic cigarettes or vaping. The government also pushed through amendments to the Human Rights Commission of Malaysia (Suhakam) Act in November to give it "teeth", allowing it to visit any detention centre to probe alleged human rights abuses, and the appointment from Suhakam of commissioners for children.

Controversies

Certain government moves caused concern or confusion:

The concentration of executive power: First, the prime minister kept the finance minister's portfolio despite Harapan's previous opposition to the practice. Calls for him to appoint a second finance minister reflected concerns that the critical ministry was not receiving adequate political and policy oversight.

Second, questions had been raised about the government's commitment to reform given its stalling on earlier promises to separate the role of the attorney general and public prosecutor, impose a ten-year term limit for prime ministers, subject key appointments like election commissioners and the chief of the Malaysian Anti-Corruption Commission to parliamentary oversight, and legislate political funding, as well as its defence of the Sedition Act and Security Offences (Special Measures) Act 2012, which Harapan had criticized.[5]

Its position on corruption and money politics: First, the government dropped its graft charges against Anwar's key political ally Zahid Hamidi. Second, Anwar's refusal to equalize constituency development funds between the government and opposition members of parliament gave the ruling coalition a great advantage in attracting defectors from the opposition. Harapan's acceptance of the five defectors from Bersatu undermined the spirit of the anti-hopping law and encouraged future defections and instability. Third, while Harapan had earlier criticized political appointments to government-linked companies and government agencies, Anwar appointed nineteen MPs and forty-two other politicians from the ruling coalition to at least sixty-one boardroom positions.[6]

Its position on race and religion: First, Anwar had previously criticized the abuses of race-based affirmative action and had promoted a needs-based approach, which was popular with Harapan's non-Malay supporters. But just before the August state elections he issued a harsh response to a student at a public engagement who asked about replacing the racial quotas for school admissions with a meritocratic system. His response hit supporters hard when he said that the racial quota system could not be scrapped as it would cause the unity government alliance to lose all elections. In November, in the United States, he suggested that a needs-based approach would also be important.

Second, in an interview with Radio Television Malaysia in January, Anwar said that his administration would not accept the concept of a secular state or the rights of the Lesbian, Gay, Bisexual and Transgender (LGBT) community. In August, the government banned LGBT-themed Swatch watches and related materials. The government did not allow some pop concerts to proceed amidst protests from PAS but did allow others; e.g., Coldplay, in November, stating that Coldplay was pro-Palestine.

Third, in May, Mohd Na'im Mokhtar, minister in the prime minister's department (religious affairs) replied to a question from the opposition in parliament, saying that the administration did plan to table an amendment (RUU355) to the Shariah Courts (Criminal Jurisdiction) Act 1965, pending cabinet approval. This would be tabled alongside the Shariah Courts (Federal Territories) Bill, purportedly aimed at empowering the Shariah judicial system. (Previously, PAS had sought to table amendments to allow for harsher punishments for Shariah offences by raising the Shariah courts' maximum sentencing limits to thirty years' jail, RM100,000 fines, and a hundred strokes of the cane. The existing limits are three years' jail, RM5,000 fines, and six strokes.[7] This was meant to pave the way to enacting Hudud, an Islamic criminal code.) The minister's response provoked an outcry from Harapan supporters. In November, Anwar said that a special committee, consented to by the conference of rulers, would be set up to empower and elevate the country's Syariah courts. It was unclear what that would entail.

Fourth, in June, Anwar stated that he wanted the Malaysian Islamic Development Department (Jakim) to provide greater inputs into policymaking. In August, the government announced an additional Islamic module for national schools; in response to outcries from non-Malays, it clarified that the "Imam al-Nawawi's 40 Hadith" appreciation module was intended for Muslim students. It denied it was seeking to further Islamize the system; rather, the intention was to ensure the correct understanding of Islam.

Fifth, following the attacks by Hamas on Israel on 7 October and Israel's counter-attacks in Gaza, Anwar launched a high-octane condemnation of Israel and made a point of not criticizing Hamas. This issue resonated deeply with

Malay-Muslims in Malaysia. While there was longstanding and broad sympathy among Malaysians for Palestinians, Anwar's strident position, it was feared, could alienate non-Muslims and undermine Malaysia's interests.

An anti-Israel boycott had been called, targeting Israel and companies from the West perceived to be supporting it. The government failed to take a position on this. Calls to "buy Muslim products first" stirred concerns among non-Muslims. Meanwhile, Anwar continued to woo large Western companies to invest in Malaysia.

A Palestine Solidarity Week (PSW) was announced for schools, and videos emerged of students being encouraged to desecrate the Israeli flag and join mock confrontations with toy guns in what appeared to be expressions of support for terrorism. DAP leaders and twelve non-Malay MPs from Anwar's party, PKR, expressed concern over the PSW, but the government held its ground. Schools in East Malaysia stated that they would not comply. Leaders in Sarawak and Sabah stated that they would not accept Palestinian refugees. Scholarships and assistance for Palestinians in Malaysian universities sparked unhappiness among non-Malays.

All this overshadowed the government's Budget 2024, which was being debated in parliament, as well as Malaysia's other interests, such as during the visit of Japanese prime minister Fumio Kishida and the Asia-Pacific Economic Cooperation (APEC) Leaders' Meeting in November.

Economy

Malaysia's political and governance challenges in 2023 took place against a backdrop of slower growth moderated by adverse external developments. The launch by the government of the National Energy Transition Roadmap in late August, the New Industrial Master Plan 2030 to revitalize Malaysia's manufacturing sector and the 12th Malaysia Plan Mid-Term Review in September were well-received as signposts for the government's medium-term economic goals. It had also increased cash assistance for lower-income groups and lowered the cost of internet services and maintained subsidies. But the public remained concerned about the cost of living and subdued growth. (*Menu Rahmah*, an initiative for private vendors to provide RM5 budget healthy meals, was notable among government initiatives for the rare public resonance and popularity it received when launched in January.)

According to Bank Negara, Malaysia's economy was projected to expand by around 4 per cent in 2023 and 4–5 per cent in 2024. Inflation continued to decline, but core inflation was 2.5 per cent in the third quarter, above the long-term average of 2 per cent. Headline inflation was expected to settle at 2.5–3 per cent for 2023. In October, the ringgit fell against the US dollar to its lowest level since the Asian financial crisis, to 4.885 per USD.[8] Contributing to this was high interest rates in the United States and lower inbound investments to Asia as a result of China's slow recovery. At the same time, the ringgit hit 3.5086 per SGD.

Growth in 2023 was largely on the back of domestic demand. Exports fell because of weak global demand, only partially offset by improving inbound tourism. The services, construction and agriculture sectors grew, but manufacturing declined.

Malaysia remained competitive as a global electronics hub. Intel was investing US$7 billion in a new semiconductors packaging plant in Penang. Infineon Technologies was constructing a new wafer fab module in Kulim, with around US$1.7 billion of investment. Tesla's high-profile plan to set up its Southeast Asia office in Malaysia followed the government's lifting of local ownership requirements, allowing Tesla hundred per cent ownership of its operations in Malaysia.

The government tabled two budgets, in March and October, for 2023 and 2024. Both were Malaysia's largest ever, at US$83 billion and US$85 billion, respectively. The 2023 budget was notable for its tax cuts to promote growth. The 2024 budget was disappointing for those hoping for more substantive reforms to rationalize subsidies and raise revenue, such as the introduction of a goods and services tax. Instead, the government announced a 10 per cent capital gains tax, a 5 per cent to 10 per cent high-value goods tax, and a 2 per cent hike on the Sales and Services Tax. It was commended for its pro-growth incentives and its environmental, social and governance priorities, including encouraging green technology and electric vehicles for sustainable development.

International Relations

Malaysia's foreign policy is well-established and pragmatic, aimed at sustaining friendly relations with other countries to safeguard its national security and economic and political interests. It maintains non-alignment vis-à-vis the United States and China. It seeks to lead as a Muslim middle power in matters that affect the global *ummah* (the worldwide community of Muslims), particularly those that resonate with its Malay majority. It is also an active participant in regional and international organizations, such as ASEAN, the United Nations, and the Organisation of Islamic Countries.

Anwar maintained this approach. He made the customary introductory visits to all ASEAN countries (except Myanmar) and visited the United Arab Emirates and Egypt. He visited China, Indonesia, Thailand, Türkiye and the United States twice; and Singapore and Saudi Arabia three times. He also met leaders from Jordan, Iran, Pakistan and Canada on the sidelines of multilateral meetings.

Befitting Malaysia's international standing and warm ties with several countries, it received visits from several heads of state: Germany's president Frank-Walter Steinmeier (February), Singapore's president Halimah Yacob (March) and New Zealand's governor-general Cindy Kiro (October). It also received visits from many heads of government: Indonesia's president Joko Widodo (June), the Philippine's president Ferdinand R. Marcos Jr (July), Thailand's prime minister Srettha Thavisin (October), the Netherland's prime minister Mark Rutte (October) and Japan's prime minister Fumio Kishida (November).

International relations was familiar territory for Anwar given his previous experience as finance minister and deputy prime minister. His engagement with influential Muslim countries such as Saudi Arabia, the UAE and Türkiye reinforced his image as an international Islamic leader, standing taller than his domestic political rivals. The rich Gulf states are also important sources of trade, investment and tourism for Malaysia.

For most of his visits, his team ensured that memoranda of understanding were signed and investment commitments announced to demonstrate he had delivered economic and strategic benefits for Malaysians. For instance, in San Francisco in November, he met leaders from technology giants Google, Enovix, Microsoft and TikTok. He announced that Malaysia had secured US$13.5 billion in proposed investments by Abbott Laboratories, Amsted Rail, Hematogenix, Ford, Boeing, Amazon and Lam Research, among others.[9]

While Malaysia sought to balance its relations with the United States and China, there appeared to be a slight tilt towards China under Anwar. This was typical. In the United States in November, he acknowledged the United States as a close security and economic partner, while noting that China was geographically closer and a rising source of trade and investment. Anwar chose China as the first country to visit after Southeast Asia and Saudi Arabia. The Chinese government reciprocated by granting Anwar the highest level of access and sustained bilateral trade and investments. China also actively cultivated both West and East Malaysia, whose proximity to the South China Sea and abundant natural resources were undoubtedly relevant considerations.

China has remained Malaysia's largest trading partner for fourteen consecutive years, with total trade at US$110.6 billion in 2022. It was Malaysia's biggest foreign direct investor in 2022, with approved investments totalling US$12.5 billion. Anwar gave the keynote address at the Boao Forum in March and met President Xi Jinping in Beijing. Anwar touted proposed investment deals of more than US$38 billion during his March trip. He visited China again in September to attend the 20th China-ASEAN Expo and met Premier Li Qiang.

There have also been occasions, however, where Anwar has made controversial statements, which often resulted from his eagerness to paint a positive picture of relations with Beijing. His remark that he was "open to negotiations" with China on disputed areas in the South China Sea necessitated clarification from the foreign ministry that Malaysia "is unequivocally and firmly committed to protecting Malaysia's sovereignty, sovereign rights and interests in its maritime areas in the South China Sea, as depicted by our 1979 Map".[10] He was reported to have said that Malaysia had chosen Huawei for its new 5G Dual Wholesale Network structure for 5G in September. No open tender had been called.[11]

As for the United States, in March, Malaysia reiterated its critical stance on AUKUS after it formalized plans to provide Australia with nuclear-powered submarines from the early 2030s. Later that month, Malaysia did not accept the invitation to attend the United States' second Democracy Summit. While Anwar visited the United States twice, to attend the United Nations General Assembly in New York and the APEC Leaders' Meeting in San Francisco, he had yet to hold a bilateral meeting with US president Joe Biden.

In October, Anwar stated that Malaysia had received "threats" from the West over its position on the Israel-Palestine conflict. This was then dialled down to "pressures". It emerged that the United States had requested Malaysia to urge a country (believed to be Iran) not to take advantage of the Gaza conflict by using a proxy to get involved in the war. The United States also expressed concern over Malaysia's position towards Israel and Hamas, urging the government to issue a statement showing sympathy to the people of Israel. Malaysia declined.[12] In November, in response to questions about the impact on Malaysia of the proposed Hamas International Financing Prevention Act by the United States, Anwar stated that Malaysia did not recognize such unilateral sanctions. He admitted that it could affect Malaysia if it were found to have provided material support to Hamas or the Palestinian Islamic Jihad, including investments by US companies.

Approved investments in 2022 from the United States came in second to China, at US$6.6 billion. The United States was Malaysia's third-largest trading partner, with total trade at US$57.3 billion. In remarks at Berkeley in November, in a rare admission of their close ties, he said "Malaysia conducts more bilateral and multilateral military exercises with the US than with any of our other partners: 11 bilateral and five multilateral exercises annually…. These help to build critical capacity and readiness for our forces. Between 2018 and 2022, US security assistance exceeded US$220 million, providing equipment, training, and other vital support."[13] Malaysia provided 25 per cent of the semiconductor components needed by the United States.

Malaysia also enjoyed good ties with Australia, Japan and South Korea, allies of the United States. In February, Malaysia announced the purchase of eighteen South Korean FA-50 jets, worth US$920 million. Malaysia has been seeking to replace its BAE Systems and Russian MiG-29 aircraft.

Anwar sought to strengthen relations with all ASEAN countries except Myanmar. The most significant development was the signing of the Treaty Relating to the Delimitation of the Territorial Seas of the Two Countries in the Southernmost Part of the Melaka Straits and the Treaty between Malaysia and Indonesia Relating to the Delimitation of the Territorial Seas of the Two Countries in the Sulawesi Sea during Jokowi's visit to Malaysia in June.

Malaysia and Singapore were each other's second-largest trading partners, with bilateral trade reaching US$83.53 billion in 2022, a 37.6 per cent increase from 2021. A significant announcement in 2023 was their plans to establish a Johor-Singapore Special Economic Zone to enhance cross-border flow of goods and people and strengthen their business ecosystems. They also made progress in pursuing cross-border electricity trading, where Singapore would import renewable energy from Malaysia. (Sarawak aims to provide up to one gigawatt of renewable energy to Singapore by 2032 via submarine cables, with negotiations said to be at an advanced stage.) The ascension of the Johor sultan to the kingship is expected to encourage the government to cultivate good relations with Singapore, which plays a key role in the Johor economy. The sultan had publicly pushed for the shelved High-Speed Rail (HSR) project with Singapore, and Anwar subsequently confirmed his government's interest in its revival in December.

Conclusion

As the Anwar administration marked its one-year anniversary on 24 November, Merdeka Center reported its survey findings that Anwar's approval rating of 68 per cent in December 2022 had fallen to 50 per cent in October because of public concerns about the economy. Approval for the government fell from 54 to 41 per cent. Thirty-one per cent of respondents said the country was heading in the right direction, while 60 per cent said it was heading in the wrong direction.[14]

Anwar dismissed the polls. He also reminded critics that "what's most important is that we have Malay leaders who do not steal the country's money. If anyone asks me what I am proud of this past one year, I say, praise God, I watch our leadership closely, I ask for reports, and in the past year, there have been no cases of leaders stealing the people's money."[15] But as a nod to criticisms, he promised firmer and clearer policies in the coming year.

Under pressure to raise public confidence in his government, on 12 December, Anwar announced a cabinet reshuffle, where he finally appointed a second finance minister. There were five additions: second finance minister Amir Hamzah Azizan, human resource minister Steven Sim (DAP), plantation and commodities minister Johari Abdul Ghani (UMNO), health minister Dr Dzulkefly Ahmad (Amanah), and digital minister Gobind Singh Deo (DAP); the latter three being ministers from previous administrations. Anwar retained the tainted UMNO president Zahid Hamidi as deputy prime minister, who faced internal leadership challenges. The next-most-senior leader after Zahid, UMNO deputy president Mohamad Hasan, was reassigned from defence to the foreign affairs ministry, widely seen as a demotion.[16]

The reshuffle saw only one removal—the tainted minister V. Sivakumar (DAP), who had held the human resource portfolio. While party and regional representation was respected, Anwar eschewed the traditional appointment of a Tamil-Hindu minister. V. Sivakumar was dropped without a replacement from either the DAP or PKR, causing chagrin among some quarters as Tamil-Hindu voters had been the most enthusiastic supporters of Anwar.

The recent appointment of the chief executive officer of the Employees Provident Fund, Amir Hamzah, to the finance ministry was universally welcomed, given his experience in major government-linked companies like Tenaga Nasional and businesses under Petronas, and Shell. He would bring helpful experience and attention to policymaking, oversight and implementation. Key decisions, however, would undoubtedly continue to be made by Anwar. Indeed, the cabinet reshuffle may make little substantive difference to perceptions of government performance without changes to the prime minister's approach to leadership and governance.

The administration could expect further challenges. First, calls from UMNO to release former prime minister Najib Razak could increase, but doing so would further undermine the government's anti-corruption brand and alienate its supporters. Second, race relations have not improved and could worsen, as shown by how easily groups were provoked by incidents in Malaysia over the Israeli-Palestine debacle, with little give and take. Third, groups like the ruling coalitions in Sabah and Sarawak will continue to demand more power and resources under the aegis of implementing the terms of the Malaysia Agreement 1963. The new king and his ambitions for Malaysia and policy views would have to be handled carefully by the administration.

Meanwhile, experienced Perikatan leaders were adept at pointing to weaknesses in government policies and continued to undermine confidence in the government by warning of impending defections. While PAS may be building up younger leaders like Dr Samsuri Mokhtar for national office, it would need to do more to gain broad national acceptance. It did not offer any serious alternative budget or comprehensive plan to develop the economy. It was better known nationally for its objections to pop concerts, policing of the attire of non-Muslim females from Langkawi to Kota Baru, and promoting polygamy to address the issue of single women.

In 2024, the government that was primarily centred on Anwar would have to offer a more effective and policy-oriented governing team to shore up its fiscal position, stimulate growth, increase jobs and wages, and mollify its various constituencies—from rating agencies to the civil service, rural communities, the middle class and lower-income voters.

Notes

1. Mohd Amin Jalil, "PH-BN Partnership Not the Main Reason Why Voters Chose PN: Loke", *New Straits Times*, 15 August 2023, https://www.nst.com.my/news/politics/2023/08/943203/ph-bn-partnership-not-main-reason-why-voters-chose-pn-loke.

2. Hajar Umira Md Zaki, "In Seventh Term, DPM Zahid Says 'At End of Service' as MP", *Malay Mail Online*, 5 November 2023, https://www.malaymail.com/news/malaysia/2023/11/05/in-seventh-term-dpm-zahid-says-at-end-of-service-as-mp/100363.

3. Mike Yeo, "Malaysia Adds Funds to Troubled Littoral Combat Ship Program", *DefenseNews*, 30 May 2023, https://www.defensenews.com/naval/2023/05/30/malaysia-adds-funds-to-troubled-littoral-combat-ship-program/.

4. Bridget Welsh, "On Hold: A Year of Anwar – Part 2", *Malaysiakini*, 29 November 2023, https://www.malaysiakini.com/columns/688323.

5. Bersih, "Press Release: Reforms at Snail's Pace: First Year Assessment of the Unity Government on Electoral and Institutional Reforms, 2022–2023", 23 November 2023, https://bersih.org/2023/11/23/reforms-at-snails-pace-first-year-assessment-of-the-unity-government-on-electoral-and-institutional-reforms-2022-2023/.

6. Andrew Ong, "Spoils of War: Sharing the Loot, Madani-style", *Malaysiakini*, 23 November 2023, https://www.malaysiakini.com/news/687525.

7. Shahrin Aizat Noorshahrizam, "Religious Affairs Minister Says Anwar Administration Will Table Controversial RUU 355 Once Cabinet Approves", *Malay Mail Online*, 25 May 2023, https://www.malaymail.com/news/malaysia/2023/05/25/religious-affairs-minister-says-anwar-administration-will-table-controversial-ruu-355-once-cabinet-approves/70975.

8. Hazlin Hassan, "Malaysians See Lower Profits, Cut Travelling, amid Weaker Ringgit", *Straits Times*, 12 November 2023, https://www.straitstimes.com/asia/se-asia/malaysians-see-lower-profits-cut-travelling-amid-weaker-ringgit.

9. "Malaysia Bags Investments Worth RM63.02b in US, Says PM Anwar" (Bernama), *Malay Mail Online*, 18 November 2023, https://www.malaymail.com/news/malaysia/2023/11/18/malaysia-bags-investments-worth-rm6302b-in-us-says-pm-anwar/102751.

10. Ministry of Foreign Affairs of Malaysia, "Press Release: Malaysia's Position on the South China Sea", 8 April 2023, https://www.kln.gov.my/web/guest/-/malaysia-s-position-on-the-south-china-sea#:~:text=Malaysia%27s%20position%20on%20the%20South%20China%20Sea%20is%20consistent%20and,depicted%20by%20our%201979%20Map.

11. Shannon Teoh, "Malaysia's 5G Future in Choppy Waters as Geopolitics, Commercial Interests Collide", *Straits Times*, 23 October 2023, https://www.straitstimes.com/asia/se-asia/malaysia-s-5g-future-in-choppy-waters-as-geopolitics-commercial-interests-collide.

12. Mergawati Zulfakar, "When Engagement Is Seen as a Threat", *The Star*, 5 November 2023, https://www.thestar.com.my/opinion/columnists/2023/11/05/when-engagement-is-seen-as-a-threat.

13. "PM: Malaysia, US to Formulate Plan to Further Strengthen Vital Bilateral Ties" (Bernama), *The Star*, 15 November 2023, https://www.thestar.com.my/news/nation/2023/11/15/pm-malaysia-us-to-formulate-plan-to-further-strengthen-vital-bilateral-ties.

14. Zarrah Morden, "Merdeka Center: PM Anwar's Approval Rating at 50pc, Driven by Concerns over Economy", *Malay Mail Online*, 22 November 2023, https://www.malaymail.com/news/malaysia/2023/11/22/merdeka-center-pm-anwars-approval-rating-at-50pc-dissatisfaction-on-the-rise/103511.

15. Hazlin Hassan, "Malaysia to Allow Visa-Free Entry for China, India Citizens: PM Anwar", *Straits Times*, 26 November 2023, https://www.straitstimes.com/asia/se-asia/malaysia-to-allow-visa-free-entry-for-china-india-citizens-pm-anwar.

16. Ariel Tan, "Malaysia PM Anwar's Latest Cabinet Reshuffle Is No Course Correction, but an Attempt to Maintain Power", *Today Online*, 20 December 2023, https://www.todayonline.com/commentary/commentary-malaysia-pm-anwars-latest-cabinet-reshuffle-no-course-correction-attempt-maintain-power-2329336.

The Malaysian Economy under the Anwar Administration

Cassey Lee

The Malaysian economy has made a steady recovery from the 2020–21 pandemic. As a trade-dependent country, Malaysia has benefited but also suffered from the vagaries of the global economy. The surge in demand for electrical and electronic exports cushioned the adverse shocks during the Covid-19 pandemic. But adverse global headwinds in the post-pandemic period constrained Malaysia's economic performance in 2023. The economic environment for the past year has been a fairly uncertain one with the export sector remaining relatively weak and food inflation continuing to linger.

Anwar Ibrahim, who became Malaysia's prime minister and finance minister in November 2022, has had a year to steer the Malaysian economy amidst the evolving economic uncertainties. Under his leadership, the "Unity Government", which is made up of a coalition of diverse political parties, has introduced and launched a number of economic initiatives and policies to enhance the country's economic performance. This includes the Madani Economy, a broad policy framework that encapsulates Anwar's economic aspirations and vision for the country. As the Anwar administration has only been in power for a year, a number of the economic policies that were launched during this period were initiated under previous administrations but finalized under the current government.

This essay provides an analysis of Malaysia's economic performance and the government policy responses during the first year of the Anwar administration. It will assess the government's economic initiatives and policies, which include macroeconomic stabilization policies for the short to medium term as well as longer-term economic policies.

The outline of this essay is as follows. The next section will examine Malaysia's macroeconomic performance and the government's stabilization policies. Some

CASSEY LEE is Senior Fellow and Coordinator of the Regional Economic Studies Programme at the ISEAS – Yusof Ishak Institute, Singapore.

of the long-term challenges facing the economy and the government's policy initiatives to address them are discussed after that. The final section concludes.

Macroeconomic Performance and Stabilization Policies

Macroeconomic Performance

The Anwar administration inherited an economy that was on a weakening trend. Economic growth had been on a downward trajectory for three consecutive quarters from the second quarter of 2022 to the fourth quarter of 2022 (Figure 1). But the pace of economic growth gradually began to pick up in the subsequent nine months up to September 2023. This resurgence in economic growth was driven initially by domestic sources (primarily consumption in the first and second quarters of 2023) but later by net exports (in the third quarter of 2023) (Figure 2). Government expenditures also played an important role in the third quarter of 2023, suggesting the impact of fiscal stimulus in the latter period of the Anwar administration.

The recovery in the labour market has been more consistent since the third quarter of 2021. The unemployment rate in September 2023 was around 3.4 per cent, which is only slightly above pre-pandemic levels. Across the different age groups, the unemployment rate amongst older workers (55 and above) worsened in the nine months leading to September 2023. Inflation gradually declined during the first year of the Anwar administration (Table 1). The inflation rate has dipped

FIGURE 1
Real GDP Growth (%, q/q, seasonally adjusted)

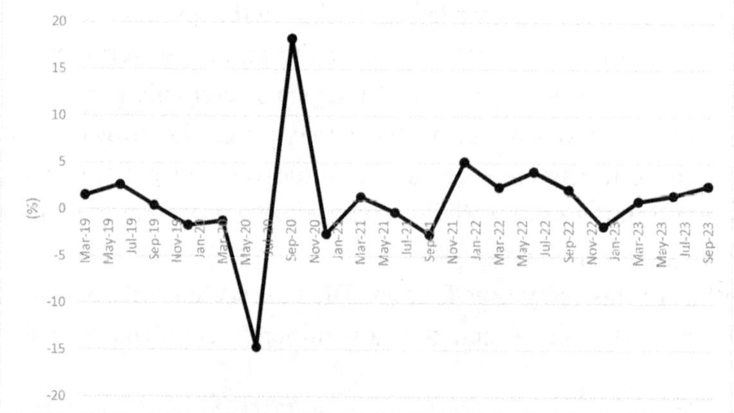

Source: Department of Statistics, Malaysia.

FIGURE 2
Share of Real GDP Change by Expenditure Type

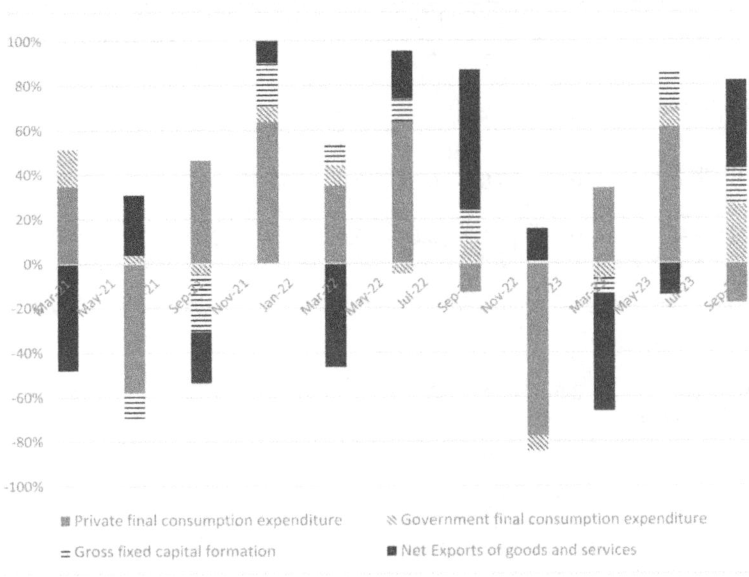

Source: Department of Statistics, Malaysia.

below 2 per cent in the later months of the year. Food inflation has also declined significantly from 6.7 per cent in February 2023 to 3.6 per cent in October 2023. Despite statistical evidence of the decline in inflation, the cost of living remains a major public concern. This can be attributed to the cumulative and ratchet effects of price increases, especially in the case of food items.

Stabilization Policies

The two key economic stabilization policies available to the Malaysian government are fiscal and monetary. In terms of fiscal policy, the Anwar-led government presided over two annual budgets (Budget 2023 and Budget 2024). Budget 2023 was delayed because of the change in government. Originally, Budget 2023 was tabled in the Malaysian parliament on 7 October 2022. However, the budget was not ratified following the dissolution of the parliament on 10 October 2022 to pave the way for the fifteenth general election (GE15). As a stop-gap measure, a temporary budget—the Consolidate Fund Bill 2022—was passed in December, primarily to cover the operating expenditures of the government (Figure 3). A revised budget—the Supply Bill 2023—was finally passed in February 2023, followed by the smaller Supplementary Supply Bill 2023. The disruptions in fiscal

TABLE 1
Inflation Rate in 2023

	Jan	Feb	Mar	Apr	May	Jun	Jul	Aug	Sep	Oct
Total	3.7	3.7	3.4	3.3	2.8	2.4	2	2	1.9	1.8
Food & non-alcoholic beverages	6.7	7	6.9	6.3	5.9	4.7	4.4	4.1	3.9	3.6
Alcoholic beverages & tobacco	0.8	0.8	0.6	0.6	0.7	0.6	0.5	0.5	0.7	0.6
Clothing & footwear	0.5	0.4	0.5	0.5	0.4	0.1	0.1	0	0.1	0
Housing, water, electricity, gas & other fuels	1.5	1.7	1.6	1.6	1.8	1.8	1.7	1.6	1.6	1.6
Furnishings, household equipment & routine household maintenance	3.5	3.4	3.1	3	2.7	2.3	1.9	1.7	1.5	1.4
Health	1.6	1.8	2.2	2.1	1.9	2	2	2.4	2.2	2.4
Transport	4	3.7	2.4	2.3	1	0	-0.4	0	-0.1	0
Communication	-1.4	-1.4	-1.4	-1.4	-3.7	-3.6	-3.7	-3.7	-3.7	-3.7
Recreation services & culture	2.7	1.7	1.9	1.8	1.8	1.6	1.1	1	0.6	0.7
Education	1.3	1.6	1.7	1.6	1.9	1.9	2	2.1	2	2.1
Restaurants & hotels	6.8	7.4	7.2	6.6	6.7	5.4	5	4.7	4.4	4.6
Miscellaneous goods & services	2.3	2.5	2.1	2.5	2.9	2.6	2.6	2.4	2.5	2.3
CPI without fuel	3.9	4	3.8	3.6	3.3	2.8	2.5	2.4	2.3	2.1

Source: Department of Statistics, Malaysia.

allocation and expenditures clearly affected the government's ability to stabilize the economy via fiscal expenditures. Fiscal stimulus via government expenditures was relatively muted in the last quarter of 2022 and first quarter of 2023 (Figure 2). Fiscal expenditures subsequently surged, especially in the third quarter of 2023.

Even though fiscal policy under the Anwar administration has been expansionary in nature, the government has been conservative. The federal government's overall deficit as a percentage of GDP declined from 6 per cent in 2022 to 5 per cent in 2023 (Table 2). This figure is projected to decline further to 4 per cent in 2024.

Monetary policy has been an important macroeconomic stabilization tool during the first year of the Anwar administration. Malaysia's central bank, Bank Negara Malaysia (BNM), is fairly independent of the government in matters of monetary policy. The central bank had progressively increased interest rates between May 2022 and May 2023 (Figure 4). BNM has not changed

FIGURE 3
Budget Allocation, 2023–24

Source: Ministry of Finance.

TABLE 2
Budget Outlook, 2022–24

	2022	*2023*	*2024*
Revenue	294,357	303,200	307,600
Operating expenditure	292,693	300,140	303,800
Current balance	1,664	3,060	3,800
Development expenditure	70,167	96,300	89,200
Covid-19 Fund	30,979		
Overall balance	−99,482	−93,240	−85,400
Deficit (% of GDP)	−6	−5	−4
Federal government debt (% GDP)	−60	−62	

Source: Ministry of Finance.

the interest rate since May 2023, when the country's inflation rate dipped below 3 per cent. The US Federal Reserve only paused its interest rate in July 2023. The aggressive interest rate hikes in the United States have weakened the Malaysian ringgit since March 2022. In the first ten months of 2023, the Malaysian ringgit depreciated by close to 10 per cent against the greenback. The option of strengthening the country's exchange rate by increasing the interest rate was not likely to be an attractive one as inflation was under control and economic growth remained uncertain during the past year. Furthermore, the cycle of ringgit depreciation during the January–October 2023 period brought the ringgit/USD exchange rate (4.76 MYR/USD in October 2023) back to the

FIGURE 4
Interest Rates and Exchange Rate

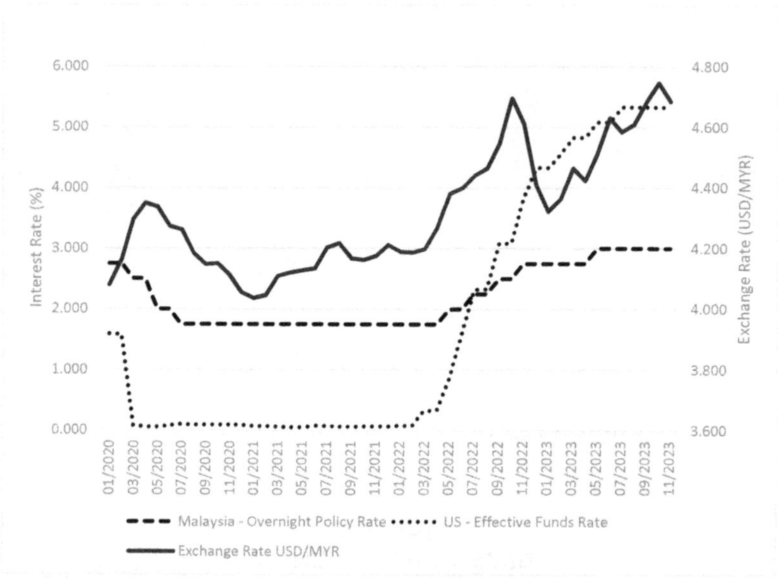

Source: CEIC.

previous level experienced after the previous cycle of ringgit depreciation (4.70 MYR/USD in October 2022).

Overall, the use of fiscal policy by the Anwar administration to stabilize the Malaysian economy has been affected by the political transition process. The timing of the general elections delayed the fiscal stimulus rollout. The ringgit also went through another cycle of depreciation in the first ten months of the Anwar administration. This likely can be attributed partly to the cumulative effects of the aggressive rate hikes of the Federal Reserve and the relatively stable and lower interest rate in Malaysia. There is no reason to believe that the Anwar administration could have done better to stabilize the Malaysian economy in its first year. The more difficult problems to tackle are the long-term challenges facing the Malaysian economy. These are discussed next.

Long-Term Challenges and Policy Responses

Economic Challenges in the Long-Term

The Malaysian economy has undergone significant structural changes since the Asian financial crisis in 1997. The country's average growth rate has experienced a long-term decline for the past twenty years (Figure 5). The Malaysian economy

FIGURE 5
Economic Growth

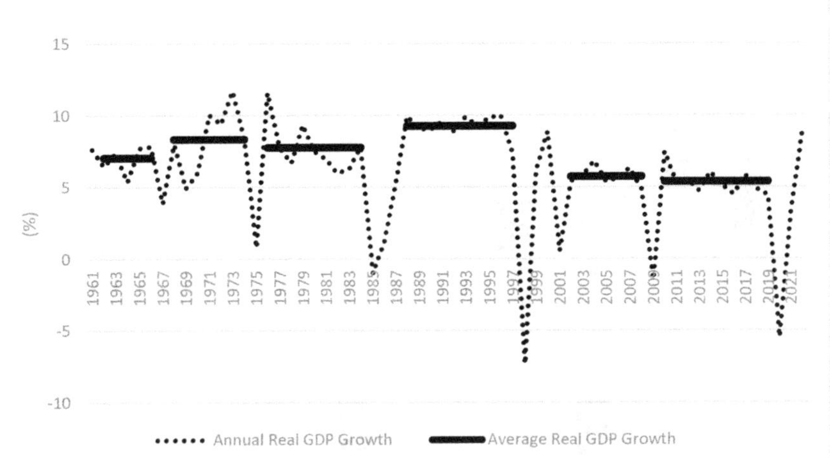

Source: World Bank.

grew at an average annual rate of 5.4 per cent between 2010 and 2019. This was lower than the 9.3 per cent growth rate achieved between 1988 and 1997.

The slowdown in economic growth is caused by low levels of capital formation (investment) and innovation (total factor productivity, or TFP). This can be seen from a growth accounting analysis of Malaysia (Figure 6). The largest contributor to growth is non-IT capital formation, which declined significantly after 2000. The rate of capital formation as a share of GDP fluctuated between 17 and 26 per cent in the period after 1999. The rapid growth in the 1970s, 1980s and 1990s was driven by two great surges in capital formation during 1976–83 and 1987–97 (Figure 7). There has also been a long-term decline in domestic savings since 2008. Though aggregate gross savings as a share of GDP have increased a little since the Covid-19 pandemic, the rate of lifetime savings for retirement is very low amongst lower income workers. In a recent parliamentary session, the deputy finance minister stated that about 35 per cent of the 274,715 members of the Employees Provident Fund (EPF) that are aged 54 and above had less than RM10,000 in their savings in January 2023.[1] Another media reported that 51.5 per cent of EPF members under the age of 55 (nearly 6.7 million people) had less than RM10,000 in their accounts at the end of 2022.[2]

The slowdown in the Malaysian economy has also been accompanied by another important change—namely, deindustrialization—which entails a relative decline in the importance of the manufacturing sector in the economy. The manufacturing sector's share of GDP peaked near 31 per cent around 1999–2004

FIGURE 6
Source of Economic Growth

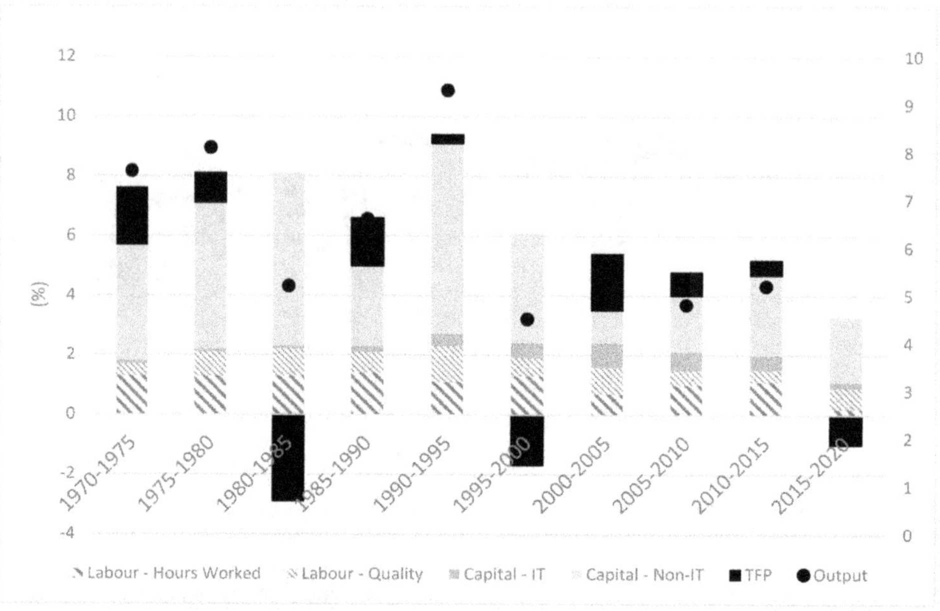

Source: Asian Productivity Organization.

FIGURE 7
Investment, Savings and FDI

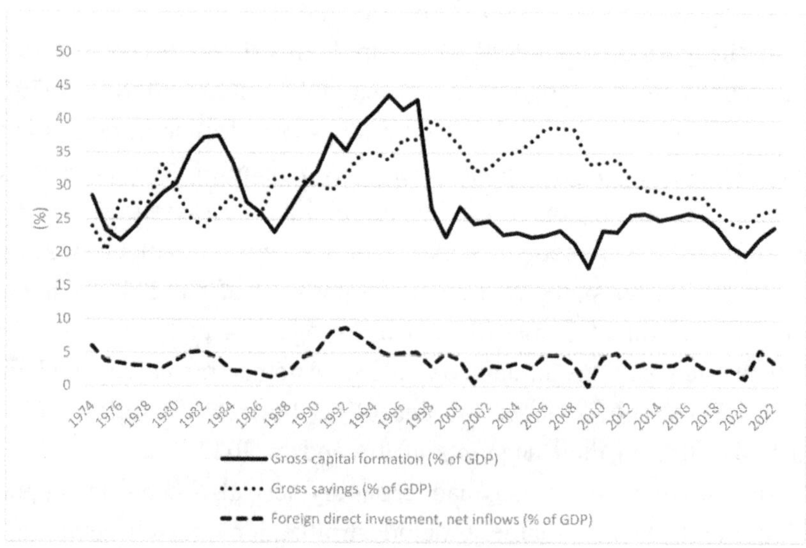

Source: World Bank.

FIGURE 8
Sectoral Composition of GDP

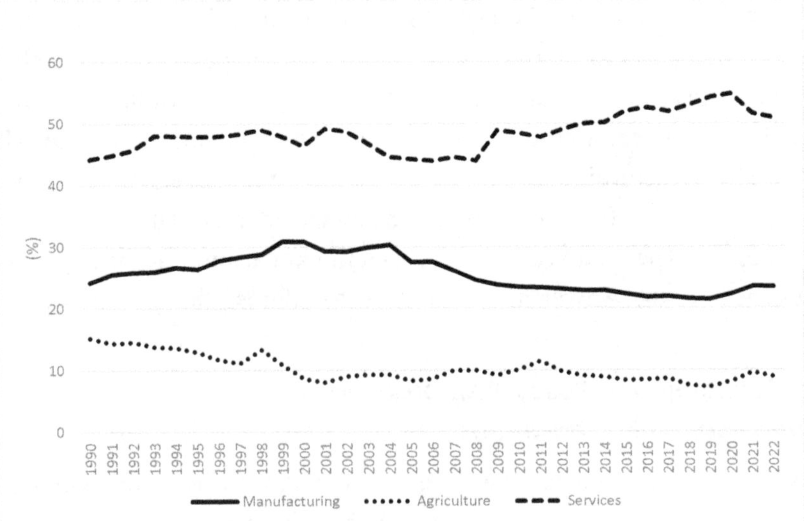

FIGURE 9
Exports and Imports as Share of GDP

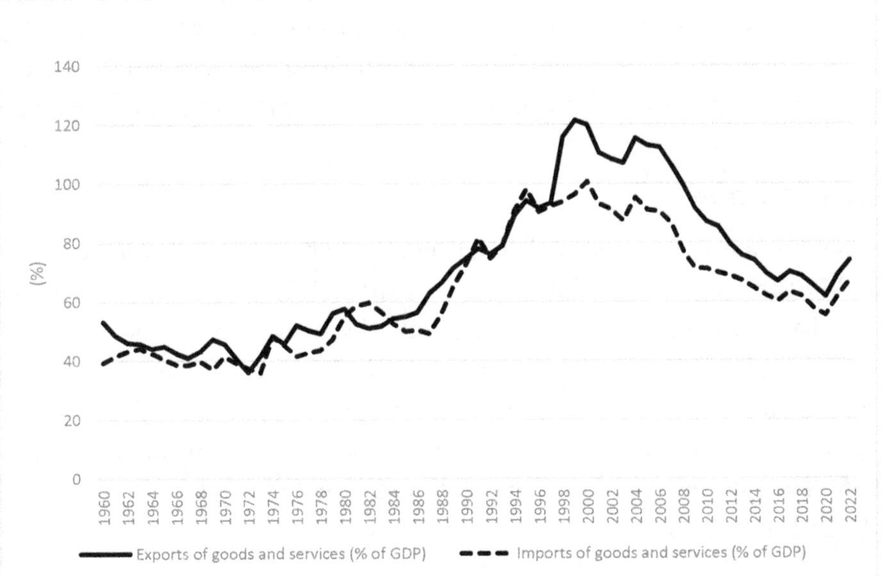

and declined to 21 per cent in 2019 (Figure 8). As Malaysia's manufacturing sector is fairly export-intensive, the country's exports-to-GDP share has declined from a peak of 121 per cent in 1999 to 62 per cent in 2020 (Figure 9). The size of the difference between exports and imports (net exports) has also shrunk. All the evidence suggests a decline in exports as a driver of Malaysia's growth.

The long-term economic challenges are quite daunting for the Malaysian economy. The structural change that underpins the deceleration of economic growth over the past two decades are deep-seated and will require significant policy responses. The next section examines the key economic strategies that have been launched by the Anwar administration to address these challenges.

Madani Economy and Policy Responses to Long-Term Economic Challenges

The Anwar administration has launched a number of economic policies since it came to power in October 2022. As a number of these policies required some time to formulate, many of them were first initiated by the previous government(s). Furthermore, the previous government was led by the Barisan Nasional (BN) coalition, which remains a member of the Unity Government. It is also not known whether the policies that were initiated earlier were extensively revised by the Anwar administration prior to their launching. Thus, the direct and full attribution of these policies to the Anwar administration can be a tricky issue. Nevertheless, it is probably fair to say that the Anwar administration bears responsibility for these policies once they are launched during their tenure (presumably after they receive cabinet approval). Each of these policies is examined chronologically.

Malaysia Madani

Malaysia Madani is a vision and broad policy framework that was launched by Prime Minister Anwar Ibrahim on 19 January 2023. "Madani" is a normative concept that envisions a society underpinned by principles of social justice and democracy.[3] The concept can be traced back to as early as the 1990s when Anwar was minister of finance (1991–98) and deputy prime minister (1993–98). Anwar incorporated moral dimensions into Malaysia's federal budget from 1992 to 1996. The concept of Madani Society (Masyarakat Madani) appeared in the Supply Bill of 1995.[4]

> In October 2022, Anwar published a book titled *Membangun Negara Madani* (Developing the Madani nation) outlining his vision and policy

> framework for the Madani Society.[5] The vision for the Madani Society
> is articulated as follows: To build a sustainable and prosperous Malaysia
> based on care and compassion, mutual respect, innovation, and trust, where
> inclusiveness and equality are embraced by the whole nation—ultimately
> a just Malaysian society based on analyses of each of the pillars across
> eight dimensions: economic/financial, legal, institutional, educational,
> social, cultural, urban, and rural.[6]

The policy framework for the Madani Society is structured by juxtaposing the six drivers of Madani (i.e., sustainability, care and compassion, respect, innovation, prosperity and trust) against its eight pillars (i.e., economic/financial, legal, institutional, educational, social, cultural, urban and rural). Thus, the book contains a total of forty-eight sections (six drivers times eight pillars) of policy recommendations and a list of thirty-six policies that should be given priority. Some of the thirty-six policy recommendations are very specific (e.g., abolish FELDA settlers' debts), while others are very general.

With its official launch, the Madani concept became an official mantra of the Anwar administration. The six drivers (now re-labelled as core values) remained intact in the official description of the concept. Efforts were made to define Madani as well as explain its mission and vision:[7]

> Definition: "MADANI is a synthesis of the Malaysian style, combining
> existing practices with new methods designed to deal with new issues
> and uncertainties. MADANI's six core values are broken down into an
> interrelated and integrated framework of policies and philosophies, with
> each reinforcing the others. MADANI was inspired based on the concept
> of willingness to accept change, taking into account the suggestions of all
> levels of society with the desire for recovery through substantive reforms
> for the sake of a more advanced and prosperous Malaysia."
>
> Mission: "Our goal is to transform Malaysia into a more prosperous and
> developed country based on six MADANI values through trust between
> the government and the people, a policy of transparency and cooperation."
>
> Vision: "Shaping the future of Malaysia with all the potential that exists
> by taking into account all forms of change that change the world, and
> aspiring to navigate Malaysia in the complicated post-normal era through
> adjusting the language, concepts and culture of local wisdom."

Even though the core elements of the Madani book became an official narrative of the government, the policy recommendations in the book were not systematically translated into government policies. This is understandable as the book is the product of one person (and his team) but government policies are formulated across ministries.

Budget 2023

The budget for Malaysia's federal government was first tabled in parliament on 7 October 2022. The budget was not ratified, however, as the parliament was dissolved on 10 October 2022 to pave the way for the fifteenth general election (GE15), which was held on 19 November 2022. Following Anwar Ibrahim's appointment as Malaysia's tenth prime minister on 24 November 2022, his ministerial cabinet was formed on 2 December and the deputy ministers were appointed on 9 December 2022. To ensure continued funding for the operating expenditures of the government, an interim first part of the new Budget 2023 was first tabled in parliament on 19 December 2022 (under the "Consolidated Fund [Expenditure on Account] Act 2022). The interim budget was made up mostly of operating expenditure. Most ministries were allocated about fifty per cent of the annual operating expenditures that were proposed in the earlier budget (tabled on 7 October 2022). Thus, it is obvious that the Anwar administration did not have sufficient time to craft a new budget that reflects its economic priorities. Two months later, on 21 February 2023, the second-part of the 2023 budget—now re-labelled as the "Madani Budget"—was tabled in parliament.

As with the interim budget, the Anwar administration still did not have sufficient time to craft a new budget from scratch, nor did it have to, as the new cabinet included political leaders who were members of the previous government. The previous finance minister from the Ismail Sabri cabinet, Tengku Zafrul, is now the minister of investment, trade and industry in Anwar's cabinet.

Thematically, the Madani Budget stated its emphasis on the following three pillars: (1) inclusive and sustainable economic growth; (2) institutional reforms and good governance to restore confidence; and (3) combating inequality through social justice. Comparing the original budget proposal and the Madani Budget, certain continuities and differences may be seen. This can be attributed to the emphasis on the three pillars. In the first pillar, the emphasis on an expansionary and responsible budget is consistent with the previous government's fiscal stance. In the case of the second pillar, a major departure is the governance of public procurement. These included the cancellation of the RM15 billion flood mitigation projects that were awarded by the previous government through direct negotiations. For the third pillar of social justice, the practice of the previous government of providing income support to low-income families and subsidies for essential goods was continued in the Madani Budget. But unlike the previous government, the Anwar administration has begun to make the tax regime gradually more progressive by increasing the tax rate for higher-income groups.

The first three months represented a steep learning curve for the Anwar administration in economic policymaking. The following months would witness continuing efforts by the government to clarify and expand its economic agenda. This began with the formulation and launch of another concept; namely, "Madani Economy". This is discussed next.

Madani Economy

The experience of revising Budget 2023 would have highlighted the need for a broad framework for economic policymaking. This policy framework was provided in Anwar Ibrahim's speech on the Madani Economy of 27 July 2023. The Madani Economy speech provides a diagnosis of the economic challenges facing Malaysia. Short-term challenges (the next one year) include the high cost of living and hardcore poverty. For the medium term, the key economic challenges are slower economic growth, declining investment, and lack of competitiveness. In response to these challenges, the policy focus for the medium-term period (the next ten years) is (1) to strengthen the national economy (to establish Malaysia as a Leading Asian Economy) and (2) to elevate the quality of life of the people (Table 3).

How does the Madani Economy relate to Malaysia Madani? The two medium-term policy focus areas encapsulate two intertwined elements of the Madani concept: enlarging economic wealth while ensuring an equitable distribution of benefits. Complementing these two focus areas are two types of medium-term reforms related to governance and fiscal matters. To measure progress in policy implementation, the Madani Economy lists seven aspirational quantitative targets (Table 3). Finally, the Madani Economy provides a listing of policies and actions to address the short- and medium-term challenges.

Overall, the Madani Economy is an interim broad economic policy framework. The list of aspirational targets is fairly limited and, to some extent, narrow. In addition, the policies and actions listed do not correspond directly to the aspirational targets. Subsequent policies are likely to expand the scope of application of the ideas promulgated in the Madani Economy and Madani Society. These include the National Energy Transition Roadmap, the New Industrial Master Plan and the Mid-Term Review of the 12th Malaysia Plan. These are reviewed next.

National Energy Transition Roadmap

Malaysia has been promoting greater use of green energy for more than two decades, beginning with the Five Fuel Diversification Policy in 2000. This was

TABLE 3
Policy Framework of the Madani Economy

Economic Challenges	Targets	Policy Focus/Actions
Short-Term: Cost of living Hardcore poverty	Eradicating hardcore poverty Expedite execution of projects for schools and dilapidated clinics	Income generation activities* Affordable food** Schools and clinics Basic infrastructure (in less-developed states)
Medium-Term: Growth Investment	Size of economy ranking: 38 to top-30 Competitiveness ranking: 27 to top-12	**Focus 1: Leading Asian Economy** Economic restructuring Economic integration Investment facilitation, promotion and incentives Local start-ups & SMEs Financial market reforms Islamic finance Energy transition Agriculture—food security
Wages	Labour share of income: 35% to 45% Female LFPR: 53% to 60% HDI: 62 to top-25	**Focus 2: Elevating Quality of Life for the People** Labour market reforms—minimum wage, working environment, foreign labour Assistance to marginalized groups Regional industrial policy Competitive, liveable and sustainable urban centres Childcare facilities Expansion of social protection Healthcare reforms Education reforms Basic infrastructure Affordable housing

Governance Reforms	Targets	Policy Focus/Actions
Medium-Term: Performance Accountability Transparency	Corruption Perception Index: 47 to top-25	Special parliamentary select committee Media freedom
Public service delivery		Digitalization—GovTech Malaysia Implementation and improvements driven by STAR Taskforce

Fiscal Reforms	Targets	Policy Focus/Actions
Medium-Term: Fiscal reforms	Fiscal deficit: 5% to 3% or less	Efficient and targeted subsidy mechanisms

Notes: * Inisiatif Pendapatan Rakyat (IPR); ** Payung RAHMAH.
Source: Cassey Lee, "Will Anwar's 'Madani Economy' Narrative Strengthen His Economic Leadership?", *Fulcrum*, 10 August 2023.

TABLE 4
Targets in National Energy Policy 2022–2040 (DTN)
and National Energy Transition Roadmap (NETR)

Levers	Sector and Key Driver	2040 DTN	2050 NETR
Energy efficiency	Industry and commercial energy efficiency savings (%)	11	23
	Residential energy efficiency savings (%)	10	20
Renewable energy	Coal share of installed capacity (%)	19	0
	RE share of installed capacity (%)	41	70
	Total installed capacity of RE (MW)	18,431	—
Hydrogen	Green hydrogen production (MTPA)	—	Up to 2.5
	Green hydrogen feedstock phase off (%)	—	100
	Hydrogen hubs	—	3
Bioenergy	Biofuel capacity (billion litres)	—	3.5
	Bioenergy power generation (GW)	—	1.4
Green mobility	Urban public transport modal share (%)	50	60
	xEV (4W) share of fleet (%)	38	80
	E2W share of fleet (%)	—	80
	Light vehicle fuel economy	—	−30
	Heavy transport fuel economy	—	−24
	Biofuel blending for heavy transport	B30	B30
	Hydrogen penetration for heavy transport (%)	—	5
	LNG penetration as alternative fuel in marine transport (%)	25	—
	Green fuel penetration in marine transport	—	40
	SAF blending mandate by 2050 (%)	—	47
Carbon capture, utilization and storage	Number of CCUS clusters (%)	—	3–6
	CO_2 storage capacity (Mtpa)	—	40–80

Sources: National Energy Policy 2022–2040 (p. 27) and National Energy Transition Roadmap (p. 22).

followed by the introduction of the National Renewable Policy & Action Plan in 2010. The National Energy Policy 2022–2040 (Dasar Tenaga Nasional, or DTN) was launched by the previous prime minister, Ismail Sabri, in September 2022, a month before the general election. The goal of the DTN is to achieve the Low Carbon Nation Aspiration by 2040.[8] Nine selected targets are listed in the DTN. To achieve these targets, a total of twelve strategies and thirty-one action plans are listed.

The Anwar administration launched the National Energy Transition Roadmap (NETR) on 29 August 2023. The goal of the NETR is to accelerate the process of energy transition in Malaysia. Energy transition entails a structural shift of energy systems towards cleaner sources of energy. A comparison between DTN and NETR suggests that there is policy continuity between the two. The NETR extends the time horizon for energy transition from 2040 to 2050. Two targets in the DTN have been dropped and the number of targets has been increased to twenty-one (Table 4).

The NETR demonstrates that there was continuity in policymaking in the first year of the Anwar administration. It is a significant long-term policy initiative that will continue to evolve in the future. Though the time horizon for the NETR is very long (around twenty-eight years), the policy will have important medium-term impacts on consumers and industries.

New Industrial Master Plan 2030

The Malaysian economy has been deindustrializing for more than two decades, resulting in a decline in the share of manufacturing in employment as well as national income. The New Industrial Master Plan 2030 (NIMP2030) was launched by Anwar Ibrahim on 1 September 2023 with the goal of revitalizing the country's manufacturing sector. Technically, the NIMP2030 is the country's fourth industrial master plan. It provides a medium-term policy framework for the development of the manufacturing sector until 2030. The vision for the NIMP2030 is encapsulated by six goals: (1) a competitive industry with high economic complexity, (2) high income and skilled workforce, (3) strong domestic linkages, (4) well-developed new and existing industry clusters, (5) balanced and inclusive participation, and (6) sustainable development. The first five of these goals are drawn from two earlier policy initiatives under previous governments; namely, the New Investment Policy (October 2022, under the Ismail Sabri administration), which is anchored by the New Investment Aspirations policy (April 2021, under the Muhyiddin administration).

TABLE 5
Structure of New Industrial Master Plan 2030

Goals					
Increase economic complexity	Create high value job opportunities	Extend domestic linkages	Develop new and existing clusters	Improve Inclusivity	Enhance ESG practices
Targets					
High-tech manufacturing and services value-added share of GDP: 15% GERD to GDP: 3.5%	Number of jobs created: 700,000 Median salary: RM4,510	Share of export-oriented SMEs: 25% Domestic value-added in manufacturing: 65%	Global market share in high-tech manufacturing exports: 6% Global market share in green and digital exports: 4%	Realized FDI and DDI share of contribution to state GDP: 25% Manufacturing value-added in less-developed states: 30–35%	Sustainalytics ESG Index: 75–100 (Grade A) Reduction in carbon emission intensity based on NDC goals: 45%
Missions					
Advance economic complexity	Tech up for a digitally vibrant nation	Push for Net Zero		Safeguard economic security and inclusivity	
5 Strategies 15 Action plans	4 Strategies 8 Action plans	4 Strategies 10 Action plans		4 Strategies 10 Action plans	
Enablers					
Mobilize financing ecosystem	Foster talent development and attraction	Establish best-in-class investor journey		Introduce whole-of-nation governance for ease of doing business framework	
4 Strategies and 19 Action Plans					

Source: Author's compilation based on the New Industrial Master Plan.

The impact of NIMP2030 is to be measured against three macroeconomic annual growth targets; namely, manufacturing value-added (6.5 per cent), employment (2.3 per cent) and the median wage (9.6 per cent). In addition, two targets have been assigned for each of the six goals. To achieve these targets, the NIMP2030 will be implemented via a "Mission-based approach" that focuses on strategies which cut across sectors. A total of twenty-one strategies and sixty-two action plans have been proposed across the four missions, supported by four key enablers (Table 5). Even the mission-based approach involves cross-sectoral implementation: a total of twenty-one sectors have been identified, with five being designated priority sectors. These priority sectors include aerospace, chemical, electrical and electronics (E&E), pharmaceutical and medical devices. In addition, four new growth areas have been identified. The new growth areas, which are consistent with energy transition, include advanced materials, electric vehicles, renewable energy, and carbon capture, utilization and storage (CCUS).

Overall, the NIMP2030 is a comprehensive and holistic industrial master plan. The process of drafting the master plan began well before the current government came to power. As with the other policies launched by the Anwar administration, the master plan reflects the ongoing work by bureaucrats. The mission-based approach is a new approach, and it will be some time before the effectiveness of this approach is known.

Mid-term Review of the Twelfth Malaysia Plan, 2021–2025 (12 September 2023)

The medium-term development strategies of Malaysia have historically been outlined in the country's five-year plans, also known as the Malaysia Plans. These plans are typically reviewed and sometimes revised at the mid-point of their implementation period. The Anwar administration presented its mid-term review of the Twelfth Malaysia Plan, 2021–2025 (MTR12) on 12 September 2023. In the MTR12, the government has presented its policy proposals in terms of seventeen "Big Bolds" (see Table 6). The list of various strategies under these suggests that a number of key areas of focus and policy initiatives that were outlined in the Twelfth Malaysia Plan (MP12) have been maintained. These include the digital economy, E&E industry, housing and MSMEs.

There are some discernible changes in the MTR12. The Covid-19 pandemic has also affected the government's policy priorities, notably its emphasis on improving social protection and healthcare services. In addition, the National

Energy Transition Roadmap has also sharpened the focus on energy transition in the MTR12. Another significant change takes the form of a new emphasis on institutional reforms. These reforms are related to strengthening public service, reducing rent-seeking and corruption, and strengthening public finance. The approach taken by the Anwar administration in the MTR12 is both sensible and practical, especially given the time constraints and that the MP12 only has two more years (2024–25) to completion. Nevertheless, the MTR12 reflects some of the key priorities of the Anwar administration. This is further reflected in the budget for 2024.

Budget 2024

Budget 2024, which was tabled in parliament on 13 October 2023, is officially the Anwar administration's second annual budget for the federal government. But, as discussed earlier, the Anwar administration was not able to structure Budget 2023 because of time constraints. Hence, Budget 2024 is the first Federal Budget that it has had time to shape comprehensively. A key thrust of Budget 2024 is strengthening the country's public finances by increasing tax revenues and improving the efficiency of government expenditures. On the revenues side, the government announced an increase in the service tax rate (from 6 per cent to 8 per cent), imposed a new capital gains tax on gains from the disposal of unlisted shares of local companies (at 10 per cent), and a new tax on luxury goods (5 to 10 per cent). To further improve public finance, the government has also tabled the Public Finance and Fiscal Responsibility Bill 2023 (or the Fiscal Responsibility Act, FRA), which will improve the governance of public finance through greater transparency and accountability.

On the expenditures side, the government has begun to restructure the subsidy programmes to reduce their fiscal burden. The government currently provides subsidies to the population as well as financial assistance to the poor. These include fuel subsidies (RM50 billion), electricity (RM15 billion) and cash assistance (RM10 billion). In Budget 2024, the government has announced the removal of subsidies for electricity consumption for the top ten per cent of consumers with the highest electricity consumption. The subsidies for eggs and chicken have also been removed by floating the prices of these products. There are also plans to have a more targeted subsidy programme for petrol and gas in the second half of 2024. Overall, the priority of the Anwar administration in Budget 2024 has been to strengthen the country's public finance, which has deteriorated in the past and has also constrained the government's fiscal space.

TABLE 6
Big Bolds and Strategies in the Mid-term Review of the 12th Malaysia Plan

Big Bold	Strategies/Initiatives
1. Governance and institutional framework	Strengthen governance and integrity to rebuild trust and confidence of the people; Improve the institutional framework to enhance efficiency of public service delivery; Enhance the role of the Special Task Force on Agency Reform (STAR); Develop the Landslide Early Warning System (SAATR) to improve disaster management
2. Legislation related to corruption	Strengthen the regulatory framework to improve accountability and transparency; Introduce an integrity plan based on the core values of MADANI; Enact laws to combat rent-seeking
3. Fiscal sustainability and financial system	Introduce the fiscal responsibility act; Accelerate the drafting of the government procurement act; Broaden the revenue base; Realign surplus funds under federal statutory bodies and government-linked companies; Enhance cost-effective project implementation; Strengthen Malaysia as a global Islamic financial centre
4. HGHV industry based on energy transition	Implement National Energy Transition Roadmap (NETR); Create electricity exchange system to enable cross-border RE trading; Increase RE capacity—solar, hydro, bioenergy and hydrogen; Introduce road map for natural gas; Accelerate the preparation of a regulatory framework for carbon capture, utilization and storage (CCUS); Formulate a long-term low-emissions development strategy (LT-LEDS); Implement carbon pricing; Accelerate ESG adoption
5. Targeted subsidies	Retarget all types of subsidies, such as electricity, diesel and RON95; Develop data repository on households, Pangkalan Data Utama (PADU)
6. Enculturation of MADANI Society	Develop a progressive society; Build self-identity based on Rukun Negara; Fuel the spirit of nationalism and unity through the flagship Kembara Perpaduan programmes; Develop MADANI people by inculcating the elements and values of Maqasid Syariah; Enhance inclusive participation in sports
7. Social protection reform	Strengthen the national social protection system through a life cycle approach; Formulate guidelines on informal workers for more comprehensive social protection; Expand the Inisiatif Pendapatan Rakyat (IPR) programme to cover the hardcore poor and poor and the B40 to increase income
8. Housing for the people	Accelerate the transition from ownership concept to shelter; Introduce attractive and sustainable housing financing packages; Harness the potential of retirement villages
9. Strengthening healthcare services	Strengthen the financing of health protection; Expand the MADANI medical scheme; Introduce a leasing mechanism for the procurement of health equipment; Establish a national institute of mental health
10. Strengthening national security and defence	Enhance national border security; Strengthen readiness and capabilities in managing security threats; Establish Prison Incorporated as a coordinator in improving prisoner rehabilitation programmes
11. Digital- and technology-based HGHV industry	Accelerate digitalization through Government Technology (GovTech); Accelerate National Digital Identity implementation; Implement national-level digital leadership and upskilling programme; Strengthen tech start-up ecosystem—focusing on angel investors and seed funding; Strengthen the INNOVATHON programme as a platform to promote innovation

TABLE 6 (cont.)
Big Bolds and Strategies in the Mid-term Review of the 12th Malaysia Plan

Big Bold	Strategies/Initiatives
12. High value E&E HGHV industry	Strengthen front-end manufacturing ecosystem to accelerate industry transition towards higher value chain; Emphasize high-value-added activities in integrated circuit design, engineering design and wafer fabrication; Enhance quality investment that prioritizes advanced technology
13. HGHV agriculture and agro-based industry	Strengthen modernization in the agriculture sector through private investment to accelerate adoption of smart farming technology; Diversify agro-based industries to reduce dependency on food imports; Promote low-carbon agriculture practices; Expand implementation of the Program Inisiatif Usahawan Tani (INTAN) under IPR as a strategy to strengthen food supply chain and increase income
14. Rare earths HGHV industry	Develop a comprehensive business model for rare earths covering upstream, midstream and downstream; Prepare detailed mapping of rare earths resources in states with potential resources; Revise the National Mineral Policy 2 to support and set the direction of the mineral industry, including rare earths; Enhance research & development & commercialization & innovation (R&D&C&I) to promote local rare earths output and product
15. Empowering MSMEs and social enterprises	Integrate MSMEs into domestic and global supply chain; Promote alternative financing for MSMEs; Accelerate the productivity growth of MSMEs through technology adoption; Scale up MSMEs through smart ventures; Encourage social enterprises to venture into innovative social entrepreneurship projects; Optimise *waqf* potential for enterprise development
16. Streamlining the public transport network	Improve first- and last-mile connectivity through expansion of the Bus Rapid Transit (BRT) and intracity bus services; Strengthen passenger mobility data; Increase accessibility and connectivity to facilitate the better movement of people and goods; Implement green aviation by increasing the efficiency of air traffic management
17. Future-ready talent	Implement a progressive wage policy; Accelerate the implementation of multi-tier levy; Conduct continuous upskilling and reskilling; Introduce the Academy in Industry (AiI) programme as a government and industry collaboration platform

Source: Mid-term Review of the 12th Malaysia Plan.

Conclusions

The Malaysian economy grew modestly during the first year of the Anwar administration. The ability of the new government to stabilize the economy through government expenditures was severely constrained in the first few months because of the dissolution of the parliament to pave the way for general elections. This delayed the rollout of fiscal stimulus by several months. External developments vis-à-vis the federal reserve's monetary policies also drove a cycle of ringgit depreciation in the first ten months of the administration.

The Anwar administration had greater success in strengthening and shaping its economic narrative and policy framework. The first few months of the administration witnessed efforts to shape its economic policy narratives based on the Madani concept. These did not necessarily translate into concrete policies in the first few months, partly because of time constraints. In the latter part of its first year, substantive polices were announced, and these can be attributed to the work of the bureaucracy, which does not appear to have been disrupted by the political transition. The formulation of major medium to long-term policies was mostly undertaken under the leadership of the previous governments (led by Muhyiddin and Ismail Sabri) but was finally completed and launched under Anwar Ibrahim's leadership. These policies include the National Energy Transition Roadmap and the New Industrial Master Plan 2030.

The influence of the Anwar administration only emerged with the Mid-term Review of the Twelfth Malaysia Plan and Budget 2024. A major priority of the new government is the strengthening of public finance by increasing tax revenues and reducing subsidies by making them more targeted. These developments are likely to enhance the government's ability to better stabilize in the medium-term and restructure the economy for long-term growth in the future.

Notes

1. Tarrence Tan, Martin Carvalho, and Junaid Ibrahim, "35% of EPF Members at Age 54 Have below RM10,000 in Savings, Dewan Rakyat Told", *The Star*, 29 November 2023.
2. Derrick Paulo, "'Worst Policy Ever': Retirement Time Bomb after Malaysia's Pension Drawdowns amid Pandemic?", CNA Insider, 29 October 2023.
3. Mohd Faizal Musa, *The Evolution of Madani: How Different is 2.0 from 1.0*, Trends in Southeast Asia no. 18/2023 (Singapore: ISEAS – Yusof Ishak Institute, 2023).
4. Khoo Boo Teik, *The Making of Anwar Ibrahim's Humane Economy*, Trends in Southeast Asia no. 18/2020 (Singapore: ISEAS – Yusof Ishak Institute, 2020).
5. The English version of the book is titled *SCRIPT for a Better Malaysia: An Empowering Vision and Policy Framework for Action*.
6. Anwar Ibrahim, *SCRIPT for a Better Malaysia: An Empowering Vision and Policy Framework for Action* (Institut Darul Ehsan, 2022), p. 23.
7. Google translation from text at https://malaysiamadani.gov.my/pengenalan/.
8. Low Carbon Nation Aspiration 2040 provides "emphasis on low carbon policies and investments to increase adoption and pursue selective leadership in low carbon sectors, such as: (i) Endeavour to no new coal power plant amid increasing renewables share; (ii) Provide financing and incentives to drive energy efficiency practices to meet the targets; and (iii) Incentivise adoption of EVs, increasing public transport modal share, and fuel economy standards" (National Energy Policy, p. 28).

Myanmar

Myitkyina
Mandalay
Taunggyi
NAYPYITAW
Pyinmana
Yangon
Pathein

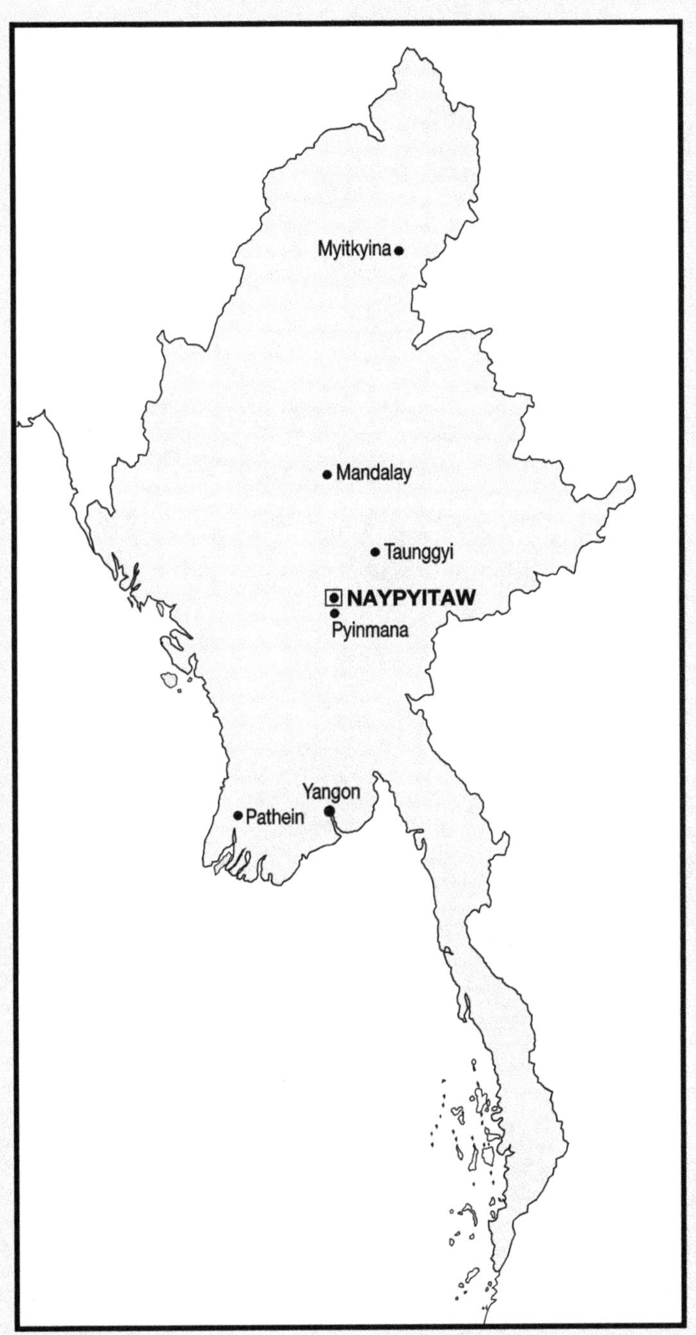

MYANMAR IN 2023:
Continued Emergency, the Transition to Strategic Terror and the Humiliation of the Military

Mary Callahan

Little will be remembered in the future—with perhaps the exceptions of intense Nay Pyi Taw political manoeuvring in January and the ramping up of deliberate mass attacks on civilians around the year—about the first ten months of 2023 in Myanmar. Instead, beginning on 27 October 2023, a shockingly successful anti-military operation launched by three much underestimated ethnic armed organizations (EAOs) in northern Myanmar led immediately to the fall of some of the most economically strategic towns, and over the next few weeks, the EAOs overran dozens of military commands, outposts and garrisons. Called "1027", the unforeseen weakness of Myanmar's Defence Services breathed life into hundreds, perhaps thousands, of cells of resistance fighters across the country. By 31 December 2023, thirty-four towns (mostly not townships) were emptied of officials associated with the State Administrative Council (SAC) and the military. On social media and even in junta-backed mainstream media, unprecedented expressions of humiliation and anger were aired by formerly pro-SAC channels on Telegram and other fora, but also from well-known retired military officers who have supported military rule since 2021. Indeed, for the first time in seventy years, the never-questioned idea held by members of the armed forces that the military was the only national institution that could hold the country together—an idea not shared by the opposition or much of the population anymore—came into question with exactly the constituency of military officers past and present who had never doubted it. Although the military is not on the verge of implosion, its "perpetual" institutional and political power is no longer a given among the officer corps.[1]

MARY CALLAHAN is an associate professor of international studies at the University of Washington and has carried out field research on and off in Myanmar for more than thirty years.

When Bad News Got to the "King"

In January 2023, there was considerable speculation among diplomats and some activists in the lead-up to the expiration of two years of emergency rule (as constitutionally stipulated) that the military junta would begin the process of establishing an interim authority to take power and hold elections in the coming year or in 2024. On 9 January, the Ministry of Immigration and Population kicked off a "census", in which it claimed it would send enumerators door to door nationwide to update the voter list and ensure the list used for its election is based on "correct data" (in the words of the SAC leader, Senior General Min Aung Hlaing). It is unclear why the SAC called a voter list update a "census" except that the information being collected goes beyond what the 2015 and 2020 voter lists contained. Questions included Citizenship Scrutiny Card (CSC) status, which is consistent with Min Aung Hlaing's position that the CSC is necessary to be a legal voter, although there is no constitutional or legal requirement as yet for CSCs. Resistance and ethnic armed groups had already come out against a SAC election, and the National Unity Government (NUG), on 5 January, specifically urged the public not to cooperate with the data collection process. In many village tracts and wards, the SAC-appointed administrators could not convince any social groups to take the forms house to house. Instead, the initiative spurred widespread local resistance, with many of the SAC administrative offices in the countryside that had survived 2021–22 burned to the ground or blown up. Those authorities who did not abandon their posts were assassinated by underground groups. By the last week of January, the entire operation was called off (with a "census" eventually postponed to October 2024).

But Min Aung Hlaing—if briefly—stayed on point about his promise of an election, with the SAC instituting a particularly demanding set of requirements under a new Political Parties Registration Law on 26 January. He had previewed the law when he addressed a Union Election Council meeting with political parties on 23 January. Therein he displayed his impatience with small parties that could not possibly represent the nation as a whole. He also restated his decision to switch from the first-past-the-post system to one of proportional representation; he seems to believe that this will give the pro-military party, the Union Solidarity and Development Party (USDP), an edge in an upcoming election. Whatever else was intended with the party registration reform, one likely anticipated result was the de-registration of the National League for Democracy, the party of former state counsellor Aung San Suu Kyi, which indeed occurred on 29 March. Throughout 2023, she remained in the prison system.

However, behind what now seem like staged scenes in Nay Pyi Taw in early January, there appears to have been considerable consternation among senior army officials about the security situation. In mid-January, *Khit Thit* news published on its Facebook page a forty-five-page memorandum documenting notes from a meeting of the Central Committee for Counter-Terrorism on 23 December 2022. State media had published a skeletal and bland portrayal of what was discussed, with the regime's then home affairs minister Lieutenant-General Soe Htut urging attendees to "strengthen preventative measures" and "improve the capacity of security members".[2] But the leaked document from the meeting acknowledged the significant security risks the regime was facing from anti-military forces and what steps would be needed to counter them. The memorandum shows that the more than fifty senior regime officials at the meeting heard that anti-military forces had expanded significantly across broad territory and that attacks were expected to increase in 2023; none of the officials present expressed confidence that the election could be held in 2023.[3] This likely would have been the moment that Min Aung Hlaing was delivered the most accurate "bad news to the king", long verboten by Myanmar cultural practices.

Rumours and speculation decisively came to an end on 31 January when the National Defence and Security Council voted to interpret Sec. 425 of the 2008 Constitution as only notional in its allowance of two extensions of emergency rule after the initial first year, thus allowing the fifth six-month extension past two years. NDSC members agreed with Min Aung Hlaing's assessment that armed resistance to junta rule constituted "unusual circumstances" and the extension was immediately approved by the regime-appointed Constitutional Tribunal.[4] The notification was published on 1 February, and on 2 February the SAC extended martial law to thirty-seven townships in Chin and Kayah States and in Magway and Sagaing Regions in statements assigning authority to the regional control commander in them or in their vicinity.[5]

Almost immediately, speeches of Min Aung Hlaing and other senior military officials dropped what had been the non-stop promotion of the SAC's election, and the UEC almost disappeared from public view after having been prominent during junta chair Min Aung Hlaing's official visits around the country and in state media for the previous two years. At the same time, China's profile emerged in promoting the so-called "peace talks" with northern EAOs. That profile appeared on 13–14 March when China's new envoy, Deng Xijung, met representatives of the seven ethnic armed groups constituting the Federal Political Negotiation Coordinating Committee (FPNCC) in Kunming.[6] In the next series of meetings on 27–28 March in Nay Pyi Taw, the junta's peace team continued to try to sell northern EAOs on the eventual election and possibly constitutional amendments vaguely associated with "federalism." While doing so, however, the junta did not even remotely recognize the fact that these EAOs held considerable leverage that puts them in a position to demand incentives from army negotiators in exchange for their staying away from the many post-2021 resistance forces, including the NUG. The junta also travelled to northern Myanmar in June for fruitless peace talks with the three armies constituting the "Three Brotherhood Alliance"—the Arakan Army, the Ta'ang National Liberation Army and the (Kokang) Myanmar National Democratic Alliance Army. None of these meetings went well, nor did the junta's attempt to force the ethnic armed groups that signed the 2015 Nationwide Ceasefire Agreement (NCA groups) to show up in Nay Pyi Taw for the 15 October anniversary celebration of the NCA signing ceremony.

Military Strategy Shift to Terror

Throughout 2023 it became increasingly apparent that the military was not only fighting against armed anti-state groups and their supporters. Instead, the military's primary intention shifted to inflicting terror upon the broader public, whether or not they had provided any kind of support to the NUG or the wide range of other armed resistance forces. This was a notable shift for the military beyond its longstanding counter-insurgency strategy, one that indicates its willingness and ability to take advantage of the changes wrought in the conflict landscape by the recent arrival of the social media age in Myanmar (which is less than a decade old). Prior to social media, military atrocities in counter-insurgency campaigns tended to have a localized impact in areas far from the centre. They could usually be covered up or obfuscated from the rest of the world; any broader impact was dulled by geographic distance and the time it took for reports to emerge.

In 2023, the Defence Services shifted into a warfare mentality that treated all residents of the country as potential enemies of the state, for the first time in history actively seeking to kill Buddhist Bamar civilians. This was a strategy of terror, perhaps not the result of any well-thought-out debates at commanding officers' conferences (as in the past) but rather a reaction to the nationwide hatred of the military. One aspect of this shift was an uptick in the number of air strikes, with some of its seventy or more aircraft dropping bombs indiscriminately in rural areas and others targeting civilian structures such as schools, monasteries, internal displaced persons (IDP) camps and hospitals.[7] Until Operation 1027, some of the worst military violence occurred in Sagaing, with thirty-seven townships, where residents in more than eighty per cent of them are ninety-five per cent Buddhist

Bamar. The 99th Division deployed its units called "Ogre Columns", or "*Sit Oo Bi Lu*" in Burmese, to Sagaing and briefly also to Magway, both heavily Buddhist Bamar areas. These columns comprise special forces trained not only in killing foes of the army but also civilians, and doing so in ferocious, public ways. In March, April, August and September, reports, photos and videos flooded social media of them decapitating, gutting or severing the limbs of dozens of villagers throughout the Dry Zone.[8] When they captured members of resistance forces, the Ogres tortured and barbarically murdered them and their families. But their main intention was to instil terror in the Buddhist heartland. The army also launched arson attacks on villages throughout the country.[9] In terms of arson to homes, the nationwide total dropped a little in 2023, but still rose that year in Sagaing. Of 29,689 household structures burned to the ground in army arson attacks in 2023, 22,009 were in Sagaing. In mid-2023, before the large-scale displacement of as many as a million people in northern Myanmar associated with the 1027 attack, Sagaing was home to 765,200 out of what was then 1.8 million IDPs. Till today, they are living mostly in informal settings in whatever forests and hilly areas they can find, and the junta has repeatedly blocked what needs to be a massive-scale humanitarian effort to a region that has no history of displacement or national or international aid. Data from the OECD shows a considerable eighty-five per cent drop in overall aid contributions since 2021—arguably at a time when intervention and support are most urgently and desperately needed.[10]

In perhaps the clearest sign the military has abandoned any hope of extinguishing armed opponents, the frequency of outright massacres almost entirely unrelated to fighting an armed opponent has been conspicuous in 2023, as has the coverage of them on social media.

- 11 March: Light infantry forces invaded Nan Nein village in Pinlaung township at dawn, with artillery support from a nearby hill lobbing in mortar rounds. The entire village was torched to ash. Most villagers fled, but a few dozen took shelter in the village monastery. At nightfall the soldiers invaded the monastery and unleashed horrific violence, killing twenty-six civilians and two monks.[11]
- 29 March: Air strikes saw bombs dropped on Khuabung village in Thantlang township in Chin State. At least ten civilians died. No resistance forces were present.[12]
- 11 April: Fighter jets and helicopter gunships attacked a breakfast celebration in Pazigyi, Sagaing. The celebration was partially for the Buddhist new year but also to honour the NUG opening a new public hall. The death toll was

more than 160, and video footage from the site indicates the possible use of thermobaric bombs by the air force.[13]

- 9 October: An air strike, followed by mortar fire, hit Mung Lai Hkyet displacement camp, close to the town of Kachin Independence Organisation headquarters in Laiza, with twenty-eight killed.[14]
- 13 November: An air strike dropped two bombs on a school in the remote hilltop village of Vuilu in Chin State. In this village of only fifty households, eleven people were killed, eight of whom were children. Again, no resistance forces were present.[15]

The fact that information and horrifically graphic images and videos about these massacres went viral on social media was likely part of the military's operational plan because it is only through such images being widely viewed that the desired effect of intimidating the broader population can be achieved.

Resistance

Clashes were on the rise in Kayah and Chin States from about March onwards, and short-term tactical alliances between EAOs (many of which have decentralized command structures) with local defence forces from ethnic nationality or Bamar-majority areas emerged throughout most of the country. But despite proclamations otherwise, at no point in 2023 did significant ethnic armed organizations come under any command structure emanating out of the NUG or its armed wing, the People's Defence Force (PDF). And the NUG's continued inability to provide arms to the hundreds of local or community armed groups in central Myanmar—not to mention humanitarian aid to the nearly one million desperate IDPs in the Magway and Sagaing regions, known as the "Dry Zone"—rankled the three hundred or more local forces in that area trying to survive and protect their communities.[16] Announcements by NUG spokespeople and headlines about the Myanmar diaspora indicated tens of millions of dollars were being handed to the NUG, but grassroots groups in many parts of the country received nothing for their service in trying to bring down the military regime.[17] Instead, many had to rotate their fighters in and out so that they could help the growing numbers of impoverished families with day labour or agricultural work. In 2023, grassroots groups called state or regionwide meetings in Chin State and Sagaing Region in attempts to harness solidarity, shore up communications and continue the revolution—with or without NUG help. There remains considerable distrust among EAOs and non-Bamar local defence forces of the NUG. Ethnic minorities are especially suspicious of the

NLD dominance of the executive of the NUG. None have forgotten that in 2020 the NLD ran an explicit campaign to wipe out ethnic political party candidates on election day, and how while in office from 2016 to 2021 its members never commented on atrocities being carried out against minorities.

There are many examples of expressions of this distrust, which are somehow lost in both sides of the extremely polarized narratives of post-2021 events. One is a recent interview with Dr Sui Khar, foreign minister of the "Chinland government" and vice chairman 3 of the Chin National Front:

> The non-Bamar in Burma have long been victims of Bamar chauvinism. The Bamar try to exert their dominance over the minorities. Seven decades have passed in this manner. The NLD has this propensity too. That is why a degree of mistrust and suspicion lingers on. The Bamars never thought of equality. We were not allowed to exercise self-determination. This engendered a sense of mistrust among us. It will take time to integrate. The non-Bamars will never hand over all self-rule to the Bamars...
> [When asked about NLD dominance of the NUG:] "NLD does not have any change to enforce its dominance in NUG at the moment. In fact, there are no indications of any such inclination. We are trying to move towards a joint leadership.[18]

Economic Losers and Winners in Myanmar's Wars in 2023

According to the World Bank, the economy in 2023 was estimated to be 30 per cent smaller than it might have been in the absence of Covid-19 and the coup. It also estimated that real GDP per capita had dropped to 13 per cent below 2019 levels, although the statistic seems to rely upon undoubtedly inflated government data. In a May 2023 survey, the Bank found that 48 per cent of farming households worry about not having enough food, up from about 26 per cent in May 2022.[19] The volatility of the kyat, the decision of the Central Bank of Myanmar (CBM) to print new 20,000 kyat notes, excessive CBM fiddling with exchange rates, the withdrawal of microfinance organizations, long-lasting electricity blackouts, and a return to aspects of the command economy established under socialism (1962–88), including bungled attempts to fix prices of commodities such as cooking oil and fuel, have led to massive uncertainty. Caloric intakes are down, migration (legal or illegal) has surged, and urban and peri-urban areas—not recently or anytime in 2023 having been the target of large-scale military violence—have swelled with domestic refugees from rural fighting. Many families have reverted to pre-2011 coping behaviours, including legal and illegal migration. One result was the highest-ever reported remittances in the SAC's balance of payments report for Jan–Mar 2023, totalling US$884.8 million.

The big winners in 2023 were operators in the illicit economy. In 2023, Myanmar rocketed to the top position globally in terms of organized criminality according to the annual report of the Global Initiative against Transnational Organized Crime.[20] The biggest change from the past came in unregulated non-renewable resource extraction (following a surge in illegal rare earth mining after the 2021 coup) and human trafficking, where cases of forced labour and of trafficking for forced criminality and marriage were exacerbated by the conflict and lawlessness across the country. Myanmar overtook Cambodia as ground zero for cyber-scam operators, mainly set up by Chinese triads, along the China or Thailand borders. The remote locations of these so-called "special economic zones" offered space for massively expanded operations in 2023 worth unknown billions of dollars. Such operations ensured impunity by paying off police, EAOs and other local Myanmar officials and military officers as well as overseas Chinese associations and organizations associated with the Chinese government in Yunnan and Beijing.[21]

In both China and the West, Myanmar's image has become one of danger, trickery and criminality. The plots of Netflix's latest season of its hit series *Jack Ryan* and the BBC's 27th season of *Silent Witness* involved portrayals of Myanmar that likened it to a cartel- or mafia-run country controlled by a few treacherous warlords and corrupt police. The two top-grossing Chinese language films of 2023—"No More Bets" and "Raid on the Lethal Zone"—depict the drug and human trafficking that victimize Chinese casualties. The setting is an unnamed Southeast Asian country, but across Asian viewing publics the consensus was that it was Myanmar. For example, the *Japan Times* polled 54,000 users on Weibo and found that 48,000 responded they would not travel to Myanmar as a result of these movies.[22] The surge in annual tourist arrivals following Myanmar's brief opening politically after 2011, which rose to well over four million, had all but disappeared by 2023. Government statistics, likely wildly overstated, reported arrivals at 1.28 million.[23] This contrast also reminds us of the thoroughly opposing narratives of rosy democratization ten years ago, and now a narco, gang-run Myanmar by 2023.

Military Humiliation: 1027

After months of low-level clashes in northern Myanmar, the Myanmar Defence Forces appeared to have been caught completely unprepared for the surprise offensive by the Three Brotherhood Alliance (3BHA) against troops along the

China border on 27 October. As the three allies—the Ta'ang National Liberation Army, Myanmar National Democratic Alliance Army and Arakan Army—quickly seized strategic border towns such as Chinshwehaw, Mong Koe and Pang Hseng as well as Namhkam and Kunlong and eventually Laukkai, resistance forces elsewhere in the country were inspired to attack what looked like a Tatmadaw in full retreat. Operation 1027, likely planned for at least many months (including during the fruitless "peace talks" with the SAC), focused mainly on northern Shan State, where the 3BHA claimed to have seized over 150 regime outposts. For the first time since the Min Aung Hlaing coup in 2021, armed anti-state organizations seized operational commands from the military. There is almost no doubt that China gave a "green light" to the operation, given that Beijing's demands that the scam centres along its borders—which have made victims of perhaps hundreds of thousands of Chinese—be shut down and their leaders turned over to the Chinese government had gone unheeded by the SAC or at least disrespected by the Myanmar military leadership. Senior General Min Aung Hlaing, who has spent his ten years as commander-in-chief enhancing ties with Russia, has long been known for his ambivalence if not outright hostility towards China.

Repeating the success of 1027 in other areas in Myanmar's conflict landscape is not easily achievable. The three EAOs involved have supported each other in battles since at least 2015 and have developed a degree of interoperability that massively supersedes the short-term tactical agreements between other EAOs and local defence forces and the PDF. As Anthony Davis, the long-time security analyst on Myanmar, warned against "guerrilla triumphalism" in his December 2023 assessment of the implications of 1027:

> [N]orthern Shan state is not Myanmar and to imagine that the conditions that produced those successes can be easily replicated in very different operational contexts in other parts of the country is surely illusory.[24]

By 31 December 2023, thirty-four towns (mostly not townships but urban areas of 15,000–30,000) were emptied of officials associated with the SAC and the military. Some have been retaken, but at immense cost to local populations. Still, the contagion effect of seeing Facebook videos of army soldiers waving white flags (sometimes just tissues) to surrender, one inflammatory photo of army generals toasting their surrender with leaders of the Myanmar National Democratic Alliance Army (MNDAA), along with the surrender of the entire Infantry Battalion 143 in Kunlong, led the coalition of groups fighting in Karenni State to launch 1111. They eventually seized military outposts in several towns and the university in Loikaw, and they continued into 2024 to fight to control the state capital.

It is almost impossible to overstate the blow taken by the Myanmar Defence Services at the end of 2023. Since 1949, the year after independence, there has never been an armed anti-state group operating successfully and freely within twenty-five miles of the capital as there is now in western Karenni and southwestern Shan states. Military officers have likely never doubted that the Defence Services was, as military propaganda has claimed for seventy-five years, the only national institution capable of holding the country together. Political scientist Joel Migdal has argued for a definition of the "state" that includes not just practice of agencies exercising the legitimate monopoly over violence (per Max Weber), but also includes its "image of a coherent, controlling organization in a territory".[25] In Myanmar, it has been the never-challenged idea of institutional capacity by those inside the military institution that has long buoyed the spirit of frontline commanders, most of whom have had no respite for three years (as opposed to the longstanding practice of six months in battle, six months in camp with families). After 1027, twelve brigadier generals were killed or captured, whereas none had died or been captured in the fighting in the previous nearly three years. Among present-day army officers, the loss of credibility of this idea of Tatmadaw resilience and of a "coherent, controlling organization" may in fact be the most important development of 2023.

SAC's Foreign Relations: Russia Rises, Neighbours Foster a Bubble and Sanctions Fail

Myanmar's foreign partners shrank to an ever smaller number of mostly equally pariah states (Russia and Belarus), while its neighbours largely catered to the SAC's intractable hold on Nay Pyi Taw. State media gave extensive coverage of frequent visits by Russian and Belarusian officials and companies to Nay Pyi Taw, and trips by the SAC's cabinet ministers to those countries. Myanmar and Russian officials issued statements throughout the year criticizing US sanctions on each other and passing out honorifics to senior leaders from each country. In 2023, the UN Special Rapporteur on Human Rights named Russia as the main supplier of weapons to Myanmar.[26] At least several thousand military officers from Myanmar were trained in Russia in the 2000s, but given their respective ongoing battlefield demands, there is probably little bandwidth in either defence establishment to undertake long-term training as in the past. However, Nay Pyi Taw residents report that the low hotel occupancy in the city appears to be mostly Russian and Belarusian guests, who probably are mechanics carrying out repairs to Russian-built aircraft and artillery, as well as supporting infrastructure projects such as the development of a small nuclear power plant by Rosatom (Russia's State Atomic Energy Corporation). Unlike China, Russia likely has little it needs to buy from Myanmar, and indeed rumours circulated in mid-2023 that Russia was buying back ammunition, tanks, missiles and artillery it had previously sold to the Defence Services and the Indian military.[27] Russia also finalized Myanmar's accession to dialogue partner status of the Eurasian multilateral organization the Shanghai Cooperation Organisation in May 2023.[28]

Myanmar's main neighbours, China, Bangladesh, India and Thailand, have withstood another of Myanmar's many postcolonial domestic crises and wars. There were initial concerns by ASEAN that the post-2021 coup and the reaction to it would lead to widespread regional instability of an order greater than earlier Myanmar crises. In fact, the post 2021 experience showed no export of war and crisis beyond borders, with the exception of occasional breaches of air space and errant artillery in unpopulated areas across the Bangladesh, Thai and Chinese borders. Some refugee flight to Manipur in India has exacerbated an already tense situation there. After Min Aung Hlaing signed, and then ignored, the "five-point consensus" reached at an emergency ASEAN meeting on 24 April 2021, ASEAN banned SAC officials from attending high-level ASEAN meetings, which continued under Indonesia's chairmanship in 2023. Before Indonesia assumed the chairmanship, its foreign minister, Retro Marsudi, had convened meetings with a variety of stakeholders from Myanmar and established an "Office of the Special Envoy to Myanmar" in the Indonesian foreign ministry. But no special envoy was ever named and ASEAN has had no visible impact on the crises in Myanmar.

Instead, before the May election in Thailand, its foreign ministry circumvented ASEAN by hosting what it called the first "Track 1.5" dialogue among "like-minded" Asian states—Cambodia, Laos and Vietnam along with China, India, Bangladesh and Japan—in March; India served as host to the second such gathering, though located in Thailand, in late April. Track 1.5 is a moniker usually used to indicate that attendees are not present in their official capacity, but the SAC's foreign minister, Wunna Maung Lwin, most decidedly was. At best, these meetings were intended to dull the international criticism and sustain open communications with Myanmar to further the national interests of the other attendees.

At the same time, as in the past, Thailand's bordering provinces have allowed relatively free movement and operation of Myanmar EAOs and non-governmental organizations (NGOs), with considerable benefit to the local economies of Chiang Mai, Mae Sot and other border towns. Politically, during the last six months of the tenure of Thai foreign minister Don Pramudwina and his special envoy, Pornpimol "Pauline" Kanchanalak", they made several trips to Nay Pyi Taw accompanied by interested Thai investors. After the 15 May election, which triggered four months of negotiations to form a new government that was sworn in on 5 September, Myanmar was largely forgotten by Thai political elites until early 2024.

For India, its main concerns with Myanmar are twofold: first, to counter China's footprint in Myanmar, which is on the verge of opening a major Chinese port adjacent to the Indian Ocean; second, India relies on collaboration with the Myanmar military to weaken insurgencies in India's northeast region along the Myanmar border.

All this said, the only important international actor inside Myanmar in 2023 was China. In the week after the 2021 coup, senior Chinese officials quietly visited Nay Pyi Taw in an attempt to influence the direction of the military, including seeking to reconcile Aung San Suu Kyi and Min Aung Hlaing. When that failed, Beijing retreated and took a wait-and-see approach, stepping up only when Chinese interests were threatened. Beginning in January 2023, however, China started engaging with the SAC on economic interests, advancing peace talks with northern EAOs as well as carrying out a pilot project to bring back to northern Rakhine State at least a small number of Rohingyas from refugee camps in Bangladesh. The SAC briefly went through the motions of attempting the latter, which led to a scandal over the UN High Commission on Refugees providing their vehicles and boats for SAC officials to visit Bangladesh.[29] Eventually, the repatriation fizzled out. At China's prompting, the SAC's National Unity and Peacemaking Coordination Committee held several meetings with northern groups. It is important not to overstate this involvement by China, which is by no means embracing the SAC. Instead, as the multiple fronts in the civil wars in Myanmar encroached on Chinese interests and investments, it had to do more to shape outcomes in Myanmar whether it really wanted to be involved or not. Given China's myriad domestic security, external security and economic challenges, it is unlikely that it would seek to be a kingmaker or invest the necessary resources to mediate peace beyond the northern EAO territories of Myanmar.

Overall, as much of the world has been focused on the Russia-Ukraine war and the potential for nuclear arms deployment, and later the Hamas attack on Israel and the Israeli Defence Force's disproportionate response to Gaza, Myanmar has attracted very little international attention.

At the political level, the United Nations Security Council is unable to move forward on any attempts to sanction the SAC as China and Russia veto any such proposals. The secretary-general has exhibited neither interest nor knowledge of the urgency of the multiple overlapping and simultaneous crises in Myanmar.[30] Moreover, his appointment of Noeleen Heyzer, who had extensive experience working with the previous junta in the aftermath of Cyclone Nargis in 2008, as his special envoy was appropriate, but her mandate was massively expanded without granting any additional resources and especially no political capital expended by the secretary-general to support her. Her resignation in June 2023 was a foregone conclusion, and there has been no urgency in naming a new one. And to date, the "Myanmar" seat in the UN General Assembly remains occupied by Kyaw Moe Tun, the NLD's appointee from prior to the 2021 military coup.

Inside Myanmar, the UN Country Team (UNCT) has had no resident and humanitarian coordinator in more than four years despite being home to one of the world's most serious and complex conflict and humanitarian crises. Instead, in 2021, the "acting in charge" resident coordinator was first the United Nations Office for Project Services (UNOPS) director, but soon followed by the UN Population Fund (UNFPA) country director until the end of 2023. Immediately after the 2021 coup, the UNCT created guidelines that established strict policies for disengaging from junta government agencies for all activities other than those required to save lives (for example, anti-retroviral treatment). It is not clear that all agencies are following the guidelines, but most agency heads have avoided Nay Pyi Taw as they are aware that such meetings will be photographed and carried front page in state media. UNFPA director Ramanathan Balakrishnan made several trips to Nay Pyi Taw over 2022 and 2023, which state media covered with photographs of him with minister of immigration and population Myint Kyaing. The accompanying state media text suggested the UNFPA would provide assistance to the upcoming 2024 population census, which Balakrishnan never refuted despite many non-state media inquiries. The Regional UNFPA office, finally, on 15 December 2023, sent an email to the *Irrawaddy* saying the agency would not support the SAC's census.[31] In general, all international organizations face difficulties obtaining visas for their staff and travel permission to leave Yangon. The implementation of humanitarian assistance programmes by various agencies is usually blocked by the SAC.

Sanctions by the United States, Canada, the United Kingdom and the European Union have continued to pile on, sometimes in a coordinated fashion, sometimes according to the logic of their own domestic politics. For example, after the 31 July extension of emergency rule and a major cabinet reshuffle of the SAC, the United States, United Kingdom and Canada placed all new cabinet members on their versions of "specially designated individuals" lists, thus imposing asset, trade and travel bans as well as other measures. Invoking Executive Order 14014 of 10 February 2021, the US Treasury Office of Foreign Assets Control (OFAC) issued instructions for winding down all transactions with the Myanmar

Foreign Trade Bank and the Myanma Investment and Commercial Bank in June; added jet fuel providers to the list of those operating in forbidden sectors of the economy in August; and banned all US involvement with the Myanmar Oil and Gas Enterprise in October.[32] Likewise, the European Union continued to add the names of human rights violators from Myanmar to a growing list of those under restrictive measures. It has not yet revoked the special trading privileges Myanmar enjoys, particularly in the garment sector, as these factories remain the only source of formal employment for tens of thousands of young workers. But growing reports of labour exploitation and trade union suppression by these factories may force the revocation of these privileges, hence the loss of limited employment opportunities for young women in the formal sector.

Notes

1. Mary Callahan, "Myanmar's Perpetual Junta: Solving the Riddle of the Tatmadaw's Long Reign", *New Left Review* no. 60 (2009): 27–63.

2. "Anti-Terrorism Central Committee Holds 1/2022 Meeting", *Infonews*, 22 December 2022, http://infosheet.org/node/3895.

3. Union of Myanmar Central Committee for Counter-Terrorism, "Memorandum of Central Committee for Counter-Terrorism Meeting 1/2022, 23 December 2022", 10 January 2023, Top Secret [in Burmese language]. Though the veracity of the document has not been confirmed, there are some indications it may be genuine: media reports in late January said a police brigadier-general had been detained over the leak, and at least one of the strategies to counter the resistance that the memorandum said was proposed at the meeting—SMS messages warning the public not to associate with "terrorists"—has since been implemented, with messages sent out to Atom (formerly Telenor) users in Sagaing Region on 31 January. The *Khit Thit* Facebook post containing the document has been removed, but the author has a copy in her possession and other news agencies picked it up. See also "Myanmar Junta Leaked Memo Shows Resistance Growing beyond Control", *The Irrawaddy*, 18 January 2023, https://www.irrawaddy.com/news/burma/myanmar-junta-leaked-memo-shows-resistance-growing-beyond-control.html.

4. Grant Peck, "Myanmar Extends State of Emergency, Delaying Expected Polls", Associated Press, 1 February 2023, https://apnews.com/article/politics-myanmar-government-min-aung-hlaing-a8feaa2812b09a95533efc9252194313.

5. See multiple announcements carried the next day in the *Global New Light of Myanmar*, 3 February 2023, https://cdn.myanmarseo.com/file/client-cdn/gnlm/wp-content/uploads/2023/02/3_Feb_23_gnlm-1.pdf.

6.   "Myanmar Armed Ethnic Coalition and Chinese Special Envoy Meet in Kunming", *The Irrawaddy*, 20 March 2023, https://www.irrawaddy.com/news/burma/myanmar-armed-ethnic-coalition-and-chinese-special-envoy-meet-in-kunming.html.

7.   UN High Commissioner on Human Rights, "Situation of Human Rights in Myanmar, (A/HRC/54/59)", 26 September 2023, https://reliefweb.int/report/myanmar/situation-human-rights-myanmar-report-united-nations-high-commissioner-human-rights-ahrc5459-advance-unedited-version.

8.   "'Ogre' Battalion Uses Brutality to Instill Terror in Myanmar", Radio Free Asia, 22 April 2023, https://www.rfa.org/english/news/myanmar/ogre-04192023150057.html; "Horrendous War Crimes of the Military Council's Ogre Column", BNI Online, 30 September 2023, https://www.bnionline.net/en/news/horrendous-war-crimes-military-councils-ogre-column#:~:text=On%20March%2030%2C%202023%2C%20during,Battalion%201%2C%20during%20the%20battle.

9.   Statistic derived from Data for Myanmar, "Burned Houses Summary", available on Facebook page at https://www.facebook.com/data4myanmar.

10. Organization for Economic Coordination and Development, "Data Explorer Page", https://data-explorer.oecd.org/vis?fs[0]=Topic%2C0%7CDevelopment%23DEV%23&pg= 0&fc=Topic&bp=true&snb=10&vw=tb&df[ds]=dsDisseminate FinalDMZ&df[id]= DSD_DAC2%40DF_DAC3A&df[ag]=OECD.DCD.FSD&df[vs]=1.0&pd=%2C&dq=.MMR..USD.Q&ly[rw]=RECIPIENT&ly[cl]=TIME_PERIOD&to[TIME_PERIOD]=false&lo=10&lom=LASTNPERIODS&lb=id.

11. Hannah Ritchie, Kocha Olarn, Heather Chen, and Angus Watson, "Myanmar Monastery Attack Kills 22 as Conflicting Accounts Emerge of Alleged Massacre", CNN, 15 March 2023, https://www.cnn.com/2023/03/15/asia/myanmar-military-monastery-attack-intl-hnk/index.html.

12. "Junta Jets Bomb Village in Western Myanmar, Killing 10", Radio Free Asia, 30 March 2023, https://www.rfa.org/english/news/myanmar/airstrike-03302023162908.html.

13. Helen Regan, Sandi Sidhu, Anna Coren, Salai TZ, and Su Chay, "'How Many More Children Have to Die?' Myanmar Airstrike Survivors Ask What will it Take for the World to Act", CNN, 20 April 2023, https://www.cnn.com/2023/04/20/asia/myanmar-sagaing-massacre-children-intl-hnk-dst/index.html; Human Rights Watch, "Myanmar: Enhanced Blast Strike Likely War Crime: 'Thermobaric' Attack in Sagaing Region Killed More than 160", 9 May 2023, https://www.hrw.org/news/2023/05/09/myanmar-enhanced-blast-strike-likely-war-crime; Rebecca Tan and Cape Diamond, "Myanmar's Military Said it Bombed 'Terrorists.' It Killed Children", *Washington Post*, 4 August 2023, https://www.washingtonpost.com/world/2023/08/04/myanmar-military-attack-civilians-children/.

14. Amnesty International, "Myanmar: 28 Civilians Killed in Military Air Strike – New Investigation and Witness Testimony", 13 October 2023, https://www.amnesty.

org/en/latest/news/2023/10/myanmar-28-civilians-killed-in-military-air-strike-new-investigation-and-witness-testimony/.

15. Jonathan Head, "Myanmar: Eight Children Killed in Military Strike on School in Chin State", BBC, 17 November 2023, https://www.bbc.com/news/world-asia-67448410.

16. "National Unity Government Lacks Chain of Command, States Analysts", *Democratic Voice of Burma*, 16 February 2024, https://english.dvb.no/national-unity-government-lacks-chain-of-command-states-analysts/.

17. International Crisis Group, "Crowdfunding a War: The Money behind Myanmar's Resistance", 20 December 2022, https://www.crisisgroup.org/sites/default/files/2022-12/328-myanmars-resistance.pdf.

18. "Entire Burma is Now a Frontline of Resistance", *Prothom Alo*, 17 February 2024, https://en.prothomalo.com/opinion/interview/dxs0bv9vkw.

19. The World Bank, "The World Bank in Myanmar", 4 December 2023, https://www.worldbank.org/en/country/myanmar/overview#1.

20. Global Initiative, "Mind the Gap: Organized Crime on the Rise in Myanmar as Resilience Wanes", 26 February 2024, https://globalinitiative.net/analysis/myanmar-organized-crime-resilience-ocindex/.

21. Priscilla Clapp and Jason Tower, "Myanmar's Criminal Zones: A Growing Threat to Global Security", US Institute for Peace, 9 November 2022, https://www.usip.org/publications/2022/11/myanmars-criminal-zones-growing-threat-global-security.

22. Alyssa Chen, "Hit Chinese Movie Raises Fears of Travel in Southeast Asia", Japan Times, 4 September 2023, https://www.japantimes.co.jp/news/2023/09/04/asia-pacific/crime-legal/china-cambodia-myanmar-tourism-cyberscams-trafficking/.

23. "2023 Sees Five-fold Year-on-Year Increase in Tourist Arrivals", *Global New Light of Myanmar*, 11 January 2024, https://www.gnlm.com.mm/2023-sees-five-fold-year-on-year-increase-in-tourist-arrivals/#:~:text=Myanmar%20attracted%201.28%20million%20international,Ministry%20of%20Hotels%20and%20Tourism.

24. Anthony Davis, "The Dangers of Guerrilla Triumphalism in Myanmar", *Asia Times*, 6 December 2023, https://asiatimes.com/2023/12/the-dangers-of-guerrilla-triumphalism-in-myanmar/.

25. Joel S. Migdal, *State in Society: Studying How States and Societies Transform and Constitute One Another* (Cambridge University Press, 2012), pp. 15–16.

26. Tom Andrews, "The Billion Dollar Death Trade: The International Arms Networks That Enable Human Rights Violations in Myanmar", May 2023, Office of the High Commissioner on Human Rights, https://www.ohchr.org/sites/default/files/documents/countries/myanmar/infographic-sr-myanmar-2023-05-17.pdf.

27. Yuko Seki and Shot Fujii, "Russia 'Buying Back' Arms Parts Exported to Myanmar and India", *Nikkei Asian Review*, 3 June 2023, https://asia.nikkei.com/Politics/Ukraine-war/Russia-buying-back-arms-parts-exported-to-Myanmar-and-India.

28. Shanghai Cooperation Organisation, "New SCO Dialogue Partners", https://eng. sectsco.org/20230505/-New-SCO-dialogue-partners-942021.html#:~:text=On%205%20 May%202023%2C%20the,Panaji%2C%20the%20Republic%20of%20India.

29. Matt Reed, "UN Refugee Agency Confirms Involvement in Junta Boat Transport", Radio Free Asia, 20 March 2023.

30. See, for example, the vague points made in the secretary-general's 150-word statement, "Secretary-General Deeply Concerned by Expansion of Conflict in Myanmar, Calls on All Parties to Protect Civilians", SG/SM/22034, 15 November 2023, https://press. un.org/en/2023/sgsm22034.doc.htm.

31. "UN Agency Says Reports It Will Support Myanmar's 'Surveillance Census' Are False", *The Irrawaddy*, 15 December 2023, https://www.irrawaddy.com/news/burma/ un-agency-says-reports-it-will-support-myanmars-surveillance-census-are-false.html.

32. OFAC, Burma Sanctions Regulations 31 CFR part 525, General License No. 5, "Authorizing the Wind Down of Transactions Involving Myanma Investment and Commercial Bank or Myanma Foreign Trade Bank", US Department of Treasury, 21 June 2023, https://ofac.treasury.gov/media/931936/download?inline; OFAC, "Determination Pursuant to Section 1(a)(i) of Executive Order 14014: Jet Fuel Sector of the Burmese Economy", US Department of Treasury, 23 August 2023, https://ofac.treasury.gov/media/932111/download?inline; OFAC, "Directive 1 Under Executive Order 14014: Prohibitions Related to Financial Services to or for the Benefit of Myanma Oil and Gas Enterprise", 31 October 2023, https://ofac.treasury. gov/media/932251/download?inline. Regarding the latter sanction to MOGE, US embassy staff in Thailand lobbied for delays in the imposition of this sanction until the post-May Thai election had established a proper government (September). Because Bangkok is highly dependent upon the natural gas from Myanmar for electricity, the United States did not want to carry out an action against Myanmar that could affect the intense negotiations among Thai political parties. Hence, it waited to announce the MOGE sanction, but also wrote it in such a way that Thailand would be able to sustain its power generation.

Myanmar's Continuing Socio-economic Challenges since the Coup

Sean Turnell and Moe Thuzar

After seizing state power on 1 February 2021, coup leader and commander-in-chief of the Myanmar military, Senior General Min Aung Hlaing, assumed the position of chairman of the State Administration Council (SAC) military regime the next day. He made his first public statement only a week later, on 8 February 2021, stating that the SAC would not change the country's foreign and economic policies, and offering assurances that Myanmar's economy would remain open to foreign investment. This was echoed by the SAC's minister for investment, U Aung Naing Oo, who highlighted on 16 February that the SAC would prioritize economic recovery from the pandemic. These pronouncements were indicative of the SAC's aspiration to legitimize its seizure of power by presiding over an economic performance better than that achieved under the National League for Democracy (NLD) during its first term in office over 2016–21.[1]

The statements by Min Aung Hlaing and Aung Naing Oo were elaborations on the commitment to "recover the businesses caused [*sic*] by [the] Covid-19 pandemic as quickly as possible" that formed part of the six-point statement announcing the military's reasons for the coup.[2] Despite these stated commitments, Myanmar's economic performance has steadily declined, as have domestic and external trust in the SAC's capacity to achieve the recovery—and attendant stability—it had promised when taking over state power in 2021. Interestingly, the SAC adapted the NLD's Myanmar Economic Recovery and Reform Plan (MERRP) as its Covid-19 response. The MERRP had been developed by the NLD as an update to and an extension of the longer-term Myanmar Sustainable Development Plan

SEAN TURNELL is a long-time researcher of Myanmar's economy and former Senior Economic Adviser to Daw Aung San Suu Kyi.

MOE THUZAR is Senior Fellow and Coordinator of the Myanmar Studies Programme at the ISEAS – Yusof Ishak Institute, Singapore.

(MSDP), with a specific aim to respond to the Covid-19 pandemic. The pandemic had presented the NLD government with an opportunity to push through "radical" liberalization reforms with the MERRP, such as public finance reforms and liberalization of interest rates and the export sector.[3] The SAC, however, dropped the "reform" element of the MERRP, and unveiled it instead as the Myanmar Economic Recovery Plan, or MERP, in August 2021.[4]

As early as April 2021, the Independent Economists for Myanmar warned that the SAC's economic and financial policies—which had triggered a full-scale banking crisis—would have far-reaching implications for the Myanmar people as the SAC's cash-strapped status would affect its spending priorities, leaving limited resources (if any) for "providing financing to import the fuel and equipment needed to generate electricity, and [the] food, fertilisers and medications people need to survive."[5] In July 2021, the World Bank forecasted an eighteen per cent contraction in the economy, with "damaging implications for lives, livelihoods, poverty and future growth".[6] Any modicum of growth reported since then has not climbed out of that double-digit contraction. Socio-economic gaps have only widened since 2021, with rising numbers of people living below the poverty line, unemployment, inflation, human capital flight (migration), dropping attendance at state education facilities, and soaring healthcare costs.

In 2024, Myanmar enters a fourth year under SAC rule. The past three years have created a bleak landscape: deteriorating economic conditions exacerbated by escalation of conflict, placing more pressure on any projected recovery. There are falling incomes, falling living standards for the bulk of the people, and high inflation resulting from the falling exchange rate of the Myanmar kyat. Power shortages have affected the manufacturing sector. Foreign direct investment (FDI) reached a new low. There is now a widespread lack of confidence in the regime's policy approach, which is geared towards economic control and extracting foreign exchange. Recent corruption scandals that rocked the SAC's highest echelons show both the extent of the country's patronage system and the severity of its economic problems. Additionally, Operation 1027, launched by ethnic armed organizations in northern Shan State on 27 October 2023, has exposed the vulnerability of the main arteries of Myanmar's border trade, with attendant socio-economic implications for communities in the conflict areas.

Sluggish Growth, Exits, and Falling Living Standards

Myanmar's economy continued to underperform across 2023. The World Bank's forecast of a mere one per cent growth for Myanmar's economy in 2023/24[7] is less than a quarter of the expected growth for ASEAN economies overall.[8] This underperformance was pronounced not just in comparison to neighbouring countries in ASEAN. It also starkly contrasts with the country's economic trend over the last decade.[9] Myanmar remains the only ASEAN member state whose GDP remains below pre-Covid levels.[10]

Prior to the coup, manufacturing accounted for seventy-five per cent of the industry in 2019 and was viewed as the sector in which the country might begin to catch up to its peers and neighbours. However, manufacturing in Myanmar continued to contract in 2023. The contraction began early in 2023 and accelerated through the year.[11] Amongst the many reasons cited by factory owners for this decline include Myanmar's worsening security and political situation, electricity shortages, input bottlenecks, customer insolvencies, and rising costs. These costs include compliance costs after the Financial Action Task Force (FATF)—an international financial watchdog—added Myanmar to its blacklist in October 2022, and mounting reputational risks.

Since the coup, several companies have left Myanmar or are planning their responsible exit strategies. Divestments and exits span various industries, including telecommunications (Telenor and Ooredoo), garments (Primark, Tesco, Fast Retailing [Uniqlo], Aldi South, C&A, Mango, Marks and Spencer, H&M and Inditex [Zara]), and oil and gas (Total, Chevron and Woodside), as well as other investors such as British American Tobacco and Keppel (Sedona Hotel). Others, such as Nestle and Nivia, have closed factories in Myanmar but continue to do business in the country.

The International Labor Organization published in October 2023 the report of its commission of inquiry formed in March 2022. The commission found that "the actions taken by the military authorities since February 2021 have resulted in far-reaching restrictions on the exercise of basic civil liberties and trade union rights". The SAC had three months to review and take action on the findings, failing which the case would be referred to the International Court of Justice. Just after the ILO report was issued, prominent global brands—including Adidas (Germany), H&M (Sweden) and Zara (Spain)—announced they would stop sourcing from Myanmar.[12] The announcements by these brands followed the decisions by Marks and Spencer (in March) and Primark (in September) to make responsible exits from Myanmar. The European Union is also pondering whether to maintain the trade privileges extended to Myanmar under the EU's Everything But Arms, or EBA, scheme. This constitutes a high-stakes decision as the EBA scheme has supported livelihoods of thousands of low-paid manufacturing jobs, held mostly by women.[13]

Myanmar's slow economic growth has thus translated into continued falling living standards for the bulk of its people. According to the World Bank, in 2023 almost half of Myanmar's households reported lower levels of income compared with the previous year. The same study estimated that forty per cent of the population now lives below the poverty line (compared with twenty-four per cent prior to the 2021 coup). This sad reality bears out the 2021 prediction by the United Nations Development Programme, based on data available immediately after the coup (which compounded the challenges already presented by the Covid-19 pandemic), that Myanmar would lose the gains made in human development and poverty reduction over the preceding decade of 2011–21, and that poverty would likely "return to levels not seen since 2005".[14]

Food insecurity is attendant with rising poverty and has been exacerbated by the conflict that has engulfed the country since the coup. Civilian displacements and increased migration, disruptions to domestic and international supply chains and to agricultural cycles (and food production)—with corresponding drops in wage/daily labour opportunities—and soaring food prices have all amplified existing food insecurity and nutrition challenges. The World Food Programme cautioned in July 2023 that "acute food insecurity is at critical levels" in various parts of Myanmar. Cyclone Mocha, a Category 5 storm, which made landfall in northwestern Myanmar, further complicated the livelihood challenges of communities in Rakhine, Chin and Kachin States as well as Sagaing and Magway regions. These states and regions are also areas where sixty per cent of internally displaced populations are located, and where conflict between the Myanmar military and resistance forces has intensified since mid-2022.[15]

High Inflation and Its Consequences

Exacerbating falling incomes and much else has been Myanmar's high inflation rate, which, at an estimated 28 per cent average across 2023, is more than six times that of the average for Southeast Asia as a whole.[16] The total increase in Myanmar's inflation rate from February 2021 to March 2023 was 47.6 per cent. Efforts to disguise inflation using price controls on key commodities by the SAC regime have failed in the usual way of such schemes.

Interventions by the SAC in the financial sector and the exchange rate could not stem the declining situation and have instead created more distrust in banks and the Myanmar kyat (MMK) as stores of value. Myanmar people have resorted again to acquiring property and gold as long-term stores of value.

Myanmar's high inflation rate was partly a function of the falling exchange rate of the country's currency, the kyat, the informal market rate of which declined around thirty per cent in the year to end-September 2023. This fall affected prices directly via consumer goods imports and indirectly via rising prices of intermediate goods and other inputs. Responding to the widening divergence between this market rate of the kyat and the official rate that fixed the currency at MMK2,100 to US$1, Myanmar's authorities undertook the time-honoured policy of arresting foreign exchange dealers.[17] Such, and similar actions, did little to halt the slide, and in December 2023 the fixed exchange rate was incompletely abandoned.[18] Remaining was the chaos of controls—increasingly whimsical, and with no vision beyond almost day-to-day crisis management.

The arbitrary exchange rate decisions by the SAC have also affected many Myanmar overseas workers. Since June, the SAC started taxing migrant workers[19] and stipulated that cash transfers to Myanmar must be through registered remittance channels.[20] With the official conversion rates set below actual market rates, workers' remittances suffered exchange losses. Needless to say, these measures by the SAC were highly unpopular among the millions of Myanmar workers whose remittances are lifelines to their families coping with the difficult situation back home. The measures also created negative externalities; many in Myanmar's business community, including those operating overseas, started trying to avoid the restrictive situation and further exposure to foreign currency risks in the country by structuring transactions and payments offshore.[21]

Another significant factor contributing to inflation in Myanmar, alongside exchange rate weakness, was the country's precarious public finances. With tax collection in disarray amidst conflict and political instability, the regime has resorted to borrowing from the central bank—also known as "printing money". According to the World Bank, two-thirds of Myanmar's budget deficit—which reached a considerable 5.6 per cent of GDP in 2023 and continues to rise—was financed this way.

Myanmar's financial sector continues to be an arena of weakness and instability. The country's banks suffer crippling levels of non-performing loans, and no viable strategy for resolving these has been articulated. High levels of liquidity held by the banks in the form of cash and government bonds, which otherwise might signal prudence, instead point simply to a lack of creditworthy projects and borrowers.[22] Trust in the banks, never high given Myanmar's volatile financial history, remained uncertain throughout 2023. Such doubts were underlined by a series of bank runs by anxious depositors. Periodic restrictions on depositors to their funds and some ill-disciplined comments about the banks by senior officials also did little to allay fears.[23] At the end of 2023, Myanmar's banking sector remained as it was at the start of the year: not dead, yet not quite alive, and providing little support in terms of the necessary capital for businesses, farmers and consumers.

Myanmar's micro-finance sector, traditionally an oasis of stability amidst the chaos and fragility of the banks, also struggled through 2023 to get on top of loan arrears. Such arrears, normally never rising above 1–2 per cent of loans outstanding, stubbornly remained near 30 per cent for most micro-finance firms. Myanmar's low growth environment and poor investment climate, resulting from disruptions to incomes and loan collections brought about by the Covid-19 pandemic in 2020–21 and compounded by the coup over 2021–22, have kept the micro-finance sector from being able to meet the demand for its small loans. Access to cash and loans, especially micro-finance, is now particularly challenging for many small business owners and farmers in Myanmar. In June 2023, PACT Myanmar Microfinance, the largest provider of micro-finance loans to millions of Myanmar people, closed its operations citing challenges presented by new SAC regulations that have "made it impossible to continue operations" in Myanmar.[24]

In July 2023, Myanmar's ruling regime introduced a new higher denomination (MMK20,000) currency note. This note was printed on paper specially imported from Uzbekistan following the post-coup withdrawal of the hitherto supplier from Germany. The initiative, which did little but to remind people in Myanmar of past new currency issues that prefaced highly damaging demonetization episodes, undermined still further what trust remained in Myanmar's monetary authorities. Promises by the Central Bank of Myanmar that the new denomination bill would be issued in small volumes and only to replace damaged and unusable notes—and not form the basis of substantial money-financing of the budget deficit—went largely unbelieved by the population at large.

The increase in administrative controls and a more restricted space generally for economic activity have increased opportunities for corruption and rent-seeking in Myanmar, perceptions of which have grown since the coup. According to Transparency International in 2023, Myanmar is now regarded as the most corrupt country in Southeast Asia.[25]

Falling External Demand and Investment Inflows

Myanmar's external trade and finances mirror the weaknesses elsewhere. For the first six months of the 2023 financial year (April to September 2023), Myanmar recorded a trade deficit of nearly US$1 billion, an increase of around 1,500 per cent from the previous year.[26] Exports fell across the first half of 2023, a function of falling international demand for Myanmar-manufactured garments and a self-imposed restriction on rice exports. The latter was a misguided effort by the ruling regime to keep a lid on rice prices. With rising external debt servicing adding to the trade reversals, Myanmar's current account deficit reached 6.7 per cent of its GDP, compared with 3.6 per cent a year earlier.[27]

Degraded and deficient infrastructure in just about all areas hampers Myanmar's economic progress, and a lack of state and other investments dictates that any improvement on this front is not in prospect. Electricity shortages are the most obvious of Myanmar's infrastructure woes. Blackouts, brownouts and chronic instability of the electricity grid have been a characteristic of Myanmar for many years, but since the reversal of sectoral reforms undertaken by the deposed NLD administration, this has grown worse. According to the World Bank, in 2023 residents of Yangon, Myanmar's commercial capital and the hub of its manufacturing capacity, regularly experienced electricity blackouts of more than eight hours per day. Beyond Yangon, the situation was worse.[28]

A persistent regime objective through 2023 was to secure as much foreign exchange as possible for the state. To bring this about, an array of controls and prohibitions have been imposed, the confusion of which has only added to the disincentives to trade and investment in Myanmar. These measures included mandatory foreign currency surrender requirements on exporters, foreign currency rationing amongst importers, prohibitions on foreign currency accounts, and newly imposed taxes on the remittances of migrant workers abroad. Efforts to confine such remittance flows to formal bank channels (where they could be monitored and, given the forced application of the unrealistic fixed exchange rates, partially expropriated) and to close off the ancient and secure *Hundi* system were conspicuous failures.

FDI into Myanmar reached a record low of just US$13.6 million in the second quarter of 2023.[29] Such FDI came from Thailand, South Korea, China, Hong Kong and Singapore.[30] Much of this, however, comprised the funds of Myanmar nationals "round-tripping" to attract various FDI tax concessions and which were otherwise prudently held offshore to guard against policy caprice. In 2023, FDI into Myanmar from beyond Asia was near to non-existent.

Once a greatly promising sector, tourism in Myanmar was a shadow of its former self in 2023. Overall numbers of tourist arrivals rebounded sharply after the SAC reopened the country to visitors in April 2022 after the Covid/coup-related shutdowns. Even so, visitor arrivals by end-2023 remained at less than half the levels of 2019.[31] International tourist arrivals are primarily very short-term visitors from China and Thailand, while Myanmar has largely disappeared from the itineraries of high-spending travellers from Europe and North America. Countries such as the United States, the United Kingdom and Australia maintain "do not travel" notices for Myanmar, citing armed conflict, civil unrest and potential wrongful detention as just some of the risk factors for their nationals. Around a quarter of Myanmar's international standard hotels have not reopened since the pandemic and the military coup.

Education and Health At Risk

Investment of all forms underperformed in Myanmar in 2023, but amongst the most damaging to the country's long-term prospects is that relating to human capital. State spending on health and education combined dropped from 3.6 per cent of GDP in 2020 to just 1.8 per cent for the fiscal year 2023. These allocations amounted to only half of military spending.[32]

The low investment in education and health has thus taken its toll. Even before the 2021 coup, Myanmar faced the problem of "a missing million" in its state schools, which meant the exit of one million youths from Myanmar's education system each year without completing high school. Despite the efforts of the NLD government, little headway was made in reforms to curriculum design, teaching facilities and methodologies, as these all require substantial and sustained investment. The coup deepened Myanmar's education challenges, already tested severely by the pandemic, and caused further disruptions. Following the coup, overall school enrolment rates fell to about ten per cent nationwide, with less than one million of the nine million students enrolled in the 2019–20 academic year. The SAC played up the rise in enrolment numbers the following year by headlining in state media that "over 91 per cent of students joyfully study at 3,207 schools in Yangon", an example of the regime's politicization of education in Myanmar. But news reports on enrolment numbers show that the registered pool of students in 2022 was six million (compared to the nine million pre-coup) nationwide. The enrolment numbers also do not reflect the choices of parents seeking alternative education options for their children, whether overseas or in parallel education programmes established by the National Unity Government.[33]

The coup also exacerbated inequalities in Myanmar's healthcare sector. Myanmar has ranked among the lowest in public health expenditures in the region, even though the public health sector in Myanmar accounts for over eighty per cent of total healthcare services. The expanding middle-class during the previous decade of opening and reform increased both health awareness and demand for healthcare services, with attendant rises in private healthcare expenditure. Since the coup, those with financial means and access to overseas travel have increasingly turned to private healthcare, but the majority of Myanmar's population—who live in semi/peri-urban or rural areas—often have no similar recourse to quality healthcare services or awareness. Electricity shortages, lack of equipment and supplies, and shortages in healthcare workers compound Myanmar's healthcare challenges. Doctors and healthcare workers started the civil disobedience movement in the days immediately following the 2021 coup and were targeted by the military for their leadership and participation in it. The military targeted both healthcare facilities and healthcare workers, politicizing the provision of healthcare support and services to people protesting the coup. Attacks on healthcare workers, damage to healthcare facilities, and denial of medical and humanitarian aid to displaced civilians in many conflict areas have continued in 2023.[34]

Debts and Sanctions

In parallel to new and emerging economic problems in the aftermath of the coup, legacies of past ruling regimes dogged Myanmar throughout 2023. Among the most significant was the substantial debt-servicing costs for past loans from China. For instance, a US$400 million loan acquired by Myanmar's cooperative sector during the Thein Sein administration in 2013 has dramatically increased in magnitude on account of the depreciation of the kyat coupled with accumulating interest and servicing charges on the debt.[35]

In 2023, economic and financial sanctions were imposed on individuals and entities connected to Myanmar's ruling regime. The ones with the biggest impact were those imposed by the United States on two of Myanmar's state-owned banks; namely, the Myanmar Foreign Trade Bank and Myanmar Investment and Commercial Bank. These banks were hitherto instrumental in connecting the regime to international payments.[36] The United States also imposed restrictions on US citizens supplying financial services to the state-owned Myanmar Oil and Gas Enterprise (the regime's largest source of foreign currency earnings), as well as on foreign entities supplying jet fuel to Myanmar.[37] Backing up US and other official sanctions, a number of international banks took precautionary moves by restricting offshore transactions with Myanmar. The US sanctions also resulted in Bangladesh's state-owned Sonali Bank freezing the accounts of the two Myanmar state-owned banks.[38] Additionally, the US sanctions added to rising compliance costs after the FATF included Myanmar in its blacklist in October 2022. These mounting costs and reputational risks may well have been key considerations for Singapore's United Overseas Bank restricting its offshore transactions with

Myanmar.[39] In 2023, Myanmar remained on the FATF's so-called money laundering "blacklist", in company with only North Korea and Iran.[40]

Conclusion

Beneath all the numbers presented here, in 2023 Myanmar's economic policy-making framework continued its shift away from the market orientation of the last decade or so towards a much more restrictive and state-centred approach. With the SAC's recent setbacks on the battlefield, this slide into dirigisme can be expected to continue for as long as the regime remains in power. A war economy does not reform make.

With the current trends of rising inflation and poverty rates, foreign businesses continuing to exit Myanmar, more human capital outflows and fewer investment inflows, the hopes of Myanmar's people for improvements in employment, livelihoods and real incomes in the near future are fading. Anger and frustration have found different outlets, including a deepening distrust of power and authority structures.

The SAC's economic miscalculations have created socio-economic implications of a magnitude that future administrations in Myanmar will need to tackle for years to come. The 2021 coup has catalysed a negative cycle where the expertise and capacities necessary to tackle Myanmar's socio-economic challenges are unable to develop and thrive in the current environment, undoing the country's promising potential of the past decade.

Notes

1. Htet Myet Min Tun, Moe Thuzar, and Michael Montesano, "An Attempt to Lead Myanmar Back to the Future? Data on the State Administration Council Regime's Union Ministers", *ISEAS Perspective* no. 2021/137, 22 October 2021.
2. Republic of the Union of Myanmar, Office of the Commander-in-Chief of Defence Services, Notification No. 1/2021, https://www.gnlm.com.mm/republic-of-the-union-of-myanmar-office-of-the-commander-in-chief-of-defence-services-notification-no-1-2021/.
3. ISEAS – Yusof Ishak Institute, "Webinar on the State of Myanmar's Economy", 29 March 2023, https://www.iseas.edu.sg/media/event-highlights/webinar-on-the-state-of-myanmars-economy/.
4. John Liu and Frontier, "Regime Seeks Economic Recovery, but Drops NLD Reform Agenda", *Frontier Myanmar*, 17 September 2021, https://www.frontiermyanmar.net/en/regime-seeks-economic-recovery-but-drops-nld-reform-agenda/.
5. Independent Economists for Myanmar, "Overview of Myanmar Military Finances", 26 April 2021, https://docplayer.net/229144644-Overview-of-myanmar-military-

finances-independent-economists-for-myanmar-iem-26-april-2021.html; see also Gwen Robinson and Rory Wallace, "Myanmar Economists Urge Curbs on Junta's Hard Currency Access", *Nikkei Asia*, 29 April 2021, https://asia.nikkei.com/Spotlight/ Myanmar-Crisis/Myanmar-economists-urge-curbs-on-junta-s-hard-currency-access.

6. World Bank, "Myanmar Economic Monitor July 2021: Progress Threatened; Resilience Tested", July 2021, https://documents1.worldbank.org/curated/en/884011627285477076/ pdf/Myanmar-Economic-Monitor-Progress-Threatened-Resilience-Tested.pdf.

7. World Bank, "Myanmar Economic Monitor December 2023: Challenges amid Conflict", https://documents1.worldbank.org/curated/en/099121123082084971/pdf/ P5006630739fd70a00a66c0e15bf7b34917.pdf.

8. International Monetary Fund, "Transcript of Press Briefing on Regional Economic Outlook for Asia and Pacific", 18 October 2023, https://www.imf.org/en/News/ Articles/2023/10/18/tr101823-transcript-of-press-briefing-on-reo-for-asia-and-pacific-singapore-october-2023#:~:text=The%20economies%20in%20ASEAN%20are,our%20 April%20World%20Economic%20Outlook.

9. World Bank, "Myanmar Economic Monitor December 2023".

10. International Monetary Fund, "Southeast Asia, Datasets", https://www.imf.org/external/ datamapper/profile/SEQ.

11. "Myanmar Manufacturing PMI", Trading Economics, 1 December 2023, https:// tradingeconomics.com/myanmar/manufacturing-pmi#:~:text=Myanmar%20Manufact uring%20PMI%20Lowest%20in,steepest%20pace%20since%20December%202022.

12. In 2023, Marks & Spencer, Primark, Uniqlo, H&M and a host of other brands announced their intentions of cutting Myanmar as a source producer. See Ria Kakked, "How Myanmar's Human Rights Crisis Is Shaking Up Fashion Retail", *Sustainability Beat*, 22 August 2023, https://www.sustainability-beat.co.uk/2023/08/22/myanmar-suppliers-retail/#:~:text=In%20March%202023%2C%20Marks%20%26%20Spencer's,risks%20 in%20the%20garment%20sector.

13. "EU Monitors Myanmar Labour Rights as Fashion Brands Exist", Reuters, 24 August 2023, https://www.reuters.com/sustainability/eu-monitors-myanmar-labour-rights-fashion-brands-exit-2023-08-24/.

14. United Nations Development Programme, "Impact of the Twin Crises on Human Welfare in Myanmar", November 2021, https://www.undp.org/sites/g/files/zskgke326/ files/2022-07/UNDP-MMR-Impact-of-Twin-Crises-on-Human-Welfare-in-Myanmar-2021-EN.pdf.

15. Food and Agriculture Organisation, "GIEWS Update—The Republic of the Union of Myanmar – The Current Critical Food Insecurity Situation Could Deteriorate in the Second Half of 2023", 31 July 2023, https://www.fao.org/documents/card/en/c/ cc7195en.

16. International Monetary Fund, "Southeast Asia, Datasets", https://www.imf.org/external/ datamapper/profile/SEQ.

17. RFA Burmese, "Junta Threatens Unauthorized Foreign Currency Holders as Myanmar Kyat Tanks", 21 August 2023, https://www.rfa.org/english/news/myanmar/currency-08212023164853.html.

18. "Myanmar Interventions Threaten to Create 3 Forex Rates", *Nikkei Asia*, 27 June 2023, https://asia.nikkei.com/Spotlight/Myanmar-Crisis/Myanmar-interventions-threaten-to-create-3-forex-rates; "Kyat Depreciates Further after Myanmar Central Bank Abandons Dollar Forex Rate", *The Irrawaddy*, 7 December 2023, https://www.irrawaddy.com/news/burma/kyat-depreciates-further-after-myanmar-central-bank-abandons-dollar-forex-rate.html.

19. "Myanmar Slaps Tax on Migrant Workers' Earnings Move by Cash-Strapped Junta Comes on Heels of Requirement to Remit 25% of Wages", *Bangkok Post*, 28 September 2023, https://www.bangkokpost.com/world/2654338/myanmar-slaps-tax-on-migrant-workers-earnings#:~:text=The%20military%20government%20of%20Myanmar,rates%2C%20according%20to%20local%20reports.

20. "'We Don't Have a Choice': Junta Puts the Squeeze on Overseas Workers", 22 September 2023, https://www.frontiermyanmar.net/en/we-dont-have-a-choice-junta-puts-the-squeeze-on-overseas-workers/.

21. Romain Caillaud, "Time to Collect: The SAC's Actions Come to Bite Myanmar's Economy", *Fulcrum*, 28 November 2023, https://fulcrum.sg/time-to-collect-the-sacs-actions-come-to-bite-myanmars-economy/.

22. Myanmar Quarterly Statistics Bulletin, Quarterly Time Series 2022–2023 (Q4), Central Statistical Organisation, Ministry of Planning and Finance, Government of the Republic of the Union of Myanmar, available at https://www.csostat.gov.mm/PublicationAndRelease/QuarterlyBulletin.

23. "KBZ Users Struggle under Junta Surveillance", *Frontier*, 28 April 2023, https://www.frontiermyanmar.net/en/kbz-users-struggle-under-junta-surveillance/.

24. Development Media Group, "Major Microfinancier Pulls Out of Military-Ruled Myanmar", 27 June 2023, https://www.dmediag.com/news/pact-mmicro-finance.html.

25. "Myanmar Plunges in Latest Corruption Index, but Vietnam Rises", Radio Free Asia, 31 January 2023, https://www.rfa.org/english/news/myanmar/corruption-perceptions-index-01312023144554.html.

26. Hein Htoo Zan, "Junta Seeks Brake as Myanmar's Runaway Trade Deficit Nears $1Bn in Six Months', *The Irrawaddy*, 23 October 2023, https://www.irrawaddy.com/business/junta-seeks-brake-as-myanmars-runaway-trade-deficit-nears-1bn-in-six-months.html.

27. World Bank, "Myanmar Economic Monitor December 2023".

28. Ibid.

29. "Myanmar Foreign Direct Investment", *Trading Economics*, 28 November 2023, https://tradingeconomics.com/myanmar/foreign-direct-investment.

30. Myanmar Quarterly Statistics Bulletin, Quarterly Time Series 2022–2023 (Q4), Central Statistical Organisation, Ministry of Planning and Finance, Government of the Republic of the Union of Myanmar.

31. "Myanmar Travel Sector Mocks Junta Tourist Claim", *The Irrawaddy*, 30 September 2023, https://www.irrawaddy.com/business/myanmar-travel-sector-mocks-junta-tourist-claim.html.

32. Ibid.

33. Aung Tun, "The Political Economy of Education in Myanmar", ISEAS Economics Working Paper 2022–5, September 2022, https://www.iseas.edu.sg/wp-content/uploads/2022/08/ISEAS_EWP_2022-5_Aung_Tun.pdf.

34. Insecurity Insight Press Release, "A Tragic Milestone: More Than 1,000 Attacks on Health Care in Myanmar since the February 2021 Military Coup", 15 November 2023, https://insecurityinsight.org/wp-content/uploads/2023/11/A-Tragic-Milestone-Myanmar-Press-Release-November-2023.pdf; See also ReliefWeb, "A Tragic Milestone: More Than 1,000 Attacks on Health Care in Myanmar since the February 2021 Military Coup", 15 November 2023, https://reliefweb.int/report/myanmar/tragic-milestone-more-1000-attacks-health-care-myanmar-february-2021-military-coup.

35. "Myanmar Junta Struggles to Repay $400 Million Chinese Bank Loan Due to Jump in Dollar Price", *Mizzima*, 13 August 2023, https://www.mizzima.com/article/myanmar-junta-struggles-repay-400-million-chinese-bank-loan-due-jump-dollar-price.

36. US Department of State, Press Statement by Antony J. Blinken, "Sanctioning Two State-Owned Banks and the Ministry of Defense for the Burma Military Regime's Atrocities", 21 June 2023, https://www.state.gov/sanctioning-two-state-owned-banks-and-the-ministry-of-defense-for-the-burma-military-regimes-atrocities/.

37. US Department of the Treasury Press Statement, "Treasury Prohibits Financial Services with Myanma Oil and Gas Enterprise and Imposes Additional Sanctions on Burma Military Regime Officials and Supporters", 31 October 2023, https://home.treasury.gov/news/press-releases/jy1856; US Department of State Press Statement, "Expanding Burma Sanctions Authorities and Imposing Sanctions on Additional Jet Fuel Suppliers", 23 August 2023, https://www.state.gov/expanding-burma-sanctions-authorities-and-imposing-sanctions-on-additional-jet-fuel-suppliers/.

38. "Key Bangladeshi Bank Freezes Myanmar Regime Accounts", *Asia Financial*, 23 August 2023, https://www.asiafinancial.com/key-bangladeshi-bank-freezes-myanmar-regime-accounts#:~:text=Sonali%20Bank%2C%20a%20state%2Downed,US%20Treasury%20on%20June%2021.

39. Gwen Robinson, "Key Singapore Bank UOB Moves to Cut Off Myanmar", *Nikkei Asia*, 9 August 2023, https://asia.nikkei.com/Spotlight/Myanmar-Crisis/Key-Singapore-bank-UOB-moves-to-cut-off-Myanmar.

40. Financial Action Taskforce Statement, "Myanmar's Progress in Strengthening Measures to Tackle Money Laundering and Terrorist Financing", 9 November 2023, https://www.fatf-gafi.org/en/publications/Mutualevaluations/fur-myanmar-2023.html.

Philippines

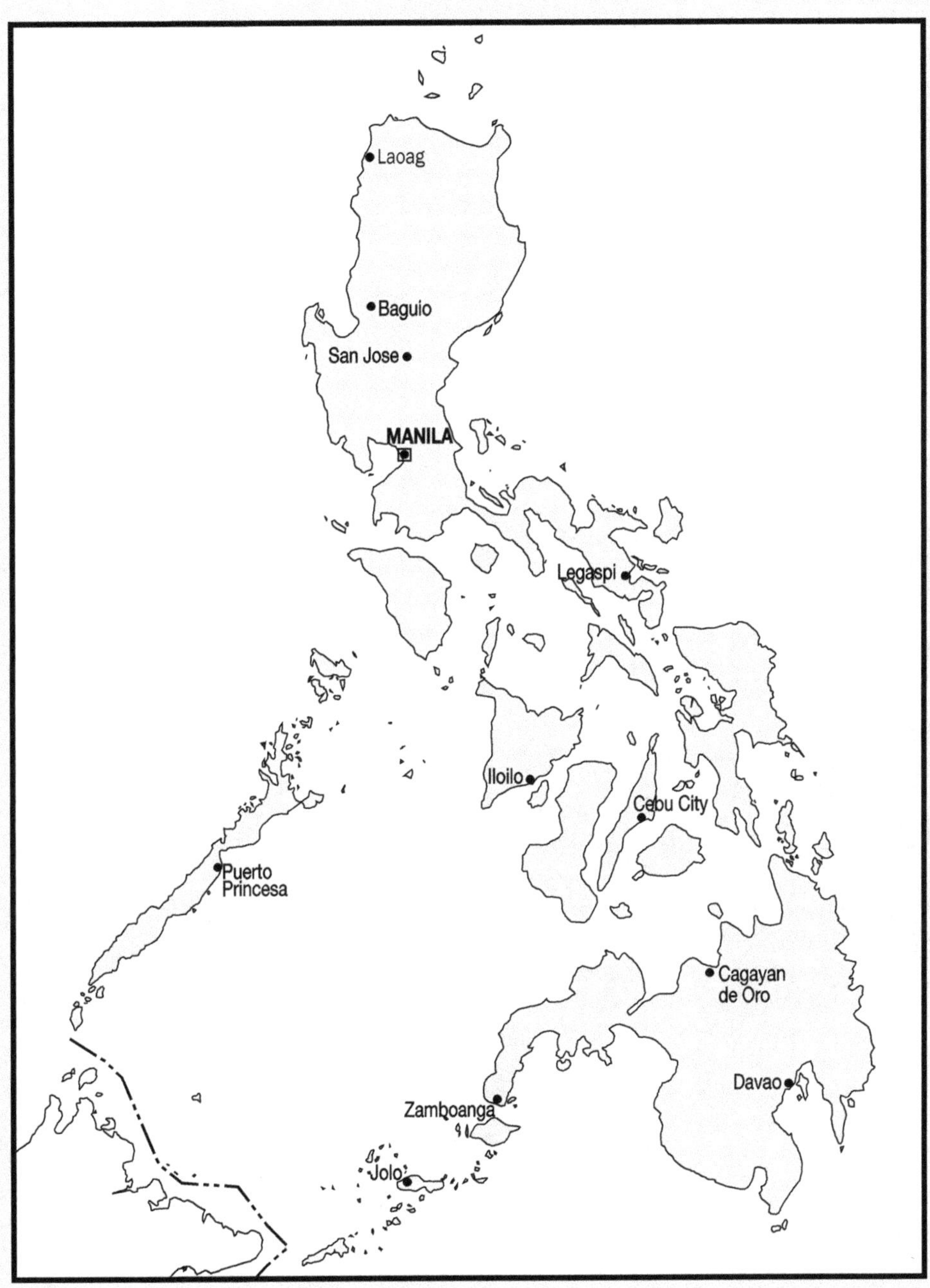

THE PHILIPPINES IN 2023:
Post-pandemic Challenges and Fraying Political Alliance

Ruth R. Lusterio-Rico

The year 2023 was arguably one of the most challenging for Filipinos, particularly as the country continued to struggle to recover from the impact of a global pandemic. This is the first full year of the administration of Ferdinand Marcos Jr., who was elected president in a landslide victory in the May 2022 national elections. By the middle of 2023, an end to the pandemic was announced in the country through a presidential proclamation lifting the state of public health emergency resulting from Covid-19. It was expected, therefore, that the Philippines would bounce back from the gruelling effects of the pandemic on the economy. In 2022, a survey conducted by the Social Weather Stations (SWS) reported that 45 per cent of the adult population of the country were optimistic that the quality of their lives would improve in the next twelve months, while 39 per cent believed there would be no change.[1] A year later, the optimism remains at the same level of 46 per cent. This is despite the high prices of basic commodities—including rice—a soaring inflation rate, and more than two million Filipinos being unemployed.[2]

In the political realm, observations of a crack within the ruling political alliance that enabled the electoral victory of President Marcos and Vice-President Sara Duterte, the daughter of the former president, became more pronounced. Talk of the disintegration of President Marcos and Vice-President Duterte's UniTeam alliance abounded as conflicts among personalities associated with both leaders began to emerge. This was accompanied by the emergence of controversial proposals such as the establishment of the Maharlika Investment Fund and the huge allocation of confidential funds for the use of the Office of the Vice-President and the Department of Education headed by the current vice-president.

RUTH R. LUSTERIO-RICO is Professor of Political Science, College of Social Sciences and Philosophy, University of the Philippines Diliman.

Interestingly, the trust and approval ratings of the two highest officials of the country remained relatively high. Although there was a double-digit drop in the approval ratings of both leaders by the third quarter of 2023, such ratings still indicate a majority approval of their leadership. According to a Pulse Asia survey conducted in September 2023, the approval rating of Marcos dropped to 65 per cent from 80 per cent in June 2023, while Sara Duterte's approval rating moved downwards from 84 per cent to 73 per cent. The Pulse Asia survey was conducted from 10 to 14 September 2023, when deliberations for the 2024 budget were ongoing in the Philippine Congress and when rice price caps were imposed through the issuance of Executive Order No. 39.[3]

This review of the key political and economic developments in the Philippines in 2023 gives particular attention to what has been generally observed as the weakening of the Marcos-Duterte alliance. The economic challenges confronting the country continue to be the main concern as the Philippine public rate the performance of the country's two highest officials. Some key political developments will also be highlighted as these are seen to have a significant impact on the preservation of the ruling political coalition. Seemingly absent in the current Philippine political scene is an opposition group or party that can pose a challenge to the ruling political alliance. Some prospects for the Philippines in 2024 will be offered to conclude this chapter.

A Recovered Economy?

Ferdinand 'Bongbong' Marcos Jr. won a landslide victory in the elections of May 2022. He beat his closest rival, Maria Leonor 'Leni' Robredo, with a commanding 59 per cent of the vote. Political analysts attributed the Marcos victory to the political alliance or power-sharing arrangement that was forged among groups that supported either Bongbong Marcos or Sara Duterte.[4] Former political opponents Joseph Estrada and Gloria Macapagal Arroyo were among those who brokered the grand coalition that took the name "UniTeam" and adopted the vague theme of unity for its political campaign. Thus, it is expected that all eyes will be on this coalition over the six years of the Marcos administration.

No concrete policies or programmes for post-pandemic economic recovery were laid out by Marcos during his campaign for the presidency. But when he delivered his first state of the nation address in July 2022, the revival of the Philippine economy was promised through the implementation of sound fiscal management and tax administration reforms, among others. One year later, in his second state of the nation address, the president claimed that his administration had accomplished a lot, citing the highest economic growth rate achieved at 7.6 per cent. Marcos proclaimed that the Philippine economy is now "revived and rejuvenated, backstopped by a favorable enabling environment and the strong rule of law".[5] But the purported economic growth rate had little impact on ordinary Filipinos as prices of food and basic commodities continued to increase in 2023. Unemployment also remained high at 4.5 per cent,[6] although it had dropped from 4.8 per cent at the start of the year. A research group further notes that the Marcos administration has not really improved the economy's capacity to generate meaningful jobs.[7] Many Filipinos are involved in informal and part-time work. The reported new jobs often entail precarious employment that struggling Filipinos take on to survive. What has increased significantly is the number of part-time workers, the self-employed, and unpaid family workers, which IBON Foundation estimates to be 42.1 per cent of those who were employed in August 2023. It is also worth noting that a considerable number of Filipino households depend on remittances from overseas work. The 2022 Survey of Overseas Filipinos estimates the total number of Overseas Filipino Workers at 1.96 million.[8] The total amount of remittances for 2023 is expected to reach US$37 billion. This is higher than the total remittances in 2022, which was at US$36.1 billion and which accounted for 8.9 per cent of the country's gross domestic product (GDP) and 8.4 per cent of its gross national income (GNI).[9] Thus, overall, it cannot be claimed that the current Philippine government has addressed the long-time problem of unemployment and underemployment.

A recent national survey conducted by the Social Weather Stations reported that 28 per cent of Filipinos believed that their quality of life got better over the past twelve months, 30 per cent said they are worse off now compared with the past twelve months, and 41 per cent say that their quality of life has stayed the same.[10] In the same survey, 48 per cent of Filipinos rated themselves as poor and 38 per cent said that they are food poor. These findings indicate that a recovered and rejuvenated Philippine economy has not translated into tangible benefits for ordinary Filipinos. Moreover, the September 2023 survey by Pulse Asia revealed that 56 per cent disapprove of what the government is doing to control inflation and 36 per cent disapprove of government efforts towards poverty reduction. Their three most urgent national concerns were controlling inflation, increasing the pay of workers and creating more jobs.[11]

Clearly, the promises made by Marcos are quite far from reality. Some observers note that the output in terms of legislative measures to support the administration's programmes for economic recovery have not been impressive, considering that only three out of those that had been certified as urgent bills have been passed into law thus far. One of the bills whose approval appears to have been fast-tracked is the controversial Maharlika Investment Fund Act of 2023. The proposed bill, which aimed to establish the Philippines' sovereign wealth fund, passed third reading in the House of Representatives in December 2022 and was approved in the Senate in May 2023. On 18 July 2023, Republic Act No. 11954, or the Maharlika Investment Fund Act of 2023, was signed into law by President Ferdinand R. Marcos Jr. This happened despite the scepticism and apprehension expressed from various sectors, including financial experts, economists and investors.

A Vehicle for Economic Growth?

The Maharlika Investment Fund (MIF) is referred to as a sovereign wealth fund and described by the government as a vehicle for economic growth designed "to catalyze economic development and accelerate the country's growth by optimizing the use of government financial assets and promoting their intergenerational management".[12] The creation of the MIF has also been described as a "game-changer for the Philippine economy". Although it is not really a novel idea, some people are inclined to believe that this is the brainchild of the current president and it has been pushed to help propel economic development in the Philippines via investment capital, infrastructure development, foreign investment and good governance.

When news of the plan to establish the MIF came out, scepticism and apprehensions were already expressed by some sectors, including economists. The swift approval of the law that created the fund was not surprising considering the support the president enjoys from a super majority in both the House of Representatives and the Senate. There was little chance of the minority opposition in the legislature being able to block the legislation. Overall, the scepticism is based on provisions in the law that "could affect the independence of government financial institutions and the central bank".[13] Moreover, some financial experts believe the fund could become a space for corruption or, worse, be used for money laundering. On the part of the public, perception of the creation of the MIF is vague to say the least, because people—including legislators—know little about it. In the first quarter of 2023, a national survey of public opinion on the MIF undertaken by the Social Weather Stations revealed that the majority of the public were not aware of or knew nothing about the fund. Perhaps because the passage of the law was fast-tracked, public consultations to discuss the establishment of the fund and the provisions of the proposed law were not conducted. Even after its approval, financial experts and academics still raised the basic flaws of the law. Faculty members of the School of Economics of the University of the Philippines Diliman wrote in a discussion paper that the MIF "violates fundamental principles of economics and finance and poses serious risks to the economy and the public sector".[14]

On 12 October 2023, the implementing rules and regulations (IRR) of the MIF Act were suspended through a memorandum issued by Executive Secretary Lucas Bersamin upon the directive of the president. The memorandum directs officials to suspend the implementation of the MIF law pending its further study. No explanation was provided for the suspension, but it appears that questions over transparency and the accountability of officials who would govern the Maharlika Investment Corporation (MIC) were raised from various sectors, including economists and financial experts. One speculation is that the suspension has something to do with the selection of officials who will govern the MIC. Meanwhile, according to secretary of the Department of Finance Benjamin Diokno, the MIC will start operating by end-2023.

The Confidential Funds Controversy

Another major controversy that erupted in the Philippines while budget proposals were being deliberated in Congress is the allocation of confidential and intelligence funds (CIF) for agencies of the executive branch of government. These funds are commonly used by law enforcement agencies for surveillance and intelligence-gathering operations, and they are exempted from standard auditing rules because of the nature of the activities for which the funds are to be spent. Vice-President Sara Duterte figured prominently in this controversy as her office, the Office of the Vice-President (OVP), asked for PHP500 million in confidential funds and the Department of Education (DepEd), which she heads, also sought a PHP150 million budget for the same item. Opposition legislators expressed concern and questioned why civilian agencies should be provided this type of fund. In the course of deliberation and questioning, it was found that the OVP used CIF in December 2022, although Congress did not allocate any CIF to the OVP in that year. It was revealed further that the OVP had accessed confidential funds through a transfer made by the Office of the President. The amount provided was PHP125 million, which was spent in only eleven days.[15] Opposition legislators and critics feel there was no justification to provide such funds to the OVP or the DepEd. Moreover, the transfer of funds from the Office of the President was also criticized and regarded by some as illegal and unconstitutional. For her part, Sara Duterte defended and justified her use of CIF in the name of national security and to provide a safe learning environment for teachers and students. She called her critics "enemies of peace" or "enemies of the state" and insisted that her offices are entitled to the use of such funds.

As concern over the CIF allocation for Sara Duterte and other civilian agencies grew, members of major parties in the House of Representatives agreed to remove the controversial item and realign the budget to other civilian agencies whose functions are directly related to securing the country's borders and territory. The disapproval in the House of Representatives of the requested budget for CIF for civilian agencies, including the OVP and DepEd, apparently led to the withdrawal of this budget item request when it was about to be taken up in the Senate. The reason for the withdrawal, according to the vice-president, is that the issue had become "divisive". Some analysts noted that Sara Duterte might have backtracked from her original position in defending the CIF for the offices she headed because of the double-digit drop in her approval ratings. Some said that it could also be a political strategy so that Sara Duterte can appear as the underdog and eventually get the public on her side.

The rejection of Sara Duterte's request for confidential funds led her father, former president Rodrigo Duterte, to accuse Speaker of the House of Representatives Martin Romualdez, a cousin of President Marcos, and all members of the legislative chamber of being engaged in corrupt practices. He also described the House of Representatives to be the "most rotten institution" in the country. The older Duterte made these statements in his programme over the media network Sonshine Media Network, Inc. (SMNI). In response to the tirades of the former president, members of the House of Representatives adopted House Resolution 1414, which upheld the institution's integrity and honour and pledged support for its current leader, Romualdez. Two Duterte supporters did not sign the resolution and were stripped of their leadership positions in the House. One of these is former president Gloria Macapagal Arroyo, who was first deposed as senior deputy speaker in May 2023 after rumours emerged of her plan to oust Romualdez as House Speaker. This demotion of Arroyo led Sara Duterte to resign from the Lakas-CMD party, which had "adopted" her when she ran as vice-president.

On one occasion, the vice-president, through a speech, gave a hint that there is indeed a crack within the UniTeam coalition.[16] She mentioned that she does not want to say the middle name of the president.[17] Although the parties involved have all denied the existence of a rift, speculations of a crack within the Marcos-Duterte coalition persist. A rumour that the vice-president would be impeached surfaced in the wake of the controversy over the confidential funds. Legislators from the former president's party, PDP-Laban, transferred to Romualdez's party, Lakas-CMD, which is now the dominant party in the coalition and positions Romualdez—as head of the party—as a strong contender to be the next president of the country. It is certain that the older Duterte is not pleased with this development since he had initially wanted his daughter to run for president. It has now become evident that Sara is being eased out to pave the way for another member of the Marcos family to become president.

As the political influence of the Romualdez-Marcos family consolidates in the House of Representatives, the Senate is another story. While the older Duterte might be losing his hold on former allies in the lower chamber, he might still have a strong influence in the Senate given that his prominent supporters are very much present in the upper chamber. The president's older sister, Senator Imee Marcos, has declared her unwavering support for the Dutertes. Aside from her, there are senators who owe their position to the former president, including his long-time allies who were elected senators, Ronald Dela Rosa and Christopher 'Bong' Go. The rumour that at least nine senators were in favour of restoring the confidential funds requested by the vice-president possibly indicated the influence that the former president still has among the senators. In the meantime, members of the ruling political alliance must attend to the pressing issues confronting the country. As they continue to manoeuvre their positions in the power matrix, they must not neglect the watching public, whose support is important in keeping them in those positions.

A Foreign Policy Turn?

In his first address to the nation in July 2022, President Marcos declared that his administration would maintain an "independent foreign policy, with the national interest as our primordial guide".[18] In this speech, the new president did not mention any specific country or major power. China, which was always mentioned by his predecessor in his speeches, was not cited. Marcos's statements were broad and not specific and simply referred to the promotion of "stronger and multifaceted partnerships". The Philippines' foreign policy under the Marcos presidency had originally been described as "balanced" and "flexible", specifically in reference to the country's relations with the United States and China. In his speeches, the president declared that the Philippines seeks to enhance existing cooperation—in particular, with ASEAN, Japan, the United States and China—for shared security and economic concerns.

The "balanced foreign policy" appears, however, to have taken the direction of renewing the Philippines' alliance with the United States. Less than a year after his election as president, Marcos revived the country's Enhanced Defense Cooperation Agreement (EDCA) with the US. Originally signed in 2014, this agreement supplements the previous Visiting Forces Agreement and reaffirms the alliance between the two countries. The implementation of EDCA was not realized, however, because of legal and political challenges presented by various opposition groups. And when Rodrigo Duterte became president in 2016, the prospects for the implementation of EDCA further diminished. But EDCA was given new life under the Marcos administration. In 2023, the Philippines gave the US access to four more military bases in the country in addition to the five that had been granted previously. The two countries also issued an updated set of bilateral defence guidelines that effectively signalled the renewed commitment of the Philippines and the United States in each other's interests.[19] Moreover, in May 2023, Marcos paid US president Biden a visit, which indicated an intention to deepen the Philippines' relationship with the United States. This move was considered "unique" given that many Southeast Asian states have turned more towards China in recent years.[20]

Apart from rekindling the country's alliance with the United States, the Philippines under Marcos has also strengthened its security partnerships with Japan and Australia, which are considered strong US allies in the region. The Philippines and Japan have agreed to begin talks about a Visiting Forces Agreement, strengthen military cooperation and work closely with the United States. On the part of the Philippines and Australia, the two countries upgraded their bilateral ties through the signing of a strategic partnership agreement in September 2023. These efforts to strengthen the Philippines' ties with the United States and its allies took place amid growing tensions in the South China Sea. In particular, the Philippines and China have traded accusations of committing actions that endanger peace and stability in the region. The Philippines has condemned Chinese actions in the South China Sea, in particular China's use of water cannons to shoot Philippine civilian vessels near Scarborough Shoal. For its part, China accused the Philippines of provoking conflict by sending construction supplies to the Second Thomas Shoal (also known as Ayungin Shoal in the Philippines) and of brushing aside its goodwill and restraint. Based on these developments, it has become evident that the Philippines now leans more towards reviving and strengthening its ties with the United States and its allies as it confronts the challenges presented by China, which was the preferred ally of Marcos Jr.'s predecessor.

An Unexpected Turn: De Lima's Release

On 13 November 2023, former senator, secretary of justice, and human rights commissioner Leila De Lima was granted bail after being detained in jail for more than two thousand days. A staunch critic of former president Rodrigo Duterte's war on drugs, De Lima was accused of taking bribes from imprisoned drug traffickers and using the funds for her senatorial campaign. Three cases were filed against her; she was acquitted in two of them, and in the third case bail was finally granted after five witnesses recanted their testimonies.

Political observers note that the release of De Lima could indicate a rift within the Marcos-Duterte alliance. The Duterte camp definitely does not approve of the release. But the move could have been taken as a way for President Marcos to improve both his and the Philippines' image in the international community. For several years, various international human rights groups and individuals from the United States and the European Union have called on the Philippine government to release De Lima. Her detention was clearly politically motivated because De Lima was the one who initiated the investigation of human rights violations committed by the infamous Davao Death Squad in Davao City where Rodrigo Duterte was former mayor. With the end of Duterte's term of office in 2022, an opportunity opened for the groups to start negotiating with the new administration.

Upon his assumption to the presidency, Marcos declared that the "deepening of the Philippines' alliance with the United States and other Western governments" is a cornerstone of his administration's foreign policy.[21] This is clearly a departure from his predecessor's strong pro-China position. Marcos had visited the United States and had hosted visits of US officials in the country. In August 2022, a delegation led by US senator Edward Markey visited De Lima in jail and met with President Marcos and his justice secretary to discuss human rights. In October 2022, Senator Markey and his colleagues wrote a letter to Secretary of Justice Remulla and stated that he and President Marcos "can turn the page on President Duterte's abuses and demonstrate your commitment to the rule of law in the Philippines".[22]

Another significant development was the approval of resolutions in the House of Representatives urging the government to allow the International Criminal Court (ICC) to come to the country and cooperate in its investigations of Duterte's war on drugs and extrajudicial killings. Earlier, statements made by President Marcos were interpreted to mean that he is open to the idea for the Philippines to rejoin the ICC. His executive secretary has, however, clarified that this matter is still being studied and that the country will not be rejoining the ICC anytime soon.

These two developments—De Lima's release from prison and the House resolutions urging the government to cooperate with the ICC investigations—further reinforce the view that there is indeed a serious rift within the Marcos-Duterte alliance. Despite denials and statements that claim that all is well in the ruling coalition, the public can clearly discern that a power struggle is taking place. Whether the cracks in the coalition will widen to a complete rift remains to be seen.

Maintaining the UniTeam

The question now is would maintaining the unity within the UniTeam be beneficial to all parties? At the outset, the "unity" that was forged between the two main camps—the Marcoses and the Dutertes—had been quite volatile. The coming together of the various forces that constitute the UniTeam had been referred to as a "marriage of convenience". The principal aim of forging the alliance was really to secure the main seat of power in the country. Thus, talks of power-sharing arrangements surfaced. For the electoral campaign, the alliance conveniently used the vague term "unity" to represent the different groups and personalities that came together to get the top positions in government. After electoral victory was secured, the struggle for positions ensued.

It appears now that the issue is who will succeed Marcos as the next president. Political manoeuvrings of the president's cousin—the Speaker of the House of Representatives—are already quite evident in the lower chamber of the legislature. Politicians from former president Duterte's party have already transferred to Romualdez's Lakas-CMD. The allegiance of legislators in the House of Representatives has also been clearly expressed through the adoption of House Resolution 1414, which it released after the former president lambasted the lower chamber for not approving the request of his daughter to be given confidential funds. What remains to be seen is how another former president and staunch Duterte supporter, Gloria Arroyo, will move against the current House leadership in favour of Sara Duterte.

For her part, Sara Duterte may be enjoying an advantage because of the public support she inherited from her father. In fact, some observers have pointed out that of the two highest officials of the country, Sara Duterte is the one with the more significant political capital. Her popularity is shown in the pre-electoral surveys as well as in the number of votes she garnered to become vice-president. It is also said that Marcos owed his election as president to Sara Duterte. But public perception of her leadership cannot be taken to be constant. The approval ratings of both the president and the vice-president have dropped considerably in recent months as a result of the continuing problems of inflation and unemployment, a lack of transparency in governance, and allegations of corruption. These are crucial issues that are significant for the public. If Sara Duterte fails to give adequate attention to them, it will erode public trust in her. And if such issues remain unresolved, any politician's popularity would hang precariously.

A Possible Opening for the Opposition?

Ideally, the rift within the ruling political alliance combined with the pressing issues facing ordinary Filipinos should provide an opportunity for a political opposition that could challenge dynastic politics to emerge. In the case of the Philippines, though, politics has always been about personalities. This is the reason why only alliances emerge. Political parties serve the interests of individuals; essentially, they do not have platforms of action or ideologies. They exist simply to push the candidacies of politicians. Membership is based generally on which party can provide the most benefit. Thus, politicians shift allegiance from one party to another very easily. Some politicians, especially senators who are voted nationally, choose not to belong to any political party, and they do survive politically.

What, then, is the future political outlook for the Philippines? Obviously, the public will follow keenly the developments in the drama between Sara Duterte and Martin Romualdez. The roles the former presidents will play and how they will use their political capital will also be interesting to watch. At the centre of the ongoing rift is President Marcos, whose actions will be critical. Will Sara Duterte allow herself to be sidelined? Or will she turn out to be the opposition? Some observers have already noted that she may be positioning herself as the underdog in order to gain public sympathy.

In the meantime, those who have been pushed to the sidelines because of the political strategies employed against them during the last elections can prepare and plan their next moves. The political cards may be on the side of the likes of Marcos and Sara Duterte right now. But people can be disillusioned, and their political preferences can change.

Notes

1. Social Weather Stations, Third Quarter 2022 Social Weather Survey, 29 September – 2 October 2022 National Survey, https://www.sws.org.ph/swsmain/artcldisppage/?artcsyscode=ART-20221209074723.
2. The Philippine unemployment rate was reported by the Philippine Statistics Authority to be at 4.5 per cent in June 2023. See Ralf Rivas, "Unemployment Rate Increases

to 4.5% in June 2023, Unpaid Workers Still Rising", *Rappler*, 9 August 2023, https://www.rappler.com/business/unemployment-rate-philippines-june-2023/.

3.   Jean Mangaluz, "Bongbong Marcos, Sara Duterte's Approval Ratings Fall – Pulse Asia", *Inquirer.net*, 2 October 2023, https://newsinfo.inquirer.net/1839616/bongbong-marcos-and-sara-dutertes-approval-ratings-fall-pulse-asia#:~:text=and%20Vice%20President%20Sara%20Duterte,percent%20in%20the%20same%20period.

4.   J. Baquisal and A. Arugay, "The Philippines in 2022: The "Dance" of the Dynasties", in *Southeast Asian Affairs 2023*, edited by Daljit Singh and Hoang Thi Ha (Singapore: ISEAS – Yusof Ishak Institute, 2023), p. 242.

5.   Official Gazette of the Republic of the Philippines, "Ferdinand R. Marcos, Jr., Second State of the Nation Address, July 24, 2023", 24 July 2023, https://www.officialgazette.gov.ph/2023/07/24/ferdinand-r-marcos-jr-first-state-of-the-nation-address-july-24-2023/.

6.   The Philippine Statistics Authority estimated the unemployment rate at 4.5 per cent in September 2023: Philippine Statistics Authority, "Labor Force Survey", 7 February 2024, https://psa.gov.ph/statistics/labor-force-survey.

7.   IBON Foundation, "More Part-Timers, Unpaid Family Workers Underscores Admin's Inability to Create Quality Jobs", 6 October 2023, https://www.ibon.org/more-part-timers-unpaid-family-workers-underscores-admins-inability-to-create-quality-jobs-ibon/.

8.   Philippine Statistics Authority, "2022 Survey of Overseas Filipinos (Final Result)", 11 October 2023, https://psa.gov.ph/statistics/survey/labor-and-employment/survey-overseas-filipinos/node/1684061314.

9.   CNN Philippines Staff, "BSP: OFW Remittances Could Hit $37 Billion in 2023", *Balita News*, 18 November 2023, https://balita.org/n/bsp-ofw-remittances-could-hit-37-billion-in/8076.

10. Social Weather Stations, "Social Weather Report: Gainers Minus Losers Falls to −2 in September from +11 in June", 25 November 2023, https://www.sws.org.ph/swsmain/artcldisppage/?artcsyscode=ART-20231125092510.

11. See Pulse Asia Research Inc., "Ulat ng Bayan", www.pulseasia.ph.

12. Republic of the Philippines, Department of Finance press release, "Newly Enacted Maharlika Investment Fund to Serve as Vehicle for Growth", https://maharlika.dof.gov.ph/newly-enacted-maharlika-investment-fund-to-serve-as-vehicle-for-growth/ (accessed 29 November 2023).

13. Kyle Aristophere T. Atienza, "Economists Still Skeptical about Maharlika Fund after Congress Approval", *BusinessWorld*, 2 June 2023, https://www.bworldonline.com/top-stories/2023/06/02/526343/economists-still-skeptical-about-maharlika-fund-after-congress-approval/.

14. JC Punongbayan, "Maharlika Fund: New Law, New Lies", *Rappler*, 19 July 2023, https://rappler.com/voices/thought-leaders/analysis-maharlika-investment-fund-new-

law-lies/; "Maharlika Investment Fund: Still beyond Repair", UP School of Economics Discussion Papers, https://econ.upd.edu.ph/dp/index.php/dp/article/view/1551/1035.

15. Dwight De Leon, "Duterte's OVP Spent P125-M Confidential Funds in 11 Days – COA", *Rappler*, 25 September 2023, https://www.rappler.com/nation/office-vice-president-duterte-spent-confidential-funds-11-days-coa/.

16. Cristina Chi, "Public Barbs by UniTeam Leaders Signal Brewing Showdown", *Philippine Star*, 8 June 2023, https://www.philstar.com/headlines/2023/06/08/2272366/public-barbs-uniteam-leaders-signal-brewing-showdown.

17. In the Philippines, the middle name is the mother's surname. In this case, what is referred to is Romualdez.

18. F.R. Marcos, "State of the Nation Address", 25 July 2022. The full text of the speech is available at https://www.rappler.com/nation/full-text-transcript-president-marcos-jr-state-nation-address-2022/.

19. Felix K. Chang, "US-Philippines Enhanced Defense Cooperation Agreement Revived", Foreign Policy Research Institute, 14 June 2023, https://fpri.org/article/2023/06/us-philippines-enhanced-defense-cooperation-agreement-revived.

20. Joshua Kurlantzick, "President Marcos Jr. Meets with President Biden – But the US Position in Southeast Asia Is Increasingly Shaky", Council on Foreign Relations, 2 May 2023, https://www.cfr.org/blog/president-marcos-jr-meets-president-biden-us-position-southeast-asia-increasingly-shaky.

21. Sui-Lee Wee and Camille Elemia, "Leila De Lima, Critic of Duterte's Drug War, Is Released on Bail", *New York Times*, 13 November 2023, https://www.nytimes.com/2023/11/13/world/asia/leila-de-lima-release-philippines.html#:~:text=Though%20she%20was%20never%20convicted,president%27s%20brutal%20war%20on%20drugs.

22. Congress of the United States, "Letter Addressed to Jesus Crispin Remulla, Secretary of the Department of Justice of the Republic of the Philippines", 12 October 2022, https://www.markey.senate.gov/imo/media/doc/bicameral_letter_to_philippines_soj_-_october_2022.pdf.

The Philippines: Disinformation and Democracy

Yvonne T. Chua

The next election in the Philippines is scheduled for May 2025 and won't even involve the often fiercely contested positions of president and vice president. But the interval between elections so far remains fraught with disinformation, which has plagued the Philippine political landscape and exacerbated the polarization of society.

Referred to as "patient zero" and the "petri dish" in the global disinformation epidemic,[1] the Philippines persistently serves as a prime example of a country where government, politicians and their allies employ disinformation both online and offline to manipulate public opinion, suppress critics, advance controversial policies and consolidate power.

Truth under Siege

The Philippines caught global attention in 2016 when the elderly Rodrigo Duterte, a longtime local politico with a minimal national political base at the time, successfully deployed a highly coordinated army of mostly paid "keyboard warriors" on social media. This strategy amplified his populist appeal and undermined his rivals during his presidential run.

The disinformation machinery would stay intact throughout his six-year presidency, helping him justify his brutal war on drugs, vitriolic attacks on the media and opponents, unequivocal defence of the late Ferdinand Marcos Sr. and his authoritarian rule, and contentious "pivot" away from the United States towards China, among others.

The 2019 midterm election serves as a further reminder of the Duterte camp's effective social media playbook. A vicious volley of false or misleading narratives

Yᴠᴏɴɴᴇ T. Cʜᴜᴀ is Associate Professor in the Department of Journalism, University of the Philippines—Diliman.

primarily targeted the eight-member senatorial slate of the opposition coalition Otso Diretso. All of its candidates—even Manuel Roxas II and Paolo Benigno Aquino IV, who had the biggest chances of winning according to pre-election surveys—lost their bids. Conversely, nine bets of the administration electoral alliance Hugpong ng Pagbabago, managed by Duterte's daughter Sara, made it. They included Marcos's eldest daughter, Imee, whom Duterte previously admitted helped bankroll his 2016 campaign.[2]

Electoral disinformation reached a new level of sophistication in the 2022 poll, which saw a rematch between Ferdinand Marcos Jr., the late dictator's son and namesake, and Leni Robredo, to whom he lost the 2016 vice presidential race.

Months of a relentless barrage of disinformation, disseminated across multiple formats and platforms and unprecedented in the country's history, approximated what the US-based think tank Rand Corp. describes as the "firehose of falsehood" strategy: high-volume and multichannel; rapid, continuous and repetitive; and lacking commitment to objective reality and consistency.[3] Amid an avalanche of positive messages skewed in his favour, Marcos beat Robredo by a landslide to become the country's seventeenth president, marking the return of the Marcoses to Malacañang Palace thirty-six years after their ouster from power through the People Power Revolution.

A growing body of research sheds light on the evolving nature of political disinformation in the Philippines, particularly during elections.

V-Dem (Varieties of Democracy), a global democracy tracker, confirms the "substantial" use of social media (2.983 out of a possible high score of 3) among major political parties and candidates in the Philippines to sway the population.[4] Government and political parties and candidates alike frequently use online platforms to circulate misleading viewpoints or false information on many key political issues at home and abroad.

The pool of disinformation actors, meanwhile, has significantly diversified. From pro-Duterte bloggers and macro-influencers and pseudonymous social media accounts in 2016, it expanded to micro- and nano-influencers in 2019. By 2022 the landscape further evolved to encompass "knowledge influencers" (self-proclaimed experts), hyperpartisan news anchors, and even streaming by attractive "AFAM" (foreign or non-Filipino) personalities that engaged Philippines political content.[5]

Covert political influencers have been categorized into at least seven types: "amateur" commentators and curators, hyperpartisan influencers, "stan" or fan accounts, trending influencers, alt-news and entertainment media, mainstream popular influencers, and polarizing influencers. They reportedly raked in a conversative PHP600 million to 1.5 billion (US$10.9 million to 27 million) from the 2022 presidential and vice-presidential races alone.[6]

Arguably, one of the most significant fallouts from the divisive 2022 presidential election was the further erosion of traditional media's gatekeeping role during polls, coupled with what a group of researchers call "parallel public spheres".[7] These spheres, the researchers said, represent two distinct and unequal information ecosystems aligned with the political identities of Marcos and his running mate Sara Duterte's UniTeam and of Robredo and her running mate Francis Pangilinan's Kakampinks.

Marcos's dominance in this realm comes as no surprise. The pro-Marcos political reality is said to have been made possible "by a well-funded, full-service media-information-fantasy complex capable of diversified content production".[8]

This machinery predates his presidential bid by years, evident in the persistent "Tallano gold" myth used to justify the Marcoses' wealth and refurbish their image. Descendants of the fictitious pre-colonial Tallano royalty supposedly paid Marcos 192,000 tons of gold for legal services in 1949 before he entered politics. This tall tale has been traced to a website article published as early as 2007 and proliferated across platforms in recent years as social media became popular.[9] While the Marcoses have officially distanced themselves from the narrative, it is repeatedly spun, reinforcing the illusory truth effect, a psychological phenomenon where false information, if repeated enough times, comes to be perceived as true.

Negative messaging about Robredo likewise long preceded the 2022 elections. It started soon after she was elected vice president in 2016, when both the Marcos and Duterte camps unleashed a barrage of false narratives, including allegations of electoral fraud and misogynistic attacks.

Marcos himself has leveraged social media to his advantage for over a decade, gaining a head start on many other politicians. He established his YouTube and Twitter (now X) accounts in May 2009, a year before his Senate run, followed by Facebook and Instagram after securing his seat. More recently, he joined TikTok. Several of his vlogs have been fact-checked as disseminating false or misleading information, particularly concerning his own or his family's achievements.

Marcos's robust online presence has enabled him to craft what a pundit describes as "virtual hypermasculinity". Unlike his predecessor Duterte, who projected a tough guy persona in real time, Marcos "simulate(d) his strongman rule through disinformation pertaining to political legacies of the Marcos family, distorting or augmenting the reality of martial law, and benefitting from the ongoing online targeting of opposition forces".[10]

Some Old, Some New

While the searing intensity of political disinformation seen during the 2022 election has subsided, Filipinos remain immersed in a steady stream of falsehoods. A nationwide post-election survey revealed a sobering ninety per cent of the country's adult population encountering false news about government and politics. According to respondents, these untruths permeate primarily online and on television, but their reach extends through radio, friends, family and even community leaders as well.

Some things, it seems, refuse to wither and die. The historical distortions and myths surrounding the Marcos family are a sad testament to this.

When Marcos first proposed the Maharlika Investment Fund, the country's first sovereign wealth fund, and faced fierce opposition, bad actors opportunistically regurgitated the "Marcos gold" myth and tied it to the initiative. This mythical hoard, allegedly stashed away in European banks, was to be retrieved and used to seed the fund, allowing it to be shared with Filipinos according to the supposed dying wish of Marcos Sr. This narrative was readily paired with the oft-repeated myth of the Marcos era as a "golden age" for the Philippine economy, stoking authoritarian nostalgia during the election campaign.

Fears of historical revisionism also escalated after the education department mandated a change in the new Grade 6 social studies curriculum, replacing "*Diktadurang Marcos*" (Marcos dictatorship) with the more generic "*Diktadura*" (dictatorship).[11] Critics denounced the move as an attempt to obscure the severity of the human rights abuses and systematic repression that occurred during martial law.

Researchers at the University of the Philippines also discovered 143 sites established on Luzon, the country's largest and most populous island, to memorialize the Marcos family. The sites range from historical markers to museums and other structures named after or dedicated to the Marcoses. They glorify the late president's fabricated war exploits, fictionalize or embellish his achievements, document Marcos Jr.'s electoral victory, or show uncritical adulation of the Marcos family.[12]

Three key events provided Marcos supporters with ample opportunity to resurrect false narratives of the Marcos family's "victimhood" and the Aquino family's "villainy": the anniversary of Marcos Sr.'s declaration of martial law (September 1972), the commemoration of the assassination of opposition leader and Marcos Sr.'s chief rival Benigno Aquino Jr. (August 1983), and the anniversary of the People Power Revolution, which ended the dictatorship and swept Aquino's wife, Corazon, or Cory, to power (February 1986).

The late senator Aquino continues to be falsely labelled a "fake hero" and "red-tagged" for alleged collusion with the Communist Party of the Philippines

(CPP) and its armed wing, the New People's Army (NPA). This smear campaign persists on social media, including from accounts and pages associated with law enforcement agencies, provincial and municipal police stations, and even attached units of the Philippine National Police.

Red-tagging, considered a pernicious form of disinformation, has been defined as "the act of labelling, branding, naming, and accusing individuals and/or organizations of being left-leaning, subversives, communists or terrorists [used as] a strategy ... by state agents, particularly law enforcement agencies and the military, against those perceived to be 'threats' or 'enemies of the State.'"[13]

Red-tagging intensified under Duterte and became institutionalized with the creation of the anti-communist National Task Force to End Local Communist Armed Conflict (NTF-ELCAC). It continues under the Marcos administration. The attacks came not only from state agents, but also former public officials, and even private individuals and organizations. Political opponents, critics, activists, student leaders, human rights defenders, development workers and journalists are easy targets.

The NTF-ELCAC, opposing a proposed human rights defenders protection bill, labelled human rights groups Karapatan and Philippine Alliance of Human Rights Advocates and lawyers' groups National Union of Peoples' Lawyers and Free Legal Assistance Group as "communist terrorist groups".[14]

On occasion, hate speech formed part of the rhetoric. For instance, an LGBTQIA+ rights group openly critical of the Marcos government was baselessly accused of being a communist front during Pride Month in June. Social media posts employed vulgar language and incited violence against its chairperson.

Members of the opposition and progressive lawmakers are among those who have continually been under fire.

At a Senate hearing, Raoul Manuel, a Kabataan party-list representative in Congress, faced false accusations of communist affiliations. Senator and former police chief Rolando de la Rosa levelled the charge, echoing the allegation made by two individuals claiming to be former rebels.[15] Months earlier, Manuel was harassed online. Social media posts raised innuendos about his sexuality and a veiled death threat urging him to reunite with a slain teacher-activist whom the army had linked to the NPA.

The often red-tagged Kabataan party list belongs to the Makabayan bloc, a coalition of party lists within the House of Representatives that are constantly labelled as communist or terrorist. Notably, the bloc has filed a resolution supporting the International Criminal Court's investigation into crimes against humanity arising from Rodrigo Duterte's anti-drug campaign. Dela Rosa served as police chief during the campaign and is named as a respondent in the case.

In another incident, lone opposition senator Risa Hontiveros was accused of shielding CPP's recruitment activities in schools when she opposed the education department's surveillance operations in schools.[16]

In May, Marcos appointed vice president and concurrent education secretary Sara Duterte as co-vice chair of NTF-ELCAC. But even before this, she had labelled the Alliance of Concerned Teachers (ACT), a public school teachers' union, and its affiliated party-list organization as "terrorists", "communist-inspired" and a "lover" of the communist ideology for criticizing her office's and government's shortcomings in aiding teachers.[17]

In October, she lambasted critics of the PHP650 million (nearly US$12 million) confidential and intelligence funds she requested from Congress for her two offices, calling them "enemies of peace" and "enemies of the state".[18] Among the first to have questioned the funds was ACT party-list representative France Castro. ACT also belongs to Makabayan.

The vice president withdrew her request to lawmakers regarding the funds. However, smarting from attacks on his daughter over the funds, former president Rodrigo Duterte singled out Castro on his weekly television talk show, saying communists like her are those he wanted to kill. He again red-tagged and threatened Castro weeks after she sued him in court for grave threats,[19] forcing Castro to file a supplementary complaint.

Duterte's talk show, *Gikan sa Masa, para sa Masa* (From the masses, for the masses), is hosted on Sonshine Media Network International (SMNI), a broadcasting network owned by Kingdom of Jesus Christ pastor Apollo Quiboloy, who is wanted in the United States in connection to an ongoing sex and human trafficking case. The hyperpartisan SMNI vehemently endorsed the Marcos-Duterte tandem in the 2022 election. The presidential debate it organized during the election was the only one Marcos attended.

Like the NTF-ELCAC, SMNI still engages in serial red-tagging through programmes like Duterte's weekly show and Laban Kasama ang Bayan hosted by former NTF-ELCAC spokesperson Lorraine Badoy and Jeffrey Celiz, a self-described ex-rebel. The array of individuals and organizations they have red-tagged is wide and diverse, and this time it has landed them in trouble. The Makabayan bloc and progressive groups, members of Church groups (including a Roman Catholic bishop), student organizations, a Manila judge, media groups and journalists were among those who were falsely labelled.

A coalition of news organizations documenting attacks on the media found that red-tagging accounted for the biggest proportion of attacks on journalists: 31 of 75 incidents logged from Marcos's assumption of office until 30 April 2023.[20]

Interestingly, the current disinformation scenario strongly suggests fissures within the Marcos-Duterte political alliance, with once staunch supporters, from influencers to ordinary netizens, busily lobbing disinformation at each other's camp with a ferocity previously reserved for their adversaries. It has turned into a three-ring circus amid speculation that House Speaker and Marcos's cousin Ferdinand Martin Romualdez plans to run for president in 2028 against Sara Duterte.

Numerous attacks against Marcos and Romualdez originated from SMNI. Over SMNI, former president Rodrigo Duterte accused the Speaker of conspiring with communists in connection with his plan.[21] SMNI host Celiz asserted that Romualdez had spent PHP1.8 billion (US$32 million) for travel in a year. The Speaker earlier defended his chamber's decision to realign the confidential funds Sara Duterte had sought for her two offices. On social media, allegations of corruption in the House swirled, as did unfounded posts that Marcos had removed Romualdez as Speaker.

Several anti-Marcos narratives revolved around unfounded electoral fraud allegations against Marcos and his wife Liza. A once pro-Marcos influencer, who has since changed her tune, suggested Liza's involvement in onion smuggling through her brother. The first lady was also purported to be anti-Duterte, to allow those associated with the opposition Liberal Party into the government (Liza and Roxas, LP's standard bearer in the 2016 polls; both hail from the prominent Araneta clan), and to be poised to take over the presidency. Meanwhile, another narrative emerged that Sara Duterte was supposed to replace Marcos as president in 2025 as part of a "term sharing" agreement (the Philippine Constitution does not provide term sharing for presidents).

At the height of the controversy over the confidential funds, conflicting accounts circulated regarding Sara Duterte's hold on the vice presidency. One version claimed she was removed from her post by Congress, another said she resigned, and yet another suggested that the Communist Party was behind moves to impeach her. All three were false.

The situation marked a departure from the 2022 election, when false or misleading narratives about Marcos and Duterte were almost invariably positive.

Beyond Domestic Politics

What the Philippine government has seemingly become increasingly aware of and has started responding to are influence operations from China. Influence operations may involve, but do not always necessitate, the dissemination of disinformation or deceptive content. Instead, they encompass "coordinated efforts to manipulate or corrupt public debate for a strategic goal", including deceptive behaviour. Campaigns could be covert, such as the use of fake identities, or overt, such as employing authentic and influential voices by state-controlled media to promote messages that may or may not be false.[22]

The European Union has identified Russia and China as the main threat actors in what it terms "foreign information manipulation and interference" (FIMI). FIMI refers to "a mostly non-illegal pattern of behaviour that threatens or has the potential to negatively impact values, procedures and political processes. Such activity is manipulative in character and is conducted in an intentional and coordinated manner. Such activity may be undertaken by state or non-state actors, including their proxies inside and outside of their own territory".[23]

China's attempts to influence Philippine politics came to light in 2020 when Facebook took down a network of fake accounts based in China supporting Duterte and his daughter Sara, who was then touted to run for president. The accounts also promoted China's position on the South China Sea, where it has territorial disputes with the Philippines.[24]

China has rejected a ruling issued by an international arbitration tribunal in 2016 in favour of the Philippines. The ruling declared China's nine-dash line, land reclamation activities and other activities in Philippine waters unlawful. Duterte, however, set aside the ruling in favour of fostering closer ties with China.

China Index, a cross-regional project that measures China's overseas influence, ranked the Philippines as the seventh most influenced nation by China among eighty-two countries assessed in the index for 2021. This ranking spans nine domains, including foreign policy, domestic politics, media, academia, law enforcement, and the military.[25]

After reaffirming its defence ties with the United States and other allies and taking a firmer stance on contested waters, the Philippines in 2023 found itself under a barrage of Chinese influence operations. These online and social media campaigns aimed to undermine Philippine claims and sway public opinion in favour of Beijing's aggressive actions, including the firing of water cannons on Philippine vessels near the Second Thomas Shoal (claimed by the Philippines as Ayungin Reef and by China as Ren'ai Shoal).

As tensions with China over the South China Sea intensified, the Philippines' National Security Council finally acknowledged the existence of online "operators" and "proxies" amplifying pro-Beijing narratives and defending China's aggression.[26] These social media accounts, some reportedly formed during the Duterte administration, parrot China's talking points and downplay its actions in the disputed waters.[27]

Aftermath

Does disinformation contribute to democratic backsliding?

A 2023 global study provides evidence supporting this claim by analysing disinformation levels in 179 countries over a dozen years. The study suggests that higher levels of disinformation in democracies increase the likelihood of "autocratization onsets".[28] According to the research, the inherent potential of disinformation to polarize society and erode trust in democratic institutions contributes to a preference for non-democratic regimes.

The Philippines, where disinformation has become normalized,[29] exemplifies the findings to a significant extent.

Data from V-Dem's 2023 report confirm an increasingly polarized Philippine society, with the degree of polarization falling within the range of "serious" since 2016. This indicates substantial differences in opinions on key political issues leading to major clashes of views.

Among the democratic institutions suffering from low public trust is the Philippine news media, which is relentlessly red-tagged and demonized. Only thirty-eight per cent of adult Filipinos trust the news, lagging the global average (forty per cent) and remaining the lowest among the five Southeast Asian media markets covered in the annual Digital News Report.[30] The same report identifies a correlation between low media trust and high levels of media criticism in the Philippines and other countries.

Red-tagging not only harms reputations but also puts targets in physical danger. The Philippines' Commission on Human Rights found in a national inquiry that human rights defenders were red-tagged before facing harm, including being killed, injured, illegally arrested, or charged with trumped-up cases.[31]

Forced abductions of activists and community organizers who have been red-tagged by state agents or their proxies now occur at a faster rate under Marcos than they did under Duterte, according to a human rights group. The military and police continue to be implicated in these abductions, initially blaming communist rebels for the incidents.[32]

Since 2016, the Philippines has slipped from a democracy to an autocracy, a trend underscored by the Democracy Report 2023,[33] which characterizes the country as "autocratizing further". The liberal democracy index of the Philippines has declined significantly over the past decade, placing it 101st among 179 countries, or among the bottom fifty per cent of countries.

Freedom House continues to categorize the Philippines as "partly free",[34] attributing this status in part to highly organized disinformation campaigns that undermine fair political competition. The report points specifically to social media platforms engaging in the widespread propagation of disinformation and hyperpartisan online news outlets consistently spreading misleading content.

The adverse impact of disinformation on the political engagement of young Filipino voters should not be underestimated. A study encompassing nearly 24,000 college students revealed that individuals who were uncertain about the accuracy of their political information because of misinformation were less inclined to vote.[35] On the other hand, those who expressed trust in mainstream media or had confidence in their ability to discern false or misleading political content exhibited a higher likelihood of voting.

A related study observed that polarized young supporters of Rodrigo Duterte were more prone to inaccurately identify both false and real news.[36] This pattern mirrors findings in the United States, where Republicans were found to be more susceptible to misinformation. This research was conducted during Duterte's presidency.

Pushing Back

The Philippines is not lacking in initiatives to combat disinformation. Numerous sectors work actively to resist the spread of false information, including media organizations, educational institutions, civil society organizations, the private sector, funders, and even individuals such as social influencers, Wikipedians, artists, lawyers and the youth.[37] Collaborative efforts, in the form of coalitions or consortiums, have been established to tackle the issue more effectively and promptly. These efforts encompass various strategies, such as promoting media and information literacy, conducting fact-checking and debunking activities, engaging in disinformation studies, providing legal assistance to disinformation victims, and engaging government entities and online platforms.

In 2023, stronger steps were taken to address disinformation actors.

A series of civil suits were filed against Badoy and Celiz, individuals who engaged in red-tagging through their programme on SMNI. Journalist Atom Ataullo, veteran activist Carol Araullo, and former Makabayan lawmaker Teddy Casiño each sought approximately PHP2 million (US$36,000) in compensation.

In a separate case before the Office of the Ombudsman, Badoy and another ex-NTF-ELCAC official, Antonio Parlade, were found guilty of conduct prejudicial to the best interest of the service because of their serial red-tagging, but they got off with a reprimand.[38] The administrative case was filed by the National Union of People's Lawyers.

Action against SMNI extended to various platforms. In July, YouTube terminated SMNI and Laban Kasama ang Bayan channels for violating its terms of service. Two months later, the Facebook page of SMNI became unavailable.

Following Celiz's accusation of Speaker Romualdez's substantial travel expenses, the House committee on legislative franchises initiated an inquiry into SMNI's alleged peddling of false news, reportedly a violation of its franchise. Both Badoy and Celiz were detained at the House for about a week in December for being disrespectful and refusing to answer questions.

On 20 December, the Movie and Television Review and Classification Board suspended two programmes on SMNI—*Gikan sa Masa* and *Para sa Masa*—in response to complaints about alleged death threats and profane language from its host, former president Duterte. Laban Kasama ang Bayan was suspended over Romualdez's alleged PHP1.8 billion travel expenses.

Two days later, the National Telecommunications Commission suspended SMNI's entire operations for thirty days in compliance with a House resolution citing multiple violations, including baseless red-tagging.[39] This government action sparked a debate on whether the suspension was, among other things, an issue of press freedom or a response to disinformation and dangerous speech. SMNI has sought legal recourse to challenge the suspension.

Meanwhile, SMNI and Laban Kasama ang Bayan have continued to broadcast on YouTube by creating new channels shortly after their termination. SMNI also uses a different page on Facebook. This practice is common among bad actors and further underscores the need for more effective and lasting responses to disarm disinformation.

Notes

1. Facebook's global politics and government outreach director Katie Harbath used the phrase "patient zero" to describe the extent of digital disinformation in the Philippines' 2016 election, while Cambridge Analytica whistleblower Christopher Wylie used the phrase "petri dish" to describe the Philippines as a testing place for electoral disinformation techniques and technology.

2. Duterte did not list Imee Marcos among his campaign donors. But he disclosed the support at a gathering of local officials on 4 October 2016 and in an interview with CNN Philippines on 29 December 2016. In exchange he said he promised to allow her father's burial at the heroes' cemetery. Marcos Sr. was buried with full military honours on 18 November 2016.

3. Yvonne T. Chua, Maria Diosa Labiste, and Felipe Gonzales, "Firehose of Disinformation Floods Run-up to Election", *Tsek.ph*, 8 May 2022, https://tsek.ph/firehose-of-disinformation-floods-run-up-to-election.

4. The V-Dem Dataset, V-Dem, March 2023, https://v-dem.net/data/the-v-dem-dataset/country-year-v-dem-fullothers-v13/.

5. Rossine Fallorina et al., *From Disinformation to Influence Operations: The Evolution of Disinformation in Three Electoral Cycles* (Philippines: Internews, 2023).

6. Fatima Gaw et al., *Political Economy of Covert Influence Operations in the 2022 Philippine Elections* (Philippines: Internews, 2023).

7. Jonathan C. Ong et al., *Parallel Public Spheres: Influence Operations in the 2022 Philippine Elections. The Media Manipulation Case Book* (Internews and Harvard Kennedy School Shorenstein Center, 2022).

8. Ibid.

9. Ronald U. Mendoza et al., "When Fake News Infects Political Networks: Case Study of the Tallano Gold Myth in the Philippines", *Media Asia* 50, no. 4 (2023): 501–27.

10. Maria Tanyag, "Marcos Jr. and the Dangers of Virtual Hypermasculinity", *Fulcrum*, 4 April 2023, https://fulcrum.sg/marcos-jr-and-the-dangers-of-virtual-hypermasculinity.

11. Faith Argonsino, "DepEd Slammed over Memo to Remove 'Marcos' from 'Diktadurang Marcos' Term", *Inquirer.net*, 10 September 2023, https://newsinfo.inquirer.net/1829447/deped-slammed-over-memo-to-remove-marcos-from-diktadurang-marcos-term.

12. Rick Berdos, "UP Study Discovers 143 Sites in Luzon Dedicated to Marcos Family", *Vera Files*, 30 September 2023, https://verafiles.org/articles/up-study-discovers-143-sites-in-luzon-dedicated-to-marcos-family.

13. Supreme Court Associate Justice Marvic Leonen's definition in Zarate vs. Aquino III (G.R. No. 220028) promulgated on 10 November 2015.

14. Amnesty International, "Deadly Practice of 'Red-Tagging' Continues under Marcos Administration", 22 March 2023, https://www.amnesty.org.ph/2023/03/deadly-practice-of-red-tagging-continuesunder-marcos-administration.

15. Sherrie Ann Torres, "Dela Rosa Vows Probe into Kabataan Rep's 'Communist Links'", ABS-CBN News, 29 November 2023, https://news.abs-cbn.com/news/11/29/23/dela-rosa-vows-probe-into-kabataan-reps-communist-links.

16. "FACT CHECK: Risa Hontiveros Not Affiliated with CPP-NPA", *Rappler*, 10 September 2023, https://www.rappler.com/newsbreak/fact-check/risa-hontiveros-not-affiliated-with-cpp-npa.

17. Department of Education, "Statement by Deped Secretary Sara Duterte on Act Teachers Support to the Transport Strike", 4 March 2023, https://www.deped.gov.ph/2023/03/05/statement-by-deped-secretary-sara-duterte-on-act-teachers-support-to-the-transport-strike.

18. Giselle Ombay, "Sara Duterte: 'Ang Kontra sa Confidential Funds ay Kontra aa Kapayapaan'", GMA Integrated News, 5 October 2023, https://www.gmanetwork.

com/news/topstories/nation/884236/vp-sara-ang-kontra-sa-confidential-funds-ay-kontra-sa-kapayapaan/story.

19. "Ex-president Duterte Threatens Castro Again after Court Summons", CNN Philippines, 16 November 2023, https://www.cnnphilippines.com/news/2023/11/16/duterte-court-summons-wednesday-tv-interview.html.

20. Melinda Quintos de Jesus, "State of Media Freedom in the Philippines", Center for Media Freedom and Responsibility, 3 May 2023, https://pcij.org/article/10122/2023-state-of-press-freedom-in-the-philippines.

21. "Ex-president Duterte Links Romualdez with Reds for 2028 Polls; Speaker Denies", GMA News, 18 November 2023, https://www.gmanetwork.com/news/topstories/nation/888764/ex-president-duterte-links-romualdez-with-reds-for-2028-polls-speaker-denies/story.

22. Facebook, "Threat Report: The State of Influence Operations 2017–2020", May 2021, https://about.fb.com/wp-content/uploads/2021/05/IO-Threat-Report-May-20-2021.pdf.

23. Nicolas Hénin, *FIMI: Towards a European Redefinition of Foreign Interference* (EU DisinfoLab, 2023).

24. Ben Nimmo, C. Shawn Eib, and Lea Ronzaud, *Operation Naval Gazing: Facebook Takes Down Inauthentic Chinese Network* (Graphika, 2020).

25. Doublethink Lab, "Philippines: China Index 2022", 15 November 2022, https://china-index.io/country/philippines.

26. Camille Elemia, "Pro-China Narratives Philippines Confronts Unlikely Adversary in SCS Row: Filipinos Echoing 'Pro-Beijing' Narratives", *Philippine Center for Investigative Journalism*, 23 October 2023, https://pcij.org/article/10888/philippines-confronts-unlikely-adversary-south-china-sea-row-filipinos-echo-pro-beijing-narratives.

27. Pauline Macaraeg, "How Pro-China Propaganda is Seeded Online in the Philippines", *Rappler*, 1 November 2023, https://www.rappler.com/newsbreak/investigative/ways-how-china-propaganda-seeded-online-philippines.

28. Yuko Sato, Felix Wiebrecht, and Staffan I. Lindberg, "Disinformation and Episodes of Regime Transformation", V-Dem, 11 September 2023, https://www.v-dem.net/media/publications/wp_144.pdf. The study also concluded that disinformation stabilizes authoritarian regimes.

29. Freedom House, "Philippines: Freedom on the Net 2023", https://freedomhouse.org/country/philippines/freedom-net/2023.

30. Yvonne T. Chua, "Media Criticism Linked to Low Trust in News—Digital News Report 2023", *Philippine Star*, 11 April 2022, https://www.philstar.com/headlines/2023/06/14/2273808/media-criticism-linked-low-trust-newsdigital-news-report-2023.

31. Commission on Human Rights, "Statement of the Commission on Human Rights on the Attempt to Trivialize and Justify the Dangers of Red-Tagging", 11 April 2022,

https://chr.gov.ph/statement-of-the-commission-on-human-rights-on-the-attempt-to-trivialize-and-justify-the-dangers-of-red-tagging.

32. Nick Aspinwall, "Activists Keep Disappearing in Marcos's Philippines", *Foreign Policy*, 9 November 2023, https://foreignpolicy.com/2023/11/09/philippines-marcos-disappeared-activists-duterte-tamano-castro.

33. V-Dem Institute, *Democracy Report 2023: Defiance in the Face of Autocratization* (Sweden: University of Gothenburg, 2023).

34. Freedom House, "Philippines: Freedom in the World 2023", https://freedomhouse.org/country/philippines/freedom-world/2023.

35. Gabrielle Ann Mendoza et al., "Misinformed or Overconfident? Fake News and Youth Voting Likelihood in the Philippines", SSRN, 23 March 2022, https://ssrn.com/abstract=4064584.

36. Imelda B. Deinla et al., "The Link between Fake News Susceptibility and Political Polarisation of the Youth in the Philippines", *Asian Journal of Political Science* 30, no. 2 (2022): 160–81.

37. Rachel E. Khan and Yvonne T. Chua, "Countering Disinformation Tools and Initiatives in the Philippines", *International Media Support*, May 2023, https://www.mediasupport.org/publication/countering-disinformation-tools-and-initiatives-in-the-philippines.

38. Dempsey Reyes, "Ombudsman Reprimands Badoy, Parlade", *Inquirer.net*, 22 September 2023, https://newsinfo.inquirer.net/1835152/ombudsman-reprimands-badoy-parlade.

39 "NTC Suspends SMNI Operations for 30 Days", CNN Philippines, 21 December 2023, https://www.cnnphilippines.com/news/2023/12/21/NTC-suspends-SMNI-operations-for-30-days.html.

Singapore

Woodlands
Central
Catchment Area
Pulau Ubin
Pulau
Tekong
Changi
International
Airport
Central
Business
District
Tuas
Jurong
Island
Pulau Bukom
Sentosa

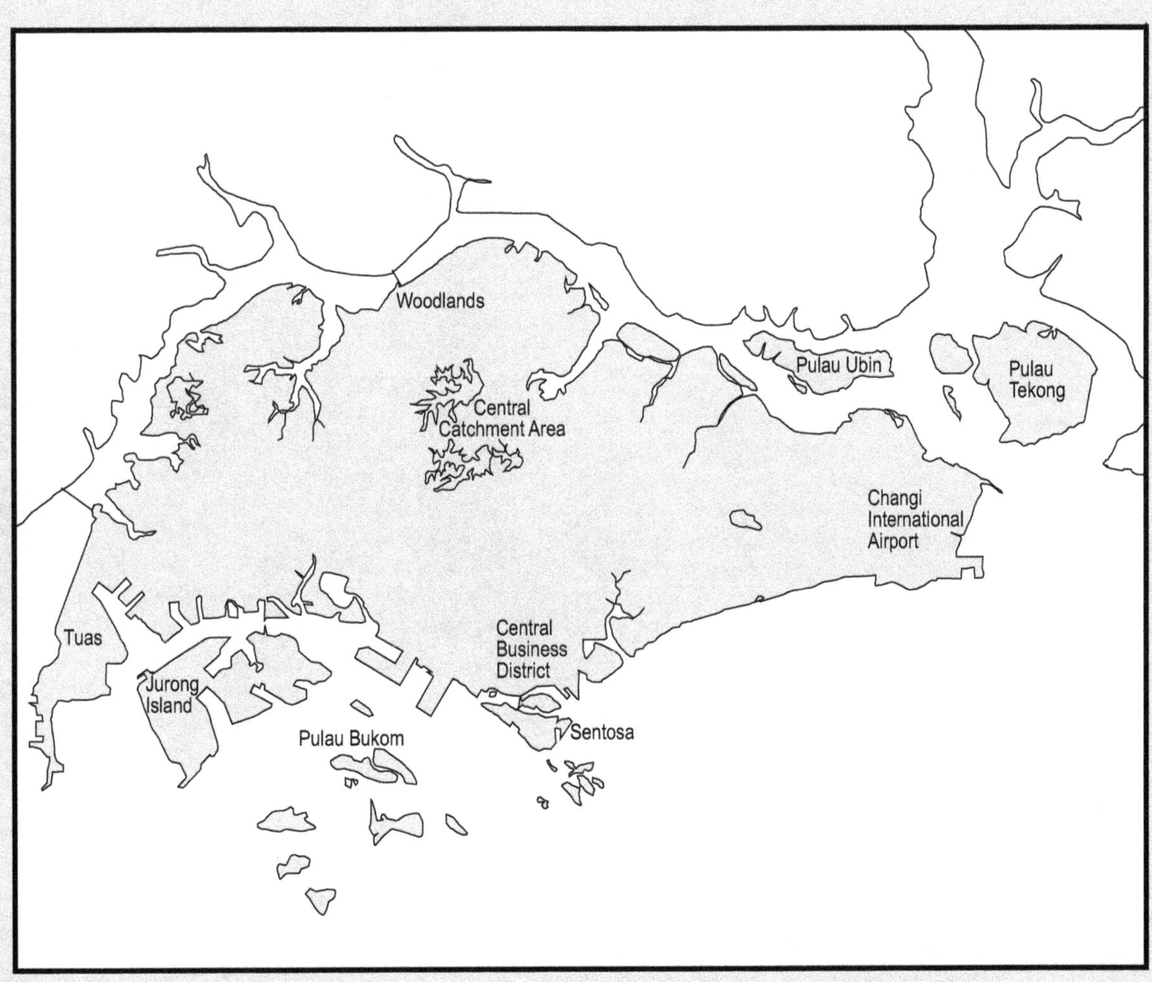

SINGAPORE IN 2023:
Of Political Setbacks and Succession, Revitalizing the Middle Ground, and Keeping Spirits Up

Eugene K.B. Tan

In normally placid Singapore, 2023 witnessed the political succession entering a critical phase with a more definitive timeline announced amid political controversies and scandals involving the ruling and leading opposition party capturing the attention of Singaporeans. The government's plans for a revitalized social compact were also unveiled after more than a year of consultations and engagements with Singaporeans under the auspices of the Forward Singapore exercise. The economy still awaits the strong post-pandemic recovery—it grew by 1.1 per cent, against the GDP growth forecast of 0.5 to 2.5 per cent. Coming on the back of the pandemic, making sense of the continuing uncertainty was not only challenging but also demanded a steely resolve from everyone to keep spirits up.

Watchful Waiting for Post-pandemic Economic Recovery

The International Monetary Fund had forecasted that a third of the world economy would be in recession in 2023, with the United States, European Union and China all slowing down simultaneously. Multiple global crises have confronted the world simultaneously on an almost unprecedented scale since 2022, including the Russian invasion of Ukraine, intense geopolitical rivalry between China and the United States, cross–Taiwan Straits tension, nuclear weapons on the Korean peninsula, and the lingering effects of the Covid-19 pandemic.

Domestically, the economy was a key concern, with inflation and the cost of living being top of the mind and creating uncertainty and anxiety for workers,

EUGENE K.B. TAN is Associate Professor of Law at the Yong Pung How School of Law, Singapore Management University.

consumers and businesses alike, especially when the inflation rate surpasses wage growth. With reduced real purchasing power, consumers tend to spend less, affecting business outlook, spending and investments. In turn, job insecurity and uncertainty among workers regarding whether salaries would remain stagnant or even be cut are generated. It's a vicious cycle that economic uncertainty drives, and which necessitated the government to provide ongoing assurance.

In 2023, the government rolled out a slew of measures such as various rebates, vouchers, subsidies, Medisave top-ups, and even cash payouts throughout the year, with low-income families receiving subsidies almost every month.[1] The bulk of these came under the SG$8 billion Assurance Package to cover food and groceries, utilities and healthcare to partly manage the Goods and Services Tax (GST) increase, from 7 to 8 per cent effective 1 January 2023, with another 1 percentage point increase in 2024. As an economy dependent on export and investment, Singapore is bound to be affected by global economic storms. But the GST hike bore the brunt of the blame for the inflationary prices even as the rationale for the two-phased GST increase had been regularly explained. In part, it may indicate that Singaporeans still lack a competent understanding that being plugged into the international economic grid means Singapore is not spared from the vicissitudes of its external environment.

Although the employment rate fell in 2023, the labour market remained tight.[2] The weaker and uncertain economic outlook slowed labour market improvements in the short-term even as labour underutilization indicators continued to improve: more were in permanent jobs; the incidence of workers discouraged from seeking work remained stable and low; and the time-related underemployment rate fell.

Self-employed persons, including platform workers such as private-hire car drivers and delivery workers, declined to pre-Covid-19 levels after four years of increases. The number of regular platform workers fell by about twenty per cent, with most of those who exited being delivery workers. This was attributed to the easing in demand for deliveries compared to the immediate post-pandemic period.[3]

Nominal incomes continued to rise, but real incomes fell in 2023 after taking inflation into account. For example, at the twentieth-percentile income level, workers earned S$2,826 monthly in 2023, up from 2022's $2,779. After accounting for Workfare Income Supplement (WIS) and related payments, real wages for these workers still declined by 2.1 per cent. Real incomes for resident workers at the twentieth percentile salary level fell 3 per cent year on year. Similarly, median wage resident workers saw a 2.3 per cent decrease year on year.

A barometer of economic recovery is Changi Airport. It was the world's seventh-busiest airport for international passenger traffic in 2019, but dropped to the ninety-fifth spot in 2021 with borders shut and air travel demand having plunged during the pandemic. In October 2023, 5.12 million travellers passed through the airport. This represented 90.7 per cent of 2019 levels, the highest percentage since Covid-19 struck and the first time monthly passenger traffic crossed 90 per cent of pre-pandemic levels.

Another indicator is the population number comprising citizens, permanent residents and non-residents. The first two categories are relatively stable, while the number of non-residents is closely connected to economic activity. Table 1 highlights the size of the various categories of people living in Singapore between 2019 and 2023.

The recovering economy and the lifting of pandemic-related border controls contributed to the rise in the number of non-residents between 2022 and 2023, resulting in the total population at the highest level ever. Population concerns remain salient, even sensitive. Singapore's resident total fertility rate was at an all-time low of 0.97 in 2023, dipping below the previous low of 1.05 in 2022 and 1.12 in 2021. The government remains undaunted and continues to bolster support for parents and families. Budget 2023 doubled the amount of government paid paternity leave for eligible working fathers to four weeks for children born in 2024. Families with children and younger married couples applying for public housing flats for the first time now have greater priority, including an additional ballot. Housing grants for families buying resale flats for the first time increased by up to S$30,000. The government has also increased the baby bonus cash gift by S$3,000 and will contribute more to the Child Development Account.

TABLE 1
Population of Singapore by Citizens, Permanent
Residents and Non-residents, 2019–23 (millions)

Year	Citizens	Permanent residents	Non-residents	Total
2023	3.61	0.54	1.77	5.92
2022	3.55	0.52	1.56	5.64
2021	3.50	0.49	1.47	5.45
2020	3.52	0.52	1.64	5.69
2019	3.50	0.53	1.68	5.70

In line with the global effort to ensure a more transparent tax environment, it was announced in Budget 2023 that Singapore would introduce a global minimum effective tax rate of 15 per cent for large Singapore multinational enterprises (MNEs) starting on or after 1 January 2025. A domestic top-up tax will be introduced to raise the effective tax rate here for large MNE groups to 15 per cent. This move will affect overseas subsidiaries of Singapore parent companies and MNEs operating here. These changes come under the Base Erosion and Profit Shifting initiative, or BEPS 2.0, a global framework for the reform of international tax rules.[4]

Preparing for a Super-Aged Singapore: Majulah Package for Young Seniors

Singapore is likely to become "super-aged" in 2026. By 2030, one in four citizens will be aged 65 and above, up from one in six now.[5] At the National Day Rally, PM Lee unveiled the Majulah package for "young seniors" (Singaporeans born between 1960 and 1973) to help them meet their basic retirement needs, especially for lower- and middle-income Singaporeans. About 1.4 million, or close to a quarter of Singaporeans, will benefit from the package, including those born before 1960. The package is largely custom-made to meet the needs of the young seniors who have benefited relatively more from Singapore's progress and are generally less disadvantaged than the Pioneer and Merdeka generations in terms of education, income, life chances and retirement adequacy.[6]

The skeletal details of the package are an annual "Earn and Save" bonus of up to $1,000 a year to help grow Singaporeans' Central Provident Fund (CPF) savings while they are still in full-time or part-time employment. Another component, the Retirement Savings Bonus, is a one-time CPF bonus of up to $1,500 for those whose CPF balances have not reached the CPF basic retirement sum. This will benefit, among others, homemakers who may have set aside their careers to raise their families. The third component is a one-time MediSave Bonus of up to $1,000 for medical expenses and insurance premiums. The Majulah package is estimated to cost S$7 billion in addition to the earlier packages for the Pioneer and Mederka generations pegged at S$9 billion and S$6.1 billion respectively.

With the three generational packages, cohorts born in 1973 or earlier have dedicated programmes to help prepare them for retirement. As with the Pioneer and Mederka Generation packages, the full lifetime costs of the Majulah package will be financed from the fiscal resources of the current term of government. This ensures that even such significant outlays to benefit the current generation will not burden future generations or draw on the past national reserves.

Political Controversy and Scandals and a Minister Arrested for Corruption

Controversy over Cabinet Ministers Renting State Properties

Reform Party leader Kenneth Jeyaretnam first wrote about the rented state-owned black-and-white bungalows in a 6 May blog post stating that he had "received information from a number of sources" that two ministers were "occupying two of Singapore's most prime residential properties in Ridout Road". He questioned whether they were paying the "market rent". In response to media queries on the issue on 12 May, the Singapore Land Authority (SLA), which manages state properties, stated that Home Affairs and Law Minister K. Shanmugam and Foreign Minister Vivian Balakrishnan had rented the properties through a bidding process. Mr Shanmugam was the sole bidder for 26 Ridout Road, and Dr Balakrishnan the highest bidder for 31 Ridout Road.

But the floating of mere suspicion of inappropriate conduct, amid the lack of further information from the authorities, not only generated intense public interest but also spawned online commentary often accompanied by spurious arguments, salacious untruths and wild conjectures. These included mature trees being cut down illegally, SLA paying for improvement works such as a car porch and a swimming pool, and of Mr Shanmugam's son being awarded SLA contracts for renovation works on the Ridout Road properties. There was also over-exuberant speculation online about the circumstances under which the ministers came to rent the properties. Allegations of conflict of interest and preferential treatment accorded to the ministers, unethical conduct or even criminal wrongdoing swirled online. In short, there was no lack of misinformation and disinformation as well as potentially defamatory statements made against the ministers. And these had certainly spiked public interest and generated heightened concern and speculation.

Prime Minister Lee directed the Corrupt Practices Investigation Bureau (CPIB) on 17 May 2023 to investigate the matter. Subsequently, on 22 May 2023, he instructed Senior Minister Teo Chee Hean to conduct a separate review to address wider potential process or policy issues, which go beyond the scope of CPIB's investigation. Investigations by the CPIB had established there was no evidence of corruption or criminal wrongdoing in the two rental transactions.[7] The Attorney-General's Chambers had reviewed the investigation papers and agreed with CPIB's findings. In Parliament's much anticipated examination of the controversy, there was unanimity among ruling party and opposition parliamentarians that the allegations of corruption and abuse of power against the two ministers were unfounded. But most of the clarifications sought in Parliament laboured on matters ancillary to the core issue of whether the rental transactions were tainted with corruption, abuse of power or conflict of interest. The opposition flagged the "optics" of where and how elected officials lived and whether their residential addresses enervated them of their commitment to serve and reduced their empathy for the masses. This episode demonstrated vividly the abiding reality that social media is always replete with unverified allegations, weaponized rumours and untruths. Facts seem not to matter as much as perceptions do. This is the harsh reality of today's political climate.[8] Although parliamentary scrutiny matters immensely for public accountability and democratic governance, what matters as much, or even more, is how the scrutiny is done.

Affairs of the Heart and Repercussions

Extramarital affairs by PAP and opposition MPs resulted in three parliamentary seats being vacated in July. Speaker of Parliament Tan Chuan-Jin and fellow PAP MP Cheng Li Hui stepped down from their positions on 17 July following the revelation of their having an extramarital affair. The pair resigned from the party after Prime Minister Lee found out in July that the pair had continued their relationship despite being counselled years earlier.[9] That same day, a video of Workers' Party MP Leon Perera and WP Youth Wing chair Nicole Seah sharing an intimate moment was circulated online. Both opposition leaders later resigned from the party.

Both the PAP and the WP sought to provide a full account of the high-profile resignations. The jury is still out as to whether the public was persuaded that there was full accountability and that appropriate action was meted out swiftly and decisively. In explaining why he took more than two years to act on the PAP MPs, Prime Minister Lee said, "In retrospect and certainly now knowing how things eventually turned out, I agree. I should have forced the issue sooner. But let me explain my general approach, as well as my thinking at that point in time. These sorts of relationships happen from time to time … what we do depends on many factors: the circumstances, how inappropriate or scandalous the behaviour was, the family situations. We also have to be conscious of the impact on innocent parties—particularly the spouses and children."

Lee highlighted at least three situations: First, "where the individuals involved will be talked to, and if they stop, the matter ends there. No further action need be taken." Second, where immediate action must be taken such as when one party has supervisory power over the other party. Third, "where the relationship raises some questions of propriety, beyond it being an extra marital affair per se. The parties will be talked to, but the matter cannot end there. Even if the affair stops, some action has to follow. But what that action is and when it is taken, depends on the nature of the facts and the boundaries that have been transgressed."[10]

Earlier, Speaker Tan had apologized to WP MP Jamus Lim for using "unparliamentary language" that was caught on a hot mic during a Parliament sitting in April. Mr Tan was heard muttering "****ing populist" on the microphone after Mr Lim had spoken of doing more to help the lower-income groups, including having an official poverty line.[11]

Corruption probe and a Minister Interdicted from Duty

On 11 July, Transport Minister S. Iswaran was brought in by CPIB and subsequently released on bail. Tycoon Ong Beng Seng was arrested the same day in relation to the same probe.[12] While investigating another matter, CPIB came across some information concerning the minister that merited looking into. CPIB alerted the prime minister on 29 May. On 5 July, CPIB's director briefed PM Lee on the findings CPIB had at that point and indicated that CPIB would need to interview Mr Iswaran to take the investigation further. CPIB sought PM Lee's concurrence to open a formal investigation, which he gave on 6 July. Upon Iswaran's arrest, Lee instructed Iswaran to take leave of absence until the investigations were completed. Being interdicted from duty, he was placed on a reduced monthly pay of S$8,500 until further notice.[13] In Parliament, PM Lee stated that the CPIB must be allowed to do its work of investigating the matter "fully, thoroughly and independently". He said that the process was clear: when the investigation was completed, CPIB would submit its findings to the Attorney General's Chambers, which would then decide what to do with them. PM Lee added that, "Whichever way the facts come out, the case will be taken to its logical conclusion. That has always been our way."[14]

The Ridout Road controversy, the extramarital affair, and the corruption probe were significant setbacks for the PAP government. For much of July and August, it was in damage control mode. Repairing any damage done to its standing and legitimacy will take longer. These issues may not hog the public narrative and consciousness for an extended period of time, but the ruling party knows it has to demonstrate that it is equal to the task of governing Singapore with an electorate more receptive to a more diverse and competitive political landscape. The resignations of the three MPs from the PAP and WP should generate soul searching not just by the WP and PAP but by all parties and Singaporeans on the standards expected of anyone seeking political office. Are they too high, too low, or just right? How can political parties ensure that politicians are men and women with the right attributes? Voters also must ask whether they hold parties to the same exacting standards as well.

Similarly, the CPIB probe involving Minister Iswaran is a severe test for the Singapore government and governance, which has long prided itself and benefited from the commitment to clean governance and incorruptibility. While there is no perfect system, and zero corruption is an aspiration, what the latest case might bring to light in terms of flaws in processes, safeguards and controls, oversight and early warning, and selection of men and women for the top positions will come under intense scrutiny. In other words, whether there had been complacency, judgement failures and leadership inadequacies will feature long after the investigations and the judicial process are concluded. There will be a political price to pay—indeterminate for now—for sure. The PAP's public perception challenge is to rebuild trust and confidence that it can and does uphold the high standards it sets for itself.

Political Succession—Another Milestone

Towards the end of 2023, political succession hogged the limelight after the earlier controversies. Prime Minister Lee, the PAP secretary-general, at his party's Awards and Convention on 5 November, declared: "I intend to hand over to DPM Lawrence [Wong] before the next general election. After that, I will be at the new PM's disposal.... So if all goes well, I will hand over by the PAP's 70th birthday next year...". At the same event, his presumptive successor stated emphatically that he was "ready for [his] next assignment".[15] Earlier, in his nineteenth annual National Day Rally in August, PM Lee had stated that the leadership succession plans were "back on track" with Covid "behind us". He said, "my original plan was to hand over and step down as Prime Minister by 2022, before my 70th birthday. But the pandemic disrupted this plan. I promised Singaporeans that I would see the nation through the crisis, together with both the current and the 4G leadership."

The wholehearted endorsement by Mr Lee of his deputy and his team was made to urge voters to keep faith with the party, especially the fourth generation (4G) leadership. The stage is now set for Mr Lee to hand over the party leadership to Mr Wong at the latest around November/December 2024, which coincides with the PAP's seventieth anniversary and its biennial Central Executive Committee election. The possibility of Mr Wong taking over earlier cannot be discounted given how political developments and calculations can be unpredictable and dynamic.

In setting the timeline for Mr Wong to take over, Mr Lee gave his strongest endorsement yet of Mr Wong and the 4G team and of their readiness to take the reins of power. It also provides clarity and makes it definite that Mr Wong will be the next prime minister and the first to be born post-independence—should the PAP win the next general election. Put simply, where the ruling party and government is concerned, the leadership renewal and succession is settled. The overarching narrative is a smooth handover of power from the 3G to the 4G and of how that enhances stability in and confidence of Singapore. It remains to be seen whether Mr Lee will hand over to Mr Wong the party leadership and premiership at the same time. There remains some vagueness, deliberate of course, to allow for some flexibility. It could be politically advantageous to the ruling party for Mr Wong to take over the premiership baton only after securing the mandate at the next general election, which must be held by November 2025. Mr Lee marks twenty years as premier and forty years in politics in 2024—the PAP could leverage on his political capital and standing in the hustings. But it may well be that this approach of going into the pivotal general election with Mr Lee remaining as PM and Mr Wong as party leader does not fit into the overall narrative of political renewal and succession.

Forward SG: Promoting and Protecting the Middle Ground

In April and again in September 2023, Deputy Prime Minister Lawrence Wong characterized the Forward Singapore exercise, a nationwide engagement to solicit views on the country's roadmap for the next stage of development, as advancing the well-being of the broad middle. In October, he unveiled its report, *Building Our Shared Future*, which advocated seven policy shifts.[16] Ultimately, they seek to build a vibrant, thriving and resilient society where the broad middle enjoys progress, the vulnerable receive care, and the better-off do their part to improve the lives of fellow citizens. Strengthening this broad middle ground has been a tenet of Singapore politics under the PAP government. Then prime minister Lee Kuan Yew highlighted in a speech to the British Labour Party in October 1967 that the fruits of hard work and sacrifice had to be "fairly and justly distributed" across the country. In 2018, Prime Minister Lee Hsien Loong exhorted his party to be "a broad tent, a broad church", bringing different groups together.

About two-thirds to three-quarters of the population identify as middle class, and this majority overlaps significantly with the middle ground in Singapore. Even so, the middle ground is less defined by their socio-economic status than by their political inclinations and sensibilities. With a disposition towards moderation and centrism in politics, the middle ground avoids identity politics, trenchant ideological positions and political correctness. As such, they exert restraint on politically charged issues. Politics consequently remain conducive to moderate, non-partisan public policymaking.

Losing this broad middle ground has dire consequences. Society's core will become fragmented. Public distrust may evolve into a distaste for government, politicians and the political process. Recognizing these dangers, PM Lee noted in 2018 that when the middle ground weakens or withers away, "the extremes will grow, politics will have to follow and become a zero-sum game.... Once our society goes this way, we're in that downward spiral, and it'd be practically impossible to rebuild centrist politics again and bring Singaporeans together again."

The refreshed social compact is fundamentally about keeping politics, economics and society inclusive and ensuring that government and politics enjoy broad-based support and a unity of purpose. Much political hope is placed on the refreshed social compact, and it is likely to feature significantly in the next general election. Whether it can hold the centre and prevent Singapore from falling into divisive, populist politics is the real litmus test. These policy shifts must now form the cornerstone of national policies and of how Singaporeans relate to each other, especially those unlike them.

Not "Importing" Foreign Conflict: The Hamas-Israel Conflict

The 7 October Hamas attacks on Israel and Israel's retaliatory strikes in Gaza precipitated a "noticeable increase" in anti-Singapore sentiment from around the region on social media.[17] The government was naturally concerned about the impact events in the Middle East could have on Singapore's hard-earned social cohesion and harmony. A parliamentary motion was passed in November acknowledging, among other things, Israel's right of self-defence while unanimously condemning the violence against innocent civilians.[18] What the debate demonstrated was that Singaporeans can hold very strong views on the tragedy unfolding in the Middle East and yet come to a consensus on how Singapore and Singaporeans should respond.

Singapore's longstanding and principled position is that it supports a negotiated two-state solution consistent with all relevant UN Security Council resolutions.[19] Singapore firmly believes that Israelis and Palestinians have the right to live in peace, security and dignity. There is absolutely no contradiction in Singaporeans taking the position of how callously Palestinians have been treated since the creation of the state of Israel and to empathize with their plight whilst also taking the firm stance that the attacks on Israel cannot be justified by any rationale. Similarly, it is possible to support Israel's right to defend itself and for Israel to avail itself the use of force to protect its legitimate interests, but at the same time to demand that Israel's response be consistent with the rules and requirements of public international law so that the safety, security and wellbeing of civilians are safeguarded.

Singapore has warm and friendly relations with both the Palestinian Authority (PA) and Israel. The PA's President Abbas and Prime Minister Mohammad Shtayyeh have invitations from the Istana and PM Lee, respectively, to visit Singapore. Singapore is actively supporting the PA with capacity building through the S$10 million Enhanced Technical Assistance Package for the Palestinians. During the pandemic, Singapore also provided a special healthcare assistance package worth about S$750,000. Furthermore, Singapore has publicly disclosed its intention to establish a representative office in Ramallah. This is coupled with Singapore's commitment to the legitimate right of Palestinians to a sovereign and independent state to defend its citizens and its territorial integrity. Similarly, there is the commitment to international humanitarian law.

Public assemblies on matters related to the Israel-Hamas conflict were prohibited given real public safety and security concerns. The police had also advised that promoting or supporting terrorism through the display of apparel or paraphernalia that carry logos of terrorist or militant groups—such as Hamas or its military wing, Al-Qassam Brigades—would not be condoned. The Singapore government recognizes that the conflict and violence have elicited strong emotions in Singapore and will continue to do so. The developments could affect Singapore's internal situation; the foremost consideration for Singapore's authorities is to maintain Singapore's racial and religious harmony, and that external events must not affect this fundamental attribute. Singapore is determined not to "import" foreign conflicts onto its shores. Civil society and faith communities have been encouraged to put their focus on humanitarian assistance to those affected by the conflict. This can help the ground situation in Gaza, whereas protests make for good social media posts and rabble rousing but will not move the needle on the conflict.

A Sensation of Lawlessness: The "Fujian Gang" in the "Switzerland of Asia"

In mid-August, the authorities conducted simultaneous raids in an anti-money-laundering blitz that saw ten foreigners arrested and the freezing and seizure of luxury properties, cars, gold bars, designer handbags and jewellery worth—as at October 2023 —S$2.8 billion. More arrests and seizures are expected in what is

Singapore's largest money laundering case.[20] Dubbed the "Fujian Gang" (because they mostly originated from China's Fujian province), those arrested led lavish lifestyles, which captured the interest of Singaporeans and which media reports have covered assiduously.[21] Media reports also indicated that several of those arrested were allegedly linked to individuals who were investigated in China for organized crime activities overseas, such as scams and online gambling.[22] They hold foreign passports from countries such as China, Türkiye, Cyprus, Cambodia and Vanuatu. The high-profile effort to impose the full force of the law on the alleged money launderers and fraudsters is intended to signal that lawlessness is not tolerated and that Singapore must not be a venue for such illegal activities.

This unprecedented case of money laundering threw a spotlight on privately held family offices and also highlighted Singapore's attractiveness as a place for the region's wealthy to domicile their funds, necessitating robust anti-money-laundering and anti-forgery controls. As the "Switzerland of Asia", a haven for wealth (notwithstanding some criticisms of Singapore as a tax haven), flights of capital to Singapore are not unusual. In early 2023, there were media reports and public commentary on fund flows from China into Singapore even as the authorities insisted that the sources of overall inflows into Singapore are diversified from different markets.

It should not surprise us then if Singaporeans see their city-state as becoming a playground for the rich and locals feel increasingly priced out. The wealth being flaunted by some ultra-high net worth individuals and families offends the sense of egalitarianism that many believe is or should be a hallmark of Singapore society. It adds to the perception that Singapore is a playground for the rich and famous and those seeking financial safe havens.[23] DPM Wong, when asked how Singapore manages "the perception of growing inequality and the focus on wealth, said it engages the new arrivals and reminds them about Singapore's values and our way of life: "[We] tell them that Singapore is an inclusive society. We are placed with an informal and egalitarian ethos, where people can interact freely with one another comfortably as equals, where we frown on ostentatious displays of wealth. So these are our house rules. If you would like to be here, please follow our norms, follow our rules. If you think they are not for you, that is okay. You can take your money elsewhere. We will not hold it against you."[24]

Adieu to President Halimah and Welcome to President Tharman[25]

President Halimah Yacob, Singapore's first woman head of state, completed her six-year term on 12 September 2023. In May, she announced her decision not to seek re-election. Madam Halimah was elected in 2017 without a contest as she was the only Malay applicant who received a certificate of eligibility from the Presidential Elections Committee. Following amendments to the Singapore Constitution in November 2016, the 2017 election was reserved for the Malay community as it had not had a member as the president in the five most recent presidential terms.[26]

During the Covid-19 pandemic, which Prime Minister Lee had described as the "crisis of a generation", Madam Halimah worked closely with the Council of Presidential Advisers and the government to approve draw down on the country's past reserves of up to $52 billion in the 2020 financial year, $11 billion in 2021 and $6 billion in 2022 to fund crisis measures to protect lives and livelihoods. Her weekly schedule was packed with numerous visits to social service agencies, non-profit organizations and companies that promoted the social causes she supported passionately, such as gender equality, protecting older workers, and mental well-being. During her term, the President's Challenge had focused on empowering people with disabilities, building a digitally inclusive society, and supporting caregivers, among others.[27] Madam Halimah has long been a strong proponent of building interfaith relationships and encouraging multicultural dialogue. She mooted and convened in 2019 the inaugural International Conference on Cohesive Societies, organized by the S. Rajaratnam School of International Studies.

In his speech at President Halimah's farewell ceremony, Prime Minister Lee described her as "a powerful symbol of unity for all Singaporeans…. Throughout your tenure, you showed the way with grounded leadership, and a warm heart for the people. Your ability to empathise and resonate with Singaporeans from all walks of life has brought our nation closer together and reminded us that we all have a role to play to make Singapore a better home."

Singaporeans headed to the polls on 1 September for the sixth presidential election. The initial scepticism that there would be another uncontested election did not materialize. About 2.5 million voters cast their ballots for the three candidates on the ballot sheet: Ng Kok Song (former chief investment officer of Singapore's sovereign wealth fund GIC Pte Ltd), Tharman Shanmugaratnam (former senior minister and deputy prime minister) and Tan Kin Lian (former chief executive officer of insurer Income). In a massive victory undergirded by a dignified and consistent campaign, "Respect for All", emphasizing his track record, Mr Tharman won 70.4 per cent (1,749,261 votes) of the popular vote to become the first president to be elected in a contest who was not an ethnic Chinese. Mr Ng polled 15.72 per cent (390,636) while Mr Tan, who was making his second presidential bid, had 13.87 per cent (344,584). Prior to the election, there were expectations that Mr Tharman's performance would be hurt by his being a former PAP stalwart and the recent political controversies involving his former party colleagues.

Voters made it clear, however, that they wanted a non-partisan president and that prior affiliations, even political ones, need not be determinative. They wanted a president who not only has the requisite experience and ability to be a custodian of Singapore's national reserves and the public service's integrity but who also has a track record of being a unifying figure. Despite claiming to be the only "truly independent candidate", Mr Tan's candidacy was endorsed by an array of opposition leaders.

It was a commanding display of unity, meritocracy and multiracialism by the Singaporean electorate as they came together to give Mr Tharman an overwhelming mandate. Mr Tharman's victory can be attributed to his being a compelling candidate for many Singaporeans. Had the leading candidate from the establishment possessed a less-than-compelling track record or lacked the independent mindedness, experience and ability of Mr Tharman, it is likely that both Mr Tan and Mr Ng would have polled better as the differentiation among the three candidates would have been less distinct.

Most importantly, voters knew what was at stake even in a presidential election and were clear about not short-changing themselves through blind loyalties to political manoeuvrings and that the presidency was not a political prize to be captured for instrumental ends by political parties. There were also sufficient voters, even those with non-establishment leanings, who appreciated that the presidency must be non-partisan and above the political fray for it to be a unifying institution.

Should the PAP retain power in the next general election, DPM Lawrence Wong can benefit from the counsel and advice of President Tharman. On the campaign trail, Mr Tharman had indicated that he recognized the president's role in this leadership transition, and that was one of the reasons he had put himself forward for the position: "Singapore society is changing, Singapore politics is changing, and I think the relationship between the president and the prime minister, the new prime minister, should be a constructive one; and I believe we can make that work." With the strong mandate from the people, the Tharman presidency can be an additional ballast for stability and unity during the political transition against the backdrop of a more diverse and competitive political landscape.

'Long Island' Project: Singapore's Climate Adaptation Imperative

Singapore is extremely vulnerable to the impact of sea level rise. As about thirty per cent of the city-state lies five metres below mean sea level, the threat of rising sea levels is real and an existential one. On 28 November 2023, Mr Desmond Lee, minister for national development, announced technical studies and public consultations on the "Long Island" endeavour, intended as a long-term solution to protect homes, businesses, infrastructure, and public spaces such as East Coast Park.[28] This announcement of Singapore taking another step towards climate adaptation and mitigation coincided with the start of the COP28 talks in Dubai.

First announced by Prime Minister Lee Hsien Loong at the 2019 National Day Rally, Long Island was first mooted in the 1991 Concept Plan.[29] It is an integrated solution envisaged to comprise land approximately twice the size of Marina Bay (by land area) reclaimed off the East Coast. It could take the form of islands located some distance away from the existing coastline. It offers the prospect of meeting multiple national needs beyond coastal protection and flood resilience, such as water resilience and creating more land to meet future development needs, as well as new recreational opportunities.

Long Island is expected to take a few decades to plan, design and implement. In view of the urgency to protect the East Coast from sea level rise, agencies will commence technical studies from early 2024 and concurrently engage stakeholders and the public as part of the process. The technical studies, including engineering studies and environmental impact assessments, will also explore ways to better integrate coastal protection measures with land reclamation through a combination of engineering and nature-based solutions while minimizing potential impact to the environment and existing uses.

Foreign Policy: Relevance and Giving Singapore More Strategic Space

Moving Forward in Bilateral Relations with Closest Neighbours

The year 2023 was a busy one for Singapore's diplomatic calendar that saw a full schedule of outgoing visits by Singapore's leaders and incoming visits by foreign leaders to the country. The tenth Singapore-Malaysia Leaders' Retreat, the first to be held since the Covid-19 pandemic, saw Malaysian prime minister Anwar Ibrahim visit Singapore in October to discuss bilateral issues and explore new areas of cooperation. It was also PM Anwar's first such retreat since he was sworn in as prime minister in late 2022. Both countries intend to enter into a memorandum of understanding (MOU) to explore the feasibility of a Johor-Singapore Special Economic Zone (SEZ). The SEZ can improve the flow of goods and people between both sides of the Causeway, which marks its centenary in 2024, and enhance the ecosystem of the Iskandar development region and

Singapore. Singapore is Iskandar Malaysia's second-largest foreign investor, with S$9.5 billion (RM33 billion) committed between 2006 and June 2023.

Knotty issues were deliberated by both leaders. They agreed to formulate a set of mutually agreed principles and outcomes for both civil aviation authorities to move forward as expeditiously as possible on the provision of air traffic services over southern peninsular Malaysia that would accommodate current and future operational needs.[30] On maritime boundary delimitation, both leaders agreed to convene a joint meeting to resolve outstanding bilateral maritime boundary delimitation issues and to implement the International Court of Justice's 2008 judgment on Pedra Branca, Middle Rocks and South Ledge. Similarly, they noted the good progress made at the first meeting in June of the technical working group on delimiting precisely the territorial waters' boundary in other parts. Both countries will resume discussions on the prices of raw and treated water without prejudice to each other's long-declared positions on the right to review prices under the 1962 Johor River Water Agreement. They also agreed to resume discussions on how to safeguard the Johor River's water quality and increase the yield to ensure a sustainable supply that meets the 1962 water agreement.[31]

Earlier in March, Prime Minister Lee Hsien Loong met Indonesian president Joko Widodo in Singapore for the Singapore-Indonesia Leaders' Retreat. This was Mr Lee's sixth Leaders' Retreat with President Widodo, and the first to be hosted in Singapore since the pandemic. The retreat came a year after both countries signed three landmark agreements in 2022 on longstanding bilateral issues of airspace management, defence cooperation and extradition of fugitives. Under the Expanded Framework, both countries will bring the three agreements into force on a mutually agreed date. The resolution of these longstanding issues will be a boost for bilateral relations. Six MOUs in emerging sectors such as the digital economy, sustainability, and human capital development, as well as in traditional areas like security, were also inked.

Singapore, China and the United States

Sino-American rivalry continued to keep policymakers occupied. During the Foreign Ministry's budget estimates, Foreign Minister Vivian Balakrishnan noted that Singapore (and the countries in the region) want to maintain good relations with both China and the United States. He reiterated that Singapore did not wish to be forced to choose sides, noting that all three countries participated in multiple initiatives that have overlapping memberships but do not always include both China and the United States. Singapore's bottom line: "We have always put

Singapore's national interest first and we take principled positions impartially, even if it does not always please one or the other superpower. We need the quiet confidence and the national unity to do so consistently for the long term. Given the grave implications for the world, we, like most countries, hope that the US and China work out a modus vivendi between themselves."[32]

Prime Minister Lee elaborated on Singapore's concerns with the increasing geopolitical contestation, which "affects every country and region in the world". He observed that "neither the US nor China seeks conflict. But the issues that divide them are deep. Increasingly each sees the other as an adversary. And the risk of accidents and miscalculation is ever present, especially in dangerous hotspots like the Taiwan Strait. This worries Asian countries a lot. We are close to ground zero. We will be impacted economically too. 'De-risking' is understandable, but 'de-risking' is risky and costly. It may result in bifurcation, and it will likely have more than just economic consequences. But the picture is not all gloomy. Because while different countries will align more closely with one side or the other, nearly all still want to be friends with both."[33]

Similarly, Defence Minister Ng Eng Hen offered three broad tracks that China could do to promote stability in the region and globally. First, China must continue to grow economically and further integrate its markets with the rest of the world. Second, China must continue to promote multilateralism and uphold the rule of law: "That is China's greatest assurance to other nations, big or small, that … as China grows economically and militarily, it does not seek to supplant or replace others based on its own national interests." Third, China including the People's Liberation Army, must lead to reduce tensions in the region: "Whether China accepts it or not, wants it or not, it is already seen as a dominant power and must therefore act as a benevolent one."[34]

In August, China's newly reappointed foreign minister Wang Yi visited Singapore, Malaysia and Cambodia in his first foreign visit after his reappointment. The visit served to highlight Beijing's strong commitment to Southeast Asia and that there was continuity in China's foreign relations and its Southeast Asia policy following Qin Gang's removal as foreign minister. Earlier in March, Prime Minister Lee visited China for his first visit to China since 2019. Both countries agreed to upgrade their ties in an "All-Round High-Quality Future-Oriented Partnership", reflecting the aim of having more ambitious goals in bilateral cooperation. Besides meeting President Xi Jinping, Mr Lee had individual meetings with three top leaders: Beijing Party Secretary Yin Li, National People's Party Congress chairman Zhao Leji, and Chinese People's Political Consultative Conference chairman Wang Huning. Both sides agreed to work towards resuming flight connectivity and restoring people-to-people exchanges to pre-pandemic levels.[35] PM Lee also visited Guangdong and Hainan provinces.

Leading a delegation of 4G leaders, DPM Wong also visited China in December, where he and Chinese vice-premier Ding Xuexiang co-chaired the Joint Council for Bilateral Cooperation, related joint steering council meetings, and commemorative events on the fifteenth anniversary of the Tianjin Eco-City. DPM Wong noted that the bilateral ties provided for mutual learning and collaboration even as Singapore had to constantly find ways to provide value to China.[36] A new visa-free arrangement from early 2024 was also announced: Singaporean and Chinese nationals can visit the other country for up to thirty days without a visa.[37]

PM Lee made two working visits to the United States in March and November 2023. It was his first visit to the US under the Biden administration, which took office in January 2021. In science and technology, Singapore and the United States deepened their collaboration. In 2021, both countries signed the "Partnership for Growth and Innovation (PGI)", which seeks to advance bilateral cooperation in the areas of digital economy and smart cities, energy and environmental technologies, advanced manufacturing and supply chain resilience, and healthcare. Deputy Prime Minister Lawrence Wong made a high-profile working visit to Washington DC in October, where both countries agreed to further collaboration in critical and emerging technology, including artificial intelligence, critical infrastructure, and biotechnology, among others. During the visit, the US-Singapore Critical and Emerging Technology Dialogue was inaugurated to "promote candid and sustained exchanges on risks, opportunities, and key national security implications associated with the rapid advancement of technologies across these six focus areas".[38]

Singapore's President as Chief Diplomat

In her final year as head of state, President Halimah Yacob made several state visits, including to the Republic of Kazakhstan and the Republic of Uzbekistan in May 2023, the first state visits by a Singaporean president to Central Asia. In March 2023, President Halimah made a state visit to Malaysia—the first such visit since 2013. Her last state visit was to Qatar in June. Qatar's emir, Sheikh Tamim bin Hamad Al Thani, was the first visiting head of state Madam Halimah hosted in Singapore after she assumed office in 2017. In total, President Halimah made twelve state visits abroad during her term of office. In an interview, she observed of her role as the chief diplomat and said that: "whether it's developed countries or developing countries, we do have a brand name. And they do know that when they enter into any negotiations with us, whether it is for economic initiatives or for other kinds of initiatives, they know that we are a trusted partner.... There is a lot of respect for Singapore, for our governance, for our efficiency, for our clean government."[39]

Prime Minister Lee also made his first official visits to South Africa and Kenya in May. He also made an official visit to Vietnam in August 2023, reciprocating Vietnamese premier Pham Minh Chinh's official visit to Singapore in February 2023. This exchange of visits coincided with the fiftieth anniversary of bilateral relations and tenth anniversary of Singapore's strategic partnership with Vietnam. PM Lee also made official visits to Saudi Arabia and the United Arab Emirates in October 2023 amid the Hamas-Israel conflict. At the COP28 in Dubai (The Conference of the Parties to the UN Framework Convention on Climate Change), Singapore announced that it would not be claiming from the loss and damage fund to help countries most vulnerable to climate change cope with its effects. Singapore is also unlikely to contribute to the fund despite having to invest very significantly in climate change mitigation efforts such as coastal protection. Instead, it is committed to helping developing countries by sharing best practices in climate adaptation and resilience under the Sustainability Action Package under the Singapore Cooperation Programme through activating financing and technology and bringing solutions to cities. At the request of United Arab Emirate's COP28 president Sultan Al Jaber, Minister for Sustainability and the Environment Grace Fu co-facilitated with Norwegian foreign minister Espen Barth Eide ministerial consultations to successfully reach consensus on various mitigation efforts to keep the 1.5°C goal within reach. Singapore also played a key role in facilitating the conclusion of the first Global Stocktake, which reviewed the collective progress towards the achievement of the goals of the Paris Agreement.

Conclusion

The year under review was a challenging one for the PAP government amid the final phase of the leadership handover. Despite the setbacks, the ruling party was determined to press on with its agenda of action laid out in the President's Address at the opening of the second session of the 14th Parliament in May, including the Forward Singapore exercise, which will likely be a key plank of the 4G PAP election manifesto. The challenge is to secure buy-in from Singaporeans and inspire the necessary support from all stakeholders—government, businesses, civil society and individuals—for the refreshed social compact. How the PAP government steers the export-oriented economy amid geopolitical headwinds will matter immensely. While the economy has been projected to grow by 1 to 3 per cent in 2024, global economic uncertainty affecting Singapore's exports and interest rates could result in domestic anxiety and perhaps a downgrading of the government's performance legitimacy at a time when it can ill afford it.

The year ahead will see earnest preparations for the pivotal general election, which could be called in 2024. In the July 2020 general election—held during the pandemic and despite the existential and economic crisis—the Workers' Party made significant gains by winning the largest number of seats by an opposition party in a general election post-independence. There was no flight to safety that voters had previously demonstrated in earlier elections when there was an economic downturn or a serious security threat. The year 2024 will provide valuable insights into whether the pandemic has caused a significant change in how Singaporeans view the state of government and politics in Singapore and whether a generational change of leadership will inspire optimism. Whether and how Mr Lawrence Wong and his 4G team will inspire Singaporeans and earn their electoral support, against the backdrop of increasing global disorder, will determine the trajectory of the PAP's one-party dominance, which stretches back to 1959.

Notes

1. See the prominent advertisement titled "Assurance in FY2023" in *The Straits Times* of 3 and 20 December 2023.
2. *Labour Force in Singapore Advance Release 2023*.
3. Ibid.
4. The two pillars in the framework are (1) reallocating profits of the largest and most profitable MNEs from where activities are conducted to where consumers are located, and (2) introducing a fifteen per cent global minimum effective tax rate for MNE groups with annual global revenues of €750 million or more.
5. The United Nations defines a country as "ageing" if the proportion of its population aged sixty-five and above crosses 7 per cent. It is "aged" if the proportion exceeds 14 per cent, and "super aged" when it reaches 21 per cent. See "Initiatives in Place to Tackle Ageing Issues as S'pore Hits 'Super-Aged' Status in 2026: Health Minister", *Straits Times*, 20 April 2023.
6. Such tiered support, tied to one's income and CPF savings, demonstrates the commitment to the equitable sharing of Singapore's prosperity: those who need more help will receive more help; those who do not need help will receive less or nothing.
7. See Prime Minister's Office statement of 28 June 2023 on "Rental of State Properties at Ridout Road by Minister K Shanmugam and Minister Vivian Balakrishnan", CPIB Report of 23 June 2023, and Senior Minister Teo Chee Hean's report of 26 June

2023 at https://www.pmo.gov.sg/Newsroom/Rental-of-State-Properties-at-Ridout-Road-by-Min-Shanmugam-and-Min-Vivian-Balakrishnan.

8. This episode reminds us of the immense challenge Singapore faces in attracting people to consider entering politics, regardless of political affiliation, given how their personal lives and that of their families would be relentlessly probed or even unfairly targeted.

9. PM Lee said that he first learnt of their relationship sometime after the 2020 General Election in November 2020. The pair were both spoken to, and counselled, separately and they said they would stop the affair. In February 2023, Lee spoke to them again, separately. Mr Tan admitted that what he did was wrong and offered to resign, which Lee accepted. But Lee said that before Tan actually resigned, Tan had first to make sure residents in Kembangan-Chai Chee (his ward) and Marine Parade (his GRC) were taken care of. See "Transcript of Ministerial Statement by Prime Minister Lee Hsien Loong on the CPIB Investigation Involving Minister Iswaran and the Resignations of Former Speaker and a PAP MP on 2 August 2023", https://www.pmo.gov.sg/Newsroom/Ministerial-Statement-by-PM-Lee-Hsien-Loong-on-investigation-and-resignations-Aug-2023. See also "Statement by Prime Minister Lee Hsien Loong on Speaker of Parliament Tan Chuan-Jin's Resignation on 17 July 2023" and the exchange of letters, https://www.pmo.gov.sg/Newsroom/Statement-by-PM-Lee-Hsien-Loong-on-Speaker-Tan-Chuan-Jin-resignation.

10. According to PM Lee, this was not a new position but the PAP's long-standing practice since the days of Mr Lee Kuan Yew. See "Transcript of Ministerial Statement by Prime Minister Lee Hsien Loong on the CPIB Investigation Involving Minister Iswaran and the Resignations of Former Speaker and a PAP MP on 2 August 2023", https://www.pmo.gov.sg/Newsroom/Ministerial-Statement-by-PM-Lee-Hsien-Loong-on-investigation-and-resignations-Aug-2023

11. Mr Tan wrote on Facebook that "When I listen to speeches made, like everyone, I do form views on them. What was said were my private thoughts which I had muttered to myself and not to anyone…. However I should not have expressed them aloud or in unparliamentary language, and I apologise for that. I have also spoken to [Prof Lim] … to make that apology as well, which he has kindly accepted." See "Speaker Tan Chuan-Jin Apologises to Jamus Lim for 'Unparliamentary Language' Caught on Hot Mic", *Straits Times*, 11 July 2023.

12. Through his company, Singapore GP, Ong owns the rights to the Formula One Singapore Grand Prix as its chairman. In 2008, the first night race in F1 history was held in Singapore. In January 2022, Singapore signed a deal to continue hosting the race for another seven years. This was the fourth renewal and the longest extension so far. Mr Iswaran had been actively involved in the government's engagements with F1.

13. As PM Lee observed, incidents involving ministers are rare (the last would be then national development minister Teh Cheang Wan in 1986). Lee noted that "there is no rule or precedent on how to effect an interdiction on a Political Office Holder. Hence, I used the current civil service practice as a reference point. The specific details in Minister Iswaran's case follow generally how the civil service would deal with a senior officer in a similar situation. But this was my decision as Prime Minister, because the political contexts for a minister and a civil servant being investigated and interdicted are different."

14. See "Transcript of Ministerial Statement by Prime Minister Lee Hsien Loong on the CPIB Investigation Involving Minister Iswaran and the Resignations of Former Speaker and a PAP MP on 2 August 2023", https://www.pmo.gov.sg/Newsroom/Ministerial-Statement-by-PM-Lee-Hsien-Loong-on-investigation-and-resignations-Aug-2023.

15. See Lee's and Wong's speeches at https://pap-dr-wp.s3.ap-southeast-1.amazonaws.com/2023/11/05173042/Checked-Speech-by-PAP-Secretary-General-Lee-Hsien-Loong-at-PAP-Awards-and-Convention-2023.pdf and https://pap-dr-wp.s3.ap-southeast-1.amazonaws.com/2023/11/05173105/Checked-Speech-by-PAP-Deputy-SecGen-Lawrence-Wong-PAP-Awards-and-Convention-2023.pdf, respectively.

16. The seven key policy shifts are: Embracing Learning beyond Grades, Respecting and Rewarding Every Job, Supporting Families through Every Stage, Enabling Seniors to Age Well, Empowering Those in Need, Investing in Our Shared Tomorrow, and Doing Our Part as One United People. The report is available at https://www.forwardsingapore.gov.sg/.

17. See "Rise in Anti-Singapore Sentiment Online since Outbreak of Israel-Hamas Hostilities: Shanmugam", CNA, 27 November 2023, https://www.channelnewsasia.com/singapore/shanmugam-anti-singapore-sentiments-online-after-oct-7-hamas-israel-3948091.

18. The "Solidarity, Security and Peace: The Israel-Hamas Conflict" motion debated read as follows: "That this House, having regard to the terrorist attacks by Hamas against Israel and the deepening humanitarian crisis arising from Israel's military operations in the Gaza strip: (a) Expresses its deepest condolences to all innocent victims and civilian casualties; (b) Advocates the urgent delivery of humanitarian aid to the civilian population in Gaza; (c) Condemns those responsible for the terrorist acts and violations of international law; (d) Calls for all parties to ensure the safety and security of civilians, including the release of all hostages; (e) Reiterates Singapore's longstanding commitment to a negotiated two-state solution consistent with the relevant UN Security Council resolutions; and (f) Urges all Singaporeans to safeguard and uphold our multi-racial and multi-religious peace and harmony."

19. Singapore's approach is premised on the faithful observance of international law, especially the independence and sovereignty of nation-states. Singapore's stance is that the two-state solution is most conducive for a durable, just and comprehensive

20. resolution of the longstanding dispute and conflict. This will enable Palestinians to have their sovereignty and distinct identity, which could facilitate Israel and Palestine to live side-by-side in peace and security.

20. "How Suspects Laundered Billions in Singapore for Years", Bloomberg, 4 December 2023.

21. See "Property, Nightclubs, Collector Items: How 'Fujian Gang' Lifestyles Aided Money-laundering Activities", *ThinkChina*, 31 August 2023, https://www.thinkchina.sg/property-nightclubs-collector-items-how-fujian-gang-lifestyles-aided-money-laundering-activities.

22. "Suspects in Billion-Dollar Money Laundering Case in S'pore Allegedly Linked to China Gambling Groups", *Straits Times*, 21 August 2023.

23. "Can the Growing Number of Ultra-rich in Singapore Live in Harmony with the Average Joe?", *TODAY*, 2 June 2023.

24. "DPM Lawrence Wong at the Milken Institute Asia Summit 2023", 13 September 2023, https://www.pmo.gov.sg/Newsroom/DPM-Lawrence-Wong-at-the-Milken-Institute-Asia-Summit-2023.

25. For a fuller discussion, see the chapter by Benjamin Joshua Ong in this volume.

26. The last Malay president before Madam Halimah was Mr Yusof Ishak, Singapore's first head of state, who held office from 1965 to 1970. He was the Yang di-Pertuan Negara between 1959 and 1965 when Singapore was self-governing (1959–63) and a state within the Federation of Malaysia (1963–65).

27. The President's Challenge is an annual fund-raising campaign to help the less fortunate in society. The beneficiaries are annually selected by the President's Office.

28. This section is drawn from information available on "Long Island", https://www.ura.gov.sg/corporate/planning/Master-Plan/Draft-Master-Plan-2025/Long-Island.

29. Reviewed every ten years, the Concept Plan is Singapore's strategic land use and transportation plan to guide development in the next forty to fifty years. It aims to ensure there is sufficient land to meet anticipated population and economic growth and to provide a good living environment. See the write-up on the Ministry of National Development's website at https://www.mnd.gov.sg/faqs/land-planning-and-conservation/general.

30. The existing arrangements for safe and efficient air traffic management were recommended and approved by the International Civil Aviation Organisation (ICAO) in 1973 and implemented through the Operational Letter of Agreement between Kuala Lumpur and Singapore Area Control Centres concerning Singapore Arrivals, Departures and Overflights 1974.

31. Under this agreement, Singapore can draw and use 250 million gallons daily from the Johor River. Singapore is, in turn, obliged to provide Johor with treated water up to 2 per cent of the water Singapore imports.

32. Speech by Minister for Foreign Affairs Dr Vivian Balakrishnan at MFA's Committee of Supply Debate, 27 February 2023, https://www.mfa.gov.sg/Newsroom/Press-Statements-Transcripts-and-Photos/2023/02/Min-COS-2023.

33. Remarks by Prime Minister Lee Hsien Loong at the Closing Dialogue for the Asia Future Summit 2023 on 5 October 2023, https://www.pmo.gov.sg/Newsroom/PM-Lee-Hsien-Loong-at-the-Asia-Future-Summit-2023.

34. Speech by Minister for Defence Dr Ng Eng Hen at the 10th Beijing Xiangshan Forum, Third Plenary Session on "Asia-Pacific Security Architecture: Present and Future" on 31 October 2023, https://www.mindef.gov.sg/web/portal/mindef/news-and-events/latest-releases/article-detail/2023/October/31oct23_speech.

35. China only reopened its borders to foreign tourists on 15 March 2023, when it restored the issuance of all types of visas to China. Prior to the pandemic, there were about four hundred direct flights a week between China and Singapore. At the end of 2023, flights between both countries were at seventy-five per cent of pre-pandemic levels.

36. "Singapore to Keep Finding Ways to Add Value to China, says DPM Lawrence Wong", *Straits Times*, 8 December 2023.

37. Until the change, China passport holders needed a visa to enter Singapore, while Singaporeans could visit China for up to fifteen days visa-free.

38. See White House fact sheet, "Upgrading the U.S.-Singapore Strategic Technology Partnership", 12 October 2023, https://www.whitehouse.gov/briefing-room/statements-releases/2023/10/12/fact-sheet-upgrading-the-u-s-singapore-strategic-technology-partnership/.

39. "Singapore a Consistent and Reliable Partner: Halimah Yacob on a Key Message when Travelling as President", *TODAY*, 12 September 2023, https://www.todayonline.com/singapore/singapore-consistent-and-reliable-partner-halimah-yacob-key-message-when-travelling-president-2252356.

Singapore's 2023 Presidential Election: The Presidency Continues to Evolve

Benjamin Joshua Ong

Singapore's Presidency: An Ever-Evolving Institution

Singapore's state institutions were modelled originally on their British counterparts but have undergone transformations to meet local needs and challenges. Further—partly because of modern Singapore's youth, partly because of new challenges, and partly because Singapore's political order allows institutional arrangements to be adjusted swiftly—this process of transformation is an ongoing one.

Singapore's presidency is no exception. When Singapore became a sovereign independent state in 1965, the president was like the monarch in the United Kingdom: he was the head of state and a symbol of the nation, and official functions were performed in his name, but he was not involved in the formulation and execution of law or policy.

Things changed in 1991, following fears that a future rogue government could effect irreversible change to Singapore—say, by squandering Singapore's reserves on poorly thought out or outright populist measures, with the aid of state institutions packed with cronies. The solution was this: in addition to his existing ceremonial duties and "soft" role as a unifying figure, the president would now have the power to veto proposed key public appointments or any attempts by the government of the day to draw down on reserves built up by previous governments.

In many cases, the veto could be overridden, but only if the president's veto was contrary to the views of the appointed Council of Presidential Advisers *and if* the government introduced a motion in Parliament to overrule the president that Parliament agreed to by a supermajority—which would certainly come at a political cost. So the president took on what were known as "custodial" functions:

BENJAMIN JOSHUA ONG is an Assistant Professor of Law at the Yong Pung How School of Law, Singapore Management University.

while he could not stop what he saw as unwise spending or a bad appointment, he was to serve as an important safeguard.

To perform the new custodial functions, the president would have to be independent of the incumbent government. So the presidency was transformed into a popularly elected office, with elections taking place every six years. Since the first popularly elected president, Ong Teng Cheong, took office in 1993, the office of the presidency has continued to evolve: early assumptions were clarified, points of friction between the presidency and the government were smoothed over, and rules on who can be president were reformed.

Presidential polls do not take place frequently. Of the six election cycles so far, three have been walkovers. This is because of tight rules on who may qualify to run in an election in the first place. Conversations about these rules are inevitably tied up with conversations about what the president's job is and should be. Such debates swell around the time of presidential elections.

The 2023 election saw these debates continue, perhaps more intensely than ever before. One aspirant, George Goh, was not granted the certificate of eligibility necessary to stand in the election. Three people were. One of them, Tan Kin Lian, turned out to have a history of making social media posts that cast doubt on his character. Mr Tan and the other two candidates, Tharman Shanmugaratnam and Ng Kok Song, found themselves the subject of debates about how truly "independent" they were. These were not just matters of legal interpretation; they raised broader questions about the nature of the presidency and of Singaporean democracy more generally.

For these reasons, the 2023 election, and the laws and norms that scaffold the institution of the presidency more generally, are worthy of careful study, even now that the dust has settled and Mr Tharman has begun his work in office as Singapore's popularly elected president.

Who Can Be the President?

Background to the Qualifying Criteria

Prior to 1991, the president—then a mainly ceremonial office—was "elected" by Parliament. This involved a "low-key closed-door affair"[1] that could be trusted to produce someone worthy of being called head of state. The office took on a certain dignity, not unlike (say) the monarchy of the United Kingdom.

When the presidency became popularly elected, this dignity had to continue. Not just anybody could stand to be president. The president had to have "integrity, good character and reputation" and the requisite "ability" and "experience" to do the job, and the electoral process alone might not weed out all unsuitable candidates.[2] So there is a Presidential Elections Committee (PEC), which screens candidates according to certain criteria; only candidates who meet them receive a "certificate of eligibility", which is required to stand in an election.

One might argue that the stringent criteria "make the office of president fundamentally elitist".[3] Yet one can appreciate the rationale behind pre-qualification: the stakes are too high to take the risk that an unsuitable candidate might be popularly elected. There was another risk: the process of open elections could devolve into a style of politicking that could dissuade suitable candidates from participating in the electoral process.[4]

The last major change to the qualifying criteria took place in 2016, following several recommendations of the Constitutional Commission, which was headed by the chief justice and staffed by prominent public- and private-sector figures, and which conducted a wide-ranging public consultation exercise. The biggest change was the new "reserved election" system: because one task of the president is to represent Singapore—whose society is multiracial—new rules were put in place, such that if in the past five presidential terms no president was from the "Chinese community", "Malay community", and/or "Indian or other minority communities", then the next election would be reserved for candidates from that community/those communities. That aside, the basic framework remained the same as in 1991, subject only to certain tweaks.

The Qualifying Criteria Today

As of 2017, the criteria (set out in Article 19 of the Constitution) have been as follows. To qualify to stand in a presidential election, a person must meet certain basic requirements: he must be a Singapore citizen, at least forty-five years old, not a member of a political party, not be an undischarged bankrupt, and not have been convicted of an offence above a certain level of seriousness, among others. Further, the PEC must be satisfied that the person is "a person of integrity, good character and reputation". The person must also have a certain track record that demonstrates the ability and experience to serve as president.

This track record may be proven in one of two ways.

First, a person automatically qualifies if he or she has held one of several public-sector offices—such as chief justice, Speaker of Parliament, minister, or chief executive of GIC or Temasek Holdings (Singapore's sovereign wealth funds)—or has served in a large company with at least SG$500 million (US$374 million) in shareholders' equity as the "chief executive", which means the "most senior executive … principally responsible for the management and conduct of the [company's] business and operations".

Second, under what is called the "deliberative" or "discretionary" track, one can qualify on the basis of what the PEC considers "experience and ability that is comparable" to a person who meets the "automatic" criteria, provided that the PEC is also satisfied that "the person has the experience and ability to effectively carry out the functions and duties of the office of President".[5]

Either way, the qualifying criteria are stringent. In short, candidates must have had experience in being personally responsible for making complex, high-stakes decisions, and must have met a certain minimum standard of conduct.

The 2017 election cycle was the first to take place after the changes following the commission's recommendations. The election was reserved for candidates from the Malay community. Several applied, but only one—Madam Halimah Yacob—met all the criteria. The qualifying criteria therefore came to the fore in the period leading up to the 2023 election.

George Goh Testing the Boundaries of the Private-Sector Criteria

One aspirant, George Goh, tested the boundaries of the private-sector criteria. He presented himself as a self-made businessman, known for establishing the presence of Harvey Norman (an Australia-based retailer) in Singapore. But he could not point to a single sufficiently large company of which he was chief executive. Instead, he sought to persuade the PEC, under the "deliberative" track, that he had had roles in five different companies that were, in substance, a single organization. This was not impossible—under the deliberative track, one need not be the chief executive of a "company", but rather an "organisation", an undefined term that could in principle consist of multiple companies that work together. But it was unprecedented.

Mr Goh was not granted a certificate of eligibility. While the PEC does not ordinarily publicize the reasons for its decisions (instead communicating them privately to applicants who may publicize them if they wish), this time it did. This was because Mr Goh had alleged publicly that the PEC had not "explain[ed] the rationale behind its decision".[6] In response, the PEC invoked its power to publish its reasons if it is "in the Committee's opinion, necessary to respond to any public allegation made against the Committee".[7]

The PEC had clearly accepted that, in principle, five companies can be "owned, managed and operated" such that they are, for all intents and purposes, one "organisation". However, on the facts, the five companies were not in substance one "organisation", nor did Mr Goh have experience tantamount to that of the "chief executive of a typical company" whose size was the combined size of the five companies.

The PEC did not—as Mr Goh alleged—take a "very narrow interpretation" of the qualifying criteria. It—as lawyers and accountants do—rightly considered substance over form. Nonetheless, the public eye focused on the broader issue of why the qualifying criteria are what they are. The fundamental question is: is the voting process alone sufficient to guarantee that the victor will be a good president? That difficult question goes right to the heart of representative democracy.

Tan Kin Lian and the "Character" Requirement

Three people—Ng Kok Song, Tan Kin Lian and Tharman Shanmugaratnam—received certificates of eligibility. Then there was a second incident, which re-ignited public debate about the qualifying criteria.

It turned out that Tan Kin Lian had, in past years, made several questionable posts on social media. These included photographs of women whom he described as "pretty girls" (including one of a woman's partially exposed buttocks), as well as a photograph of people with dark skin on a public bus in Singapore together with a caption that Mr Tan "found that [he] was in Mumbai".[8] These posts drew criticism[9] and a bizarre non-apology from Tan (followed by two ham-fisted apologies).[10]

By this point, the PEC had issued Tan a certificate of eligibility, which meant that it had been satisfied as to his "integrity, good character and reputation". The PEC therefore found itself in a somewhat awkward position. It had no legal power to rescind the certificate, and so had to stop at saying that it had never known of the social media posts and so could not be taken to have endorsed them.

One might ask whether the PEC should have dug deeper. Yet there are broader questions of principle: why should the "integrity, good character and reputation" requirement even exist; what precisely does that phrase mean; and who should be the judge? Some have argued that that requirement should be scrapped, and the electorate alone should be the judge of character.[11] This writer would suggest that only specific wrongs—such as having been found civilly liable for negligence in certain serious cases or having been convicted of certain serious criminal offences (both of which one currently must disclose on the application form)—should disqualify one from running in the election.

Finally, Iris Koh, an anti-vaccine activist, objected to Mr Tharman's candidacy on the purported ground that he would be unable to serve independently as president because of a risk of "foreign interference" arising from his "affiliations with foreign entities".[12] Underlying these views were various conspiracy theories relating to the World Economic Forum and the United Nations. These views were plainly baseless.

Ms Koh attempted to file a formal objection with the Elections Department, and also supported an attempt by M. Ravi (a lawyer and activist, apparently supported by another lawyer, Joseph Chen) to apply to court for an order that Mr Tharman be disqualified.[13] Koh did not successfully submit her objection—quite likely because the purpose of the objection process is to allow prospective candidates to object to other prospective candidates, not for members of the public to do so. Further, Mr Ravi's application failed chiefly because he had not shown that it was unlawful for Mr Tharman to be a candidate. In short, they had only argued that Mr Tharman was undesirable; but undesirability is dealt with through elections, not legal processes.

These attempted applications, founded as they were on faulty reasoning, misleading misstatements of fact, and/or outright falsehoods, inadvertently highlight an important point: the qualifying criteria set high standards, but they are only minimum standards, and are no substitute for the judgment that voters must exercise as to the merits of each candidate. If anything, Ms Koh and Mr Ravi should have directed their efforts towards attempting to persuade voters, rather than towards having Mr Tharman disqualified altogether.

The Campaign

Campaigning took place through traditional means such as banners, posters, walkabouts (in-person campaigning at public places), and televised messages and debates, as well as candidates' social media. Mr Ng took the somewhat risky step of choosing not to put up banners and posters—an environmentally friendly approach, but one that may have come at a cost given that the other two candidates did not follow suit. One can only speculate on what impact Mr Ng's decision had on the outcome.

The Theme of "Independence"

While George Goh did not qualify as a candidate, his attempt at candidacy played a prominent role in public discourse. Goh focused on how he had developed his businesses despite not having great educational qualifications—he did not gain a university degree until 2022, when he was sixty-two years old. Some mocked him for how he spoke—for example, how he pronounced "change". In response, he, maintaining the image he had sought to cultivate, released a series of videos called "Time For Chain"[14] in which he described himself as being from an "ordinary" family and not "the elite group", displayed his ability to speak in Chinese and Malay, and showed footage of him being coached in public speaking in English. Goh portrayed himself as a down-to-earth person who had pulled his way up in the "private sector" independently without being "endorsed by the establishment".

This last theme—independence from "the establishment"—became a locus of debate. Mr Tharman was highly qualified and experienced. He had been a ruling-party Member of Parliament and minister since 2001 and the chairman of the Monetary Authority of Singapore (Singapore's central bank) since 2011. But some wondered whether someone who was such a senior member of the political establishment could then serve as an effective check and balance against that same establishment. In response, Tharman highlighted his roots as a "student activist" and his former career as a civil servant, which he said were proof of his being "independent-minded".[15]

Mr Ng stressed that he, unlike Tharman, was independent of any political party.[16] But he was not independent of the public sector. He had sought to qualify as president based on his experience as former chief investment officer of GIC (which GIC's website calls a "fund manager for the Government of Singapore"). This position gave him the requisite experience, but it also raised questions about his independence. Such questions were unwarranted. The government "neither directs nor interferes in GIC's investment decisions", and neither does the president. Further, the president has the power to veto a proposed appointment or removal of GIC's chairman and directors.

Finally, Tan initially emphasized his independence, but he later boasted of having the support of two opposition politicians. Ng and others criticized this as an attempt at politicizing the office.[17]

The fact that the concept of "independence" came to the fore perhaps signals that the president's custodial role (as opposed to other roles) was foremost on some voters' minds. We will return to this below. Ultimately, popular discussion about "independence" created more heat than light. As Eugene Tan, a law academic and political analyst, pointed out, the ultimate question is whether someone can "faithful[ly] execut[e] … the powers of the presidency".[18] Therefore, when considering "independence", we must bear in mind what the president can and cannot do, seen against the backdrop of the president's formal institutional role as well as soft powers of persuasion. Indeed, one might argue that a president with a history of a good working relationship with the government will be better placed to advocate for position through informal means, doing through persuasion what cannot be done through an openly adversarial relationship.

The Limits to the President's Role

The question of precisely what the president can and cannot do also came to the fore. Tan Kin Lian pushed the boundaries. In a draft of a speech that was to be televised, he had proposed to say that he would "highlight [a certain] overall investment strategy ... to the professional investment managers to achieve the desired results" and "use the president's office to influence policies that will make a better life for the people of Singapore".[19] The Infocomm Media Development Authority asked him to remove those paragraphs from his script because they "had inaccuracies about the President's role".[20] Tan complied.

One might debate about the precise basis for IMDA's request. The Elections Department had stated that the president's role was initially "modelled on the Sovereign in the United Kingdom", who "must not express his personal views on matters of state" and is "not entitled to take a public position that is different from the government".[21] But one might question whether this position—which in the United Kingdom is a matter of convention, not law—has been inherited by Singapore and has survived the transition to the popularly elected presidency.

In response, it would be useful to contrast Tan's approach with Ng's. This writer has not seen Tan's proposed script in full, but acknowledges the possibility that his words, in context, could have been misleading. By contrast, when speaking to the media, Ng expressed a view on what would be the "right kind of policy" to tackle income inequality, but was quick to stress that the president could play only an indirect role in that regard: "what the president can do in regard to the cost of living is to make sure that we safeguard our reserves, so that the Singapore dollar will remain strong.... And when the Singapore dollar is strong, it helps to reduce the cost of living."[22]

Perhaps, then, the point was not that the president cannot exercise soft influence—he plainly can—but rather that this should be clearly distinguished from a legal power, or even a duty, to exercise such influence. Paradoxically, an exercise of soft power, by its nature, must not be seen to be an exercise of power at all. Further, as Mr Tharman said: "If the President and Prime Minister have respect for each other, then the President would have greater ability to be able to provide independent advice and will know that it's taken seriously."[23]

The Poll

The Elections Department (ELD) was as meticulous as ever in conducting the poll. Its job was certainly easier than during the 2020 general election, when it had to contend with public health requirements. At the same time, there were challenges in the form of new forms of voting that Parliament had provided for. It is not too far-fetched to think that the presidential election was meant to test these new schemes with a view to possibly rolling them out at the next Parliamentary election. There were two main changes.

New Modes of Voting

First, polling stations were set up at certain nursing homes that housed a "significant number of electors" who would be unable to vote at polling stations outside the home "except with great difficulty".[24] Despite possible challenges such as "managing voters who may lack the mental capacity to vote", this writer hopes that something similar will be done at future elections, not only at more nursing homes, but also at hospitals and possibly even prisons.

Second, Singaporeans living overseas could vote by post instead of travelling to one of the ten polling stations in embassies overseas. This experiment, if successful, could pave the way for more forms of postal voting in future elections. While it is not clear that the change has caused more overseas Singaporeans to vote,[25] this writer remains hopeful about the potential benefits of postal voting.

There were also smaller operational improvements. At polling booths, instead of pens, there were stamps that would mark the traditional "X". The aim, it appears, was to reduce the number of inadvertently spoiled votes.

Problems—Some Minor, Some Less So

The election was largely smooth. There were three minor hiccups, which were quickly overcome. First, some were initially unsure how to use the stamps. Second, some voters received multiple polling cards with different serial numbers; whatever trust may have been lost through this oversight was regained as these voters were ultimately not hindered from voting. Third, there were delays with the electronic registration system; these caused inconvenience, but "[t]here was no evidence that this was caused by cyberattacks."[26]

There were two more serious matters, however. The first arose from an administrative problem at the 2020 Parliamentary election, as a result of which several voters were wrongly recorded as not having voted. Their names had been automatically removed from the official register of electors, and they could not vote in 2023. While their votes could not have swung the election, it is somewhat troubling as a matter of principle. Then again, one might fault these voters for not checking the official register and raising a complaint early—which they had been entitled to do (through a process that had been publicized through the media), and which others successfully did. Nonetheless, the government sensibly announced that, in future, the ELD would contact each individual who was entitled to vote but who had been recorded as not having voted, presumably to notify them of their right to apply to be restored to the register of electors.

Second, while 2,997 voters had downloaded the forms to cast postal votes, only 1,345 were received by the deadline; the rest either arrived late or "were found torn, unsealed or opened, or had absent, faint, illegible or late postmarks". Again, this is somewhat troubling: the postal voters, if they had known that their vote would not be counted, might well have taken the trouble to vote in person at an overseas polling station. Then again, Singapore has had no prior experience with postal voting. Given the large number of Singaporeans living overseas—more than 200,000 by the most recent count—the way forward should not be to abandon the idea of postal voting, but rather to improve the process.[27]

Giving More People the Opportunity to Vote

The new systems of postal voting and voting in nursing homes should be seen in the following context. In Singapore, voting in elections is compulsory in the sense that a person who does not vote will be barred from voting in future. Such a person so barred can, however, regain the ability to vote by paying $50 or by proving that he had a good reason for not voting, such as being overseas, or being physically unable to travel to a polling station in Singapore (for example, due to illness or imprisonment). So the law accepts that not everybody will be able to vote. Nonetheless, in principle, voting is a constitutional right (and a civic duty), and any steps that would enable more people to vote are therefore to be welcomed.

The Result of the Election

Mr Tharman gained 70 per cent of the vote and was elected president. Mr Ng and Mr Tan gained 16 per cent and 14 per cent, respectively. It will be fruitful to consider what led to this outcome. But, for now, this writer will stop at making the following observation.

The 2023 presidential election cycle, unlike the next most recent one in 2017, was not reserved for any ethnic community. Mr Tharman is of Indian ethnicity—a minority in Singapore. Ideally, this fact would be unremarkable. But it took on significance for the following reason.

The authorities have not seen Singapore as having yet "arrived" as a "race-blind community". This is not without justification. In a 2011 survey, "a substantial proportion of respondents" did not positively agree that "a person of an ethnic minority group can be elected as president through the current system", and there has always been a soundbite that Singapore is "not ready for a non-Chinese prime minister". Such views justify two institutions that are designed to ensure minority representation: the reserved presidency, and the group representative constituency system. But now Mr Tharman, an ethnic minority, has succeeded in a non-reserved election. That might say something about the maturity of Singapore's electorate in making other choices—say, in general elections—for reasons other than race.[28]

The Presidency beyond Singapore

Mr Tharman has held various appointments in international organizations. For example, he has been the co-chair of the United Nations Human Development Report Advisory Board. Such roles came into the spotlight in November 2023, when Lawrence Wong, the deputy prime minister (speaking on the prime minister's behalf), stated that Tharman continued to hold these roles with the cabinet's blessing.

The government, however, thought that he ought to hold these roles in his *private* capacity, such that he would be free, in these roles, to express views that are not identical to those of the government's. So, shortly after Mr Tharman took office, the government introduced, and Parliament passed, an amendment to the Constitution. This stated that the president can "accept and hold an office in a foreign or international organisation in his private capacity", but only if cabinet agrees that it would be "in the national interest" for him to do so; and that the cabinet has the power to require the president not to say or do a particular thing in that office.

In this writer's view, it was not necessary for the constitutional amendment to be backdated, because it has always been lawful for the president to participate in any organization in his private capacity. It is not as though the constitutional amendment had retroactively rendered lawful what had been unlawful. Anyway, there is no reason to doubt Mr Wong's statement that when Mr Tharman took office, he continued in his roles in international organizations in his official capacity "with the advice and support of the Cabinet".

Whatever view one takes, the effect of the constitutional amendment has clearly been to reassert—if not tighten—the cabinet's control over what the president does, even purportedly in his private capacity. This is not unusual: there are codes of conduct that restrict the conduct of judges and ministers too. Moreover, it makes sense; even when the president purports to act in his private capacity, he cannot hide the halo of the presidency that he bears—he will inevitably be seen as an eminent representative of Singapore (which may well be the reason why he was appointed in the first place).

Mr Wong made this last point in response to questions from opposition MPs Gerald Giam, Dennis Tan and Leong Mun Wai about whether the president's ability to serve Singapore independently would be diminished. Wong's response was that, even when acting in a private capacity, the president is "contributing to his national responsibilities" and "undertaking his presidential duties" as "Singapore's top diplomat".

This last remark is interesting. The president's role has always encompassed keeping Singapore's flag flying high on the international stage. The government has now rightly affirmed this, but this is the first time that this has been said explicitly through law. Before 1991, when the president's role was similar to that of the sovereign in the United Kingdom, it was merely assumed to be the case. After 1991, the president's new custodial powers were set out in law, but the more long-standing duties were not.

Perhaps, then, what ruffled the feathers of those who opposed Mr Tharman's holding other appointments was as follows. The point of making the presidency an elected office was that only an elected office holder could effectively exercise custodial powers. The election process has, in drawing attention to these powers, taken the focus away from the president's other roles, including domestic ceremonial duties and international positions. Indeed, those roles have been somewhat amorphous because they have not been set out in law, and crystallizing a non-legal practice into a legal rule is rarely a smooth process.

Conclusion

It is useful to conclude on this last note. More than three decades have passed since the elected presidency was introduced, yet the precise nature of the institution has not been fully settled. The elected presidency was an innovation. As with all innovations, there have been successive versions, each of which sought to improve on the last. All the issues discussed above, from debates during the pre-campaigning process to the recent constitutional amendment, demonstrate this.

Given the presidency's institutional features, its evolution will have no fixed end point. The president's role, and therefore the surrounding rules and norms, is the product of an "acceptable compromise" that seeks to maximize the president's ability to discharge all of his various functions—constitutional check and balance; familiar face and national unifying figure; diplomat and representative—effectively and meaningfully, without turning the president into an "alternative or even a competing centre of power".[29]

Some have proposed alternative models, from making the presidency a "three- or four-man office" to abolishing the elected presidency and having a separate elected senate perform the custodial function.[30] None of these ideas is perfect; neither was the system as originally created in 1991 (hence, the various adjustments over the years); and neither is the present system. Ultimately, much depends on whether the leaders in power have the right skills, ideas and values to be up to the task—and what that task is is itself open to evolution. Ensuring that is an ongoing challenge.

Notes

1. Huang Jianli, "The Head of State in Singapore: An Historical Perspective", in *Managing Political Change in Singapore: The Elected Presidency*, edited by Lam Peng Er and Kevin Tan (London: Routledge, 1997), p. 13.
2. Seventh Parliament of Singapore, *Report of the Select Committee on the Constitution of the Republic of Singapore (Amendment No. 3) Bill [Bill No. 23/90]*, Parl. 9 of 1990, 18 December 1990, https://sprs.parl.gov.sg/selectcommittee/selectcommittee/download?id=301&type=report, para. 6–13 and 14(d); See also the White Papers, *Constitutional Amendments to Safeguard Financial Assets and the Integrity of the Public Services* (Cmd. 10 of 1988, 29 July 1988) and *Safeguarding Financial Assets and the Integrity of the Public Services: The Constitution of the Republic of Singapore (Amendment No 3) Bill* (Cmd. 11 of 1990, 27 August 1990) (available through the National Archives: https://www.nas.gov.sg); and the attendant debates in Parliament: *Singapore Parliamentary Debates, Official Report*, vol. 51, col. 529–638 (11 August 1988); vol. 56, col. 459–569 (4–5 October 1990); vol. 56, col. 717–53 (3 January 1991). (Records of Parliamentary debates are available through Parliament's website: https://sprs.parl.gov.sg.)
3. Kevin Tan, "The Presidency in Singapore: Constitutional Developments", in *Managing Political Change in Singapore: The Elected Presidency*, edited by Lam Peng Er and Kevin Tan (London: Routledge, 1997), pp. 70–72; See also Kevin Tan, "The Elected

Presidency in Singapore: Constitution of the Republic of Singapore (Amendment) Act 1991", *Singapore Journal of Legal Studies* (1991), p. 190.

4.   See the *Report of the Constitutional Commission 2016*, 17 August 2016, https://www.gov.sg/docs/default-source/media/gov/elected-presidency/report-of-the-constitutional-commission-2016.pdf, para. 4.6–4.17.

5.   For a summary of the eligibility criteria, see Annex 2 accompanying the speech of Deputy Prime Minister Teo Chee Hean, in *Singapore Parliamentary Debates, Official Report*, vol. 94 (7 November 2016), https://www.pmo.gov.sg/-/media/PMO/Newsroom/Files/Media-Release/022020Eligibility.ashx.

6.   Grace Yeoh, "George Goh Says Presidential Elections Committee Took 'Very Narrow Interpretation' of Requirements in Rejecting His Application", CNA, 18 August 2023, https://www.channelnewsasia.com/singapore/george-goh-presidential-election-narrow-interpretation-3707511.

7.   Elections Department, press release, 18 August 2023, https://www.eld.gov.sg/press/2023/PEC%20statement_18%20Aug%202023.pdf, para. 2; Presidential Elections (Certificate of Eligibility) Regulations 2017, r. 11(3)(c).

8.   Instagram post by @wakeupsingapore, "These Were Some of the Facebook Posts That Presidential Candidate Tan Kin Lian Published Previously…", 22 August 2023, https://www.instagram.com/p/CwNpFfXxpll (archived at https://perma.cc/5S2Y-MHBM); Reddit post by /u/Yftian, "Collection of Tan Kin Lian Shitposting", 18 August 2023, https://old.reddit.com/r/singapore/comments/15uebh3/collection_of_tan_kin_lian_shitposting/ (archived at https://perma.cc/LGB5-Z5B4); Kirsten Han, "Nope: The Presidential Election Edition", *We, The Citizens*, 22 August 2023, https://www.wethecitizens.net/presidential-election-nope/ (archived at https://perma.cc/ABK4-7BU5).

9.   Nicole Lam, "PE 2023: 'Horrid' or 'Not Wrong'? Tan Kin Lian's 'Pretty Girls' Posts Draw Sharp Reactions; Some Say PEC Can't Police Morality ", *TODAY*, 22 August 2023, https://www.todayonline.com/singapore/pe-2023-tan-kin-lian-pretty-girls-reactions-pec-2238166.

10. Tang See Kit, "Tan Kin Lian Apologises to Those Who Feel 'Uncomfortable' over His 'Pretty Girls' Social Media Posts", CNA, 22 August 2023, https://www.channelnewsasia.com/singapore/tan-kin-lian-apologises-pretty-girls-social-media-posts-3715931; Matthew Mohan, "Tan Kin Lian Apologises Again to Those Offended by Social Media Posts", CNA, 30 August 2023, https://www.channelnewsasia.com/singapore/tan-kin-lian-presidential-election-apology-pretty-girls-social-media-3734096.

11. Representations of Eugene K.B. Tan, annexed to the *Report of the Constitutional Commission 2016* (17 August 2016), vol 1, pp. 5–6; representations of AWARE (Association of Women for Action & Research), annexed to the *Report of the Constitutional Commission 2016* (17 August 2016), vol 2, p. 4.

12. TikTok post by @iriskoh11, "I'm objecting to Tharman's Candidacy for the Singapore Presidential Election", 22 August 2023, https://www.tiktok.com/@iriskoh11/video/7269980732343225601 (archived at https://perma.cc/KNJ6-AR59); Facebook post by Iris Koh, "…I was at the elections office just now to file my objection to Tharman's candidacy…", 22 August 2023, https://www.facebook.com/iriskoh/posts/pfbid02qAyS2vca3e6EjjYY5RFW2FakmvvwFStYscYjHKwW9G8fFxd6CQW68tVvUKGE9zu7l (archived at https://perma.cc/E7VX-EK9L); Facebook post by Iris Koh, "I Spoke to the Press about Why I Am Objecting [*sic*] Tharman's Candidacy…", 22 August 2023, https://www.facebook.com/iriskoh/posts/pfbid0tKFDyAXV69ZxmPLYDPiGi2gxE7efhthdBnLtq4Pw6NjGRBMJY7j6AGph916Ttc5Ll (archived at https://perma.cc/3VJD-K5J8); Iris Koh, "Stop the 'Moonlighting' Bill. Tharman to Resign First" (formerly titled "Objection to Tharman's Candidacy for the Singapore Presidential Election" and "Please Resign from WEF and Other International Affliations [*sic*] or as President of Singapore"), https://www.change.org/p/stop-the-moonlighting-bill-tharman-to-resign-first (previous versions archived at https://web.archive.org/web/20230905075238/https://www.change.org/p/objection-to-tharman-s-candidacy-for-the-singapore-presidential-election and https://web.archive.org/web/20230925032412/https://www.change.org/p/objection-to-tharman-s-candidacy-for-the-singapore-presidential-election; latest version as of 13 December 2023 archived at https://perma.cc/Q7SQ-GWMT).

13. Facebook post by Iris Koh, "Thank You Ravi", 29 August 2023, https://www.facebook.com/iriskoh/posts/pfbid02zSHbzpGdneo3kkeGW2s2Lo8n1mJFUWDvW5rAb6gXQLP65gRf4mtBkerh3TaJQt5Ll (archived at https://perma.cc/E3M9-DLN8); TikTok post by Iris Koh with ID 7273460368675048722, 31 August 2023 (now removed; copy on file with the author). The author gratefully acknowledges that the Supreme Court granted him permission to inspect the official case file relating to Mr Ravi's application to court, which is known as High Court/Originating Application No. 880 of 2023. This allowed the author to confirm what Mr Ravi's arguments were and form an opinion about them.

14. George Goh Ching Wah, "Time For Chain (change) // Episode 1: Eligibility", https://www.youtube.com/watch?v=IutcCGHORpY, especially at 1:23 and 4:19; "Time For Chain (change) // Episode 2: "Goh for Independence", https://www.youtube.com/watch?v=W0oxKITYhJE, especially at 1:38; "Time For Chain (change) // Episode 3: Family", https://www.youtube.com/watch?v=K-Uxpci3Mzw; "Time For Chain (change) // Episode 4: Goh, Going, Gone?", https://www.youtube.com/watch?v=IutcCGHORpY.

15. Tham Yuen-C, "Tharman on His Independence and How President's Role of Safeguarding Reserves Will Evolve", *Straits Times*, 15 August 2023, https://www.straitstimes.com/singapore/politics/tharman-on-his-independence-and-how-president-s-role-of-safeguarding-reserves-will-evolve.

16. Justin Ong, "PE 2023 Campaign Broadcast: Ng Kok Song Calls for Non-partisan President as 'Ownself Check Ownself' System Unreliable", *TODAY*, 24 August 2023, https://www.todayonline.com/singapore/pe2023-ng-kok-song-campaign-broadcast-non-partisan-president-2239721.

17. Renald Loh, "PE 2023: Analysts Say Opposition Backing, '3-in-1 Presidents' Claim Cast Doubt over Tan Kin Lian's Independence", *TODAY*, 28 August 2023, https://www.todayonline.com/singapore/pe-2023-tan-kin-lian-independent-doubt-analysts-2242211.

18. Louisa Tang, "Presidential Candidates Have Tried to Establish Their 'Independence' to Varying Degrees of Success: Analysts", CNA, 28 August 2023, https://www.channelnewsasia.com/singapore/presidential-election-2023-independence-analysts-ng-kok-song-tharman-tan-kin-lian-3729611.

19. Tan Kin Lian, "My Participation in PE 2023 is Caused by Fate", *#HearMeOut*, 24 August 2023, https://tklcloud.com/Feedback/feedback2.aspx?id=5846 (archived at https://perma.cc/L4MZ-FHCN).

20. Elections Department, "Media Statement: Tan Kin Lian's Presidential Candidate Broadcast (PCB) Speech", 24 August 2023, https://www.eld.gov.sg/press/2023/Media%20statement%20on%20Tan%20Kin%20Lian%E2%80%99s%20Presidential%20Candidate%20Broadcast%20(PCB)%20speech.pdf.

21. Elections Department, "Explanatory Material on the Role of the President under the Constitution of the Republic of Singapore", https://www.eld.gov.sg/Resources/Explanatory%20Material%20on%20Role%20of%20the%20President%20under%20the%20Constitution%20of%20the%20Republic%20of%20Singapore.pdf, citing Walter Bagehot, *The English Constitution*; and Vernon Bogdanor, "The Monarch and the Constitution", *Parliamentary Affairs* 49 (1996): 407–22.

22. Isabelle Liew, "Presidential Hopeful Ng Kok Song Submits Forms, Stresses Importance of Singapore's Reserves", *Straits Times*, 4 August 2023, https://www.straitstimes.com/singapore/politics/presidential-hopeful-ng-kok-song-submits-forms-stresses-importance-of-s-pore-s-reserves.

23. Nur Hikman Md Ali, "PE 2023: A President's Ability to Advise the PM Depends on Their Relationship, Says Tharman", *TODAY*, 24 August 2023, https://www.todayonline.com/singapore/pe-2023-presidents-ability-advise-pm-depends-their-relationship-says-tharman-2239126.

24. Presidential Election Act 1991, s. 30A(2).

25. There were 6,649 registered overseas voters—not many more than the 6,570 in the 2020 general election. Elections Department, "Press Release: Total Votes Cast for Presidential Election 2023", https://www.eld.gov.sg/press/2023/PR%20on%20Total%20Votes%20Cast%20for%20PE2023.pdf; "Restoration of Names to Registers of Electors", in *Singapore Parliamentary Debates, Official Report*, vol. 95 (11 May 2021) (He Ting Ru, Chan Chun Sing), written answer to oral question 25.

26. "Lessons from Incident where 10,000 Voters in Tanjong Pagar Received Two Poll Cards" and "Random Audit Checks of Registers of Electors", in *Singapore Parliamentary Debates, Official Report* vol. 95 (18 September 2023) (Joan Pereira, Ng Ling Ling, Chan Chun Sing), oral answer 61 and written answer 2.

27. Jean Iau, "2 in 5 Postal Votes for Presidential Election That Arrived on Time Disallowed for Counting: ELD", *Straits Times*, 19 September 2023, https://www.straitstimes.com/singapore/2-in-5-postal-votes-for-presidential-election-that-arrived-on-time-disallowed-for-counting-eld; National Population and Talent Division et al., "Population in Brief 2023", p. 20, https://www.population.gov.sg/files/media-centre/publications/population-in-brief-2023.pdf.

28. *Report of the Constitutional Commission 2016* (17 August 2016), para. 5.9; Nicholas Yong, "COMMENT: Heng Swee Keat's Minority PM Remark Echoes PAP's Position", *Yahoo! News*, 31 March 2019, https://sg.news.yahoo.com/comment-heng-swee-keats-minority-pm-remark-echoes-paps-position-091203481.html; Mathew Mathews, "Tharman is President-Elect. Is Singapore a Post-race Society?", *Straits Times*, 6 September 2023, https://www.straitstimes.com/opinion/tharman-is-president-elect-is-singapore-a-post-race-society.

29. *Report of the Constitutional Commission 2016* (17 August 2016), para. 2.61; Eugene K.B. Tan, "Perfecting Singapore's System of Political Governance: Privileging Elites in the Quest for Good Governance", in *Constitutional Change in Singapore: Reforming the Elected Presidency*, edited by Jaclyn L. Neo and Swati Jhaveri (London: Routledge, 2020), p. 88, at 101.

30. *Report of the Constitutional Commission 2016* (17 August 2016), para. 5.24; *Singapore Parliamentary Debates, Official Report* vol. 94 (8 November 2016, 2.31 p.m.) (Sylvia Lim).

Thailand

Chiang Rai
Chiang Mai
Udon Thani
Nakhon
Ratchasima
BANGKOK
Surat
Thani
Phuket
Songkhla
Hat Yai
Pattani
Narathiwat

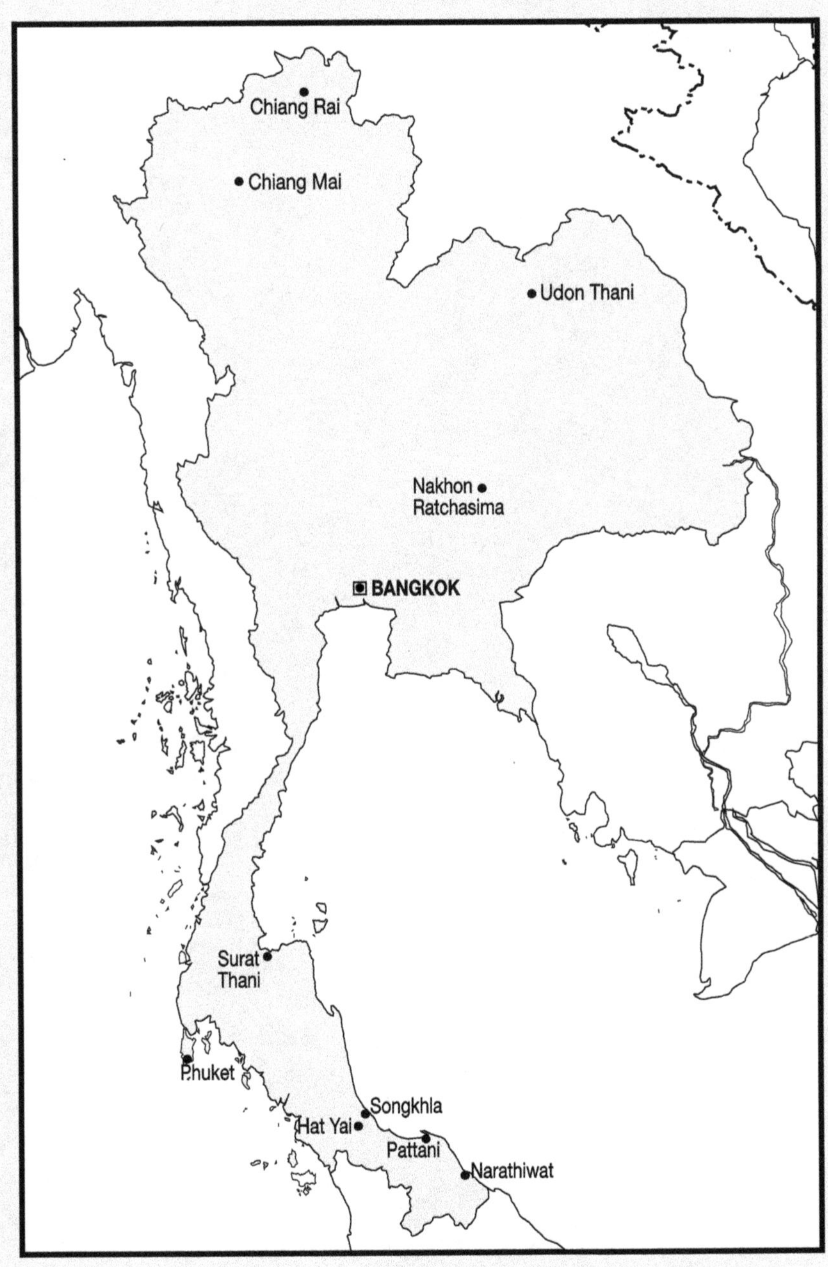

THAILAND IN 2023:
Political Realignments and the
Quest for Resilience and Stability

Napon Jatusripitak

In 2023, Thailand continued to grapple with the challenges posed by growing economic vulnerability and geopolitical uncertainty. These challenges have been amplified by a crisis of confidence in the country's political trajectory emanating from the outcomes of the 14 May general election. While the election marked a definitive end to General Prayut Chan-o-cha's military-dominated regime, it paradoxically resulted in the formation of a government that appears to diverge from the clear mandate expressed by Thai voters.

Although the Move Forward Party (MFP) emerged as the winner in the election, securing 151 seats in the 500-member House of Representatives, it was unable to form the government. The party's leader and prime ministerial candidate, Pita Limjaroenrat, was rejected twice in parliament despite having the support of an eight-party coalition that held a comfortable majority in the House. Their exclusion from power appeared to be sealed from the outset by a complex interplay between the institutional legacies of the May 2014 coup d'état—specifically, the existence of a military junta-appointed 250-member Senate with the power to jointly select the prime minister alongside the House—and a deal brokered behind the scenes between former prime minister Thaksin Shinawatra and the conservative establishment.

On 22 August, coinciding with Thaksin's return to Thailand from a fifteen-year self-imposed exile, Srettha Thavisin of the Pheu Thai Party was elected as prime minister. He was supported by eleven parties, including the military-backed United Thai Nation Party (UTN) and Palang Pracharath Party (PPRP), as well as senators aligned with Prayut. Just ten days later, Thaksin's sentences were reduced from eight years to one via a royal pardon. Although the exact

---

Napon Jatusripitak is Visiting Fellow at the ISEAS – Yusof Ishak Institute, Singapore.

relationship between Thaksin's return, his pardon and the government formation process remains elusive, the timing and significance of these events strongly hint at the emergence of an alliance between Thaksin and the conservative establishment. This alliance appears to have facilitated both Thaksin's return to Thailand and Pheu Thai's rise to power, on the understanding that the new Pheu Thai–led government would act as a safeguard for the conservative establishment, shielding it from the reformist demands of the MFP and broader pro-democracy movements. Ultimately, it required an extraordinary realignment among the Thai elite, the most significant since the coup that ousted Thaksin in 2006, to stifle the growing calls for change in Thai society.

This chapter begins with an overview of the transformation in Thailand's political landscape in the wake of the 2023 general election. In addition to examining the electoral dynamics, it explores how Pheu Thai managed to rise to power despite finishing second in the election and discusses the implications that this holds for Thailand. The chapter then broadens its focus to Thailand's economic landscape. It identifies the structural barriers impeding Thailand's efforts to foster economic development, while evaluating the new government's capacity to navigate these barriers. The third section offers an analysis of Thailand's positioning in the international arena, focusing on the country's struggle to strike a balance between two distinct yet interconnected goals: establishing itself as a hub for investment and tourism, and navigating the evolving dynamics of global power politics.

The Road to the 14 May General Election

The atmosphere in the lead-up to the 2023 general election mirrored that of 2019, with political parties aligning themselves along a pro-military to pro-democracy spectrum. Beneath the surface, however, significant changes were already in motion, fuelled by rumours of internal conflicts between the generals associated with the May 2014 coup and subsequent military-dominated governments: Prayut Chan-o-cha, Prawit Wongsuwan and Anupong Paochinda. In early January, with only two years remaining in his tenure if re-elected as prime minister, as per the Constitutional Court's verdict, General Prayut formally joined the UTN, a newly formed political party with former Democrat MP Pirapan Salirathavibhaga as its leader and former People's Democratic Reform Committee (PDRC) leader Akanat Promphan as secretary-general.[1] This move officially marked Prayut's separation from the ruling PPRP, confirming long-standing speculation about his strained relationship with PPRP leader Prawit, who had been his deputy and closest ally.

The rift between the two generals had been simmering for some time, especially following Prawit's decision to turn a blind eye to PPRP secretary general Thammanat Prompao's bid to undermine Prayut during a no-confidence debate in 2021.[2] Tensions escalated towards the end of August 2022 when Prawit assumed the interim prime minister role during Prayut's one-month suspension, openly displaying his own prime ministerial ambitions. This unfolded amidst whispers of an informal alliance forming between the PPRP (Prawit) and Pheu Thai (Thaksin), leading to a fracture within the PPRP. Factions within the party rallied behind either Prawit or Prayut as the next prime ministerial candidate, with notable figures who supported Prayut, such as Labour Minister Suchart Chomklin and Prime Minister's Office minister Anucha Nakasai, subsequently defecting from the PPRP to join the UTN.

Prayut's move to the UTN, however, did not yield the momentum required for the UTN to emerge as a major force in the election. Approaching nine years in power, Prayut no longer enjoyed the same level of popularity he had in 2019. Furthermore, he no longer held the expansive powers of Article 44 previously granted to him as the head of the National Council for Peace and Order (NCPO) before its dissolution following the 2019 elections. Meanwhile, the PPRP, without Prayut, experienced a substantial decline in popularity and a series of defections by its MPs, not only to the UTN, but also to the Bhumjaithai Party (BJT) and Pheu Thai. While Prayut and Prawit retained disproportionate influence over the formation of the next government through the NCPO-appointed 250-member Senate, which had the power to choose the prime minister alongside the 500-member House, their failure to present a united front ultimately weakened their ability to co-opt politicians. This lack of cohesion introduced an element of unpredictability and created opportunities for political manoeuvring by various actors, including Thaksin, who aimed to leverage the generals' power struggle to their advantage.

Beyond the conflict between Prayut and Prawit, the shifting political landscape, characterized by changes in formal electoral rules and significant events over the last two years, added to the uncertainty surrounding the election. Prompted by constitutional amendments in 2021 and new organic laws enacted in January 2023, the electoral system was changed from the single-ballot, mixed-member apportionment (MMA) system used in 2019 to a dual-ballot parallel voting system akin to those employed in 2001 and 2011. The modifications to the rules were expected to benefit larger parties at the expense of smaller ones, specifically those lacking a geographically concentrated electoral base. Consequently, this caused parties such as Kla, led by former finance minister Korn Chatikavanij, to merge with the Chart Pattana Party, under Suwat Liptapanlop's de facto leadership, in an attempt to mitigate the adverse effects of the election rule change. The changes were widely seen as an attempt to undermine the MFP by making constituency elections the locus of competition, stripping away some of the advantages that the MFP's predecessor, the now-dissolved Future Forward Party, enjoyed in terms of winning party-list seats.[3] The same changes, however, also made the electoral strategies of the military-backed parties in 2019—a tactic of divide and rule aimed at fragmenting larger parties like Pheu Thai and co-opting the support of small and single-seat parties to form a pro-military coalition—unlikely to succeed again.

Against this backdrop, Pheu Thai projected a landslide victory—a claim that appeared credible given its strong track record and recent triumphs in provincial administration organization (PAO) by-elections.[4] Doubling down on this promise, Thaksin's youngest daughter, Paetongtarn, was designated as the head of the Pheu Thai Family, an organizational umbrella aimed at reuniting former party leaders and the Red Shirt grassroots communities. This sent a strong and unmistakable signal about the Shinawatra family's unwavering commitment, not only to stage a political comeback, but also to position Paetongtarn, a Shinawatra scion, as Pheu Thai's prime ministerial candidate and, eventually, successor to Thaksin. During the campaign, Pheu Thai adhered to its usual pattern of making ambitious campaign promises, including a policy to distribute a one-time 10,000 baht (US$284.58) payment of digital money to every Thai citizen aged sixteen and above—a flagship policy unveiled by real estate tycoon Srettha Thavisin, who became one of Pheu Thai's prime ministerial candidates alongside Paetongtarn and Chaikasem Nitisiri.

Yet, in a surprising twist, as the elections approached, the MFP seized the momentum from Pheu Thai and shifted the campaign focus from economic agendas, which were hardly distinguishable across parties, to deeper ideological and structural issues concerning the military and monarchy. This shift in political discourse is best understood as the aftershock of the pro-democracy movements in 2020 and 2021, during which unprecedented waves of street protests began calling for reform of the monarchy, breaking a long-held taboo in Thailand. These movements brought forth a generation of politically engaged youth who were not afraid to make demands for a more democratic society. Although the movements lost much momentum because of the Covid-19 pandemic, these demands resonated with a section of the populace and were carried forward by several youth activists who shifted their focus to urging political parties to take a stand on the controversial *lèse-majesté* law, or Article 112.

Distinguishing itself from other parties—especially Pheu Thai, whose focus remained largely on economic issues—the MFP emerged as a party that inherited these lingering aspirations for structural reform. While it was not the only party to take a stance on the *lèse-majesté* law, it stood out as the only party with a credible commitment to amend the law—a stance bolstered by the MFP's prior involvement in translating the demands of the pro-democracy movement into a legislative agenda, bailing out detained activists, and recruiting some of these activists into its ranks as candidates for the general election. Building on this reformist stance, the MFP pledged not to form alliances with parties affiliated with Prayut and Prawit, adopting the slogan "where there are uncles, there is no us" (มีเราไม่มีลุง มีลุงไม่มีเรา).[5]

By contrast, Pheu Thai struggled to convey a clear rejection of the conservative status quo from the outset. The party initially kept its stance strategically ambiguous, allowing for the possibility of forming a government with parties outside the pro-democracy camp. In the final stretch of the election campaign, fuelled by social media enthusiasm and a dedicated political following that actively engaged with the party both online and offline, the MFP and its leader, Pita, saw a surge in the polls.[6] Not only did they eclipse Pheu Thai and Paetongtarn in terms of popularity, but they also successfully overturned the narrative of the election, moving it away from the age-old power struggle between the Shinawatra family and the military towards a more comprehensive referendum on change and structural reform. The stage was set for an exceptionally unpredictable electoral landscape, one in which the emergence of new political dynamics had the potential to disrupt longstanding patterns and established stakeholders in the Thai political system.

Political Disruption

The day after the election, which saw a turnout of approximately 75.71 per cent of the 52 million eligible voters nationwide, the Election Commission announced that both the MFP and Pheu Thai secured 112 constituency seats.[7] But the MFP, with the backing of more than 14 million in the popular vote—a lead of about 3 million over Pheu Thai—earned an additional 39 party list seats, surpassing Pheu Thai's 29, thereby establishing itself as the decisive winner of the election. With a tally of 151 and 141 seats, respectively, the MFP and Pheu Thai significantly outperformed parties affiliated with the military regime, like the PPRP, which claimed 40 seats, and the UTN, which garnered 36 seats. Meanwhile, the BJT emerged as the third-largest party, securing 71 seats across the Northeast and South regions, while the Democrat Party, once a significant force in Thai politics, only won 25 seats. This outcome, as shown in Table 1, represents first and foremost a strong rejection of military influence in politics. The most remarkable aspect of the results, however, was not merely the overwhelming support for change away from the post-2014 status quo, but how this support translated into the MFP's unexpected victory over Pheu Thai, a party that had dominated every election since 2001.

The MFP's stunning achievement was underpinned by a succession of smaller victories that defied traditional boundaries and broke from established patterns in Thai electoral politics. Demonstrating robust support for the MFP among urban voters, the party won all but one seat in Bangkok. Surprisingly, this wave of success extended beyond Bangkok, reaching into many provinces in Central Thailand, historically the domain of entrenched political dynasties. In the North, the MFP made significant inroads, winning seven out of ten seats in Chiang Mai, a province widely regarded as a Shinawatra stronghold. These disruptions can be understood through two key transformations taking place at the national and subnational level. First, long-standing regional and political divisions rooted in

TABLE 1
Thailand 14 May General Elections Results

Party	Constituency Seats	Party List Seats	Total Seats (% share)	Constituency Votes (% share)	Party List Votes (% share)
Move Forward	112	39	151 (30.2)	9,665,439 (25.99)	14,438,830 (38.49)
Pheu Thai	112	29	141 (28.2)	9,340,089 (25.12)	10,962,526 (29.22)
Bhumjaithai	68	3	71 (14.2)	5,133,455 (13.8)	1,138,204 (3.03)
Palang Pracharath	39	1	40 (8)	4,186,443 (11.26)	537,632 (1.43)
United Thai Nation	23	13	36 (7.2)	3,607,580 (9.7)	4,766,390 (12.7)
Democrat	22	3	25 (5)	2,278,856 (6.13)	925,349 (2.47)
Chart Thai Pattana	9	1	10 (2)	585,205 (1.57)	192,498 (0.51)
Prachachart	7	2	9 (1.8)	334,051 (0.9)	602,645 (1.61)
Thai Sang Thai	5	1	6 (1.2)	872,893 (2.35)	340,179 (0.91)
Pheu Thai Ruam Palang	2	0	2 (0.4)	94,345 (0.25)	67,691 (0.18)
Chart Pattana Kla	1	1	2 (0.4)	297,946 (0.8)	212,676 (0.57)
Teachers for People	0	1	1 (0.2)	4,464 (0.01)	175,184 (0.47)
Thai Counties	0	1	1 (0.2)	1,202 (0)	201,410 (0.54)
New Democracy	0	1	1 (0.2)	13,583 (0.04)	273,413 (0.73)
Fair Party	0	1	1 (0.2)	9,653 (0.03)	184,819 (0.49)
Social Power	0	1	1 (0.2)	20,353 (0.05)	177,378 (0.47)
Thai Liberal	0	1	1 (0.2)	277,006 (0.74)	351,376 (0.94)
New Party	0	1	1 (0.2)	1,365 (0)	249,732 (0.67)

economic concerns and polarized opinions about Thaksin Shinawatra—issues that have become salient since 2006—have been supplanted by growing generational and ideological divides focused on issues related to the monarchy and the military. Second, traditional local power structures, characterized by money politics, patronage networks and political dynasties, have been disrupted by new modes of political engagement, party building and campaign strategies facilitated by the rise of social media and social movements.

The MFP's performance in the party list elections tells a story that is equally remarkable. Across all 400 constituencies, the MFP consistently ranked either first or second in terms of the party list vote. It claimed the top spot in 223 constituencies, including some within the traditionally conservative Southern region, as well as those won by candidates belonging to parties from the opposite ideological spectrum, including the UTN, PPRP and BJT, indicating a pattern of ballot splitting in favour of the MFP. Collectively, these results underscore the widespread appeal of the MFP. It soon became apparent, however, that a strong electoral mandate alone was not enough to ensure a straightforward path to power.

New Realignment, Old Politics

Following the election, the MFP swiftly declared the formation of an eight-party coalition with Pheu Thai, consisting of 312 MPs. But the junta-appointed Senate loomed as a significant obstacle to the coalition's chances of success. This was due to the transitory provisions of the 2017 constitution that mandated the prime minister be chosen jointly by the 500-member House and the 250-member Senate for the first five years after establishing the first National Assembly under this constitution. Despite having a strong majority in the House, the MFP-led coalition was still 64 votes short of the 376 needed for a simple majority in the combined 750-member parliament. In the weeks leading up to the selection of the prime minister, many senators attempted to justify their reservations about supporting Pita, the MFP's candidate, by citing unresolved cases related to his alleged illegal ownership of shares in a media company and concerns over his party's proposed amendments to the controversial *lèse-majesté* law, which were perceived as potential breaches of campaign laws.

On 12 July, just one day before the joint parliamentary session to select a new prime minister, the Election Commission referred the media shareholding case to the Constitutional Court, seeking an order to halt Pita from carrying out his duties as an MP and to rule on his eligibility as an MP. On 13 July, the vote on Pita's prime ministerial candidacy resulted in 324 votes in favour (only 13 of which were from senators), 182 votes against and 199 abstentions, effectively blocking Pita from becoming prime minister. The second voting took place one week later, on 19 July, but by then Pita's fate was already sealed. Citing Rule No. 41 of parliamentary rules and procedures, Pita's opponents argued that his nomination in the first round of voting constituted a failed motion and, therefore, could not be resubmitted for consideration within the same parliamentary session. The voting on this motion took place—mere hours after Pita was suspended as an MP by the Constitutional Court and forced to leave parliament—with 395 members voting in favour of barring Pita from being re-nominated. This second rejection prompted a reshuffling of alliances, which had likely been anticipated, and even counted on, by Pheu Thai, the second runner-up that was poised to gain from Pita's failed bid despite its claim to wholeheartedly support the MFP-led coalition.

The next round of selection was then postponed in response to the Constitutional Court's anticipated ruling on the case concerning the constitutional validity of the parliamentary vote that blocked Pita's re-nomination. This plunged Thailand into an extended period of uncertainty, with no new government in sight.[8] However, by early August, Pheu Thai had already made clear its intention to establish a government without the MFP and proposed Srettha Thavisin as the prime ministerial candidate. It promptly sought support from various parties, beginning with the BJT and Chartthaipattana, both of which signalled their readiness to join the Pheu Thai–led coalition under the condition that the MFP be excluded from the coalition and that there would be no amendments to Article 112. In a move widely seen as an attempt to marginalize the MFP and a departure from its pledge to uphold a pro-democracy alliance, Pheu Thai then broadened its outreach to include military-aligned parties like the UTN and the PPRP. These coalition-building efforts were made into public spectacles, with party leaders photographed toasting with cups of choc-mint[9] and holding back-to-back joint press conferences that, almost in unison, advocated for the exclusion of the MFP and a commitment to leave Article 112 untouched. Altogether, the new crossover alliance led by Pheu Thai produced a coalition consisting of thirteen parties and 314 MPs, excluding the MFP.

Despite having only one more MP than the MFP-led coalition, the Pheu Thai-led coalition was perceived as having a much stronger chance of success. This perception stemmed partly from Pheu Thai's strategic inclusion of parties affiliated with Prayut and Prawit in the coalition, which granted access to individuals capable of influencing the Senate to secure the necessary votes for Srettha. A critical moment unfolded on the morning of the third round of prime minister selection on 22 August when Thaksin Shinawatra landed at Bangkok's Don Mueang

Airport. This indicated a possible deal facilitating Thaksin's return, presumably in exchange for Pheu Thai's role in upholding the conservative establishment's interests once in government. Although the specifics of this deal remain unclear, its implications became evident when Srettha garnered an overwhelming majority in parliament, receiving 482 votes, including 152 from senators allied with Prayut. This development defied initial predictions that Prawit would emerge as the kingmaker for a Pheu Thai prime minister or even take up the prime minister's role himself with Pheu Thai's backing.

Srettha and his cabinet, representing a power-sharing agreement among various stakeholders both within and outside the coalition government, were sworn into office on 5 September, almost four months following the election. Reflecting its priorities, Pheu Thai controls most economic ministries, with Srettha also chairing the finance portfolio. Setting a historical precedent, Pheu Thai's Sutin Klungsang became the first civilian to hold the position of minister of defence without being a prime minister. Yet, the cabinet composition also highlights the substantial influence held by Pheu Thai's coalition partners, who collectively outnumber Pheu Thai in terms of the number of MPs and represent conservative and oligarchic interests that Pheu Thai cannot afford to alienate.[10] Similarly precarious, Srettha holds no formal position in Pheu Thai's hierarchy, played no role in choosing Pheu Thai MP candidates, and possesses limited influence over neither the composition nor functioning of his own cabinet.[11]

Having come to power by betraying their pledge to voters, both Srettha and Pheu Thai now face immense pressure to deliver on economic and policy fronts, especially the party's flagship 10,000 baht digital wallet scheme, which has encountered strong resistance from the opposition, technocrats and intellectuals.[12] The Srettha administration has so far prioritized meeting the short-term objectives outlined in a policy statement unveiled by Srettha upon taking office. These include economic relief and stimulus measures, such as implementing an agricultural debt moratorium and reducing energy costs.[13] This government's emphasis on immediate economic priorities has raised some concerns because of its perceived lack of a clear long-term developmental vision, particularly in areas like education. Furthermore, the government's commitment to political reforms remains in doubt because of its alliance with parties or actors representing the conservative establishment.

In the long run, the stability of this government will depend not only on its policy performance but also on its (or Thaksin's) ability to maintain a delicate alliance with the conservative establishment that, historically, has determined the longevity and boundaries of Thai democracy. On the one hand, there is a strong likelihood that the alliance will persist as long as the perceived threat to the royal institution from the MFP and the broader pro-democracy movements remains imminent, and as long as Pheu Thai can remain useful as a key player in maintaining the democratic façade. On the other hand, the viability of the alliance remains uncertain as it rests on a fragile equilibrium of mutual interests and common enemies among elites who have been at odds for the past two decades. A crucial test of this alliance will come after May 2024 with the end of the current Senate's term, which will remove the Senate from its role in the prime ministerial selection process, potentially leading to yet another reconfiguration of alliances.

The Thai Economy: Short-Term Recovery, Long-Term Uncertainty

In 2023, the Thai economy continued on its trajectory of recovery from the shocks of the Covid-19 pandemic, with tourism and private consumption serving as the primary engines of economic rejuvenation. The new government's policy to exempt visa fees for tourists from designated countries and extend a temporary visa waiver has played a part in reinvigorating the tourism sector, aiming for an influx of more than 25–30 million international tourists for the year.[14] Tracking closely, private consumption shows an upward trajectory, with 8.1 per cent in the third quarter, an improvement from the 7.8 per cent and 5.8 per cent growth in the previous two quarters, signifying a resurgence in domestic demand.[15]

The favourable momentum in tourism and private consumption has not been enough, however, to maintain a steady upward trajectory in Thailand's economic recovery. Thailand's deep integration with the world economy continues to render it susceptible to external shocks and global market volatilities. Ongoing geopolitical tensions, especially the Russia-Ukraine conflict, have led to increased energy prices and supply chain disruptions that, in turn, resulted in higher costs of living and production costs. Furthermore, the slower-than-anticipated economic rebound among major trading partners, especially China, has resulted in a softened demand for Thai manufacturing exports.[16]

The global financial market, characterized by rising interest rates and inflationary pressures, added another layer of complexity to Thailand's economic recovery trajectory. Specifically, the decision by the US Fed to hike interest rates to curb inflation has stirred global financial market fluctuations, leading to capital outflows from Thailand, thereby affecting its currency value, bond yields and stock market performance. The depreciation of the Thai baht,[17] in the context of subdued demand for Thai exports, has meant that the anticipated boost in export competitiveness from the weakened Thai baht has not been fully realized. In September, the Monetary Policy Committee of the Bank of Thailand nudged the policy rate up by 0.25 percentage points to 2.50 per cent. But given the need to fund economic stimulus measures through government debt, this rate hike may pose an obstacle for the government in terms of driving economic growth through its proposed policies.

As Thailand grapples with the ramifications of global economic fluctuations, it also faces pressing internal challenges. Specifically, the country has been dealing with the compounding issue of soaring household debt, which reached 90.7 per cent in the second quarter of 2023,[18] and high public debt, amounting to 62.1 per cent of GDP in the third quarter.[19] These high levels of debt could restrict domestic consumption and government expenditure in the long term, impeding economic growth and constraining the government's capacity to invest in needed sectors and weather future crises.

Collectively, these challenges highlight the necessity for a multifaceted approach to navigate the complex interplay between global economic volatility and Thailand's inherent economic vulnerabilities. However, the effectiveness of the new government's array of economic policies in successfully guiding Thailand out of its current predicaments remains uncertain. In fact, many of these short-term initiatives—including the digital wallet scheme, the agricultural debt moratorium and the energy subsidies—have raised concerns about Thailand's long-term fiscal health, mainly because of the substantial financial commitments they entail. This includes direct funding of the programmes, assuming the burden of interest payments, and handling the repayment or restructuring of debt terms with state-owned institutions that play a role in subsidizing or financing these initiatives. These debt-financed recovery measures, compounded by the absence of a clear strategy for sustaining growth without compromising fiscal discipline, have triggered warning signals about the risk of a credit downgrade for Thailand.[20]

As 2023 drew to a close, two contrasting narratives emerged, propelled by the government and its opposition, regarding Thailand's economy: the former views the economy as undergoing a crisis, urgently requiring stimulation, while the latter acknowledges the economy as dysfunctional, yet not in a critical state, calling for economic restructuring. The National Economic and Social Development Council reported that Thailand's GDP growth decreased to 1.5 per cent in the third quarter of 2023, well below market expectations. Earlier, in September, the Bank of Thailand had already reduced its GDP forecast for the year from 3.6 per cent to 2.8 per cent, attributing the slowdown to soft external demand and a delayed recovery in exports and tourism.[21] In a similar vein, the World Bank has revised its forecast for Thailand's economic growth in 2023 from 3.6 per cent to 3.4 per cent.[22] These indicators, while not decisively supporting either narrative, point to a continuing phase of subdued growth for Thailand compared to its neighbours. Yet, Thailand must also contend with the future challenges of an ageing society, including a diminishing workforce, increasing healthcare costs and rising inequality, all against a backdrop of technological disruptions.

Ultimately, the prevailing economic circumstances in Thailand call for a thorough re-evaluation of its developmental framework. It is imperative for the country to strike a balance between short-term initiatives and long-term strategies aimed at bolstering economic resilience. Enhancing the competitiveness of existing sectors through innovation and technology, as well as diversifying into industries with more resilient supply chains, will be key to fortifying the economy against external shocks. Furthermore, accelerating the transition to renewable energy and reducing reliance on oil are vital steps to mitigate risks from global energy market fluctuations and geopolitical uncertainties.

Significant progress has been made in this direction, particularly in Thailand's efforts to establish itself as a manufacturing hub for electric vehicles (EV). The National Electric Vehicle Policy Committee, led by Srettha, has approved a new EV incentive package, named EV3.5, reaffirming the country's commitment to becoming a major player in the EV sector. This initiative, approved in November, aims to sustain and further enhance Thailand's recent success in drawing investments, which now constitute a significant share of foreign direct investment in the automotive sector, from major Chinese electric vehicle manufacturers such as BYD Co., Great Wall Motor Co., SAIC Motor Corp, and Chongqing Changan. But despite these advances in the EV sector, there remains a palpable risk of Thailand being trapped in a prolonged period of economic stagnation and vulnerability. This is partly due to a political climate that has not spurred the necessary political will to enact comprehensive economic reforms and foreign policies that appear inadequate to meet the challenges of the changing global landscape.

Foreign Policy Continuation or Recalibration?

Since the 2014 coup, Thailand has increasingly gravitated towards China in both economic and security spheres, leading to a cooling of relations with its Western allies. This shift has disrupted the delicate balancing act that Thailand traditionally strived to maintain. The recent transition from a military-dominated government to a civilian-led one, a change that occurred after almost a decade, was expected to reinvigorate efforts to restore the geopolitical equilibrium, particularly through ASEAN as a forum. But Thailand's commitment to do so remains uncertain as the prevailing emphasis on economic security, with China as a strategic partner, has come to overshadow, or even substitute for, broader security policies aimed at managing the competing influences of major powers such as China and the United States.

Upon his election as prime minister in late August, Srettha met Chinese ambassador to Thailand Han Zhiqiang ahead of envoys from other countries, including those representing ASEAN member states, aiming to secure visa-free entry for Chinese visitors to rejuvenate Thailand's tourism sector. In October, accompanied by private sector delegates, Srettha undertook a four-day visit to attend the 3rd Belt and Road Forum for International Cooperation (BRF) in Beijing. He met with China's president Xi Jinping, Prime Minister Li Qiang, Standing Committee chairman of the National People's Congress Zhao Leji and other Chinese business leaders to enhance trade and investment collaboration between Thailand and China, focusing on target industries such as electric vehicles, batteries, semiconductors and clean energy, aligning with Thailand's bio-circular and green economic development model (BCG). Among the discussed initiatives to attract Chinese investments, Srettha voiced his intention to continue a Land Bridge megaproject initiated by the Prayut administration entailing the construction of deep-sea ports in Chumphon and Ranong provinces, linked by a ninety-kilometre rail and road network, to provide an alternative trade and transportation route to the Strait of Malacca.

Clearly, the Srettha administration has placed a high priority on attracting Chinese tourists and investments as a central aspect of its foreign policy. This economic focus is not limited to China alone. Srettha made a similar pitch to American business leaders regarding the Land Bridge megaproject at the APEC Summit in November. Moreover, after the event, he claimed credit for securing investments from major US tech firms such as Google, Amazon and Facebook. Beyond China and the United States, Srettha spent twenty days of his first sixty days in office visiting six other countries and Hong Kong, with the aim of strengthening bilateral ties, expanding Thailand's free trade agreements and securing foreign investment. These activities earned Srettha the nickname of a "salesman prime minister", a title that resonates with his message to the world: Thailand is "open for business".[23]

However, in a global environment where market access, technology transfers and supply chains are increasingly subject to geopolitical considerations, Thailand's aggressive pursuit of foreign investment without adequately factoring in these realities may be short-sighted. As diversification and hedging strategies become harder to maintain because of the pressure to choose sides, this business-centric approach runs the risk of fostering structural dependencies that could weaken

Thailand's bargaining power and autonomy, as well as impede its ability to address broader concerns such as environmental sustainability, human rights and regional security.

The Thai government's handling of the controversial submarine procurement deal with China serves as a case in point. The deal, which involved purchasing a Chinese-built Yuan Class S26T submarine equipped with German engines, came to a standstill when Germany, complying with the European Union's arms embargo, stopped exporting its engines to China. Thailand neither withdrew from the deal nor made any attempt to hold China accountable for failing to fulfil its end of the agreement. Instead, citing that amending the deal would be better for fostering Thailand-China relations than revoking it, Thailand's defence minister, Sutin Klungsang, announced in October that the government has accepted a proposal by the Royal Thai Navy to procure a frigate as a substitute.[24] This change is expected to increase the cost by a billion baht (US$28,450,720), as well as render any investments in parts and facilities for the intended submarine redundant. This situation not only highlights issues of transparency and accountability, as the specifics of the deal and the proposed modifications remain undisclosed as part of a government-to-government agreement. It also brings into focus critical questions about Thailand's autonomy in shaping its defence strategies and national security policies, especially when these decisions may be heavily influenced or compromised by the necessity to maintain favourable economic ties with China.

From this standpoint, despite adopting a more outward-looking and business-oriented approach to international relations, Thailand continues to struggle in crafting a foreign policy that adeptly manoeuvres through a world where economic blocs are increasingly fragmented by more rigidly defined geopolitical alliances. Nonetheless, the recent change in government appears to have produced more noticeable changes in other domains. Previously, under Prayut, Thailand's engagement within the ASEAN framework had been compromised by a series of heavy-handed diplomatic efforts to advocate for ASEAN to re-engage the Myanmar junta, whose leaders maintain close ties with Prayut and other high-ranking generals in Thailand. Most notably, a 14 June letter from Foreign Minister Don Pramudwinai to his ASEAN counterparts unveiled a proposal by Thailand to fully re-engage Myanmar and to convene an informal meeting aimed at finding a resolution to the crisis there.[25] This meeting, which Indonesia, Malaysia and Singapore declined to attend, drew widespread criticism because of its inclusion of the Myanmar military's foreign minister, Than Swe. This action not only goes against the earlier agreement by ASEAN leaders to bar the junta from its meetings because of its failure to adhere to the Five Point Consensus, but also undermines the efforts of ASEAN chair Indonesia to facilitate inclusive discussions with all parties involved in Myanmar. This blatant disregard for ASEAN's unified stance on Myanmar was further affirmed in July when Don claimed during the ASEAN foreign ministers meeting that he had met with Myanmar's ousted leader Aung San Suu Kyi, a meeting allegedly facilitated by the State Administration Council (SAC).[26]

The newly appointed foreign minister serving under Srettha's cabinet, Parnpree Bahiddha-Nukara, has reaffirmed Thailand's commitment to the ASEAN Five-Point Consensus and pledged to coordinate with ASEAN counterparts regarding any informal engagement with Myanmar. Whether this stance represents a rhetorical shift or a substantive strategic realignment, it will have important implications not only in terms of reshaping Thailand's role in ASEAN, but also in addressing pertinent issues for Thai policymakers such as refugee problems, illegal call centre operations along the Thai-Myanmar border, and the looming threat of further US sanctions on Myanmar Oil and Gas Enterprise (MOGE), which will affect gas exports from Myanmar to Thailand.

In October, the Israel-Hamas conflict presented another significant foreign policy challenge for Thailand because of the presence of around thirty thousand Thai workers in Israel, many stationed in agricultural areas near Gaza. The efforts of the Thai government focused on evacuating Thai workers and securing the release of Thais held hostage by Hamas. These tasks became even more complicated following Srettha's diplomatic misstep in the wake of the attack. In a move that could be seen as prematurely siding with Israel, Srettha posted on X (formerly Twitter) condemning the attack and expressing condolences to Israel without mentioning Palestine or distinguishing it from Hamas. Although this incident did not escalate, thanks in part to the Ministry of Foreign Affairs swiftly backpedalling on Srettha's statement in an effort to maintain neutrality, it exposed the government's lack of preparedness and expertise in effectively responding to international conflicts and navigating sensitive global issues. Such gaps in Thailand's ability to manage other aspects of international relations beyond fostering economic ties and attracting foreign investments underscore the need for a more comprehensive foreign policy strategy that can address a broader range of diplomatic, security and economic challenges on the global stage.

Conclusion

The year 2023 ushered in the most significant transformation in Thailand's domestic political landscape witnessed in the past two decades. A rather peculiar equilibrium has emerged between Thaksin and the Pheu Thai Party on one side and the conservative establishment on the other, effectively forcing the closure of an era of colour-coded political conflict between pro- and anti-Thaksin forces. Yet it also inaugurates a new chapter in Thailand's political narrative as underlying ideological differences surrounding the role of the monarchy and the military have become central to political divisions. This critical turning point arrived during a phase of economic vulnerability, with traditional economic engines proving no longer capable of delivering sustainable growth in the face of ongoing geopolitical and technological disruptions that are largely outside Thailand's control. The reconfiguration of Thailand's foreign relations, now merely a by-product of the domestic political and economic landscape, holds the potential to play a pivotal role in guiding the country towards lasting political stability and economic resilience.`

Notes

1. Chairith Yonpiam, "Prayut Signs Up with United Thai Nation Party", *Bangkok Post*, 9 January 2023, https://www.bangkokpost.com/thailand/politics/2478609/prayut-signs-up-with-united-thai-nation-party.
2. Termsak Chalermpalanupap, "Thai PM Remains Vulnerable without a Party of His Own", *Fulcrum*, 11 October 2021, https://fulcrum.sg/thai-pm-remains-vulnerable-without-a-party-of-his-own.
3. "ธนาธร ชี้สูตรหาร 100 พรรคก้าวไกลเสียเปรียบ" [Thanathorn points out new election rule puts the Move Forward Party at a disadvantage], Thai PBS News, 30 November 2022, https://www.thaipbs.or.th/news/content/322095.
4. "Pheu Thai Win at Roi Et Polls Fuels Party's Landslide Hopes", *Bangkok Post*, 26 September 2022, https://www.bangkokpost.com/thailand/politics/2400638/pheu-thai-win-at-roi-et-polls-fuels-partys-landslide-hopes.
5. Hataikarn Treesuwan, "วิเคราะห์ : 'มีลุงไม่มีเรา' ขวาง 'แลนด์สไลด์' เพื่อไทย หยุด 'ก้าวข้ามความขัดแย้ง' ของ พปชร." [Analysis: "Where there are uncles, there is no us" blocks "landslide" for Pheu Thai, stops "reconciliation" of PPRP], BBC Thai, 7 May 2023, https://www.bbc.com/thai/articles/cmj7kgxy70do.
6. "Thailand's Pita Tops PM Poll as Opposition Leads Opinion Surveys", Reuters, 5 May 2023, https://www.reuters.com/world/asia-pacific/thailands-pita-tops-pm-poll-opposition-leads-opinion-surveys-2023-05-05/.
7. "ผลการเลือกตั้ง2566 : กกต.แถลงผลไม่เป็นทางการ ก้าวไกลอันดับ 1" [Election results 2566: The Election Commission announces unofficial results, Forward Party ranks first], Thai PBS, 15 May 2023, https://www.thaipbs.or.th/news/content/327802.
8. During this period of uncertainty, Vacharaesorn Vivacharawongse, the estranged son of King Maha Vajiralongkorn, also made a short trip to Thailand, presumably for reasons unrelated to the formation of the government. Nevertheless, his presence

sparked significant speculation about the potential for changes within the royal institution and line of succession.

9.   Rebecca Ratcliffe, "Final Straw: Choc Mint Drink Becomes Symbol of Political Betrayal in Thailand", *The Guardian*, 25 July 2023, https://www.theguardian.com/world/2023/jul/25/final-straw-choc-mint-drink-becomes-symbol-of-political-betrayal-in-thailand.

10. For example, BJT leader Anutin Charnvirakul controls the interior ministry, a pivotal position for influencing the allocation of government resources and personnel. PPRP secretary-general Thammanat Prompao controls the agriculture ministry, traditionally seen as vital for cultivating political support. Finally, the UTN's Pirapan Salirathavibhaga presides over the energy ministry, signifying the enduring influence of the same oligarchic interests that had propped up the Prayut administration.

11. Srettha's seeming lack of de facto power as prime minister was the subject of much speculation in October following the screening of the movie *Sap Pa Rer* (The undertaker), attended by cabinet ministers and Paetongtarn. When a reporter referred to Srettha as "Prime Minister", he jokingly replied, "Which prime minister? I hear we have two." Srettha's standing was called into further question after a Pheu Thai Party meeting two days later, when Srettha congratulated Paetongtarn on becoming the party's leader with a hand kiss and a bow. These gestures inadvertently highlighted the ambiguity surrounding the real locus of power in the government. See Tulsathit Taptim, "Paetongtarn's Rise Gives Birth to Some Strange Theories", Thai PBS World, 3 November 2023, https://www.thaipbsworld.com/paetongtarns-rise-gives-birth-to-some-strange-theories/.

12. At the time of writing, the 10,000 baht digital wallet scheme has been scaled down and may encounter further obstacles as a result of legal reviews, the need for parliamentary approval, and the possibility of being vetoed by the constitutional court.

13. "Policy Statement of the Council of Ministers Delivered by Prime Minister Srettha Thavisin to the National Assembly, Monday, 11 September B.E. 2566 (2023)", Secretariat of the Cabinet, 31 October 2023, https://www.soc.go.th/wp-content/uploads/2023/09/Policy_66.pdf.

14. "TAT Confident of 4 Million Chinese Arrivals by End of Year", Thai PBS World, 11 October 2023, https://www.thaipbsworld.com/tat-confident-of-4-million-chinese-arrivals-by-end-of-year/.

15. National Economic and Social Development Council, "Thai Economic Performance in Q3 and Outlook for 2023", Macroeconomic Strategy and Planning Division press release, 20 November 2023, https://www.nesdc.go.th/ewt_dl_link.php?nid=14551&filename=QGDP_report.

16. Bank of Thailand, "Monetary Policy Report Q2/2023", 14 July 2023, https://www.bot.or.th/content/dam/bot/documents/en/our-roles/monetary-policy/mpc-publication/monetary-policy-report/MPR_2023_Q2.pdf.

17. Somruedi Banchongduang and Nareerat Wiriyapong, "Baht Dips Further to 37 per Dollar", *Bangkok Post*, 4 October 2023, https://www.bangkokpost.com/business/general/2656993/baht-dips-further-to-37-per-dollar.

18. Bank of Thailand, "Monetary Policy Report Q3/2023", 8 November 2023, https://www.bot.or.th/content/dam/bot/documents/en/our-roles/monetary-policy/mpc-publication/monetary-policy-report/MPR_2023_Q3.pdf.

19. National Economic and Social Development Council, "Thai Economic Performance in Q3 and Outlook for 2023", Macroeconomic Strategy and Planning Division press release, 20 November 2023, https://www.nesdc.go.th/ewt_dl_link.php?nid=14551&filename=QGDP_report.

20. Suttinee Yuvejwattana, "S&P, Fitch Say Thailand Must Sustain Growth to Avoid Ratings Cut", Bloomberg, 5 October 2023, https://www.bloomberg.com/news/articles/2023-10-05/s-p-fitch-say-thailand-must-sustain-growth-to-avoid-ratings-cut.

21 Apornrath Phoonphongphiphat, "Thailand Central Bank Surprises by Raising Key Rate to 2.5", *Nikkei Asia*, 27 September 2023, https://asia.nikkei.com/Economy/Thailand-central-bank-surprises-by-raising-key-rate-to-2.5.

22. Somruedi Banchongduang, "World Bank Cuts Thai Growth to 3.4%", *Bangkok Post*, 3 October 2023, https://www.bangkokpost.com/business/general/2656390/world-bank-cuts-thai-growth-to-3-4-.

23. Patpicha Tanakasempipat, "Thailand's 'Salesman' Prime Minister Travels the World to Court Investments", Bloomberg, 9 November 9 2023, https://www.bloomberg.com/news/articles/2023-11-08/thailand-s-salesman-pm-travels-the-world-to-court-investments

24. Wassana Nanuam, "Sutin Eyes Cheaper Chinese Ship", *Bangkok Post*, 25 October 2023, https://www.bangkokpost.com/thailand/general/2670674/sutin-eyes-cheaper-chinese-ship.

25. Panu Wongcha-um, Poppy Mcpherson, and Ananda Teresia, "Thailand Seeking to Re-engage Myanmar Junta with ASEAN Meeting: Letter, Sources", Reuters, 17 June 2023, https://www.reuters.com/world/asia-pacific/thailand-seeking-re-engage-myanmar-junta-with-asean-meeting-letter-sources-2023-06-16/.

26. Nana Shibata and Erwida Maulia, "Thai Foreign Minister Says He Met with Myanmar's Suu Kyi", *Nikkei Asia*, 12 July 2023, https://asia.nikkei.com/Spotlight/Myanmar-Crisis/Thai-foreign-minister-says-he-met-with-Myanmar-s-Suu-Kyi.

Beyond the Comprehensive Strategic Partnership: Taking Stock of Thailand-Japan Relations

David M. Malitz

On 17 November 2022, visiting Japanese prime minister Fumio Kishida and Thai prime minister Prayuth Chan-o-cha agreed to elevate bilateral relations to a Comprehensive Strategic Partnership to reflect the deepening as well as broadening of bilateral ties over the last decade. While Japan and Thailand also signed a first bilateral defence agreement in May 2022, the partnership remains, first of all, an economic one, as the Joint Statement of both prime ministers made clear. Prime Minister Kishida had already stressed the economic importance of the relationship in an article published in a Thai newspaper during his inaugural visit to Thailand in May 2022.[1] In it, he pointed out that six thousand Japanese companies had invested in the country, which eighty thousand Japanese are calling home, and also mentioned the substantial Japanese investments in infrastructure. This view is shared by the Thai public according to a survey by the Japanese Ministry of Foreign Affairs from 2021. Thais perceive Japan as an economic power and technological leader but also a country with beautiful nature and appealing traditional and popular culture.[2]

This mutually beneficial economic partnership is faced with challenges, as acknowledged in the Joint Statement, because of demographic and technological change, and the pressure to make both economies and the supply chains connecting them more sustainable. Clearly, China's influence has also increased in Thailand. According to the 2021 survey and ISEAS's State of Southeast Asia survey 2023, Japan remains the most trusted international partner of Thailand, but China is already seen today as the most important one.

The trajectory of Thailand-Japan relations in their multiple dimensions makes clear that while Japan will not be Thailand's single-most important partner

DAVID M. MALITZ is a Senior Research Fellow at the German Institute for Japanese Studies in Tokyo.

anymore, the relationship will remain an important and beneficial one for both countries in the foreseeable future.

From Amity to a Comprehensive Strategic Partnership

The Thailand-Japan partnership is the oldest bilateral relationship that Japan enjoys with a Southeast Asian partner. This is, of course, due to the fact that the then Kingdom of Siam was never colonized. As the starting point of formal diplomatic relations, the Declaration of Amity and Commerce of 1887 is generally recognized and serves as a reference point in official statements. Permanent embassies were, however, only established following the 1898 Treaty of Friendship, Commerce and Navigation. This was an unequal treaty granting consular jurisdiction to Japan in exchange for Japanese support for the codification of Siamese law, which was a prerequisite to renegotiating Siam's unequal treaties with the Western colonial powers. The treaty was renegotiated after World War I. But only in 1937 a treaty based on equality was signed. During World War II, Japan and Thailand were allies, and so there were little bitter feelings after 1945. Bilateral relations were already rekindled during the US occupation of Japan and formalized immediately after its end. The main issue in the immediate post-war period was the repayment of Japanese wartime debt, which was resolved through an agreement in 1957. Otherwise, Japanese diplomacy concentrated on trade and investment.

By the 1970s, Japanese products had a dominant position in Thailand, as in other countries in the region. This led Thailand's influential *Social Science Review* to label Japan a "yellow peril". Students responded by organizing protests and boycotting Japanese consumer goods in 1972. But one must not overestimate anti-Japanese sentiment. A contemporary survey shows that while nearly 90 per cent of students considered Japanese trade "economic imperialism", only 40 to 50 per cent of farmers and labourers concurred.[3] The lack of promising job opportunities for university graduates combined with the preference of Japanese companies to hire expatriate staff might have played a role in the different perceptions.

In response to this and similar protests in the region, but also criticism from other Southeast Asian countries, the Japanese government agreed in 1973 to enter into a dialogue with ASEAN to work out a mutually beneficial solution to the issue of synthetic rubber imported from Japan. This was the main economic point of contention at the time, which demonstrated the dominance of Japanese goods in Southeast Asian markets to the detriment of local producers.

Consultations between ASEAN and Japan thus established were formalized in 1977 with the establishment of the ASEAN-Japan Forum. Thus from the

1970s onwards, Thailand-Japan relations were managed on two tracks, directly and bilaterally on the one hand and regionally through the growing number of ASEAN-Japanese fora on the other hand.

The year 1977 also saw the declaration of the Fukuda Doctrine, defining the principles for the engagement with Southeast Asian states. The relationship was to be based on mutual trust and "heart to heart" relations. This was reaffirmed in the Joint Vision Statement of the Commemorative Summit for the 50th Year of ASEAN-Japan Friendship and Cooperation in December 2023.[4] The Fukuda Doctrine promised to support the economic development of Southeast Asia while renouncing any military role for Japan. The Japan-ASEAN relationship was then further strengthened by Japan's signing of the Treaty of Amity and Cooperation in Southeast Asia in 2004, and the opening of a permanent mission to ASEAN in 2011.

Simultaneously, Japan embarked on a campaign of cultural diplomacy through the Japan Foundation, which was founded in 1972, and through significantly increased official development assistance and scholarships. This multipronged approach is generally seen as having turned the perception of Japan in Thailand around, making the country the most trusted and highly liked partner of the present. Certainly, the massive inflow of Japanese investment from the mid-1980s onwards must be considered another factor. This created jobs, including many for university graduates, and increased standards of living in Thailand.

The Economic Partnership Agreement of 2007 further boosted trade and investment, contributing to Thailand reaching upper-middle-income status in 2011. The next year also saw the elevation of relations to a Strategic Partnership, which aimed to formally include political and security aspects into Thailand-Japan cooperation on bilateral and regional levels. The further elevation of relations to a Comprehensive Strategic Partnership in 2022 was to a certain degree symbolic. It did not actually expand the scope of the partnership beyond the 2012 Joint Statement, but rather re-emphasized its economic aspects. This largely symbolic elevation of the partnership might have been driven by the wish for a visible achievement on the occasion of the tenth anniversary of the Strategic Partnership while simultaneously demonstrating a continuous strengthening of Thailand-Japan relations.

Trade and Investment: Indispensable and Co-creation Partners

The economic exchanges on which the recent Joint Statement has refocused attention have from the beginning nearly always been the backbone of Japan-

Thailand (Siam) relations. In fact, the very first historically recorded contact can be found in the chronicle of the Kingdom of Koryŏ. It contains a passage describing merchants from Siam who claimed to have spent a year in Japan prior to sailing to the Korean kingdom. In the early seventeenth century, trade flourished, and a Japanese settlement was established in the royal capital of Ayutthaya. Today it is a popular tourist spot, and its two best known inhabitants, Yamada Nagamasa and Maria Guyomar de Pina, have inspired pop-cultural works in Japanese and Thai. The works of Japanese craftspeople such as swordsmiths were in high demand in Siam, while deer leather, shark skin, and fragrant wood for making incense were essential raw materials on the Japanese islands. Traders from Ayutthaya would continue to sail to Nagasaki until the early eighteenth century, long after most Europeans had been banned from Japan's shores.

In the late nineteenth century, even before embassies were opened, mass-produced items of the Japanese light-industry, starting with matches, captured larger and larger market shares in Siam. Japanese exports increased especially from World War I onwards, and Japan became Siam's most important trading partner in the 1930s. As the writer, public intellectual, and one-time prime minister Kukrit Pramoj observed, Japanese products were popular because they were good enough in quality while being cheaper than those of Western competitors.[5] Before and during World War II, Siamese—often Sino-Siamese—businessmen created relationships with Japanese entrepreneurs and officials. These links proved to be of great value after the war by providing access to Japanese capital and products. Strengthening the economic relations between both countries was supported by the United States, with the goal of supporting economic development and political stability in both countries to inoculate them against Communist subversion. Already in 1961, Kukrit found the quality of Japanese goods to be at least as good as that of Western goods. By the early 1970s, Japanese products, partly produced in Thailand under the import substitution policy, dominated the economy, triggering the above-mentioned anti-Japanese boycott by Thai students.

The turning point for the economic relationship was the appreciation of the yen after the Plaza Accord, which made production in Japan uncompetitive. Only shortly before, the Thai government had embraced an export-led development strategy inviting foreign investment. Japanese capital has flown to Thailand ever since. This made the kingdom a regional manufacturing hub, particularly for automotives, and a middle-income country. Hosting a large number of Japanese production facilities, Thailand has become Japan's "indispensable economic partner", as Fumio Kishida put it when he visited Bangkok as foreign minister in 2016.[6] In Asia, only Singapore and China have attracted more Japanese investment.

But in recent years, Thailand has been losing competitiveness. Surveys by the Japanese Chamber of Commerce reveal that, among respondents, the proportion of investment for replacement rather than expansion has trended upwards and reached seventy per cent for the manufacturing sector in the first half of 2023. The kingdom's ageing workforce, a lack of reforms of the education system, rising labour costs, and a shortage of engineers are concerns for manufacturers.[7] Anecdotal evidence meanwhile indicates that because of lower pay and rigid corporate cultures, Japanese companies are becoming less attractive as employers.[8] These are not new developments. Already in the 2000s, the Thailand-Plus-One strategy had been advertised as a means to overcome these weaknesses by shifting labour-intensive processes to neighbouring countries and employing Thailand's workforce in more knowledge- and capital-intensive parts of the value chain. To fully exploit the potential of this strategy, substantial investments in hard, cross-border connectivity, and soft, especially education, infrastructure are necessary. Japan has contributed substantially to both since the 1950s and continues to do so. What has changed, however, is that there are now viable regional competitors for Japanese direct investments, such as Vietnam.

A further challenge for the Thailand-Japan economic partnership is changes in demand. The shift to electric vehicles is the most prominent example. As has become plainly visible on Bangkok's streets, as of now, Chinese manufacturers are leading the transformation of the automotive industry in Thailand. The market share of Japanese automotive manufacturers has dropped from 90 to below 80 per cent.[9] While Japan remains the most important investor in the Thai economy and maintains the highest percentage of FDI stock, with approximately 30 per cent, its advantage has shrunk, with China in particular making headway and catching up.[10]

When in Tokyo in December 2023 to attend the ASEAN-Japan Commemorative Summit, newly elected Thai prime minister Srettha Thavisin also met with Japanese investors, the Japan External Trade Organization (JETRO), and the Japanese Ministry of Economy, Trade and Industry. In comments to the press, the prime minister promised tax incentives for the production of electric vehicles by Japanese firms in Thailand, but also admonished them for falling behind, and reminded them that they were "not alone in the world".[11]

Related to this development are new regulatory challenges towards making the whole supply chain of products more sustainable. Additionally, economic growth across the region has resulted in more ASEAN- and Thailand-based multinational companies and more sophisticated consumers. This makes the top-down Japanese-led approach much less suitable for the future.[12] Recognizing these developments, the Japanese Ministry of Economy, Trade and Industry announced in January 2022 the ASIA-Japan Investing for the Future Initiative to guide economic cooperation between Japan and ASEAN towards strengthening supply-chains and developing sustainable economies towards a "co-creation partnership". Based on these ideas, in November 2022 the Five-Year Joint Action Plan on Japan-Thailand Strategic Economic Partnership Towards a More Resilient and Sustainable Future was agreed upon, detailing specific objectives to enhance Thai human resources, make the Thai economy more sustainable by synergizing the Thai Bio-Circular-Green Economy with the Japanese Green Transformation strategies, and investing in and enhancing hard and soft infrastructure. These initiatives on making ASEAN-Japan—and therefore also Thailand-Japan—economic relations more sustainable were confirmed in the Implementation Plan of the Joint Vision Statement on ASEAN-Japan Friendship and Cooperation in December 2023.[13]

ODA: From Foreign Advisers to Development Partners

Closely intertwined with increasing Japanese investment in Thailand during the 1980s was the flow of Japanese Official Development Aid (ODA), which significantly contributed to the infrastructural foundations of Thailand's boom. One might consider the employment of a small number of Japanese experts by Siam during the reign of King Chulalongkorn as its forebear. The most famous among them was the Yale-educated lawyer Tōkichi Masao (1871–1921), who assisted in codifying the Siamese penal code. Furthermore, a number of Siamese princes, including the future king Vajiravudh (1881–1925) and other officials, visited Imperial Japan to study its modern institutions. This period also saw the very first Siamese students being sent to Japan. After the revolution of 1932 then, Japan was widely considered a role model for successful modernization visited by students, parliamentarians, military officers, and other officials.

Japanese aid to Thailand after World War II began with Japan's admission to the United Nation's Program of Technical Assistance in 1952 and the Columbo Plan in 1954. The first twenty-one Thai trainees arrived in 1954. The repayment of the wartime debt ended in 1970, one year after the first development aid loan was granted, and one year prior to the first grant aid provided by Japan. Amounts increased significantly following the Fukuda Doctrine, making Japan the top donor to Thailand's infrastructural needs. While the kingdom ceased to be eligible for grant aid in 1993, it continued to receive loans, with the 1990s being the decade with the highest cumulative amount given.

The launch of the Japan-ASEAN Exchange Projects in 1988 marked the additional launch of transregional Japanese ODA benefitting Thailand directly or indirectly. The Japan-ASEAN Integration Fund, founded in 2006, has funded concrete projects fostering the integration of ASEAN member states. A recent example of an important project in Thailand financed by this fund is the ASEAN-Japan Cybersecurity Capacity Building Centre, which opened in 2019.

Infrastructure remains a focus of Japanese ODA in the region because of its substantial needs for investments. In response to China's Belt and Road Initiative, the Partnership for Quality Infrastructure was announced in 2015, followed by ASEAN's own Master Plan on ASEAN Connectivity one year later. Through the Japan-ASEAN Connectivity Initiative of 2020, Japan is managing its contributions in line with both frameworks. Revised in 2023, the Japan-ASEAN Comprehensive Connectivity Initiative has a total investment budget of US$19 billion.

The end of Thailand's eligibility for Japanese grant aid in 1993 also marked the beginning of bilateral development cooperation for the benefit of third countries. For example, under the Japan-Thailand Partnership Programme, renewed in 2019, both countries' development agencies jointly support sustainable development in the Mekong region, its integration with the rest of ASEAN, and promote the adoption of universal health coverage.

Security: Alliance to Multilateral Cooperation

By offering training on cyber defence, the ASEAN-Japan Cybersecurity Capacity Building Centre is not only supporting digital connectivity across ASEAN but it is also an example of Japan-led multilateral security cooperation. In the Thai case, security or defence cooperation is usually traced to the leaders coming to power after the revolution of 1932, who acquired military hardware, including, famously, submarines from Imperial Japan. And of course, during World War II, the two countries became military allies. In fact, military relations had already begun in the reign of King Chulalongkorn, when Siamese princes went to Japan and observed the Japanese military. Siam also bought Japanese equipment and even warships after the Russo-Japanese War, and a future leader of the 1932 revolution, Phraya Phahonphonphayuhasena (1887–1947), was sent to Japan for a study trip in the 1920s. This relationship was quickly rekindled after 1945. Thai cadets were in 1958 the first foreign students at Japan's National Defense Academy and have been the largest group of foreign students since.[14]

Apart from education, however, security cooperation remained very limited throughout the Cold War. Only after the fall of the Soviet Union did the Japanese government cautiously respond to mounting international pressure by making more active contributions to global security, especially after the lack of recognition accorded to Japan's mere financial contributions to the First Gulf War. Because of the restrictions of Japan's pacifist constitution, these contributions were geared towards multilateral cooperation to promote human security and centred on Southeast Asia and maritime security—which naturally led to cooperation with Thailand. Japanese participation in the UN peacekeeping in Cambodia was the first overseas deployment of the Japanese Self Defense Forces. In 2004, both Japan and Thailand were founding members of the Regional Cooperation Agreement on Combating Piracy and Armed Robbery against Ships in Asia that had been initiated by Japan. Both countries then participated in counter-piracy patrols in the Malacca Strait. Since the following year, the Japanese Self Defense Forces have participated in the annual Thai-US Cobra Gold exercises. That participation is limited, however, to non-combat activities such as evacuation operations, disaster relief and, more recently, cyber defence.

Fora for defence cooperation between Japan and ASEAN include the ASEAN Defence Ministers' Meeting Plus since 2010 and the Japan-ASEAN Defence Ministers' Informal Meeting since 2014. Drawing on these consultations, Japan introduced in 2016 the Vientiane Vision as the guiding principle for defence cooperation with ASEAN and to link Japan's national security with its foreign policy towards ASEAN. It was revised in 2019 to be in line with Japan's Free and Open Indo-Pacific Vision and the ASEAN Outlook on the Indo-Pacific. The vision offers an umbrella framework incorporating both ASEAN-wide and bilateral security cooperation with Japan. But in contrast to those ASEAN member states that have territorial and maritime disputes with China, Thailand has shown little interest in expanding bilateral security relations with Japan. Furthermore, the Thai military is very much army-centred, whereas Japan's cooperation efforts are focused on maritime security. Japan is also not seen as a military power in Thailand, and because of the Japanese-US alliance, cooperation would not contribute to Thailand's efforts to hedge between the United States and China. While in May 2022 the Agreement Concerning the Transfer of Defense Equipment and Technology was signed by Thailand, no concrete projects have been revealed to be in the works. Nor does there seem to be Thai interest in products of Japan's defence industry. It is noteworthy that in the press readouts of the Japan-Thailand summit meetings on 15 November and 17 December 2023, Prime Minister Kishida expressed the Japanese wish to "promote … cooperation on the security front" and "maintain and strengthen a free and open international order". Thai prime minister Srettha, meanwhile, focused mainly on the economic aspect, saying that he "attaches importance to investment from Japan".

Cultural and People-to-People Exchanges

The 2021 survey of the Ministry of Foreign Affairs showed that both Japanese traditional and popular culture appeal to the Thai public and have indeed done so for a long time. Exchanges with Japan have also shaped the Thai culture of everyday life. Japanese foodstuffs had already been introduced in seventeenth-century Siam, and an early nineteenth-century king praised a Japanese sauce in a poem. Japanese food slowly gained mass appeal from the 1980s onwards, making the kingdom today one of the most important markets for Japanese cuisine. On the flipside, Thai cuisine has also gained popularity in Japan, presumably driven by larger numbers of Japanese expatriates in the kingdom as well as the beginning of mass tourism from the mid-1980s onwards. In recent years, standard Thai dishes have appeared in supermarkets as ready-cooked meals, while restaurant chains offer Thai-inspired fusion food—and the Thai term for coriander, *phakchi*, has informally been adopted into Japanese.

Already in the early twentieth-century, expatriates and members of Siam's upper-class had been known to have travelled to Japan to enjoy its milder climate. Traveling to Japan long remained a prerogative for Thailand's affluent class. Only the proliferation of low cost airlines and the introduction of a visa-on-arrival in 2013 turned Japan into a popular destination for less-affluent Thai tourists. The devaluation of the yen since early 2022 further boosted Thai tourism to Japan, making the first half of 2023 the first time period in which more Thais travelled to Japan than vice versa.

Each country also hosts a sizable expatriate community from the other country, who—based on anecdotal evidence as well as, in the Thai case, surveys about the perceptions of Japan—are generally very well liked. According to the records of the Japanese Ministry of Foreign Affairs, the Japanese community of Thailand is the fourth largest outside Japan, with 51,000 in Bangkok, making the city the second-largest overseas Japanese city after Los Angeles.[15] Japanese immigration records meanwhile show that among the 57,000 Thais in Japan, only 4,000 are students.[16] The remainder are permanent residents, dependents of Japanese citizens, or are on working visas—with the arguably most visible occupations being Thai chefs, masseurs and masseuses, and Muay Thai instructors, services that few, if any, Japanese can offer. Strikingly, seventy per cent of the Thai community in Japan is female.

Also, other exchanges can be identified that have shaped Thai society and the culture of everyday life. In the early twentieth century, the cinema was introduced by a Japanese businessman, and two famous early novels were partly set in Japan. In the post-war period, the famous tuk-tuk was introduced from Japan. Later, affordable motorbikes greatly increased mobility outside Bangkok. Japanese manga have been commonplace in Thailand since the 1970s, followed by dubbed anime. Today, Doraemon has even been incorporated into temple murals. In 1984, *Oshin*, the rags to riches story of a woman born in the Meiji period, was the first Japanese TV series to become a great hit in Thailand. Since the turn of the twenty-first century, J-pop and Japanese series have become overshadowed by the Korean Wave and its more attractive product offerings. This is probably best exemplified by the global success, particularly in Thailand, of K-pop girl group Blackpink, with its Thai member Lisa Manoban, and the much more limited appeal of the BNK48 girl group, a spin-off of the Japanese idol group AKB48. Both started in 2016. During the pandemic, Thai-produced "Boys' Love" television series about male homoerotic relationships marketed at women gained a global following. The genre was first introduced to Thailand from Japan in the early 1990s through pirated manga. The year 2007 then saw the first highly successful locally produced movie of the genre. Realizing its international appeal, the Thai Department of International Trade Promotion started in 2021 to actively promote Thai "Boys' Love" series abroad—including in the genre's country of origin.[17]

The Panda in the Room

Any meaningful discussion of Thailand-Japan relations and the two countries' Comprehensive Strategic Partnership cannot avoid addressing the fact that over the course of the last two decades, Japan's influence in Thailand has declined relative to that of China, today considered Thailand's most important partner. China has been Thailand's most important trade partner since 2013, and the most important market for Thai tourism since 2014. Chinese foreign direct investment has also been increasing and in 2019 surpassed for the first time—and, so far, only time—that of Japan. As mentioned above, Chinese manufacturers have largely captured the Thai market for electric cars and are scaling up their production facilities in the country. Driven by the expanding economic relations, cultural exchange also expanded significantly. Thai universities host sixteen Confucius Institutes, and approximately thirty thousand Thais were reported to study in China before the pandemic—more than seven times the number of Thai students in Japan. Chinese cultural diplomacy has also been successful in reaching out to middle-aged to older Sino-Thais, who still feel a cultural connection to their ancestors' homeland.

Especially since the 2014 coup, Thailand-China security relations have expanded significantly. The Thai military has increased arms purchases from China and has sent more officers to study at Chinese military academies. Joint exercises have increased in number and frequency. Chinese companies are also backing the prestige projects of high-speed rail links connecting Bangkok with the new U-Tapao airport and with Nong Khai at the Lao border. During the pandemic, the provision of Chinese vaccines through donations and sale, coupled with a robust public relations campaign, led to Chinese aid being much more highly valued than Japanese aid, which was much less visible because of the lack of a Japanese vaccine.[18]

Moving Forward

It is unlikely that Japan will regain its place as Thailand's paramount foreign partner that it arguably had in the 1990s and 2000s. And for Thailand—and also for Japan—a decoupling from China is not a possibility. Yet neither should one assume that the relationship will cease to be of great importance to both sides in the near future, given the sheer size of Japanese investment and its contribution to both countries' prosperity.

Ensuring the longevity of this economic backbone of the Comprehensive Strategic Partnership against the headwinds of technological change, decreasing competitiveness, and the new pressure to become more sustainable necessitates considerable effort and coordination not only between the two governments but also between them and their countries' private sectors. The Five-Year Joint Action Plan demonstrates that both sides are aware of these challenges and are committed to overcoming them. During the first meeting of Prime Minister Kishida with Thai prime minister Srettha Thavisin, which took place in November 2023 during the APEC summit, the latter promised to support Japanese manufacturers during the transition phase towards electric mobility and incentivize further investments, demonstrating the commitment of the new Thai government to the economic relationship. The support through tax incentives was then reaffirmed in December 2023 during the ASEAN-Japan Commemorative Summit. Meanwhile, Japanese manufacturers have likewise shown their commitment to Thailand by announcing investments to scale up the production of electric cars and motorbikes. A positive sign here is that ASEAN business executives are very optimistic that Japanese automotive companies will manage the transition.[19] And, as of the end of December 2023, the stock market has rewarded Toyota's cautious approach towards the transition to electric mobility.

The Japanese government in the meantime will not be able to match Chinese investments in ASEAN connectivity dollar for dollar. But this has never been the

Japanese approach, as the rejection of support for a high-speed rail link between Bangkok and the Northern city of Chiang Mai has shown, which was assessed to be uneconomical by Japanese experts. Rather, the declared Japanese focus on relative quality and sustainability should prove its worth to Thailand and Japanese investors over the years.

Bilateral defence and security relations have not developed as much as the Japanese side might have wished, and there is no indication that this will change in the near future as the Thai government is very much focused on the economic aspect of the relationship. To focus on multilateral engagement for the time being seems to be, therefore, the reasonable way forward. But as South Korean firms have found their way into the Thai defence market, it cannot be ruled out that Japanese defence manufacturers might find success in the future as well, if the right products can be developed and offered.

The unique advantage that Japan has is, of course, the general goodwill that it enjoys across party lines and, indeed, generational lines. General Prayuth, the former coup leader who oversaw a tilt towards China, chose to travel to Japan when in brief retirement between stepping down as prime minister and being appointed to the Privy Council. Pita Limjaroenrat, the prime ministerial candidate of the progressive Move Forward Party who gained the most votes in the 2023 general election, has meanwhile frequently expressed his admiration for Japan. Asked about his favourite word in an interview, he chose *kintsuki*, the name of a Japanese traditional technique to fix broken pottery that emphasizes rather than disguises breakages through the mixing of gold dust into the lacquer used as glue.

As a final observation, one can point out that Japanese engagement with Thai civil society has been limited. In particular, Japan has largely been loath to advertise its political system. Democracy as a shared value was mentioned in the Joint Statements of 2007 and 2012 and also stressed by former prime minister Shinzo Abe as crucial immediately after the 2014 coup. But references were then quietly dropped from joint communiqués and also do not appear in the 2022 Joint Statement.[20] Thais across the political spectrum, meanwhile, have tended to attribute Japanese prosperity and technological progress to Japanese discipline, a view promoted for example also through the *Oshin* TV-series. But Thai society is changing, as the last two general elections and the student protests of 2020/21 have shown. And some younger and more progressive Thais have discovered Japan as a role model because of its democratic institutions and its welfare state—it is reasonable to expect their numbers to grow as a result of generational change.[21] Additional, co-creation of economic values has been identified as crucial to a mutually beneficial relationship in the future. A major hurdle to achieving such mutually beneficial collaborations on the Thai side is the high social inequality and the oligopolistic structure of its economy, stifling innovation and competitiveness. It might therefore be of mutual benefit, if in the future Japan was able to nudge Thailand's conservative forces in business and bureaucracy towards more fundamental institutional change. Given Japan's standing with the kingdom's old guard, the country might be uniquely capable of doing so. Already after the 2014 coup, the Japanese business community contributed to Thailand's return to a more democratic regime by convincing its political leaders at the time of the need to do so. Their ability to frame democracy in terms of rule of law rather than civil liberties played an important role in this regard.[22]

Notes

1. Fumio Kishida, "Sanchak Nai Fumio Kishida, nayok ratthamontri Yipun", *Matichon*, 1 May 2022, p. 12.

2. Japanese Ministry of Foreign Affairs, "Kaigai ni okeru tai-Nichi yoron·chōsa, Reiwa 3 nendo: ASEAN" [Survey of foreign attitudes towards Japan: ASEAN], 2021, https://www.mofa.go.jp/mofaj/files/100348514.pdf.

3. Khian Thirawit, *Raingan phonnganwichai rueang thatsana khong khon Thai thi mi to Chin lae Yipun* [Research about the Thai perception of China and Japan] (Bangkok: Social Research Institute, Chulalongkorn University, 1975), pp. 52–53.

4. Ministry of Foreign Affairs, "Joint Vision Statement on ASEAN-Japan Friendship and Cooperation: Trusted Partner", 17 December 2023, https://www.mofa.go.jp/files/100597190.pdf.

5. Kukrit Pramoj, *Chak Yipun* [Japanese scenes] (Bangkok: Dokya, 2010), p. 290.

6. Ministry of Foreign Affairs of Japan, "ASEAN Policy Speech 'Diversity and Connectivity – Role of Japan as a Partner' by H.E. Mr. Fumio Kishida at Chulalongkorn University Bangkok, Thailand", 2 May 2016, https://www.mofa.go.jp/a_o/rp/page4e_000424.html.

7. JCC Economic Survey Team, "Survey on Business Sentiment of Japanese Corporations in Thailand for the 1st Half of 2023", 27 June 2023, https://www.jetro.go.jp/ext_images/thailand/pdf/JCCSurvey1H2023ENG.pdf.

8. Nakamura Katsuhiro, "Naze Thaijin ha Nikkei kigyō o yameru no ka?" [Why are Thais quitting Japanese firms], *ArayZ*, October 2023, pp. 14–17.

9. Toru Takahashi, "Japan's Battle for Thailand, Indonesia Auto Markets No Lost Cause", *Nikkei Asia*, 16 October 2023, https://asia.nikkei.com/Spotlight/Comment/Japan-s-battle-for-Thailand-Indonesia-auto-markets-no-lost-cause.

10. ASEANStatsDataPortal, "Stocks of Inward Foreign Direct Investment (FDI) at Year-End", https://data.aseanstats.org/fdi-by-hosts-and-sources-stock.

11. Kyodo News, "Srettha Urges Japanese Firms to Make Quick Decisions", *Bangkok Post*, 15 December 2023, https://www.bangkokpost.com/thailand/general/2706878/srettha-urges-japanese-firms-to-make-quick-decisions.

12. Mie Oba, "Japan Now Has to Deal with ASEAN on a More Equal Footing", *East Asia Forum*, 3 September 2023, https://www.eastasiaforum.org/2023/09/03/japan-now-has-to-deal-with-asean-on-a-more-equal-footing/#more-2100949.

13. Ministry of Foreign Affairs, "Implementation Plan of the Joint Vision Statement on ASEAN-Japan Friendship and Cooperation Trusted Partners", 17 December 2023, https://www.mofa.go.jp/files/100597130.pdf.

14. Ministry of Defense, *Defense of Japan 2023* (Tokyo: Ministry of Defense, 2023), p. 429.

15. Ministry of Foreign Affairs, "Kaigai zairyū hōjinsū chōsa tōkei" [Statistics of Japanese citizens living overseas], 1 October 2020, https://www.mofa.go.jp/mofaj/toko/tokei/hojin/index.html.

16. E-Stat Seifu tōkei no sōgō madoguchi, "Zairyū gaikokujin tōkei" [Statistics of foreign residents], December 2022, https://www.e-stat.go.jp/stat-search/files?page=1&stat_infid=000040068660.

17. Piya Pongsapitaksanti, "The Development of Thai Boys' Love (BL) Drama: Characteristics, Production Process, and Its Influences", *Thai Kenkyū*, no. 23 (2023): 19–29.

18. Sharon Seah, Joanne Lin, Sithanonxay Suvannaphakdy, Melinda Martinus, Pham Thi Puong Thao, Farah Nadine Seth, and Hoang Thi Ha, *The State of Southeast Asia: 2022* (Singapore: ISEAS – Yusof Ishak Institute, 2022), p. 13.

19. JETRO Singapore, "Business Sentiment Survey Report: Perception of ASEAN Businesses Towards Japan 2022", p. 8.

20. David M. Malitz, "Japanese-Thai Relations through Two Coups: Back to Business", *Kyoto Review of Southeast Asia* 36 (2023), https://kyotoreview.org/issue-34/japanese-thai-relations-through-two-coups-back-to-business.

21. For a concrete example, see "Poetchai Suphakon, phak kao klai, kap aidia ha siang baep Yipun" [Opening up: Suphakon from the Move Forward Party and the idea to canvass for votes like in Japan], *Post Today*, 8 April 2023, https://www.posttoday.com/thailand-election-2023/692841.

22. Nobuhiro Aizawa, "The Japanese Business Community as a Diplomatic Asset and the 2014 Coup 'État", in *The Courteous Power: Japan and Southeast Asia in the Indo-Pacific Era*, edited by John D. Ciorciari and Kiyoteru Tsutsui (Ann Arbor: University of Michigan Press, 2021), p. 168.

Timor-Leste

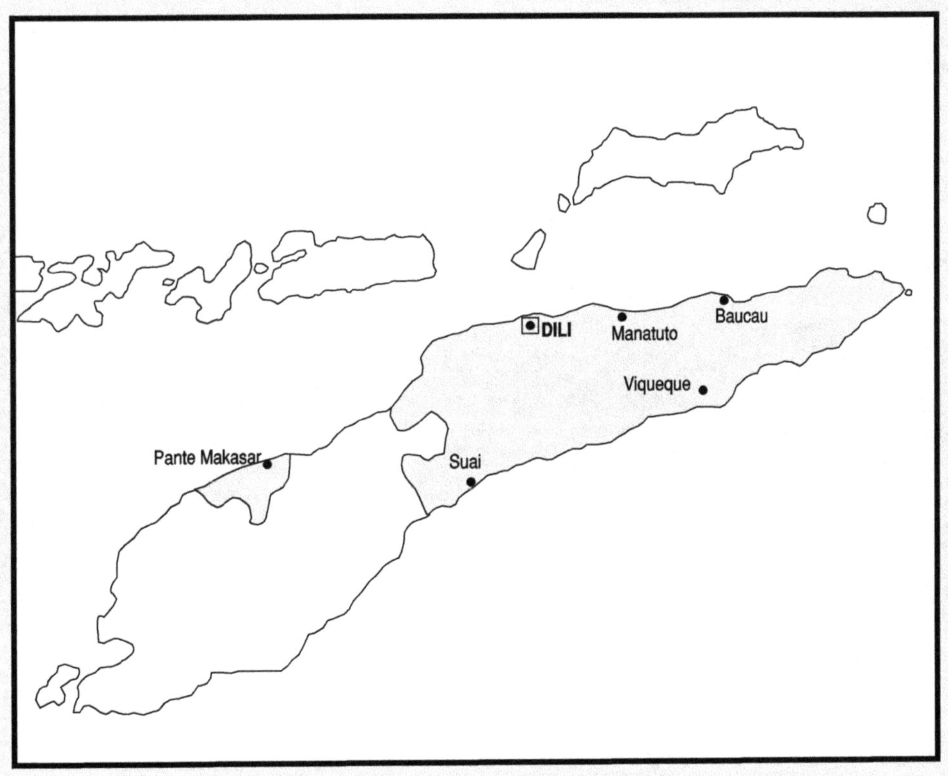

TIMOR-LESTE IN 2023:
The Return of the 'Old Firm'

Michael Leach

The 2023 parliamentary election in Timor-Leste saw voters return to the "old firm" of Xanana Gusmão and Jose Ramos-Horta, reminiscent of the 2007 elections, which took place in the wake of the 2006–7 political-military crisis. Given the advancing age of these historical leaders, however, there are expectations that overdue political transitions to a younger generation of leaders would likely unfold during the current parliamentary term. As the new government took office in July 2023, Timor-Leste embarked on a crucial decade for its future amid the looming threat of a "fiscal cliff". The country is entering what could prove the final decade of the solvency of its oil and gas sovereign wealth fund unless new revenues flow from the Greater Sunrise fields. As a result, the nation must intensify efforts to diversify its economy further and reduce excessive dependence on the oil and gas sector. At the same time, it is faced with various policy challenges arising from a major demographic "youth bulge".

The Political-Economic Context of the 2023 Elections

In the second-round presidential election that took place in 2022, Jose Ramos-Horta won a comfortable victory over the incumbent president, Francisco 'Lu Olo' Guterres from the Revolutionary Front for an Independent East Timor (FRETILIN), by a margin of 62 per cent to 38 per cent. The support of Xanana Gusmão, the leader of the National Congress for Timorese Reconstruction (CNRT), played a significant role in securing Ramos-Horta's election, marking a pivotal step for Gusmão's return to power. Ramos-Horta's CNRT backers advocated for an early parliamentary election in 2022 as they believed that Ramos-Horta's presidential

MICHAEL LEACH is a Professor in Politics and International Relations at Swinburne University of Technology in Melbourne, Australia, and is a co-founder of the Timor-Leste Studies Association, https://tlstudies.org/.

win signalled a potential surge in votes for CNRT. However, Ramos-Horta chose not to dissolve the incumbent parliament, which completed its five-year term in May 2023. Throughout 2022, President Ramos-Horta demonstrated his ability to moderate previously heated political tensions between the FRETILIN-dominated government and Gusmão's CNRT. His middle-of-the-road leadership style and general inclination towards consensus solutions have helped alleviate the intensity of political standoffs. In the first year of Ramos-Horta's second tenure as president, the efforts to open the doors of the presidency to the wider public were even more pronounced than in his first term. His personal touch and direct approach demonstrably endear him to the people. With an ally in the presidency, the parliamentary election of 2023 provided the opportunity for Xanana Gusmão's CNRT party to make a comeback to government.

As ever in Timor-Leste's proportional system, the key contest was between the two major parties, FRETILIN and CNRT, but with smaller parties likely essential to form a majority. Since 2020, Timor-Leste has been governed by a coalition comprising three parties—FRETILIN, the People's Liberation Party (PLP) and the Kmanek Haburas Unidade Nasional Timor Oan (KHUNTO). In fact, the latter two originally had formed part of a winning coalition with CNRT at the 2018 poll. That coalition, however, collapsed in 2020—in part under the influence of the former president, FRETILIN's Francisco 'Lu Olo' Guterres, who refused to install a number of CNRT ministers. Unhappy with the efforts of the PLP's Prime Minister Taur Matan Ruak to address the issue, a failed effort by the CNRT to force an early election in 2020 saw them oppose their own coalition government's budget. The move backfired, aided by President Guterres, with FRETILIN entering the government to support the two smaller parties PLP and KHUNTO during Timor-Leste's initial Covid-19 response in 2020. This alliance allowed the PLP's Taur Matan Ruak to continue as prime minister, forcing Gusmão's CNRT into opposition.

Ramos-Horta's resounding victory in 2022 clearly boded well for CNRT's return, with the three government parties—FRETILIN, PLP and KHUNTO—running separately in 2023 despite their expressed willingness to form a post-electoral coalition. Though FRETILIN's historical vote share hovered around the thirty per cent mark in recent elections, a few pre-election polls reflected a prevailing national mood for change after a few difficult years of pandemic, floods and economic contraction.[1]

The lack of pre-electoral coalitions was a notable feature of the 2023 election—a clear response to Ramos-Horta's well-known constitutional positions. While FRETILIN has always maintained that government should be first offered to the most-voted party—a position that fostered pre-election coalitions while FRETILIN's Lu Olo was president—Ramos-Horta had made it clear in his first term as president from 2007 to 2012 that he would accept a post-electoral coalition that controlled a simple majority in the parliament even if led by the second-largest party. The absence of pre-electoral coalitions meant that the real horse-trading would take place after the 2023 election.

In 2023, however, Ramos-Horta was at pains to point out that this principle would not extend to parties associated with controversial Martial Arts Groups (MAGs). His position squarely targeted KHUNTO and the new party Os Verdes (The Greens), both of which have organizational links to major MAGs. The growing collaboration between political parties and MAGs, including the employment of MAG members in state agencies, has raised concerns among civil society organizations about the rising "MAG-ification" of politics.[2] This, in turn, reflected growing public concern over episodes of open conflict in Dili's streets, which had become a recurring feature in news reports. KHUNTO emerged in the previous election cycle with a strong base among MAG members, and the newer party Os Verdes, linked to a competing MAG, entered the fray for the 2023 election. As ever, the capacity of these actors to cause social unrest was closely tied to national economic performance, with youth unemployment being a key driver of MAG activity.

The 2023 election also held pivotal importance for the economic future of Timor-Leste, which is facing a looming "fiscal cliff" as its Petroleum Fund approached what might be its final decade of solvency unless new funds from the untapped Greater Sunrise oil and gas fields start to flow in. The country's annual budget over the past years has exceeded the sustainable limit of withdrawals from that fund, prompting calls for Timor-Leste to economically diversify and to promote new job-creating industries before the oil wealth is depleted. The PLP-KHUNTO-FRETILIN government acknowledged the need for economic diversification and developed a Covid-19 recovery plan based on promoting new job-creating industries, though little progress had been made, other than in labour mobility agreements, discussed further below.

While in office, Gusmão championed the Tasi Mane downstream oil and gas processing mega-project on Timor-Leste's south coast as the solution. He opposed the alternative of sending the raw product to existing facilities in Darwin, arguing that the former would yield increased returns to the nation, notwithstanding the daunting upfront capital expenditure costs. After taking power in 2022, the PLP-KHUNTO-FRETILIN government changed the leadership of key petroleum agencies and stalled any major investment in the Greater Sunrise gas field project, effectively putting it on the back burner. The government failed, however, to develop a clear and comprehensive policy alternative to Gusmão's Tasi Mane vision. This was, in part, a tribute to Gusmão's own charismatic legitimacy, even while in opposition, and his ability to tie the successful maritime boundary campaign with Australia to the separate issue of how the remaining oil wealth should be best managed. The enduring nationalist fervour associated with the maritime boundary victory has made it politically difficult for opponents to resist the Tasi Mane mega-project.

Another noteworthy feature of the 2023 election was the generational factor. While the birth rate has slowed down and Timor-Leste's median age has risen from 18 to 21 in recent years, a large percentage of the electorate would be casting their votes for the first time in 2023. This meant that all parties needed to offer an effective suite of youth policies. Key issues in this regard included the provision of job and training opportunities for large numbers of school graduates annually. This demographic, as a percentage of the population, surpasses countries like Australia, which has a median age of 38.

Even more significantly, another major generational shift was under way, with the 2023 election likely serving as the last contest of the key figures of the 1975 generation of political leaders, who have dominated Timor-Leste politics since the restoration of independence in 2002. Gusmão will turn 80 in 2026, and other major figures of his generation, including Ramos-Horta and FRETILIN leader Mari Alkatiri, are not far behind. As most observers have noted, the transition to a new generation of leaders will have to be well managed to maintain political stability.

As the campaign unfolded, the implications of a possible CNRT victory became apparent: the Tasi Mane mega-project would return as the top agenda of economic policy, with implications for the relationship with Australia. Australia continues to argue that the decision lies with the commercial joint venture partners, led by Woodside, which are yet to agree to downstream processing in Timor-Leste. Meanwhile, political developments in Australian climate politics have made the alternative option of processing in Darwin a more vexed one.[3] The difficult bilateral legacy of the maritime boundary campaign resurfaced in July when the new Australian foreign minister, Penny Wong, publicly acknowledged the "disappointing" actions of previous Australian governments, stating that they were "not in the spirit of our friendship".[4] As the final election of the 1975 generation approached, the links between economic sustainability, the "youth bulge" and Timor-Leste's long-term political stability became evident, making the 2023 election—and the new government to be established—highly significant for the country's future.

2023 Elections: Parliamentary and Village Votes

The 2023 Parliamentary Election

Timor-Leste's 890,000 voters went to the polls on 21 May following a remarkably calm thirty-day campaign, with many locals commenting on the contrast with the atmosphere of political tensions during the past few years. Twenty-one years on from the restoration of independence and the young country had established itself as among the most democratic in Southeast Asia, registering a Press Freedom Index score higher than Australia's.[5] The election day progressed smoothly, with a competent and well-organized performance by Timor-Leste's Technical Secretariat for Electoral Administration.

Soon into the vote count it became apparent that Xanana Gusmão's CNRT party was poised to return to government with an impressive 41.6 per cent of the votes. CNRT secured a clear lead over its chief rival FRETILIN, which garnered 25.8 per cent. The participation rate was healthy, with 79.3 per cent of the registered voters turning out, a slight decrease of 1.7 per cent compared with the 2018 election.

Despite CNRT's hopes for a majority in its own right, and a major swing in its favour, it fell two seats short of a 33-seat majority in the 65-seat parliament. A post-election coalition with the Democratic Party (PD), which performed well with 9 per cent of the votes and added one more seat to its parliament representation, was announced in the following days. The two minor parties from the outgoing government, KHUNTO and the departing prime minister's PLP, successfully surpassed the 4 per cent threshold for securing seats. But the combined votes of KHUNTO, PLP and FRETILIN did not measure up to the substantial vote share garnered by CNRT.

Despite repeated warnings from Ramos Horta that he would not view favourably any coalition involving either the youth-oriented KHUNTO or the new party Os Verdes, it was notable that these parties collectively received around 11

TABLE 1
2023 Parliamentary Election Results

Party	%	Seats	Change in seats
CNRT	41.63	31	+10
FRETILIN	25.75	19	−4
Democratic Party	9.32	6	+1
KHUNTO	7.51	5	0
PLP	5.88	4	−4

per cent of the vote, though Os Verdes's vote share of 3.6 per cent fell just short of the 4 per cent threshold in their first electoral participation. This represents a sizeable constituency, and it highlights both the uncomfortable level of disaffection with conventional party politics among younger voters and their concerns about national economic performance and job opportunities.

For its part, FRETILIN—with 25.8 per cent of the vote—suffered the first notable drop in its vote share since 2007, with a decrease of around 4 per cent from its usual levels. This will be disconcerting for the long-established party, which is still recovering from the leadership tensions during the 2022 presidential campaign. In that election, the former army commander Lere Anan Timur ran against the official FRETILIN candidate, then incumbent president Francisco 'Lu-Olo' Guterres. Despite internal efforts to mend the rift for the 2023 elections, the FRETILIN vote was constrained by grassroots campaigning led by Gusmão. He effectively capitalized on his time in opposition to build the CNRT grassroots party structure and garner widespread support across the country.

Significantly, as Timor-Leste emerged from a challenging period marked by the Covid-19 pandemic, floods and associated economic contraction, voters once again turned to the "old firm" of Gusmão and Ramos-Horta, as they had done previously in the aftermath of the 2006–7 political-military crisis. This underscored the public trust in the ability of the two seasoned leaders to stimulate the economy and guarantee political stability. Voters may also have recognized that this could be the final election campaign fought by the two great national leaders.

Suco Elections

Suco council elections in Timor-Leste, the equivalent of local elections, took place nationwide on 28 October. During this process, 452 villages (*suco*) and 2,322 hamlets (*aldeias*) voted to choose their local representatives. Political parties have been banned from formal participation in these elections since 2009. This was a response to concerns—well founded in many cases—over the divisive effect of political party campaigning in some local communities in the earlier 2004–5 round of *suco* elections. Candidates now therefore run as independents irrespective of any party affiliations.

Though Timor-Leste has commendable rates of women's representation in the national parliament owing to a legal mandate requiring a minimum of one woman in every three candidates on party lists, female representation at the *suco* level has been low historically, at around 2–5 per cent. This year saw women represent 11 per cent of candidates for village positions. But only eighteen women were elected as *suco* chiefs, accounting for merely 4 per cent.[6] This marked a decrease in both female candidates and their victories for women in local government, with women's representation dropping from 4.7 per cent in 2016 to 4.1 per cent in 2023.[7]

Economic Realities Confronting the New Government

The ninth constitutional government of Timor-Leste was sworn in by President Ramos-Horta on 3 July, comprising a record number of ministers, vice-ministers and secretaries of state, at forty-seven in total. In domestic politics, the incoming government placed a six-month moratorium on MAGs activities in November 2023, which helped to assuage the president's concerns.[8] The incoming government promised to prioritize economic diversification and committed to the development of the Tasi Mane project as a national priority, arguing that the income stream from the gas fields would contribute to broadening the productive sectors of the economy through the flow-on effects of investment.[9] The renewed determination to proceed more aggressively with the Tasi Mane project again cast the spotlight on commercial negotiations with Woodside, the project operator. Woodside remains sceptical about downstream processing and is currently agreeable only to co-investing in the "upstream" offshore elements of the project.

Uncertain Future of the Greater Sunrise Field

Woodside's ongoing hesitation to commit to the downstream processing vision of the Timor-Leste government raises questions about who else would co-invest in the onshore components of the project, and how much of Timor-Leste's oil and gas petroleum fund of US$17 billion—on which the country's annual budget largely depends—would be spent on the daunting capital expenditure. Timor-Leste's annual budget has increased by 11 per cent per year on average, exceeding the interest generated by the fund. By most estimates, Timor-Leste's sovereign wealth petroleum fund will need to find new revenue sources by 2035 to sustain the progressively growing annual budget. In the meantime, little progress has been made towards diversifying the economy, which could undermine Timor-Leste's long-term economic viability.

With existing petroleum funds sufficient only to cover the annual budget for the next ten years, a determined effort to build consensus on necessary policies becomes imperative to ensure Timor-Leste can sustain the income stream from its offshore oil and gas domains. Reaching a settlement over the future of the Greater Sunrise fields will bring new focus to the bilateral relationship with Australia. An initial step towards this objective is currently under way through the ongoing concept study for the field development by Woodside and its joint venture partners, Timor GAP and Japan's Osaka Gas.[10]

While previous Gusmão-led governments promised far larger revenue streams than what would be received from downstream processing in Australia, civil society remains critical, including leading non-governmental organization La'o Hamutuk, which has contended that the "risks, benefits and costs" of downstream processing "have not been seriously analyzed".[11] Despite such critiques, some observers have argued that Timor-Leste has been able to avoid the political "resource curse".[12] This term refers to the paradoxical situation where abundant resource endowments can foster corruption, conflict and instability. So far, the country has consistently maintained free and fair elections, undergone regular changes of government, adhered strongly to liberal democratic norms, and achieved a Freedom House ranking surpassing those of other Southeast Asian countries, despite some concerns over rising corruption and clientelism in politics.

Labour Migration

Timor-Leste has formal labour migration agreements with Australia and South Korea. Additionally, many workers have in the past taken advantage of their Portuguese passports to work in the United Kingdom and Portugal. Timor-Leste joined Australia's Pacific Labour Scheme in 2019, and Timorese workers had also participated in the earlier Seasonal Worker Programme since 2012. There are presently some 3,830 Timorese workers in Australia under both schemes, and remittances from those workers contribute significantly to the income of their families in Timor-Leste.[13] In 2023, the Australian government announced a new Pacific Engagement visa for fourteen regional states, including Timor-Leste, with a commitment of 3,000 visas to be distributed among the Pacific Island nations. This scheme would provide "green card" style access to Australia, with the possibility of permanent residence. Other substantial labour schemes include the South Korean Employer Permit System, which has facilitated employment in South Korea for around 3,700 Timorese people since 2006. Estimates of the number of East Timorese working in Portugal and the United Kingdom, especially Northern Ireland, are less precise, but they are roughly calculated at around 20,000.[14]

Foreign Policy

Accession to ASEAN continues to remain the primary goal of Timor-Leste's foreign policy. It achieved a great stride forward in November 2022 when ASEAN agreed "in principle" to admit Timor-Leste as its eleventh member, subject to meeting certain "milestones" that would be assessed by ASEAN member states in 2023.[15] The statement adopted at the 41st ASEAN Summit during Cambodia's 2022 chairmanship considered several ASEAN fact-finding missions to Timor-Leste and granted observer status to Dili in the meantime to facilitate its access to all ASEAN meetings. The statement also required an "objective criteria-based roadmap" for Timor-Leste's full membership based on "milestones", which were latter discussed in 2023. These included "the required physical infrastructure and logistics readiness to host meetings" and "sufficient English-speaking personnel in all relevant line ministries and agencies".[16] Since meeting these requirements continues to be a big challenge for the new nation, questions arise as to when the regional organization will grant Timor-Leste's full accession and whether Timor-Leste is adequately prepared for the membership. There are also ongoing domestic debates within civil society over the merits of Timor-Leste's accession to ASEAN.[17]

In a surprising move, new prime minister Xanana Gusmão openly said that ASEAN had an obligation to resolve the human rights crisis in Myanmar,[18] and could not accept the military regime overturning elections. His outspoken position on Myanmar in 2023 essentially challenged the ASEAN principle of non-interference. Gusmão went on to state that Timor-Leste would reconsider its ASEAN application if the organization could not make progress towards peace in Myanmar. Timor-Leste also declared that it would allow Myanmar pro-democracy groups to open offices in the country and accept a number of political refugees. Notably, Zin Mar Aung, the foreign minister for Myanmar's National Unity Government, had attended Gusmão's inauguration earlier in the year. In response, the military regime in Myanmar expelled Timor-Leste's chargé d'affaires, Avelino Pereira. Timor-Leste condemned the expulsion and restated its solidary with the people of Myanmar.[19] Though Gusmão later described some of his earlier remarks as "uncontrolled" and off-script, the two Timorese leaders continued to speak out over Myanmar as the year progressed. President Ramos-Horta later explained that their position acknowledged the support of solidarity groups in Myanmar towards East Timorese people during the Indonesian occupation of East Timor, and that his country could not accept election results being overturned by force, promising to raise the issue at the UN in the near future.[20] Elsewhere, Timor-Leste has maintained its support for the self-determination process in Western Sahara, a position it has upheld since the restoration of independence in 2002.[21]

In 2023, Timor-Leste's bilateral relations with Australia, notably strained in the past, have seen significant improvement, though it remains a complex relationship. The complexity is exemplified in the 2023 recipients of the Ordem de Timor-Leste, the highest honour in the country. Among the awardees included Victorian premier Steve Bracks, who has served as a high-level adviser to Xanana Gusmão on government reform. Well-linked to both the Australian government and Xanana Gusmão, Bracks has been tasked to represent Australia in a joint review process examining the feasibility of different downstream processing options, known as the concept review process for the development of Greater Sunrise.

At the same time, the award also went to lawyer Bernard Collaery. In 2013, alongside a former agent of the Australian Secret Intelligence Service known as Witness K, Collaery came forward to reveal that Australia had bugged the Timor-Leste cabinet during the sensitive oil and gas treaty negotiations in 2004. The revelation significantly contributed to Timor-Leste's successful challenge to a 2004 oil and gas treaty, which had prevented a maritime boundary determination and focussed exclusively on revenue sharing. In 2018, both countries reached agreement on the establishment of a median-line maritime boundary. Collaery made a visit to Dili to receive the award from President Ramos-Horta, marking his first overseas trip since his passport was confiscated by the Australian government over charges that were subsequently dropped. His arrival in Dili was met with a hero's welcome at the airport.

In September 2023, Timor-Leste signed a Comprehensive Strategic Partnership (CSP) agreement with the People's Republic of China. A joint statement by Xi Jinping and Xanana Gusmão announced that the partnership heralded an era of increased cooperation and "mutual political solidarity".[22] The agreement represented a significant upgrading in the status of the bilateral relations, and domestic commentators expected the CSP with China to bring benefits to Timor-Leste, particularly through China's capacity to aid in the development of productive sectors for economic diversification.[23] This announcement raised fears in Australian foreign policy and media circles about a potential shift in Timor-Leste's foreign policy.[24] Specifically, there were apprehensions that the CSP might have been secured in exchange for China's active support for downstream processing from the Greater Sunrise fields in Timor-Leste. While these concerns were to be expected, they were likely exaggerated. Timor-Leste swiftly reaffirmed its "friends to all" approach to foreign policy. Observers also noted that there were no concrete signs of China's interest in the Tasi Mane project to date, and that China is currently reassessing its

Belt and Road investments to reduce its risk exposure.[25] While the CSP agreement mentioned the possibility of "high-level military exchanges", Timor Leste's major cooperation partners in defence remain Australia and Portugal. President Ramos-Horta accused elements of the Australian foreign policy establishment and media of "imagining Chinese ghosts",[26] and later clarified that Australia remains Timor-Leste's "preferred defence and security partner".[27]

Conclusion

The wider significance of the 2022–23 election cycles relates to the question of generational transition of leadership power. Following the 2023 parliamentary election, the "old firm" of Gusmão and Ramos-Horta was back in power. But Gusmão's victory came as he approached seventy-seven, with other key leaders, including Ramos-Horta, not far behind. This raised the expectation that long overdue political transitions to a younger generation of leaders would take place during this parliamentary term. One key aspect of this question was the likely future leadership of non-FRETILIN politics, whenever Gusmão eventually departs the stage. For its part, FRETILIN, now Timor-Leste's oldest party, is facing grave challenges of its own in terms of internal tensions and discord following its record low vote share in 2023.

As the new government took office in July 2023, Timor-Leste embarked on a pivotal decade that holds immense significance for its future. The nation faces the imperative task of diversifying its economy away from dependence on oil and gas and also faces a major demographic "youth bulge". In what could potentially be their farewell terms, the "old firm" of Xanana Gusmão and Jose Ramos-Horta was given a strong mandate to shape the legacy they leave behind, in a nation whose independence they played a pivotal role in securing. How they will deliver this will be closely watched at this critical juncture of Timor-Leste's development.

Notes

1. "Sondagem aponta CNRT como partido com mais apoio nas eleições em Timor-Leste" [Poll points to CNRT as the party with most support in the elections in Timor-Leste], *Observador*, 15 April 2023, https://observador.pt/2023/04/15/sondagem-aponta-cnrt-como-partido-com-mais-apoio-nas-eleicoes-em-timor-leste/.

2. Fundasaun Mahein, "Politicisation of Martial Arts Groups: Implications for National Security and the 2023 Parliamentary Election", *Fundasaun Mahein*, 17 April 2023, https://www.fundasaunmahein.org/2023/04/17/politicisation-of-martial-arts-groups-implications-for-national-security-and-the-2023-parliamentary-election/.

3. Jacob Greber and John Kehoe, "Labor-Greens Gas Deal Tips Scales to East Timor on Sunrise Project", *Australian Financial Review*, 3 April 2023, https://www.afr.com/policy/energy-and-climate/labor-greens-gas-deal-tips-scales-to-east-timor-on-sunrise-project-20230403-p5cxpy.

4. Daniel Hurts, "'Not in the Spirit of Our Friendship': Penny Wong Concedes Past Australian Wrongs in Timor-Leste", *The Guardian Australia*, 7 July 2023, https://www.theguardian.com/australia-news/2023/jul/07/penny-wong-concedes-past-australian-wrongs-in-timor-leste.

5. Reporters without Borders, Press Freedom Index, 2023, https://rsf.org/en/index.

6. Camilo da Sousa, "Eighteen Women Elected as Village Heads", *Tatoli*, 14 November 2023, https://en.tatoli.tl/2023/11/14/eighteen-women-elected-as-village-heads/17/.

7. Sara Niner, Therese Nguyen Thi Phuong Tam, Emily Morrison, and Maria Evelina Iman, "Feto Bele: Contemporary Perceptions and Expectations of Women's Political Leadership in Timor-Leste", *International Feminist Journal of Politics*, 2023, https://doi.org/ 10.1080/14616742.2023.2203187.

8. "Vatican Official Bats for Martial Arts Groups in Timor-Leste", *UCA News*, 20 November 2023, https://www.ucanews.com/news/vatican-official-bats-for-martial-arts-groups-in-timor-leste/103318.

9. Website of the Government of Timor-Leste, "Programme of the 9th Constitutional Government", 19 July 2023, http://timor-leste.gov.tl/wp-content/uploads/2023/07/EN-Programa-IX-Governo.pdf.

10. "Woodside Gets OK from East Timor to Start Work on Sunrise Concept Study", LNG Prime, 22 November 2023, https://lngprime.com/contracts-and-tenders/woodside-gets-ok-from-east-timor-to-start-work-on-sunrise-concept-study/98369/.

11. La'o Hamutuk, "Submission to Committee C, National Parliament of Timor-Leste from La'o Hamutuk Regarding the Proposed General State Budget for 2021", 13 November 2020, http://laohamutuk.org/econ/OGE21/LHSubOJE2021-13Nov2020en.pdf.

12. Moritz Schmoll and Geoffrey Swenson, "How Timor-Leste Escaped the Political 'Resource Curse'", *The Diplomat*, 20 October 2023, https://thediplomat.com/2023/10/how-timor-leste-escaped-the-political-resource-curse/.

13. Australian Government, "BP0019 Number of Temporary visa holders in Australia at 2023-09-30", 2023, https://data.gov.au/dataset/ds-dga-ab245863-4dea-4661-a334-71ee15937130/distribution/dist-dga-54b2d02b-45bf-4c2d-a2bd-d9a9064f365c/details?q=&fbclid=IwAR11XuB1SNy-LVC23mIB_DcRkx3TLcBNWxZds7xUSeMCpL Mo6Cb-i4u64cA.

14. Michael Rose, "The Transnational Village in Timor-Leste", *Australian Journal of Anthropology*, https://doi.org/10.1111/taja.12454.

15. ASEAN, "ASEAN Leader's Statement on the Application of Timor-Leste for ASEAN Membership", 2022, https://asean.org/wp-content/uploads/2022/11/05-ASEAN-Leaders-Statement-on-the-Application-of-Timor-Leste-for-ASEAN-Membership.pdf.

16. Parker Novak, "Timor-Leste update: Parliamentary Elections and a Roadmap to ASEAN Membership", *Lowy Interpreter*, 17 May 2023, https://www.lowyinstitute.org/the-interpreter/timor-leste-update-parliamentary-elections-roadmap-asean-membership.

17. See, for example, La'o Hamutuk, "ASEAN and Free Trade", 23 May 2013 update, https://www.laohamutuk.org/econ/ASEAN/10ASEAN.htm.

18. Lil-Li Chen, "Why Timor-Leste Decided to Take a Stand on Myanmar", *The Diplomat*, 5 September 2023, https://thediplomat.com/2023/09/why-timor-leste-decided-to-take-a-stand-on-myanmar/.

19. Filomeno Martins, "TL Condemns Expulsion of Timorese Diplomat and Reiterates Its Solidarity with Myanmar People", *Tatoli*, 28 August 2023, https://en.tatoli.tl/2023/08/28/tl-condemns-expulsion-of-timorese-diplomat-and-reiterates-its-solidarity-with-myanmar-people/16/.

20. Rebecca Tan, "Asia's Youngest Nation Emerges as Voice of Conscience on Myanmar", *Washington Post*, 3 October 2023, https://www.washingtonpost.com/world/2023/10/03/east-timor-leste-myanmar-asean-military/.

21. Sahara Press Service, "Prime Minister of Timor-Leste Calls for Application of International Law to Counter Moroccan Expansionist Ambitions", 19 November 2023, https://www.spsrasd.info/en/2023/11/19/1237.html.

22. Helen Davidson, "'Playing the China Card' or a Serious Regional Threat? Timor-Leste's New Deal with Beijing", *The Guardian Australia*, 28 September 2023, https://www.theguardian.com/world/2023/sep/28/playing-the-china-card-or-a-serious-regional-threat-timor-lestes-new-deal-with-beijing-australia.

23. Joao da Cruz Cardoso, "Why Did Timor-Leste Sign a Comprehensive Strategic Partnership with China?", *The Diplomat*, 11 October 2023, https://thediplomat.com/2023/10/what-did-timor-leste-sign-a-comprehensive-strategic-partnership-with-china/.

24. James Curran, "Dili's China Deal Gives Two Fingers to Canberra", *Australian Financial Review*, 25 September 2023, https://www.afr.com/policy/foreign-affairs/dili-s-china-deal-gives-two-fingers-to-canberra-20230925-p5e7eb.

25. Parker Novak, "Timor-Leste's Uncertain Future", *Lowy Interpreter*, 29 November 2023, https://www.lowyinstitute.org/publications/timor-leste-s-uncertain-future.

26. The partnership statement promised to "enhance high-level military exchanges, strengthen cooperation in areas such as personnel training, equipment technology, the conduct of joint exercises and training". See Helen Davidson, "Timor-Leste President Hits Back at Australian Criticism of New Partnership with China", *The Guardian Australia*, 3 October 2023, https://www.theguardian.com/world/2023/oct/03/timor-leste-president-jose-ramos-horta-hits-back-at-australian-criticism-of-new-partnership-with-china.

27. Daniel Hurts, "José Ramos-Horta Says Australian Intelligence Agencies 'Know Very Well' China Deal Is of No Concern", *The Guardian Australia*, 29 September

2023, https://www.theguardian.com/world/2023/sep/29/jose-ramos-horta-timor-leste-president-china-strategic-partnership-australian-intelligence-agencies.

Vietnam

HANOI
Hai Phong
Hue
Da Nang
Quy Nhon
Buon
Ma Thuot
Cam Ranh
Ho Chi Minh City
Can Tho

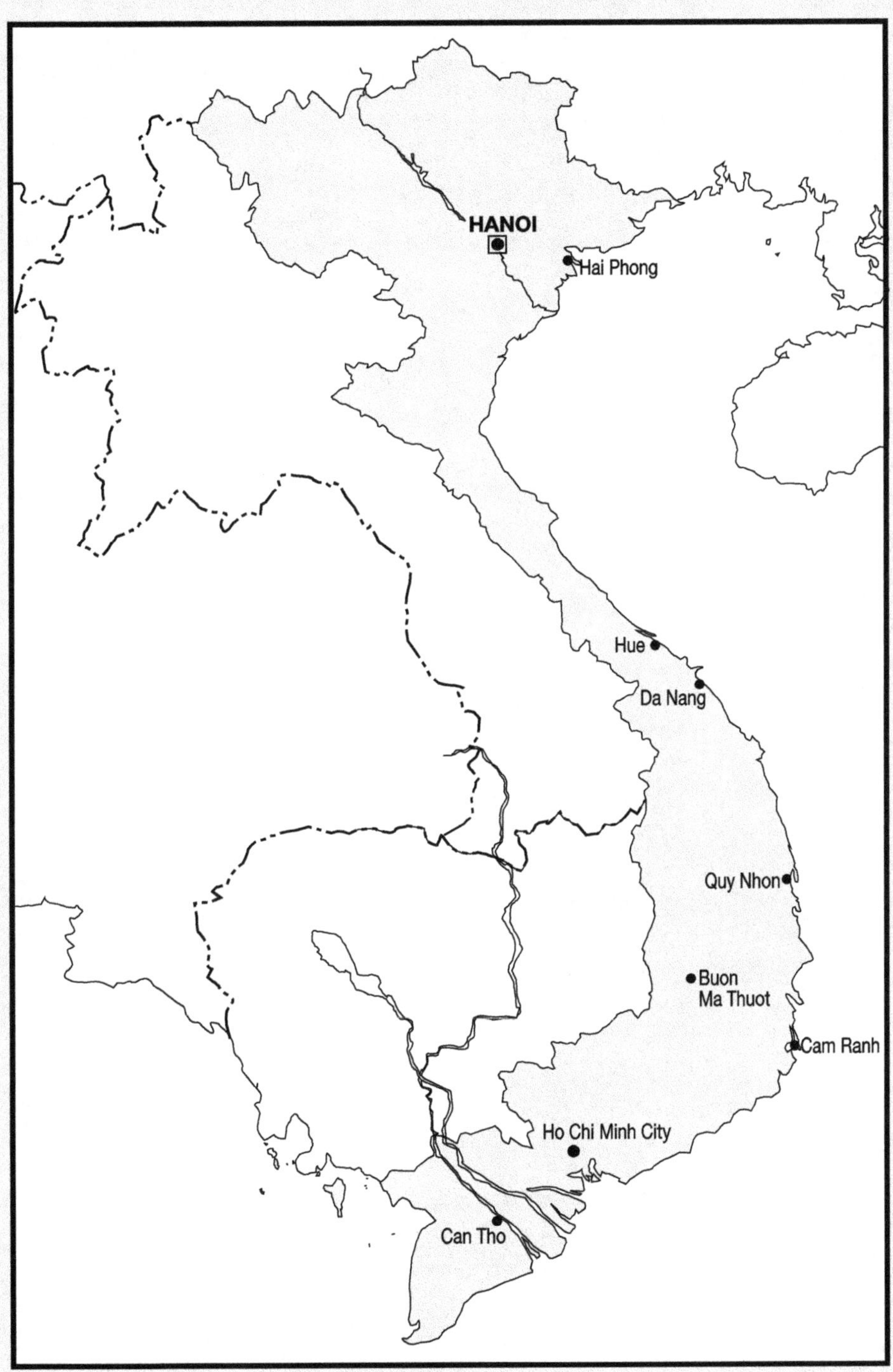

VIETNAM IN 2023:
Stoking the Embers of the "Blazing Furnace"

Edmund J. Malesky and Thiem Hai Bui

Fuelled by the scalding heat of Vietnam's "blazing furnace" (*đốt lò*) anti-corruption campaign, the year 2023 roared both in and out. In January, an investigation into bribery and overcharging for Covid-19 test kits and evacuation flights led to the dismissal of three prominent Vietnamese technocrats, including then president Nguyen Xuan Phuc. In December, an ongoing investigation into Truong My Lan—chairwoman of the Van Thinh Phat (VTP) group and one of Vietnam's highest-profile and richest tycoons—revealed a staggering graft scheme, estimated to encompass over US$44 billion and involving dozens of accomplices in the business sector, bureaucracy and government.[1] The implications of the "blazing furnace", however, are far greater than the counting of punished officials and vast sums of corruption money. The effort to root out corruption at the core of the Vietnamese regime is fundamentally altering the country's political economy. The changes that are unfolding have the potential to dramatically influence Vietnam's economic and political development trajectory in both positive and negative ways.

At the elite level, political analysts have observed that the Vietnamese leadership is more consolidated under the general secretary of the Vietnamese Communist Party (VCP), Nguyen Phu Trong, than at any time since the dawn of the Renovation (*Đổi mới*) era in 1986.[2] A key feature of Vietnam's renovation-era polity has been the implicit division of powers between the country's top leaders (general secretary, prime minister, president and national assembly speaker). The

EDMUND J. MALESKY is Professor of Political Economy at Duke University, Director of the Duke Center for International Development, and Chair of the Executive Council of the Southeast Asian Research Group.

THIEM HAI BUI is Senior Lecturer at VNU University of Economics and Business, Hanoi, and Fulbright Scholar at Duke University.

distribution of authority among these "four pillars" enabled greater diversity of opinions in the collective leadership. This structure generated veto points that facilitated thoughtful deliberation and slowed policy change. It also incentivized the redistribution of resources from regions benefitting from globalization to the more disadvantaged ones.

The downstream effects of elite consolidation are also tangible, as the press, social media and civil society, especially environmental NGOs, have come under greater scrutiny and constraints,[3] leading to what some analysts have called a "chilling effect" on public discourse. This effect was amplified on 15 November when Luu Binh Nhuong, deputy head of the National Assembly Commission for Public Petitions, a high-profile commentator on public affairs, was arrested on confusing charges of embezzlement. At the bureaucratic level, fears about being targeted by the "blazing furnace" have slowed government procurement as both officials and businesses remain uncertain of the new rules of engagement. Numerous provinces were slow to spend public money on official projects, including the country's economic capital, Ho Chi Minh City, which had only spent twenty-three per cent of its planned budget by the year's midpoint.[4] The difficulties are likely to remain until new systems are put in place that give local officials confidence that procurement can take place in a lawful and transparent manner. In terms of foreign policy, the campaign provided an important backdrop in shaping the terms of Vietnam's major foreign policy achievements, including joining the Just Energy Transition Partnership (JETP) and establishing the Comprehensive Strategic Partnership with the United States.

The Blazing Furnace Campaign

While Vietnam has attempted numerous anti-corruption efforts during its reform era, both domestic and international corruption evaluations continued to rank Vietnam as performing poorly, and most objective experts would have defined the leadership as lacking political will for anti-corruption efforts. Between 2012 and 2016, anti-corruption efforts were reinvigorated by several high-level corruption scandals involving critically important state-owned enterprises (SOEs) and several high-ranking officials. After former prime minister Nguyen Tan Dung left office and General Secretary Nguyen Phu Trong asserted power in 2017, Trong initiated a renewed effort to root out corruption at its source. He coined the term "blazing furnace" at a meeting of the Central Steering Committee for Anti-Corruption in July 2017 when he lamented the effect of corruption in holding back economic growth and vowed to punish the officials involved. He has been true to his word. Since

2016, nearly 200,000 party members, including 5 Politburo members, 36 Central Committee members and 50 military and police generals, have been disciplined. Some of these have made national headlines, including two high-flying deputy prime ministers and President Nguyen Xuan Phuc, who was officially dismissed from office for wrongdoings and violations by officials under his management because of his connections to the Viet A test-kit scandal.[5]

Two other components of the "blazing furnace" efforts have been less attention-grabbing but are equally important. First, Trong led a rewriting of VCP statutes to reduce malfeasance by limiting the permissible types of financial and business transactions. Second, the government pushed forward a series of e-governance reforms that has moved several public procedures and services online to streamline them and reduce opportunities for discretion by bureaucrats. Efforts to reduce petty corruption have spurred attempts to transform the country's e-governance with plans to move 90 per cent of the country's administrative procedures and 80 per cent of public service applications online by 2030.[6] The effort is intended to combat corruption by reducing bottlenecks in official transactions and discretion by bureaucratic gatekeepers.

On the positive side of the ledger, anti-corruption mobilization has been successful: businesses report striking declines in the frequency and size of bribe payments. Today, 43 per cent of businesses report that informal charges are common compared to 66 per cent in 2016, and only 3.8 per cent of businesses make bribe payments greater than 10 per cent of annual revenue, compared to 9.1 per cent in 2016.[7] Vietnamese citizens also report lower levels of bribery to local government in accessing public services and state employment and are more likely to believe the government is willing to combat corrupt activities.[8]

A striking feature of recent years that continued in 2023 is the willingness to target Vietnam's high-flying tycoons. Two cases stood out above the rest. First, the chairwoman and general director of Advanced International Stock Company (AIC), Nguyen Thi Thanh Nhan, was sentenced to thirty years in prison for bid rigging and paying procurement kickbacks for sixteen contracts in the supply of medical equipment to Dong Nai General Hospital. The malfeasance likely netted the powerful real estate magnate over US$6.3 million. The trial also led to the convictions of thirty-five other accomplices in business and government. While Nhan was found guilty for her role in AIC, speculation circulated in media and online that Dong Nai was part of a behaviour pattern that she had displayed in other provinces, including Quang Ninh, the home of Ha Long Bay.[9] Although the AIC scandal was distinguished for its elite political ramifications, the VTP case stands apart for its sheer size and brazenness. VTP chairwoman Truong My Lan stands accused of exploiting her financial control of Saigon Commercial Bank (SCB) to take out over US\$44 billion in customer deposits as loans. The theft, which was authorized by SCB leadership, whom she controlled, and State Bank of Vietnam officers, whom she bribed, amounts to over three per cent of Vietnam's 2022 GDP. By sheer size, it is the largest corruption scandal in world history, dwarfing Malaysia's 1MDB scandal. The Ministry of Public Security has recommended the arrest of eighty-six government, business and family collaborators.[10]

Consolidation of Elite Power

After the January resignation of President Phuc, the Politburo nominated Vo Van Thuong, a standing member of the Secretariat of the Communist Party and a close ally of General Secretary Trong, to replace him. To Lam, the powerful minister of public security, was also considered as a candidate but removed himself from consideration.[11] On 2 March, the National Assembly passed a resolution confirming the appointment, making Thuong the youngest Vietnamese president since the country's unification in 1975. Thuong has been a Politburo member since 2016 and a Central Committee member since 2011. He has had a diverse career, including stints in the party secretariats of Ho Chi Minh City and Quang Ngai Province as well as in the leadership of the Central Propaganda Department of Ho Chi Minh Youth Union. His most important credential, however, may have been his perceived role as the de facto leader of the small southern wing in the top echelon of the party leadership.

Some refer to the presidency, which is constitutionally Vietnam's head of state, as a ceremonial position.[12] But this characterization neglects the significant formal powers the president has as chairman of the Council for Defence and Security and head of the Steering Committee on Judicial Reform. It also undersells the important informal powers the president has as the second-highest rank in the Politburo.

Several Vietnamese analysts noted the close career connections that Thuong has with General Secretary Trong as well as the fact that both of them cut their teeth on the party and ideological side of the party-state as opposed to the more technocratic government apparatus. Thuong also appeared to confirm the alliance in his first speech in the office when the new president declared that he would "resolutely" continue the fight against corruption. Thus, Vietnamese experts interpreted the appointment of Thuong as another step in the consolidation of power under Trong,[13] who is already serving an unprecedented third term in office.[14] Of the current top four pillars, both Thuong and National Assembly

Speaker Vuong Dinh Hue are considered to be politically aligned with Trong, while Prime Minister Pham Minh Chinh is an independent thinker in a historically powerful position but may have had his wings clipped through exposure to another anti-corruption investigation.[15] Unlike China, Vietnam has never had clear factional divides. The system did, however, permit alliances around critical policy and personnel debates, seeing a diversity of opinions at elite levels.[16] That diversity is now severely diminished both in the Politburo and among the four pillars of elite leadership.

Legal analysts took note of how Phuc was removed from office, as the legal changes that precipitated it seemed to indicate a shift in the balance of authority to the party leadership. According to the Vietnamese constitution and Decision 260-QD/TW adopted in 2009, only the National Assembly possesses the power to remove a senior leader who seriously violates the law or party decrees. Decision 260 made clear that even a voluntary resignation, as in the case of Phuc, could be rescinded if it negatively affected the country's normal business. However, Decision 260 was withdrawn in 2021 in favour of Decision 41-QD/TW, which simplified procedures and grounds for the dismissal and resignation of public officials. The legal change removed a veto point in the punishment of senior officials, placing greater authority in the hands of the general secretary. Decision 96-QD/TW in 2023 reinforced the consolidation of authority under the party by subjecting every party and state leader to a mid-term vote of confidence by the Party Central Committee.[17]

The emphasis on anti-corruption and subsequent consolidation of authority continued at the 8th Plenum of the Party Central Committee in October—evident both in who left and who arrived. Dak Nong Province's vice party secretary Dieu K'Ré and Ben Tre Province's party secretary Le Duc Tho were both dismissed from the Central Committee after investigations by the Central Inspection Commission. Their removals were the fourteenth and fifteenth dismissals thus far during the term of the current Central Committee, which still has two years remaining—more than twice the number of dismissals in the two previous Central Committee terms. At the same time, the promotion of Le Hoai Trung, head of the Party Central Committee's External Relations Commission, paved the way for his retention at the top post overseeing the party-state's foreign affairs in the next party congress. Some speculated that this was his reward for stewarding the upgrading of US-Vietnam relations. In addition, Vu Hong Van, director of the Internal Political Security Bureau of the Ministry of Public Security (MPS) was promoted to the Party Central Inspection Commission, a strong signal that the "blazing furnace" will continue burning.[18]

Preparations are now beginning for the next party congress, to be held in 2026. First, a large-scale reshuffling of cadres between the central and the local leadership has been initiated. Many provincial leaders have been transferred to positions at the central agencies, and many new "strategic cadres" have been deployed to provinces to be trained and groomed for higher political positions. Second, study groups and research projects have been set up by the VCP to review and revise major policies for the upcoming congress. Among the most important issues on the agenda will be Vietnam's ongoing economic transformation.

Economic Performance

Vietnam's economy struggled in 2023 because of a confluence of international and domestic factors. The downturn was a severe disappointment after Vietnam recorded a real GDP growth rate of 8 per cent in 2022—one of the highest growth rates in the world and during the country's economic reform era. Vietnam's strong economic performance in 2022 appeared to signal a healthy recovery from the declines in investment and consumer confidence induced by Covid-19. In the first six months of 2023, however, the economy sputtered to a 3.7 per cent year-on-year real growth rate.[19]

As an export-oriented economy (exports account for 50 per cent of GDP), Vietnam has been negatively affected by the deceleration in global economic and trade growth. The ongoing conflict in Ukraine also had detrimental effects on the country by disrupting supply chains and causing increases in food and energy prices. In addition to the indirect effects of global inflationary pressures, Vietnam was one of Ukraine's five largest trading partners and one of its largest consumers of wheat, iron ore and corn, and one of its largest sources of electronics, garments and fish fillets. The combination of international factors culminated in a dramatic decline in exports of 11.6 per cent, from US$371 billion in 2022 to an expected US$332.82 in 2023. In November 2023, Vietnam registered a trade deficit of 8 per cent, the largest recorded in twenty-five years.[20]

Declining export and manufacturing performance in 2023 led to layoffs of a large number of workers in Vietnam's industrial hubs. PouYuen, a Taiwanese company in Ho Chi Minh City, announced severance pay of US$11.5 million after laying off 3,000 workers and failing to renew contracts for another 3,000.[21] PouYuen was far from alone. A survey by the Private Sector Development Committee found that 71.2 per cent of companies reported cutting at least 5 per cent of their workforce, and the Vietnam General Confederation of Labour reported that 48,600 workers were fired and 547,000 workers had hours reduced at 1,300 companies. As a result of the downturn, export hubs in the Southeast region, which encircles Ho Chi Minh City, reported a 62 per cent increase in the number of people receiving unemployment benefits in the second quarter of 2023. At the same time, the General Statistical Office (GSO) reported that 302,000 people were pushed into informal work as a result of layoffs.[22] Instability in the export market exacerbated a trend of employees taking early withdrawals of their one-time lump sum social insurance payments. The swell has dangerous consequences for both the long-term economic health of the employees and Vietnam's fiscal balance. The National Assembly has plans to stem the tide with a revised social insurance law in the next session. Rumours that the law will severely restrict early withdrawals, however, inadvertently created a dilemma of more workers claiming one-time payments before the legal changes take effect.[23]

While most of the layoffs occurred in the foreign manufacturing sector, one bright spot in Vietnam's international economic performance has been the country's resilient attractiveness to new foreign investors. In the first ten months of 2023, the country attracted US$15.3 billion in new projects—a 54 per cent year-on-year increase—with 73 per cent of the foreign capital being for manufacturing projects.[24] A key factor in the FDI surge is diversification away from China fuelled by the ongoing trade conflict between the United States and China as many Trump-era tariffs remain in effect.[25] In addition, investors report being attracted by Vietnam's historical growth (including the 2022 boom), an educated but relatively cheap labour force, improving infrastructure, and stable government.[26] Among the new investors is the Danish LEGO group, which is set to build a US$1.3 billion factory in southern Binh Duong province. The company has plans to build one of its most modern and environmentally friendly factories in Vietnam and to recruit thousands of new workers next year.[27] The silver lining of FDI performance was marred somewhat by news that a planned Intel expansion would be delayed and that Danish energy company Ørsted was exiting its investment in Vietnamese wind energy, claiming that its "business ethics have met hurdles", shedding new light on the ongoing need to root out corruption.[28]

The year 2023 was also a rough one for the domestic economy. Growth in domestic demand fell to 2.7 per cent in the first half of the year compared with 6.1 per cent over the same period in 2022. Industrial production fell sharply in the first half of the year, hitting a record low in January before stabilizing and recovering at the end of the year. Domestic enterprises also struggled, with over 135,000 businesses either temporarily or permanently ceasing operations. This represents a dramatic 21 per cent increase over the same period for the previous year and far exceeds the number of 116,000 newly registered businesses. Struggles are likely to continue as the PCI Business Thermometer, a leading indicator of business performance, reports that only 27.6 per cent of domestic businesses plan to increase their investments in the next year. This marks the lowest figure in the history of the survey, even falling below the 2012–13 economic crisis when 32 per cent of businesses had plans for expansion.[29]

Struggles in the domestic economy were particularly evident in the stagnation of real estate and financial markets. Several major real estate developers, which had accumulated enormous debts over the past few years, faced severe financial distress. The situation further deteriorated as global interest rates increased to counter inflation, putting pressure on the Vietnamese Dong, and anti-corruption investigators intensified their scrutiny of illegal transactions within the sector—particularly those by VTP and former chairman of FLC, Trinh Van Quyet.[30] Investigations and fears of being caught up in future land scandals impeded the acquisition of land titles and construction permits, resulting in sharp declines in sales. Licensing of residential housing projects, for instance, declined from 18,700 in the first quarter of 2022 to 7,200 in the first quarter of 2023, while over 235 real estate firms went out of business. Banks exposed to the real estate sector experienced corresponding declines in asset quality—56 real estate developers, including the country's second biggest, defaulted on bond payments in 2023. Real estate and construction accounted for over 30 per cent of corporate bond defaults and over 75 per cent of the total default value.[31]

A key controversy in Vietnam's current economic doldrums pertains to the roll-out of public investment. The urgent need for public spending, especially on critical infrastructure improvements, led the World Bank to publish a special report on the issue. The report highlighted that Vietnam's public investment had declined from 8 per cent of GDP in 2011 to 6 per cent currently, with a substantial gap of 22 per cent between budgeting and execution in 2022. Journalists and economic analysts attributed this situation to the anti-corruption campaign. They argued that provincial bureaucrats felt uncertain about proper procedures for government procurement and delayed expenditures on planned projects while waiting for legal and regulatory clarity.[32] National Assembly delegate Nguyen Huu Thong encapsulated the situation in a speech to the parliament: "State cadres and civil servants, including leaders, do not dare to work because if they do, they are afraid of making mistakes." Consequently, in the first half of the year, several provinces fell behind in their planned expenditures. By July 2023, Ho Chi Minh City had spent only 23 per cent of the money budgeted for infrastructure and construction (US$652 million), resulting in delays in crucial transportation and infrastructure projects. Other provinces were reported to have returned unspent transfers to the central government. Vietnamese authorities highlighted the importance of public investment in propelling economic growth in a public statement on the General Statistics Office website, which reported increases in both public spending allocations and their implementation in 2023.[33]

Environment and Energy

Over the past four decades, Vietnam's economic growth and dynamism have been miraculous, lifting millions out of poverty and propelling the country to middle-income status. But this sterling economic performance has not been costless. With fifteen per cent of its land below sea level and a coastline spanning 3,260 kilometres, Vietnam is already among the world's most vulnerable countries to the effects of climate change. It is also facing emerging threats from environmental degradation and pollution.[34] Air pollution caused by heavy industry (such as steel, cement, and coal-fired plants), construction and transportation is estimated to have caused roughly fifty thousand deaths annually and economic losses in the region of 4.45–5.64 per cent of Vietnam's GDP. Vietnamese citizens have been increasingly vocal in denouncing environmental accidents and have expressed strong misgivings about economic growth and investments that do not sufficiently safeguard the environment.[35] The Asian Development Bank has projected that if Vietnam maintains its current carbon-intensive energy mix, those sectors will account for 86 per cent of the country's total net emissions by 2050.

At the same time, the country's rapid economic and investment growth requires corresponding increases in energy production that cannot be met by clean energy alone. Commercial electricity consumption is expected to reach approximately 335 billion kWh by 2025 and around 505.2 billion kWh by 2030. By 2050, it is anticipated that this figure will have increased to between 1,224 billion kWh and 1,378 billion kWh. Vietnam's energy demands were acutely felt in the summer of 2023, when the government was forced to implement rolling power outages in the north of the country, which disrupted productive activities and was estimated to cost the country US$1.4 billion—roughly 0.3 per cent of GDP.

The Vietnamese government is aware of these trade-offs and has begun the task of shifting towards a more sustainable economic model. Demonstrating its commitment to low-carbon development, Vietnam has ratified the Paris Agreement and is implementing its Nationally Determined Contribution (NDC). The country is projected to require over US$27 billion in investment by 2030 to meet its NDC targets. Key investments will support renewable energy and green infrastructure, including public transport, water, and waste management. To this end, in 2022,

Vietnam signed the Just Energy Transition Partnership (JETP) with a consortium of wealthy entities, which will provide Vietnam with US$15.5 billion to reduce its coal capacity and transition towards renewable energy.

In May 2023, the government ratified Decision 500/QD-TTg approving the National Electricity Development Plan for 2021–30, with a Vision to 2050. Commonly referred to as Power Development Plan 8 (PDP8), this master plan has been in development since the 13th Party Congress in January 2021. It aims to double the maximum power that Vietnam can generate to 150 gigawatts by 2030. The PDP8 further commits to reduce reliance on dirty coal production and not to build any more coal-fired power plants after 2030. Coal production will be replaced by expanded use of domestic and imported liquefied natural gas, which will account for about 25 per cent of total generating capacity, while hydropower, wind, solar and other renewable sources will account for nearly 50 per cent by 2030.[36]

As the year was drawing to an end, at the 2023 United Nations Climate Change Conference (COP 28) in Dubai, Prime Minister Chinh announced the government's resource mobilization plan to implement its JETP commitments. Vietnam would focus on twelve specific actions, including emission reductions, further development of the renewable energy industry, and low-emissions rice production.[37]

The anti-corruption campaign was present in climate and energy activities as well. In late December, the Party Central Inspection Commission publicly announced grave discipline measures for a number of leaders of the Ministry of Industry and Trade (MOIT), including former minister Tran Tuan Anh—now a Politburo member and head of the Party Central Economic Commission—for mismanagement, resulting in "serious violations of Party regulations and State laws in advising and promulgating policies for solar and wind power development in the implementation of the adjusted Power Development Plan (PDP) VII".[38] This move officially undercut any opportunity and ambition for Tran Tuan Anh, son of former president Tran Duc Luong, to extend his political career to the top party echelons. One day later, Do Thang Hai, the vice minister of MOIT, was arrested and prosecuted for mismanagement and accepting bribes.

Civil Society

A notable trend in Vietnam's current environmental and climate transition is the absence of cooperation from non-government organizations, which for many years played an important role in research, advocacy and fundraising for environmental causes and often worked collaboratively with local authorities. Beginning with the 2022 arrest of Nguy Thi Khanh—the 2018 Goldman Environmental Prize winner—Vietnam has arrested and imprisoned six climate activists on charges of tax evasion and appropriation of official documents. The most recent arrest was of Ngo Thi To Nhien, who led an energy think tank and had been working with officials from the Ministry of Natural Resources and Environment on the JETP.

It is unclear why authorities have specifically targeted environmental organizations instead of NGOs from other sectors. Some have speculated that the Vietnamese government wants to pursue environmental change on its own terms and is suspicious of the agenda and international connections of climate activists.[39] Others questioned whether environmental NGOs pose a threat to the interests of connected businesses.

Regardless of the motivation, other NGOs believe that the arrests have cast a "chilling effect" on civil society activity in the country.[40] Tax rules for businesses and non-profits can be opaque, and under-resourced NGOs have admitted to difficulties in ensuring a hundred per cent compliance. Similarly, the sharing of documents on social networking sites like WhatsApp is a very common practice that many NGO officers are only now realizing is illegal. According to data compiled by The 88 Project, Vietnam arrested 361 "activists" between 2016 and 2023—more than triple the number of arrests made between 2003 and 2015.[41]

The chill has been heightened by aggressive policing of online media activity to "thwart self-transformation that could threaten the regime's survival and combat erroneous and hostile viewpoints", as stipulated in Central Committee Resolution 04-NQ/TW. To this end, Resolution 35–NQ/TW established a steering committee to proactively counter hostile opinions and closely monitor the ideological beliefs of party members. Specialized agencies have been created to fight ideological battles in cyberspace and remove unwanted political content. Decree 53/2022/ND-CP, enacted by the government on 22 October to implement the 2018 Cyber Security Law, has further strengthened digital surveillance and enabled the censorship of online content.[42]

In line with these developments, in July 2023, *Zing News*, the award-winning and immensely popular online magazine, took a three-month hiatus after a state review concluded it had pursued topics beyond its remit. The punishment is part of a state effort to eliminate "news-ization" (*báo hoá*), which Vietnamese authorities define as efforts by magazines and aggregated information websites to mislead the public that they are news outlets. The crackdown is part of a larger effort to consolidate and increase state influence over mainstream media. While the action has been justified as an effort to reduce bureaucracy and streamline ownership structure in the media, it opens up possibilities for misuse and potential censorship.[43]

Foreign Affairs

In September 2023, the United States and Vietnam agreed to upgrade their diplomatic relationship to a "comprehensive strategic partnership", jumping two rungs from the "comprehensive partnership" level and elevating the United States to the same status as only five other countries, including Russia and China. The upgrade surprised some sceptics, who view the 2022 anti-corruption investigations against the president and deputy prime ministers as a sign of anti-US positioning. The upgrade was agreed upon during a historic visit of US president Joe Biden to Vietnam. During Biden's visit, the two countries agreed to cooperate on innovation-driven economic growth and environmental and health issues. The visit also paved the way for major business deals in the manufacturing of semiconductors and electric vehicles, and established firmer foundations for potential defence cooperation. Hanoi secured a significant symbolic victory as President Biden, while engaging all four pillars of the Vietnamese leadership, ultimately announced the agreement on upgrading Vietnam-US ties with General Secretary Trong. This act signifies Washington's de facto acknowledgement of the legitimacy of the country's one-party system. Simultaneously, Trong's endorsement conveyed to audiences in both Vietnam and China that the agreement held the full authority of the VCP.[44]

Some Western media depicted the strengthening of the Vietnam-US relationship as Vietnam moving into the American orbit. Such portrayals were exaggerated as the upgraded relationship was in line with Vietnam's "bamboo diplomacy" of pragmatic flexibility in navigating shifts in the strategic alignments of great powers to secure its national interests without taking sides. Vietnamese leaders also took steps to underscore to their Chinese counterparts that they value the relationship with Beijing, with whom they already maintain the highest level of diplomatic relations. On 20 October, President Thuong flew to Beijing to attend the 3rd Belt and Road Forum, where he held a meeting with President Xi Jinping. On 14 December, Xi paid a state visit to Vietnam. Cooperation on economic relations, infrastructure and energy was high on the discussion list. From China's perspective, the most important achievement of Xi's visit was Vietnam's commitment to join China's "community of common destiny". While Beijing trumpeted the agreement as an upgrading of foreign relations between the two countries, others saw it as consistent with Vietnam's "bamboo diplomacy" and policy of assurances to its northern neighbour without conceding any of its important national interests, such as maritime sovereignty.[45]

Continuing with Vietnam's multi-pronged strategy, President Thuong paid an official visit to Japan in November, announcing the upgrading of Vietnam-Japan relations to a "comprehensive strategic partnership" as well. Negotiations have also been intensified for the upgrading of relations with Australia, Indonesia and Singapore to the same level. By the end of 2023, the exclusive and special status of "comprehensive strategic partnership" in the hierarchy of Vietnam's external relations has been rather diluted, which demonstrates the country's commitment to diplomatic diversification and the flexibility and resilience of its "bamboo diplomacy".

In a final diplomatic achievement on 25 November, the Vietnamese National Assembly passed a top-up tax, which requires all companies operating in the country to pay a minimum corporate income tax rate of fifteen per cent to make up for gaps caused by tax incentives or profit-shifting. The law aligns with the effort by the Organization for Economic Cooperation and Economic Development to reduce global tax avoidance and ensure companies pay taxes where they carry out their production and sales. While this move may frustrate some investors, alignment with the global minimum tax, already approved by 140 other countries, should enhance Vietnam's ability to improve revenue collection for vital infrastructure, services and human capital development, allowing it to remain attractive to investors far into the future.[46]

Conclusion

There is no question that the anti-corruption campaign has shaped the course of Vietnam in the past year. It altered elite political configurations, untangled the linkages between major business tycoons and powerful politicians, affected the risk calculations of major foreign investors, slowed service delivery and public procurement, and through tax investigations confused the operations of civil society actors. At the same time, the campaign streamlined administrative procedures, reduced bureaucratic discretion, and reduced the costs and risks of doing business for numerous small and medium-sized enterprises. Some commentators viewed the major corruption scandals as proof of rot at the core of the Vietnamese regime. After all, these scandals are eye-wateringly big—made possible by numerous bureaucrats and politicians who were either co-opted or chose to turn a blind eye.[47]

Another way to think about the events unfolding in Vietnam in 2023 is that they potentially herald a new beginning, similar to the changes that once occurred in Singapore and Taiwan. Corruption has been a thorn in Vietnam since before the reform era, which has grown and morphed alongside the opening and transformation of the Vietnamese economy. For many years, the Vietnamese leadership has been worried that it would undermine the legitimacy of the regime and thwart economic transformation. Now, strong measures are being taken to confront bribery and graft head-on. However, change cannot happen overnight. New institutions and processes need to be established and all relevant actors must learn and adapt to new rules of the game. In this light, the headline-grabbing arrests can be seen as a sign that times are changing. Earlier, these transgressions, however enormous, may have remained hidden. Slowdowns in procurement can also be seen in this light. The old rules of doing business have been cast aside, but the new ones remain inchoate. As authorities establish these new institutions, including the plans for e-governance, businesses and officials will likely regain confidence to push for ambitious investments and revive economic dynamism.

Notes

1. Le Quynh, "Vietnam Politics: Power Shift as President Nguyen Xuan Phuc Quits", *BBC News*, 17 January 2023, https://www.bbc.com/news/world-asia-64302745; "Vạn Thịnh Phát: Vì sao bà Trương Mỹ Lan bị cho là 'rút của SCB' hơn 1 triệu tỷ VND mà bị xử lý 304.096 tỷ? [Van Thinh Phat: Why was Truong My Lan accused of withdrawing more than 1 billion VND from SCB, but was fined 304,096 billion VND?]", BBC Vietnamese, 28 November 2023, https://www.bbc.com/vietnamese/articles/cqep0lz0yq2o; Pham Du, "Van Thinh Phat Chairwoman Manipulates Lender SCB in $44B Scam", *VNexpress.net*, 19 November 2023. Lan was fined US$12.5 billion for the offenses.

2. Nguyen Khac Giang, "Vietnam's Anti-corruption Campaign: Economic and Political Impacts", *ISEAS Perspective* no. 2023/41, 18 May 2023; Edmund J. Malesky, "Enhancing Research on Authoritarian Regimes through Detailed Comparisons of China and Vietnam", *Problems of Post-Communism* 68, no. 3 (2021): 163–70.

3. Dien Nguyen An Luong, *A Study of Vietnam's Control over Online Anti-state Content*, Trends in Southeast Asia, no. 5/2022 (Singapore: ISEAS – Yusof Ishak Institute, 2022); Michael Taylor, "In Vietnam, Climate Arrests Spark Calls to Halt Entergy Transition Deal", Reuters, 19 October 2023, https://www.reuters.com/sustainability/cop/vietnam-climate-arrests-spark-calls-halt-energy-transition-deal-2023-10-20/.

4. "HCMC's Public Spending Tardy in First Half Despite Great Efforts", *VNExpress International*, 15 July 2023, https://e.vnexpress.net/news/business/economy/hcmc-s-public-spending-tardy-in-first-half-despite-great-efforts-4629545.html?utm_source=substack&utm_medium=email.

5. Nguyen Manh Hung, "Vietnam in 2017: Power Consolidation, Domestic Reforms, and Coping with New Geopolitical Challenges", in *Southeast Asian Affairs 2018*, edited by Malcolm Cook and Daljit Singh (Singapore: ISEAS – Yusof Ishak Institute, 2018), pp. 407–28; Nguyen Hai Hong, "Vietnam in 2020: The Year in Transition", in

Southeast Asian Affairs 2020, edited by Malcolm Cook and Daljit Singh (Singapore: ISEAS – Yusof Ishak Institute, 2020), pp. 381–404; Nguyen Khac Giang, "Vietnam's Anti-corruption".

6. Viet Tuan, "Vietnam Spells Out Ambitious E-Governance Targets", *VNExpress International*, 5 June 2020, https://e.vnexpress.net/news/news/vietnam-spells-out-ambitious-e-governance-targets-4110846.html.

7. Edmund Malesky, Pham Ngoc Thach, Truong Duc Trong, Phan Tuan Ngoc, and Quynh Nguyen, *The Vietnam Provincial Competitiveness Index: Measuring Economic Governance for Private Sector Development, 2022 Final Report* (Hanoi: Chamber of Commerce and Industry and United States Agency for International Development, 2023), p. 71.

8. CECODES, VVF, and UNDP, "The 2022 Viet Nam Governance and Public Administration Performance Index (PAPI 2022): Measuring Citizens' Experiences", technical report (CECODES, 2023), p. 10.

9. "Hanoi Court Sentences Former AIC Chairwoman to 30 Years in Prison", Radio Free Asia, 4 January 2023, https://www.rfa.org/english/news/vietnam/aic-trial-01042023223148.html; "Vụ NSJ-AIC ở Quảng Ninh: Quan chức nhận hàng chục tỷ 'nghĩ là quà cảm ơn' [NSJ-AIC case in Quang Ninh: Officials received tens of billions thinking it was a thank you gift]", BBC Vietnamese, 11 October 2023, https://www.bbc.com/vietnamese/articles/c51wldlk5g0o.

10. Michael Tatarksi, "The VTP/SCB Fallout Continues", *Vietnam Weekly*, 28 November 2023, https://vietnamweekly.substack.com/p/the-vtpscb-fallout-continues?utm_campaign=email-post&r=chch9&utm_source=substack&utm_medium=email.

11. Le Hong Hiep, "Vietnam's Accelerated Power Transition: Glad Tidings for Investors and Foreign Partners", *Fulcrum*, 28 February 2023, https://fulcrum.sg/vietnams-accelerated-power-transition-glad-tidings-for-investors-and-foreign-partners/.

12. Vu Khanh and Francesco Guarascio, "Vietnam Parliament Elects Vo Van Thuong as New State President", Reuters, 2 March 2, 2023, https://www.reuters.com/world/asia-pacific/vietnam-parliament-elects-vo-van-thuong-new-state-president-2023-03-02/.

13. Tim Cook, "Vietnam's Xi? Nguyen Phu Trong Consolidates Power", *Georgetown Security Studies Review*, 23 October 2018, https://georgetownsecuritystudiesreview.org/2018/11/12/vietnams-xi-nguyen-phu-trong-consolidates-power/.

14. Le Hong Hiep, "Vietnam's Accelerated Power".

15. "Vietnam: PM Pham Minh Chinh Gets Embroiled in AIC Group Corruption Case", *Intelligence Online*, 30 August 2022, https://www.intelligenceonline.com/international-dealmaking/2022/08/30/pm-pham-minh-chinh-gets-embroiled-in-aic-group-corruption-case,109807825-art; "Bà Nhàn AIC bị xét xử trong vụ tham nhũng hồi ông Phạm Minh Chính lãnh đạo Quảng Ninh" [Ms Nhan AIC was tried in corruption case when Pham Minh Chinh led Quang Ninh], VOA Vietnamese, 24 October 2022, https://

www.voatiengviet.com/a/nguyen-thi-thanh-nhan-bi-xe-xu-tham-nhung-khi-pham-minh-chinh-lanh-dao-quang-ninh/7324331.html.

16. Trinh Duy, "Explaining Factional Sorting in China and Vietnam", *Problems of Post-Communism* 68, no. 3 (2021): 171–89.

17. Le Nguyen Duy Hau, "Concentrated Power: Vietnam's Communist Party Elbows the State Aside", *US-Asia Law Institute Perspectives* 3, no. 21 (2013), https://usali.org/usali-perspectives-blog/concentrated-power.

18. Nguyen Khac Giang, "Hot Furnace at Home, Cool Relationships Abroad", *Fulcrum*, 18 October 2023, https://fulcrum.sg/hot-furnace-at-home-cool-relationships-abroad/.

19. World Bank, *Taking Stock, August 2023: Making Public Investment Work for Growth* (Hanoi, 2023).

20. Author's calculations based on STATISTA (https://www.statista.com/statistics/444771/export-of-goods-to-vietnam/); Nguyen Anh, "The Impacts of Russia's Invasion of Ukraine on Vietnamese Economic Development", *Social Science Research Network*, 4 March 2023, http://dx.doi.org/10.2139/ssrn.4556234; Nguyen Thoi, "How the Russia-Ukraine War Is Impacting Vietnam's Economy", *The Diplomat*, 28 April 2023, https://thediplomat.com/2022/04/how-the-russia-ukraine-war-is-impacting-vietnams-economy/.

21. Michael Tatarski, "Is Ho Chi Minh City in Decline", *Vietnam Weekly*, 29 May 2023, https://vietnamweekly.substack.com/p/is-ho-chi-minh-city-in-decline.

22. World Bank, *Taking Stock*; General Statistical Office (GSO), *The Light and Dark Shades in the Labor Market and Employment Picture in the Second Quarter and the First Half of 2023* (Hanoi, 2023), https://www.gso.gov.vn/en/data-and-statistics/2023/07/the-light-and-dark-shades-in-the-labor-market-and-employment-picture-in-the-second-quarter-and-the-first-half-of-2023/.

23. Nguyen Tu, "Stemming Social Insurance Withdrawals in Vietnam", *East Asia Forum*, 17 October 2023, https://www.gso.gov.vn/en/data-and-statistics/2023/07/the-light-and-dark-shades-in-the-labor-market-and-employment-picture-in-the-second-quarter-and-the-first-half-of-2023/; Ai Van, "Chính phủ trình 2 phương án về vấn đề hưởng bảo hiểm xã hội một lần" [The government presented two plans on the issue of one-time social insurance benefits], *Lao Động*, 5 August 2023, https://laodong.vn/thoi-su/chinh-phu-trinh-2-phuong-an-ve-van-de-huong-bao-hiem-xa-hoi-mot-lan-1225331.ldo.

24. Sorin-Andrei Dojan, "Vietnam FDI Surges 54% in First Ten Months of 2023", *Investment Monitor*, 27 October 2023, https://www.investmentmonitor.ai/news/vietnam-fdi-growth-ten-months-2023/.

25. Edmund J. Malesky and Layna Mosley, "Labor Upgrading and Export Market Opportunities: Evidence from Vietnam", *Economics & Politics* 33, no. 3 (2021): 483–513; Sung-Ju Wu, "Foreign Profit Shifting and the Welfare Responses to the US-China Trade War: Evidence from Manufacturers in Vietnam" (Dissertation, Duke University, 2023), https://sungjuwu.github.io.

26. Malesky et al., *The Vietnam Provincial*, p. 88.

27. "Lego Group Needs Thousands of Workers to Start Operations at Binh Duong Factory", *Vietnamplus*, 18 September 2023, https://en.vietnamplus.vn/lego-group-needs-thousands-of-workers-to-start-operations-at-binh-duong-factory/268143.vnp?utm_source=substack&utm_medium=email.

28. Zachary Abuza, "Investor Caution Highlights Red Flags in Vietnam Economy", Radio Free Asia, 3 December 2023, https://www-rfa-org.cdn.ampproject.org/c/s/www.rfa.org/english/commentaries/vietnam-economy-12032023093322.html/ampRFA.

29. Malesky et al., *The Vietnam Provincial*, p. 37.

30. "Cựu chủ tịch FLC Trịnh Văn Quyết bị đề nghị truy tố" [Former FLC chairman Trinh Van Quyet was recommended for prosecution], *VNExpress International*, 8 October 2023, https://vnexpress.net/cuu-chu-tich-flc-trinh-van-quyet-bi-de-nghi-truy-to-4670034.html.

31. Mark Barnes, "Explained: Vietnam's Real Estate Market Turmoil", *VietnamBriefing*, 23 March 2023, https://www.vietnam-briefing.com/news/vietnam-real-estate-market-2023.html/; International Monetary Fund, "Vietnam: Staff Report for the 2023 Article IV Consultation", 2023.

32. World Bank, *Taking Stock*; Francesco Guarasico, "Vietnam's Anti-Graft Crackdown Chills Supply Chains, Investment", Reuters, 28 November 2023, https://www.reuters.com/world/asia-pacific/vietnams-anti-graft-crackdown-chills-supply-chains-investment-2022-11-28/.

33. General Statistical Office, "Public Investment—An Important Driver of Vietnam's Growth in the First 6 Months of 2023", n.d., https://www.gso.gov.vn/en/data-and-statistics/2023/07/public-investment-an-important-driver-of-vietnams-economic-growth-in-the-first-6-months-of-2023/.

34. Dan Southerland, "Rising Coastal Sea Levels Pose Threat to Cities in Vietnam and Thailand", Radio Free Asia, 12 November 2019, https://www.rfa.org/english/commentaries/mekong-levels-11122019164415.html.

35. Nguyen Quynh and Edmund J. Malesky, "Fish or Steel? New Evidence on the Environment-Economy Trade-Off in Developing Vietnam", *World Development* 147 (2021): 105603.

36. Mark Barnes, "Vietnam Government Approves Power Development Plan 8", *Vietnam Briefing*, 17 May 2023, https://www.vietnam-briefing.com/news/vietnam-power-development-plan-approved.html/.

37. Thanh Van, "Vietnam launches Resource Mobilisation Plan for Just Energy Transition Partnership", *Vietnam Investment Review*, 4 December 2023, https://vir.com.vn/vietnam-launches-resource-mobilisation-plan-for-just-energy-transition-partnership-107333.html.

38. "Ủy ban Kiểm tra Trung ương: Xem xét, xử lý các tổ chức Đảng, đảng viên có liên quan trong thực hiện các dự án năng lượng tái tạo" [Party Central Inspection Committee: Reviewing and disciplining party organizations and members involved in implementing renewable energy projects], *Quandoinhandan,* 20 December 2023,

https://www.qdnd.vn/phap-luat/tin-tuc/uy-ban-kiem-tra-trung-uong-xem-xet-xu-ly-cac-to-chuc-dang-dang-vien-co-lien-quan-trong-thuc-hien-cac-du-an-nang-luong-tai-tao-756309.

39. Sui-Lee Wee, "Vietnam Relied on Environmentalists to Secure Billions. Then It Jailed Them", *New York Times*, 28 November 2023, https://www.nytimes.com/2023/11/28/world/asia/vietnam-cop28-environment.html?unlocked_article_code=1.CU0.jOnx.O8CaTAMKu1eI&smid=url-share&utm_source=substack&utm_medium=email; "Vietnam's Arrest of Environmentalists Draws Fire Amid Surge of Funding for Green Transition", *Voice of America*, 8 October 2023, https://www.voanews.com/a/vietnam-s-arrest-of-environmentalists-draws-fire-amid-surge-of-funding-for-green-transition-/7301614.html.

40. Michael Taylor, "In Vietnam, Climate Arrests Spark Calls to Halt Entergy Transition Deal", Reuters, 19 October 2023, https://www.reuters.com/sustainability/cop/vietnam-climate-arrests-spark-calls-halt-energy-transition-deal-2023-10-20/.

41. The 88 Project for Free Speech in Vietnam, "2021 Human Rights Report Vietnam", n.d., https://the88project.org/wp-content/uploads/2022/05/AnnualReport-2021_final.pdf.

42. Nguyen Khac Giang and Dien Nguyen An Luong, "What Drives Vietnam's Tightened Public Sphere?", *ISEAS Perspective*, no. 2023/47, 19 June 2023.

43. Dien Nguyen An Luong, "Vietnam's Suspension of Online Magazine: When Even the Compliant Are Not Safe", *Fulcrum*, 21 July 2023, https://fulcrum.sg/vietnams-suspension-of-online-magazine-when-even-the-compliant-are-not-safe/.

44. Carlyle Thayer, "US-Vietnam Relations Post Mortem 1-4", Thayer Consultancy Background Brief, 12 September 2023.

45. Khang Vu, "Vietnam and China Announce Major Upgrade in Relations during Xi Visit", *The Diplomat*, 13 December 2023, https://thediplomat.com/2023/12/vietnam-and-china-announce-major-upgrade-in-relations-during-xi-visit/; Thuc Pham, "Xi Touts 'Community of Common Destiny' but Hanoi Lukewarm, Experts Say", *Voice of America*, 11 December 2023, https://www.voanews.com/a/xi-touts-community-of-common-destiny-but-hanoi-lukewarm-experts-say/7393515.html.

46. Nguyen Dieu Tu Uyen, "Vietnam Approves Law on Global Minimum Tax Rate", *Bloomberg Tax*, 28 November 2023, https://news.bloombergtax.com/daily-tax-report-international/vietnam-approves-law-on-global-minimum-tax-rate.

47. Abuza, "Investor Caution"; David Hutt, "How Far the Rot of Corruption Has Spread In Vietnam", *The Diplomat*, 17 November 2023, https://thediplomat.com/2023/11/how-far-the-rot-of-corruption-has-spread-in-vietnam/; Sebastian Strangio, "Vietnam Communist Party Chief Vows to Hasten Anti-Graft Campaign", 24 November 2023, https://thediplomat.com/2023/11/vietnam-communist-party-chief-vows-to-hasten-anti-graft-campaign/.

The Political Economy of Vietnam's Anti-corruption Campaign

Nguyen Khac Giang

In mid-March 2024, the Central Committee of the Vietnamese Communist Party (VCP), the nation's supreme political institution in the one-party state, convened an extraordinary plenum, during which it accepted President Vo Van Thuong's resignation and dismissed Hoang Thi Thuy Lan, the party secretary of Vinh Phuc province. Originally comprising 200 elected members, the committee saw the loss of 20 members just three years into its current term. For perspective, from 1986 to 2021, only 9 committee members lost their positions.

Vo Van Thuong and Hoang Thi Thuy Lan became the latest casualties of the unprecedented anti-corruption campaign, known in Vietnam as the "Blazing Furnace", initiated by VCP general secretary Nguyen Phu Trong in 2013. Over a decade, this campaign has targeted nearly 200,000 party members, including almost 100 Central Committee-level officials who previously enjoyed immunity because of their positions. Since the 13th VCP Congress in 2021, the campaign has intensified. Within less than two years, two presidents—Nguyen Xuan Phuc and Vo Van Thuong—and two vice prime ministers—Pham Binh Minh and Vu Duc Dam—were compelled to resign as General Secretary Nguyen Phu Trong declared the campaign to have "no no-go zones or exceptions".[1]

The persistence of the anti-corruption campaign post-2021 has taken many Vietnam observers by surprise. After all, the 13th Congress was seen as the "final victory" for Trong, who broke the VCP constitution to secure his third consecutive term without any objections.[2] He spent the entirety of his twelfth term dismantling the remnants of support for his political rival, former prime minister Nguyen Tan Dung, and he was instrumental in key personnel decisions within the VCP leadership. If the anti-corruption effort were merely a veil for power struggles among political elites, it should have decelerated post-2021, as Nguyen Phu Trong has already been the nation's most powerful politician for decades.

NGUYEN KHAC GIANG is Visiting Fellow at the ISEAS – Yusof Ishak Institute, Singapore.

The acceleration of the "blazing furnace" suggests that other determinants have influenced the dynamics of anti-corruption in Vietnam.

Approaching from a political economy perspective, this chapter aims to examine the logic of Vietnam's ongoing anti-corruption campaign, its key determinants, and the consequences for different stakeholders in both the economic and political realms. It begins by exploring recent trends in the country's anti-corruption efforts, then delves into the economic and social consequences. Subsequently, a stakeholder analysis will identify the winners and losers of the "blazing furnace" in the country's "new normal". Finally, the chapter concludes with a discussion on the future of the campaign, considering Nguyen Phu Trong's personal drive, and the necessary structural and institutional reforms required to address this deep-rooted systemic issue in Vietnam.

The Blazing Furnace: A Chronicle

Since Vietnam's market reforms in the late 1980s, corruption has been seen as a key threat to the regime's stability and legitimacy. The Politburo of the 7th Congress in 1996 identified anti-corruption as a "significant task of the current revolution", an opinion upheld by the subsequent 8th and 10th congresses. This was notably marked by the 2006 resolution on "Reinforcing the Party Leadership on Anti-corruption Affairs" and the establishment of a Central Steering Committee on Anti-corruption, supervised by the prime minister.

Actions, however, did not match the rhetoric. During this period, the VCP addressed corruption rather leniently, fearing that exposing corrupt officials would erode its legitimacy and threaten regime survival. Officials at the Central Committee (CC) level were rarely disciplined for corruption-related issues. The first major scandal erupted in 2002 with the arrest of two CC members involved in the Nam Cam organized crime case: Bui Quoc Huy, vice minister of public security, and Tran Mai Hanh, the director of Vietnam Television.[3] At the time a Politburo member, Truong Tan Sang was reprimanded for his lack of responsibility, but later became president in 2011, coinciding with Nguyen Phu Trong's first election as general secretary. Another CC member, Dao Dinh Binh, the minister of transportation, was allowed to resign when his deputy minister was implicated in a major corruption scandal.[4]

The root of these lacklustre efforts lay in the rent-seeking behaviour dominating Vietnamese politics at the time, fuelled by the exponential growth of the economy in the early 2000s. The most notable rent-seeker was, ironically, the head of the Central Steering Committee on Anti-corruption, Prime Minister Nguyen Tan

Dung.[5] After the global financial crisis in 2008 and major corruption scandals involving Dung's signature projects with state conglomerates like Vinashin and Vinalines, dissatisfaction among party conservatives grew. When Nguyen Phu Trong, a staunch Marxist theoretician, was elected general secretary in 2011, his priority was to revitalize the regime's decaying political system and to clear "bad roots"—corrupt officials, which he viewed as the main internal threat to the regime. This conservative mindset gradually replaced the "economy-first" approach of technocrats and business-friendly leaders.

The 2011–16 period was a preparatory phase during which Nguyen Phu Trong and his allies designed the necessary institutional framework for an intensified anti-corruption campaign. This included transferring the Central Steering Committee on Anti-corruption from the Prime Minister's Office to Politburo management, re-establishing key party agencies like the Central Internal Affairs Commission and the Central Economic Commission, enhancing the power of the party leadership through various decrees and resolutions, and removing potential challengers. After Trong's 12th Congress victory in 2016, the anti-corruption campaign escalated in both scale and depth. Since then, more than 139,000 party members have been disciplined, including 40 Central Committee members and 50 military and police generals.[6] Seven Politburo members—including two of the "Four Pillars", who previously were considered untouchable[7]—lost their jobs following investigations.[8] For context, no Politburo members had been dismissed for corruption in the previous thirty years since 1986,[9] and only 9 CC members faced discipline for corruption-related charges. In the first three years of the 13th Congress term, 3,523 officials were prosecuted, tripling the number in the same period from the 12th Congress term.[10]

The numbers tell only part of the story. More significantly, Trong has overhauled Vietnam's anti-corruption efforts, making it a key feature of the nation's politics in the last decade.

First, there has been a shift from government to party institutions in addressing corruption, with more rigorous disciplinary action. Trong led the Central Steering Committee on Anti-corruption in 2013, re-established the Central Internal Affairs Commission (CIAC), and empowered the Central Inspection Commission (CIC), providing the institutional capacity for the VCP to spearhead the "blazing furnace". The Ministry of Public Security (MPS), the primary enforcer of the campaign, has also come under the tighter control of the general secretary. Since 2016, Trong became the first general secretary to be a standing member of the Central Public Security Party Committee.[11]

Second, the VCP has institutionalized rules and regulations to intensify the fight against corruption. Between 2012 and 2022, the main organs of the VCP issued over 250 documents related to party building and preventing corruption, setting the regulatory backbone for 88,000 policy documents released during this period by government agencies on anti-corruption measures.[12] By early 2023, all sixty-three provinces had established their own provincial-level anti-corruption committee, which must convene and report to the central authority at least once in three months. Results in anti-corruption efforts are regarded as crucial criteria for evaluating the performance of provincial leaders,[13] prompting provincial authorities and other party-state entities to devote more attention to internal affairs and less to other duties, such as economic advancement.

Third, the anti-corruption campaign has broadened from focusing solely on party and state apparatuses to encompassing state-owned enterprises, non-state businesses and non-profit sectors, including educational entities and civil society. In 2018, the amended Law on Preventing Corruption included a section on the private sector, while VCP theorists increasingly discussed the risk of "political capture" and "interest groups".[14] This reflects the VCP's growing concern about collusion between private businesses and corrupt government officials, well reflected in the repatriation flight and the Viet A test kit scandals in 2021. As a result, there has been an increase in crackdowns in recent years on major conglomerates such as FLC, Tan Hoang Minh and Tan Hiep Phat. Most notably, the private property developer Van Thinh Phat was investigated in an alleged fraud case that resulted in losses of US$44 billion—the largest in Vietnam's history—of which Lan was accused of embezzling US$12.5 billion herself. The case also involved the bribery of senior officials from the State Bank of Vietnam.[15]

Fourth, while the term "campaign" suggests a short, intense period of mobilizing resources to achieve specific policy goals, the ongoing "blazing furnace", which began in 2013, has become the new norm in contemporary Vietnamese politics. Anti-corruption has evolved from a means to an end into an ideology in itself, with General Secretary Trong as its flagbearer. The following sections will explore the political logic of this campaign and how it will define the future of Vietnamese politics.

The Political Logic of Anti-corruption

The key drivers of fighting corruption in an authoritarian regime are to win public support and to strengthen the regime's apparatus against internal decay. Such efforts usually arise during a perceived crisis, prompting urgent action to "rectify" the regime's course.[16] But when conducted without independent third-party oversight, a strong check-and-balance system, and rigorous accountability mechanisms for civil society and the public to scrutinize government activities, the anti-corruption process risks being co-opted—intentionally or unintentionally—by the political elites in charge, often empowering them at the expense of other factions.

Vietnam's ongoing anti-corruption campaign exhibits these characteristics. The rise of Nguyen Phu Trong followed a period in the late 2000s marked by a serious legitimacy crisis for the VCP. Following the global financial crisis of 2007–8 and a series of cases of economic mismanagement, the implicit bargain between political quiescence and economic prosperity began to unravel. As performance-based legitimacy eroded, public dissatisfaction towards the ruling elites grew, especially in light of massive corruption scandals in state-owned enterprises between 2006 and 2011, such as PMU-18, Vinashin and Vinalines.

One of Trong's primary motivations for reinvigorating the anti-corruption campaign was to restore the VCP's legitimacy to rule and regain public support. In this regard, it has been hugely successful. The campaign boosted public confidence in the VCP leadership and solidified Trong's political standing, which in turn helped enhance the VCP's legitimacy.[17] The VCP Propaganda Commission claims a ninety-three per cent support rate for the anti-corruption campaign, though this figure cannot be independently verified.[18] In essence, the campaign has evolved from a means to supplement the VCP's performance-based legitimacy to an end in itself—fighting corruption to maintain regime support among the populace. This form of legitimacy became even more critical post-Covid-19 as the Vietnamese economy struggled to recover. Anti-corruption has therefore become a predominant theme in VCP narratives since 2016, rivalling, or even surpassing, economic growth in importance.

Naturally, this emphasis on anti-corruption politics has empowered its chief proponent—General Secretary Nguyen Phu Trong—regardless of whether this was one of his initial ambitions. As general secretary, Trong directs the CIC and CIAC, overseeing internal party investigations. He is also the first general secretary to be a standing member of the Central Public Security Party Committee, giving him oversight over the Ministry of Public Security's anti-corruption investigations. Essentially, he wields a double-edged sword capable of targeting virtually anyone within the system.

Trong's preference in the past decade for using party bureaucracy to address corruption has led to dominance of the party over the state, undermining the collective leadership principle foundational to Vietnamese politics since 1986. This shift is evident in key promotions post-2021. Officials with strong party or internal affairs backgrounds have replaced those ousted in the anti-corruption campaign. For example, at the provincial level, new party secretaries in provinces targeted by the campaign all have strong party affiliations. Nguyen Hai Ninh, vice chief of staff of the Central Party Office, became Khanh Hoa's party chief; Tran Duc Thang, vice chairman of the CIC, replaced Pham Xuan Thang as Hai Duong's party chief; and Nguyen Hong Linh, vice head of the Central Propaganda Commission, assumed Dong Nai's party chief role. At the central level, the promotion of President Vo Van Thuong, who previously held key positions within the party such as head of the Central Propaganda Commission and permanent member of the secretariat, exemplifies this trend. Similarly, two new vice prime ministers, Tran Hong Ha and Tran Luu Quang, have strong party records but limited national-level experience. Notably, even in sectors where technical expertise is required, the preference is for cadres with a strong ideological background. For instance, the minister of industry and trade, Nguyen Hong Dien, formerly vice head of the Central Propaganda Commission, lacks experience in trade and industrial policies. Minister Dao Hong Lan of the Ministry of Health has no healthcare background, and newly promoted vice health minister Le Duc Luan was previously an official in the State Audit Office.

Concurrently, the need to constantly carry out anti-corruption investigations also empowers internal affairs institutions, including the CIC, CIAC and MPS. The 13th Party Congress saw four out of ten "special exemptions" nominated as new Central Committee members coming from these agencies.[19] With the departure of Nguyen Xuan Phuc and Pham Binh Minh, five out of the remaining sixteen Politburo members now have police backgrounds.[20] In 2020, the CIAC was elevated to be the "permanent agency" responsible for administering the Central Steering Committee on Anti-Corruption.[21] Phan Dinh Trac, the current chief of CIAC, is the first CIAC head since 1976 to hold Politburo membership. The influence of the CIC has understandably expanded, evidenced by the increase in meetings over the past three terms to discuss and announce disciplinary measures against senior party officials. In the 11th Congress term (2011–16), the CIC convened 37 meetings, which increased to 50 meetings in the 12th Congress term (2016–21). The 13th Congress (2021–26) is just three years in and the CIC had already held 38 meetings by April 2024.

Another implication of the anti-corruption campaign is the revitalization of ideology. VCP theorists, including Trong himself, emphasize the need to strike against corruption (*chống*) and simultaneously build institutional foundations to prevent it (*xây*). As ideology is deemed fundamental to the latter, it is unsurprising that alongside the anti-corruption campaign the VCP has launched a massive ideological campaign to shore up the regime's theoretical foundations, indoctrinate millions of cadres, and shield against unwanted influences from Vietnam's increasingly open society and economy. Participation of VCP members in monthly party cell meetings and study sessions is now more stringent, with requirements including study sessions on Nguyen Phu Trong's books on ideology strengthening and anti-corruption in addition to the usual classics on Marxism and Ho Chi Minh thought. This is accompanied by various campaigns and competitions each year specifically designed for different population segments. For example, the mobilization campaign to "study and follow the moral example of Ho Chi Minh", the "Golden Hammer and Sickle" prize for media reports on party building, and the student competition to "follow the ideology, morality, and style of Ho Chi Minh".

In summary, while the initial goal of the "blazing furnace" was to eliminate "bad roots" and strengthen the VCP's internal organizations, it has created profound implications for Vietnamese politics. From a relatively balanced collective leadership system, power has decisively tilted towards the VCP in the past decade. From a relatively open and consultative authoritarian environment that was friendly to businesses and less restrictive of the activities of civil society, the one-party state has become much more conservative, prioritizing regime stability over economic development and integration. This shift has drastically effected the governance and economic systems of Vietnam.

Collateral Damage

The anti-corruption campaign was initiated with the intention of cracking down on unbridled corruption while keeping intact the economic engine that brought about Vietnam's impressive transformation since the market reforms of the late 1980s. To paraphrase from a commonly used idiom, the VCP "throws a stone at the mouse without breaking the jar" (*Ném chuột vỡ bình*).[22] But this approach ignores an inconvenient truth that corruption has been an inalienable component of Vietnam's post–Cold War political economy and played a significant part in bringing about the country's economic turnaround. The notion of corruption boosting growth, instead of impeding it, is excellently explored in a book by Yuen Yuen Yang, in which she argues that while all corruption is bad, two specific forms can boost economic performance in the short term.[23] These are *access money*, when businesses are tied with politicians to gain privileged treatments, and *speed money*, when individuals or firms pay bribes to bureaucrats to "expedite things".

Similar to the situation in China, these forms of corruption have helped firms and individuals bypass Vietnam's extremely bureaucratic system, create incentives for underpaid bureaucrats to speed things up, and encourage both national- and local-level politicians to favour business development. Without fringe income from "corrupt" practices, no one would want to work in a bureaucracy where the baseline monthly salary is about US$80 and the ceiling just over US$1,000 for the prime ministerial position—in a country where annual GDP per capita already exceeds US$3,000. This dynamic explains the high demand for government positions in the pre–Nguyen Phu Trong era despite their modest remuneration.

The anti-corruption campaign has disrupted this status quo. By targeting not only grand thefts and embezzlements but also the collusion between senior officials and big businesses (access money) and petty bribes to bureaucrats (speed money), the campaign has abruptly halted these practices. Without parallel administrative reforms, this has led to a significant slowdown in administrative processes. For instance, the disbursement rate of public investment in 2022 reached just 68 per cent of its planned target despite constant pressure from central leadership.[24] In the first nine months of 2023, the average rate of public investment disbursement stayed at 42 per cent of the prime minister's target, with many key agencies having spent less than 10 per cent of the plan.[25] The fear of being drawn into anti-corruption investigations makes even honest officials hesitant to approve projects or licences, causing significant disruptions to businesses.[26] The Ministry of Internal Affairs, which manages the bureaucracy, complained that many public officials believed that "if you don't do anything, you can't do anything wrong; it's better to stand in front of a disciplinary committee than a court".[27]

The fear of the "blazing furnace" has also led to a mass exodus from the already overloaded bureaucracy. From 2020 to 2023, about 60,000 public employees quit their jobs[28] despite reassuring messages from the top leaders.[29] Among them, 89 officials left their prestigious positions at the Government Office—out of around 500 staff—in 2022 alone.[30] It is understandable that the two sectors that are the focus of the anti-corruption campaign—education and health—have the most resignation numbers (accounting for 54.2 per cent and 26.5 per cent of the total number, respectively). The Southern provinces, which are the focus of the campaign, particularly Ho Chi Minh City, account for the highest number of resignations in term of regional distribution.

The combination of inaction and mass resignations has paralysed Vietnam's bureaucracy, leading to significant social and economic issues. Following investigations in the Ministry of Health and the Centre for Disease Control (CDC), the country has faced a severe shortage of medical equipment and supplies as a result of reluctance by officials to approve procurement contracts.[31] This has coincided with a resurgence of diseases such as dengue fever, conjunctivitis and hand, foot and mouth disease throughout the country in 2022 and 2023, which all had previously been well-controlled.[32]

The extension of the "blazing furnace" to the private sector, coupled with bureaucratic paralysis, has also had notable economic repercussions. Since 2021, major property developers like Van Thinh Phat, FLC and Tan Hoang Minh have faced allegations ranging from financial fraud to stock market manipulation and corporate bond fraud. The crackdown has not only disrupted the operations of these companies but has also had a chilling effect on the corporate bond market, which is a crucial funding source for developers. This was especially challenging given the State Bank of Vietnam's tightening of credit for the property sector as well as the lacklustre performance of Vietnam's stock exchanges. Other major players, including Nova Land and Vinhomes (a subsidiary of Vingroup), have struggled to service their domestic and foreign bond debts. Consequently, the property sector, which contributes significantly to the country's GDP, has seen a marked decline. By the third quarter of 2023, the completion of property projects and the number of transactions had decreased by 71 per cent and 57 per cent, respectively, compared to the previous year. The foreign investment sector, which has been exempted from the "blazing furnace", also experienced more delays and administrative procedures.[33] In October 2023, in a significant blow to Vietnam's ambitions as a global semiconductor hub, Intel postponed its planned chip operation expansion in the country, citing concerns about excessive bureaucracy and unstable power supplies.[34]

Regionally, provinces that have seen many senior leaders punished are struggling to attract investors and maintain adequate economic development. Ho Chi Minh City, a focal point of recent anti-corruption efforts, has been particularly hard hit. As Vietnam's economic powerhouse, the city's business environment has become increasingly challenging, with an alarming 90 per cent exit rate for new enterprises in 2022, far exceeding the anticipated 50 per cent rate. Additionally, public investment capital allocation has been woefully inadequate, with only VND 952 billion disbursed, amounting to just 2.2 per cent of the total designated capital in the first quarter of 2023.[35] For the first time in forty years, Ho Chi Minh City's GDP growth ranks in the bottom ten of the country's sixty-three provinces.[36] This issue extends to the greater Southeast region, including major manufacturing hubs like Dong Nai and Binh Duong.

The New Normal of Vietnamese Politics

As the sustained anti-corruption campaign passes the ten-year mark, it has significantly altered the country's political landscape, with two key consequences for elite politics and society.

First, there has been a notable shift in the balance of power within elite politics. Since the Renovation era (Đổi Mới), Vietnamese politics has operated under a "collective leadership" principle whereby the CC exerts restraining power over individual leaders. But with CC membership no longer guaranteeing immunity, this power has increasingly shifted to the Politburo, and particularly to General Secretary Nguyen Phu Trong. He has emerged as the most powerful Vietnamese leader in decades, attaining a supreme position akin to the country's first revolutionary leaders like Ho Chi Minh and Le Duan.

The fall of senior leaders such as President Nguyen Xuan Phuc and Vice Prime Minister Pham Binh Minh in the "blazing furnace" has further cemented Trong's authority within the VCP's collective leadership system. His pre-eminence is underscored by his seniority in both age and experience—he is thirteen years older than the second-oldest Politburo member and has served in the Politburo for six consecutive terms, while others have a maximum of two terms. Additionally, the remaining "pillars" are junior to him and rose to power with his support. For instance, National Assembly chairman Vuong Dinh Hue's career advancement from minister of finance to head of the Central Economic Commission in 2013 was orchestrated by Trong. He was also behind Vo Van Thuong's appointment as Vietnam's youngest president, although Thuong's subsequent downfall a year later has cast a shadow over this move. The reference by the VCP's mouthpiece to Trong as the "nuclear leader" (*hạt nhân lãnh đạo*) of the system reflects a status comparable to Xi Jinping's "core leader" in China.

The need to constantly carry out investigations and disciplinary work have propelled internal affairs institutions to prominence, overshadowing technocratic agencies such as the Government Office and economic-related ministries. Notable figures such as Nguyen Xuan Phuc and deputy prime ministers Pham Binh Minh and Vu Duc Dam, once key technocrats, were ousted and replaced by less-experienced party loyalists (Vo Van Thuong, Tran Hong Ha and Tran Luu Quang, respectively). Even the military has not been exempt, with no less than twenty generals being disciplined since 2016.[37] These changes indicate a securitization of the Vietnamese state, with internal affairs institutions (including MPS and disciplinary agencies) wielding increasingly overwhelming influence within the system, reflected in recent personnel promotions and policy discourse.

Beyond elite politics, the anti-corruption campaign has accelerated conservative tendencies since 2016. The heightened emphasis on ideology has led to stricter controls over the public sphere, encompassing traditional media, social media and the internet.[38] Sectors previously seen as apolitical, such as environmental protection and academic research, now face greater scrutiny as the VCP seeks to prevent any risk of pluralism and dissent. Furthermore, the decision-making process for potentially sensitive policies has slowed considerably. A prime example is the regulations on independent Worker Representative Organisations. Although agreed upon in the frameworks of the Comprehensive and Progressive Agreement for Trans-Pacific Partnership (CPTPP) and the EU-Vietnam Free Trade Agreement in 2019, the Vietnamese authorities have been hesitant to establish a structure for such organizations because of concerns over potential risks to regime stability.

Withering Away or Blazing Forward?

In communist regimes, "campaigns" signify intense mobilization periods to achieve specific policy goals, as exemplified by various initiatives during China's Mao era; notably, the Cultural Revolution. Similarly, in Vietnam, alongside the "blazing furnace", a recent example has been the Zero-Covid strategy, which employed war-like slogans (such as *chống dịch như chống giặc*—fighting the pandemic as if fighting invaders) to galvanize internal resources and public support.

While such campaign narratives can significantly boost strength and morale—akin to the effects of doping—their obvious limitation is the rapid depletion of energy for other vital governance tasks. Like doping, campaigns are effective in the short term but inevitably lead to long-term side effects. They are meant to lay the groundwork for long-term solutions, not serve as the end goal. This is evident in the eventual dissatisfaction and protests that arose from the Zero-Covid policies both in democracies (like New Zealand) and authoritarian regimes (China and Vietnam). As this chapter has examined, the anti-corruption campaign faces a similar dilemma, with both bureaucracy and society feeling the strain of a decade-long relentless "blazing furnace". This continuous intensity risks undermining the regime's legitimacy, especially as corruption remains rampant, evidenced by a 312 per cent year-on-year increase in exposed corruption cases in 2023.[39] High-profile cases, such as Viet A and the repatriation flight scandals, may further erode public trust in officials and lead to disillusionment with political institutions.[40] Amid an economic slowdown and a tightening political atmosphere, people might begin to question the rationale behind the anti-corruption campaign.

Admittedly, beyond instituting harsher punishments, the VCP also seeks to revamp its institutional framework to ensure that public servants "cannot, do not want to, dare not, and do not need to" (*không thể, không muốn, không dám, không cần tham nhũng*) engage in corrupt practices. Over the past decade, the VCP has exerted considerable efforts towards this goal. It has streamlined bureaucracy, overhauled the personnel system towards a more merit-based approach with improved remuneration, and significantly enhanced the transparency of state governance in politically non-sensitive areas. In early 2024, National Assembly chairman Vuong Dinh Hue announced that Vietnam has allocated up to US$23 billion for the implementation of public sector salary reforms by 2026. These efforts are praiseworthy. However, as evidenced by the mass exodus of public employees in the 2020–23 period, their implementation does not seem to be quick enough.

Furthermore, the top-down approach of the anti-corruption campaign presents its own challenges. Nguyen Phu Trong's emphasis on the morality and righteousness of communists to prevent "self-evolution" and "self-transformation"—terms often associated with corruption—may be effective for him and a select group of followers, but its efficacy in ensuring the integrity of over four million VCP members remains questionable.

The institutionalization of anti-corruption politics, while impressive in scope, ultimately hinges on the will of one individual—the general secretary. In fact, one could argue that the campaign has de-institutionalized Vietnamese politics, as evidenced by the erosion of the rule of law as a result of constant party intervention in government affairs and the weakening of the institutional power of the Central Committee and of the collective leadership principle of the "Four Pillars".

This leads to pressing questions about the future. What will happen when Trong, an eighty-one-year-old with health issues, eventually steps down? Will the furnace continue to blaze under a new general secretary? Will it operate in the same manner, or will it be co-opted by specific interest groups? How can the need to "clear out bad roots" be balanced against negative socio-economic effects?

These questions become more urgent considering the unresolved issue of "who guards the guardians". The top-down approach has granted substantial power to internal affairs agencies, especially the CIC, CIAC and MPS. But without a corresponding bottom-up accountability mechanism that involves the more proactive participation of citizens, civil society and media, it is challenging to contain them within the "cage of power", as Nguyen Phu Trong describes it. The immediate consequence is that internal affairs leaders—Minister of Public Security To Lam, CIAC head Phan Dinh Trac and CIC chairman Tran Cam Tu—are poised to be strong contenders for leadership roles in 2026, potentially even the top position. With a dearth of technocratic candidates, Vietnam's next leadership composition risks being disproportionately conservative at a time when technocratic expertise is crucial to address lingering structural economic and social challenges.

Looking forward, the VCP must recognize that harsh punishment alone cannot eradicate corruption. It must be accompanied by a rigorous reform of the state bureaucracy—as is currently being undertaken—and comprehensive political reform that promotes transparency and accountability and which delegates more power to non-state actors to hold the party-state accountable. In essence, the VCP needs to initiate substantial reforms both within and outside its power circle. To paraphrase the renowned economist Paul Samuelson, carrying out an anti-corruption campaign without both is like attempting to clap with one hand.

Notes

1. Nguyen Khac Giang, "Vietnam's Anti-corruption Campaign: Economic and Political Impacts", *ISEAS Perspective*, no. 2023/41, 18 May 2023.
2. Quynh Tran, "The Final Victory of Nguyen Phu Trong", *The Diplomat*, 5 March 2021, https://thediplomat.com/2021/03/the-final-victory-of-nguyen-phu-trong/.
3. "Đặc xá cho ông Bùi Quốc Huy" [Bui Quoc Huy was pardoned], BBC Vietnamese, 5 January 2005, https://www.bbc.com/vietnamese/regionalnews/story/2005/01/050131_buiquochuy.
4. Nguyen Binh and Thanh Phong, "Để tránh bị cách chức, hôm nay Bộ trưởng Đào Đình Bình xin từ chức" [Avoid being dismissed, Minister Dao Dinh Binh asks to resign], *Thanh Nien*, 4 April 2006, https://thanhnien.vn/de-tranh-bi-cach-chuc-hom-nay-bo-truong-dao-dinh-binh-xin-tu-chuc-185325064.htm.
5. Alexander L. Vuving, "Vietnam in 2012: A Rent-Seeking State on the Verge of a Crisis", in *Southeast Asian Affairs* 2013, edited by Hoang Thi Ha and Daljit Singh (Singapore: ISEAS – Yusof Ishak Institute, 2013), pp. 323–47, https://muse.jhu.edu/article/512123.
6. The data is compiled from different state-affiliated sources, including Nguyen Phu Trong, *Kiên quyết, kiên trì đấu tranh phòng, chống tham nhũng, tiêu cực, góp phần xây dựng Đảng và Nhà nước ta ngày càng trong sạch, vững mạnh* [Resolutely and perseveringly struggle to prevent and combat corruption, negativity, and contribute to building a clean and strong party and state of Vietnam] (Hanoi: National Politics Publishing House, 2023).
7. "Four Pillars" refers to the four top leaders of Vietnam: the general secretary of the Communist Party, the prime minister, the president, and the Speaker of the National Assembly.
8. The first was Dinh La Thang, party secretary of Ho Chi Minh City, who was the first incumbent Politburo member to be criminally charged and sentenced to thirty years in prison in 2018. Other people that followed include Hanoi's Party Secretary Hoang Trung Hai, two heads of the Central Economic Commission (Nguyen Van Binh and Tran Tuan Anh), two presidents (Nguyen Xuan Phuc and Vo Van Thuong), and Vice Prime Minister Pham Binh Minh.
9. Two Politburo members, Tran Xuan Bach and Nguyen Ha Phan, were dismissed from their positions on allegations of supporting pluralism and of abetting enemies during the Vietnam War, respectively.

10. "Từ đầu nhiệm kỳ XIII đến nay, số vụ án tham nhũng tăng hơn 2 lần" [From the beginning of the 13th term, the number of prosecuted corruption cases doubles], *Voice of Vietnam*, 16 August 2023, https://vov.vn/chinh-tri/tu-dau-nhiem-ky-xiii-den-nay-so-vu-an-tham-nhung-tang-hon-2-lan-post1039707.vov.

11. Anh Hieu, "Tổng Bí thư lần đầu tham gia Đảng ủy Công an Trung ương" [General secretary joins the Central Police Committee for the first time], *Cong An Nhan Dan*, 21 September 2016, https://cand.com.vn/Su-kien-Binh-luan-thoi-su/Tong-Bi-thu-lan-dau-tham-gia-Dang-uy-Cong-an-Trung-uong-i405064/.

12. Nguyen Phu Trong, *Kiên quyết, kiên trì đấu tranh phòng, chống tham nhũng, tiêu cực, góp phần xây dựng Đảng và Nhà nước ta ngày càng trong sạch, vững mạnh* [Resolutely and perseveringly struggle to prevent and combat corruption, negativity, and contribute to building a clean and strong party and state of Vietnam] (Hanoi: National Politics Publishing House, 2023), p. 95.

13. Vu Van Phuc, "Phòng chống tham nhũng, tiêu cực: "Trên dưới đồng lòng, dọc ngang thông suốt" [Anti-corruption and negativity must be done in a comprehensive approach], *Tuyen Giao*, 13 March 2023, https://tuyengiao.vn/bao-ve-nen-tang-tu-tuong-cua-dang/phong-chong-tham-nhung-tieu-cuc-tren-duoi-dong-long-doc-ngang-thong-suot-143720.

14. Nguyen Van Chung, "Kiểm soát, ngăn chặn "nhóm lợi ích" ở Việt Nam hiện nay" [Controlling and preventing 'interest groups' in Vietnam today], *Tap chi Cong san*, 12 April 2020, https://www.tapchicongsan.org.vn/web/guest/chinh-tri-xay-dung-dang/-/2018/816206/kiem-soat%2C-ngan-chan-%E2%80%9Cnhom-loi-ich%E2%80%9D-o-viet-nam-hien-nay.aspx.

15. Pham Du, "Van Thinh Phat Chairwoman Charged with Stealing \$12.5B from Lender SCB", *VnExpress*, 15 December 2023, https://e.vnexpress.net/news/business/companies/van-thinh-phat-chairwoman-charged-with-stealing-12-5b-from-lender-scb-4689378.html.

16. Baranovitch, Nimrod. "A Strong Leader for a Time of Crisis: Xi Jinping's Strongman Politics as a Collective Response to Regime Weakness", *Journal of Contemporary China* 30, no. 128 (2021): 249–65.

17. Le Hong Hiep, "Will Vietnam's Anti-corruption Campaign Endure beyond Trong?", *East Asia Forum*, 29 January 2020, https://www.eastasiaforum.org/2020/01/29/will-vietnams-anti-corruption-campaign-endure-beyond-trong/.

18. Thu Hang, "93% cán bộ, đảng viên và nhân dân tin tưởng vào sự lãnh đạo, chỉ đạo của Đảng trong cuộc đấu tranh phòng, chống tham nhũng" [93% cadres, party members, and the people trust in the leadership of the party in the anti-corruption campaign], *Tuyen giao*, 2 November 2020, https://www.tuyengiao.vn/nhip-cau-tuyen-giao/ban-tuyen-giao-tw/93-can-bo-dang-vien-va-nhan-dan-tin-tuong-vao-su-lanh-dao-chi-dao-cua-dang-trong-cuoc-dau-tranh-phong-chong-tham-130619.

19. Nguyen Khac Giang and Nguyen Quang Thai, "From Periphery to Centre: The Self-Evolution of the Vietnamese Communist Party's Central Committee", *Contemporary Southeast Asia* 44, no. 1 (2022): 56–86.

20. Prime Minister Pham Minh Chinh; To Lam, minister of public security; Phan Dinh Trac, head of CIAC; Nguyen Van Nen, party secretary of Ho Chi Minh City; and Nguyen Hoa Binh, chief justice of the Supreme People's Court.

21. See Decision 216 QĐ-TW, https://noichinh.vn/upload/others/202001/2942_QD216.pdf.

22. Xuan Linh, "Tổng bí thư: Diệt chuột đừng để vỡ bình" [Gensec: Destroy the mouse but do not break the jar], *Vietnamnet*, 6 October 2014, https://vietnamnet.vn/tong-bi-thu-diet-chuot-dung-de-vo-binh-200746.html.

23. Yuen Yuen Ang, *China's Gilded Age: The Paradox of Economic Boom and Vast Corruption* (Cambridge: Cambridge University Press, 2020).

24. Khanh Linh, "Giải ngân vốn đầu tư công 12 tháng năm 2022 ước đạt 67,27% kế hoạch" [Disbursement rate in 2022 is projected at 67.27% as planned], *Bao Chinh phu*, 3 January 2023, https://baochinhphu.vn/giai-ngan-von-dau-tu-cong-12-thang-nam-2022-uoc-dat-6727-ke-hoach-102230103173717426.htm.

25. Nguyet Bac, "Quyết liệt giải ngân vốn đầu tư công" [Proactively disbursing public investment], *Nhan Dan*, 20 September 2023, https://nhandan.vn/quyet-liet-giai-ngan-von-dau-tu-cong-post773372.html.

26. "An Anti-graft Drive Brings Down Vietnam's President", *The Economist*, 26 January 2023, https://www.economist.com/asia/2023/01/26/an-anti-graft-drive-brings-down-vietnams-president.

27. Viet Tuan, "Bộ Nội vụ đề nghị khoan hồng cán bộ sai phạm không vụ lợi cá nhân" [Ministry of Internal Affairs proposes leniency for officials who have erred without personal gain], *VnExpress*, 6 November 2023, https://vnexpress.net/bo-noi-vu-de-nghi-khoan-hong-can-bo-sai-pham-khong-vu-loi-ca-nhan-4673222.html.

28. From 2020 to July 2022, 40,000 public employees resigned. From July 2022 to July 2023, the number was 19,000. See Thanh Chung, "Mỗi tháng có gần 1.600 công chức, viên chức thôi việc" [Every month, nearly 1,600 civil servants and public employees resign], *Tuoi tre*, 18 July 2023, https://tuoitre.vn/moi-thang-co-gan-1-600-cong-chuc-vien-chuc-thoi-viec-20230718170009074.htm.

29. Since late 2022, VCP leaders have repeatedly given reassurances that cadres who "dare to think and dare to do" will be protected.

30. Thanh Chung, "89 công chức, viên chức Văn phòng Chính phủ xin thôi việc trong năm 2022" [89 public employees of the Government Office quit jobs in 2022], *Tuoi tre*, 27 January 2023, https://tuoitre.vn/89-cong-chuc-vien-chuc-van-phong-chinh-phu-xin-thoi-viec-trong-nam-2022-20230127202605736.htm.

31. N. Dung, "Lại thiếu thuốc, vật tư y tế: Bộ Y tế nói gì?" [Again a shortage of medicines and medical supplies: What does the Ministry of Health say?], *Nguoi Lao dong*, 27 October 2023, https://nld.com.vn/suc-khoe/lai-thieu-thuoc-vat-tu-y-te-bo-y-te-noi-gi-20231027150557027.htm.

32. Ministry of Health, "Sốt xuất huyết, tay chân miệng, thủy đậu đều tăng đột biến, Hà Nội khuyến cáo gì?" [Dengue fever; hand, foot and mouth disease; and chickenpox all see sudden increases, what do Hanoi authorities advise?], MoH Website, 5 April 2023.

33. Song Ha, "Quy định phòng cháy, chữa cháy "trói tay" doanh nghiệp" [Fire prevention and fighting regulations "tie the hands" of businesses], *VnEconomy*, 25 July 2023, https://vneconomy.vn/quy-dinh-phong-chay-chua-chay-troi-tay-doanh-nghiep.htm.

34. Francesco Guarascio, "Intel Shelves Planned Chip Operation Expansion in Vietnam— Source", Reuters, 7 November 2023, https://www.reuters.com/technology/intel-shelves-planned-chip-operation-expansion-vietnam-source-2023-11-07/.

35. Vien Thong, "Kinh tế TP HCM quý I tang 0.7%" [HCMC GDP growth rate at 0.7% in Q1], *VnExpress*, 30 March 2023, https://vnexpress.net/kinh-te-tp-hcm-quy-i-tang-0-7-4587581.html.

36. Huynh The Du, "Liều thuốc cho TP HCM" [A cure for HCMC], *VnExpress*, 4 March 2023, https://vnexpress.net/lieu-thuoc-cho-tp-hcm-4588575.html.

37. Le Hong Hiep, "Corruption is the Worst Enemy of the Vietnamese Army", *Fulcrum*, 22 April 2023, https://fulcrum.sg/corruption-is-the-worst-enemy-of-the-vietnamese-army/.

38. Nguyen Khac Giang and Dien Nguyen An Luong, "What Drives Vietnam's Tightened Public Sphere?", *ISEAS Perspective*, no. 2023/47, 19 June 2023.

39. Van Toan, "Tội phạm tham nhũng, chức vụ được phát hiện tăng 71,46%" [Corruption charges increase 71.46%], *Nhan Dan*, 13 September 2023, https://nhandan.vn/toi-pham-tham-nhung-chuc-vu-duoc-phat-hien-tang-7146-post772217.html.

40. Yuhua Wang and Bruce Dickson, "How Corruption Investigations Undermine Regime Support: Evidence from China", *Political Science Research and Methods* 10, no. 1 (2022), 33–48.